D1571541

spotted:

your one and only unofficial guide to *gossip girl*

crissy calhoun

Published by ECW Press, 2120 Queen Street East, Suite 200,
Toronto, Ontario, Canada M4E 1E2 / 416.694.3348 / info@ecwpress.com

LIBRARY AND ARCHIVES CANADA CATALOGUING IN PUBLICATION

Calhoun, Crissy
Spotted : your one and only unofficial guide to Gossip girl / Crissy Calhoun.

ISBN 978-1-55022-889-2

1. Gossip girl (Television program). I. Title.

PN1992.77.G66C34 2009 791.45'72 C2009-902545-0

Editor: Jennifer Hale
Cover design: Dave Gee
Text design and typesetting: Melissa Kaita
Photo section: Rachel Ironstone
Printing: Transcontinental 1 2 3 4 5

Front cover image: Edward Opinaldo /Splash News/Keystone Press. *Author photo:* © Lee Weston (leewestonphoto.com). *Photo credits:* pages 12, 111: © AP Photo/Jennifer Graylock; 25: © Sara Jaye Weiss/StartraksPhoto.com; 29: Dennis Van Tine/Retna Ltd.; 32: © Michael Simon/StartraksPhoto.com; 36: © James Veysey/Retna Ltd.; 38, 83: RD/Leon/Retna Digital; 41, 44: © Amanda Schwab/StartraksPhoto.com; 46: Andrew Marks/Retna Ltd.; 48: Sue Schneider/Moonglow Agency; 57, 131: © Tim Forbes, forbescreative.com; 62: ML Agency; 72, 123: © Sarah Dunn; 152: © Clark Samuels/StartraksPhoto.com; 167: © Albert Ferreira/StartraksPhoto.com; 173: © Albert Michael/StartraksPhoto.com; 183: © Marion Curtis/StartraksPhoto.com; 210: © Avital Aronowitz/Retna Ltd.; 234: © Gina Boyd/StartraksPhoto.com; 242: © PseudoImage/Shooting Star; 262: © AP Photo/Charles Sykes; 297: © Dave Allocca/StartraksPhoto.com; 325: © Humberto Carreno/StartraksPhoto.com; 327: © Erin Nicole Smith. (All other photos are © Crissy Calhoun.) *First photo section credits:* pages 1, 4 (girls), 5 (Blair and Chuck): The CW/Patrick Harbron/Landov; 2: Humberto Carreno/startraksphoto.com; 3 (Serena, Dan, & Jenny), 3 (Dan and Vanessa), 4 (Blair and Chuck), 8: The CW/Eric Liebowitz /Landov; 3 (Nate and Vanessa): © Dennis Van Tine/Retna Ltd.; 5 (Mean Girls): The CW/Giovanni Rufino /Landov; 6, 7: Bill Davila/startraksphoto.com. *Second photo section credits:* pages 1, 5, 6, 7: © The CW/Giovanni Rufino/Landov; 2 (Chuck and Nate): © Christopher Peterson/Keystone Canada/BuzzFoto.com; 2 (Serena & Dan), 3 (Serena), 8: © Humberto Carreno/StartraksPhoto.com; 2 (Chuck): © Freddie Baez/StartraksPhoto.com; 3 (Jenny): © Bill Davila/StartraksPhoto.com; 3 (Vanessa and Nate): © Sharkpixs/ZumaPress.com/Keystone Press; 4: © Sharkpixs/ZumaPress.com/Keystone Press.

The publication of *Spotted* has been generously supported by the Ontario Arts Council, by the Government of Ontario through Ontario Book Publishing Tax Credit, by the OMDC Book Fund, an initiative of the Ontario Media Development Corporation, and by the Government of Canada through the Book Publishing Industry Development Program (BPIDP).

Canada ONTARIO ARTS COUNCIL CONSEIL DES ARTS DE L'ONTARIO

PRINTED AND BOUND IN CANADA

for Amie and Sarah

contents

introduction

For someone now so hopelessly enamored of *Gossip Girl*, I was a late convert. A fan of YA fiction, I'd read one of Cecily von Ziegesar's *Gossip Girl* novels back in the early 2000s and dropped it in favor of smarter, funnier novels like Louise Rennison's Georgia Nicolson series. *Gossip Girl* was catty, mean, and superficial, a world so tightly embracing brand-name worship it made my skin crawl. When I saw a billboard advertising the CW's adaptation of *Gossip Girl* in fall 2007 (starring Bridget from the *Sister Pants* movie!), I took it as a sign of the apocalypse. But like Dorota, I think it's important to know thine enemies, so I tuned in. And then I tuned in again. Then my brave co-worker Sarah said that she liked the show, not liked-to-hate it, but earnestly enjoyed it. Slowly the guilty pleasure of watching *Gossip Girl* turned into me buying hairbands and suggesting Colored Tights Day at the office and talking about Serena, Dan, Chuck, Blair, Nate, and Jenny every Tuesday morning.

There's no denying that *Gossip Girl* is a soap opera full of impossibly good-looking people with drama-filled lives and conveniently connected plotlines, but what makes the show more culturally important than its daytime counterparts or savvier than its teeny-bopper predecessors like *Beverly Hills, 90210* is that it transcends the limitations of its genre by being more subversive, smarter, more self-aware, funnier, and better dressed. There's no reason to feel guilty for watching *Gossip Girl* instead of a highbrow show. Challenging, engaging television involves interwoven threadlines, narrative complexity, and a lack of "handholding," as Steven Johnson describes in *Everything Bad Is Good for You*. In *Gossip Girl*'s case it makes the viewers figure out the subtleties of character interactions and catch the rapid-fire references, allusions, and in-jokes as the plot quickly weaves and thickens all in a New York minute. It's complex and layered enough to warrant a book-length companion guide (in my humble opinion).

Meant to be read as a complement to, not a replacement for, watching the show, *Spotted*'s episode guide, bios, sidebars, and background chapters aim to help illustrate why *Gossip Girl* truly is, as *New York* magazine called it in April 2008, the "most awesomely awesome show ever." The bulk of the book is the episode guide. Before you get into it, here's a mini guide to the guide:

Each episode begins with Gossip Girl giving us some choice wisdom, so I've picked a line from her narration that encapsulates that episode best. After giving you a general analysis of the episode, I will highlight one moment, a line so funny or painful or bang-on it deserves a high five.

JTLYK: The "just to let you know" section catches intertextual references, character insights, and other pieces of interest.

Secrets & Lies: Tells you who's been lying to whom in a series chock-full of lies, secrets, ruses, and manipulation.

Scrap!: For people with so-called good social graces, the *Gossip Girl* characters get into physical altercations quite frequently. I'll catalog them here.

Not a Girl, Not Yet a Queen Bee: All about Little Jenny Humphrey and her arc through the first season.

You'll B a Woman Soon: For season 2, the focus switches to Blair Waldorf.

The Original Gossipverse: The TV world of *Gossip Girl* is adapted from Cecily von Ziegesar's book series, and here you'll find the origin of plot details and how minor characters differ from page to screen. (See page 16 for a further discussion of the adaptation.)

That's How It's Done in *The O.C.*: Creators Josh Schwartz and Stephanie Savage imported some of their best stuff — character traits, events, one-liners — from that show about beautiful, rich teenagers growing up in Califooor*nia*. Be warned: this section contains spoilers for *The O.C.*

Each episode title is named after a film (with some punning added on top for good measure). In this section, I'll give you some background on the movie (spoilers abound!) and how it relates to the episode.

Welcome to the Real World: Our quick-witted Upper East Siders make tons of off-the-cuff references to the world we live in. If one went over your head, I'll explain it here.

Locations: *Gossip Girl* is primarily filmed on location in New York City and the characters talk about real-life places they visit off-screen; plan your tour of the city with this guide.

Oops: Inconsistencies, bloopers, continuity errors, and the occasional arguable nitpick are cataloged here.

Spotted: If you were a celebrity, wouldn't you use your influence to get a walk-on role on *Gossip Girl?* Me too. Here I'll list the people of note who appear in each episode.

The Look: I will provide you with details on what the characters are wearing in this section. (But with an average of eight costume changes per character per episode, **The Look** is a highlight reel rather than an exhaustive index.)

Music: Last but not least, I will tell you what songs were playing in each scene.

Make sure you watch an episode before reading its corresponding guide — it contains spoilers for that episode (but not for anything that follows). And if there's something you think I missed, or completely read your mind about, drop me at a note at crissycalhoun@gmail.com, and/or stop by **The Calhoun Tribune** for a weekly reaction to the glory of *Gossip Girl* (calhountribune.blogspot.com).

xoxo
crissy calhoun

an auspicious beginning: cecily von ziegesar's *gossip girl*

Gossip Girl was born in a brainstorming meeting at youth marketing and media packaging firm Alloy Entertainment in the late '90s. Cecily von Ziegesar, then an editor at the company, worked up a proposal based on a name tossed out during the meeting — "Gossip Girl." Having grown up in New York City attending the Upper East Side private school Nightingale-Bamford, von Ziegesar followed the "write what you know" adage and set the story in the world she experienced as a teenager.

President of Alloy Entertainment Leslie Morgenstein said, "Cecily took the assignment and knocked it out of the park." Cindy Eagen at Little, Brown scooped up the pitch. "She seemed to have caught on to trends before they happened, with Gossip Girl being what was initially described as a 'Web mistress,' before the word 'blogger' was known. I jumped on the book right away." For CvonZ, "[Blogging] seemed like the logical thing to use within a book and it's a great literary device, allowing me to plant things in her column."

Von Ziegesar initially plotted *Gossip Girl* as an imitation of Edith Wharton's *The Age of Innocence*, but scrapped most of that version, hit her stride, and wrote the first book in just four months. "I was just so into it, it came so easily because I felt that I was writing about people that I know," she told the *Daily Telegraph* in 2002. Based on people she went to school with, the characters are "fabulously rich and wild. These kids drink, talk, dress and act like adults; they're jaded by the time they hit 18."

The initial print run of 35,000 for *Gossip Girl* was not enough copies to satisfy the ravenous YA audience. Cecily, who went on maternity leave shortly after taking on the project, never returned to her editorial position at Alloy. She kept on writing the Gossip Girl series until the eighth book (*Nothing Can Keep Us Together*). After that book, the covers read "created by" rather than "by" Cecily von Ziegesar. (The switch in authorship may account for some of the inconsistencies between books, but for the most part the changeover went off without a hitch. Cecily doesn't write the spin-off series *The It Girl* either.)

Each novel covers roughly one month in the lives of Blair, Serena, Dan, Jenny, Vanessa, and Nate as they go to parties, break up and make up, choose colleges, lose their virginity, flit off to the Hamptons, and buy $40,000 wedding dresses. What Cecily *didn't* want in the books was moralizing. "It's completely unrealistic to have a group of kids who are constantly reforming or who are being punished because they're 'naughty.' And I always resented that quality in books I'd read." To *New York* magazine, she expanded on her approach to portraying deviant behavior, "I mean, of course I want to be the responsible mother who says, 'Oh, there are terrible repercussions if you have sex, do drugs, and have an eating disorder!' But the truth is, my friends and I dabbled in all of those things. And we all went to good colleges and grew up fine. And that's the honest thing to say."

"These books are meant to be funny, so most of all I hope people laugh while they're reading them. But there are sad and touching scenes too, and I hope readers can relate to what the characters are going through. Even though they're rich and spoiled on the surface, they're still just like everyone else," explained Cecily. The difference lies in "the extraneous stuff, like the clothes that they wear and the fact that they have their own credit cards and country houses. All the important stuff is pretty much the same for teenagers wherever you go. It's the same angsty world."

While some parents were just glad their children were reading, others criticized the series. "While the activities of these youngsters are not glamorized, they are presented as business as usual," said Amy Coffin of The Book Haven, a book club for teenagers. "While older teens will be able to separate the drama from reality, younger teens could admire the vindictive natures and twisted pleasures of the cast, and adopt smoking, drinking and promiscuity as the real-life fast track to popularity." Naomi Wolf criticized the Gossip Girl series and other YA novels of its ilk in the *New York Times*: "The problem is a value system in which meanness rules, parents check out, conformity is everything and stressed-out adult values are presumed to be meaningful to teenagers. The books have a kitsch quality — they package corruption with a cute overlay."

Cecily shrugged off the criticism. "I actually think that it just makes people want to read the books. I'll stand by them. I don't think anything the kids do is there for shock value or is all that offensive. It's just based on the way kids behave. They talk about sex all the time, but whether or not they're actually doing it is another question. It's not until the fourth book that two characters actually have sex. . . . There's certainly profanity in the books, but I don't think it's gratuitous; I think it's really the way teenagers talk. And some of the characters swear more. Blair swears more because she's always pissed off.

"Also, Blair has this bulimia problem, but in the fourth book, somebody makes her admit that she has it. It's done in a way that's true to Blair. She's like, 'Oh, God. Are you gonna make me say it?' I want to reassure the reader that she's aware of it. She's not just completely insane. . . . I'm sure it's alarming to some teachers and parents. But I'm not glorifying it. I think it's actually portrayed in a pretty disgusting way. It's not anything that any reader is going to want to emulate."

The combination of no-holds-barred honesty about what teenagers can, and do, get up to in an over-the-top fantasy world of Amex Black Cards, designer everything, and ludicrous plot twists has made the Gossip Girl books bestsellers, with over 5.6 million copies sold as of August 2008. In addition to the It Girl series (which follows Jenny Humphrey at boarding school), there's another spin-off, The Carlyles, about triplets who move into the Waldorf apartment after Blair's family relocates to California (I know, as if, right?). After the 11 books in the original line, Ziegesar returned to the series, penning a prequel (*It Had to Be You*) in October 2007, shortly after the premiere of the TV show, and the original characters return to the city in November 2009's *I Will Always Love You*.

Alloy Entertainment, the company behind *Gossip Girl*, its spin-offs, and other successful YA series like *The Clique*, *The A-List*, *Pretty Little Liars*, and *Private*, works with film and television producers to develop these properties onscreen. (Alloy was behind *The Sisterhood of the Traveling Pants* movies.) Before the CW picked up the television rights for the *Gossip Girl* project, there was a feature film adaptation in the works, circa 2004, at Warner Bros.

Pictures, with Amy Sherman-Palladino (*Gilmore Girls*) attached as a writer and Lindsay Lohan set to star. Thankfully the rights reverted to Alloy, and Josh Schwartz, Stephanie Savage, and the CW were able to bring us the *Gossip Girl* we know and love.

you're nobody until you're talked about: josh schwartz, stephanie savage, and the CW

"The books are a soap opera, and TV makes a lot of sense [for an adaptation]. When we made the list of writers who would be the best to adapt *Gossip Girl* for television, Josh was at the top of the list," said Alloy Entertainment's Leslie Morgenstein to the *Hollywood Reporter*. Putting Josh Schwartz at the top of the list made a lot of sense too. Josh was famously the mastermind behind FOX's hit teen soap *The O.C.*, which debuted on August 5, 2003, when Josh was just 26 years old, making him the youngest person to create and run a TV series in U.S. history.

Born on August 6, 1976, and raised in Providence, Rhode Island, Josh, his younger brother Danny, and his sister Katie had parents with what sound like dream jobs for a kid: they were toy inventors working at Hasbro; his father became the president of Playskool. Josh quipped in a *New York Times* profile, "I was invited to a lot of birthday parties as a kid, and probably not out of actual friendship. It prepared me well for Hollywood." Describing his childhood as happy and his father as a "liberal with a Republican wallet," he loved movies and had a subscription to *Variety* by the age of 12, writing screenplays at summer camp and short stories in the backyard, and attending the independently run Wheeler School. "I guess there's a part of me that will always feel like a teenager, that sort of still feels like a teenager," he told AP in 2006. "It's such a rich time in your life. Everything is really new, you're experiencing things and everything feels like life-and-death and really huge and momentous and epic. And as you get older, you start to roll with it a little bit more and you start to become a little more cynical, a little less open to the world, I guess."

Studying film at the University of Southern California, he was surrounded by "people who looked like they were out of an Abercrombie & Fitch catalog," and didn't quite fit in. "I was highly strung, hyper analytical. And USC? Not a place for a lot of Jews." But Josh focused on his work, selling his first screenplay to Sony in 1997 when he was still a junior, and a television pilot, *Brookfield*, about wealthy kids at boarding school in New England to ABC in 2000. Josh then cooked up a pilot called *Wall to Wall Records* for the WB in 2001 about working in a music store (which would be "like my personal summer camp" to Josh). The idea of a show about California rich kids came up and Josh ran with it, using his experience at USC and a lifetime absorbing popular culture.

Not a regular viewer of *90210* or *Dawson's Creek*, Josh is more of a golden age of teen cinema guy, counting among his favorites *Fast Times at Ridgemont High* and the films of John Hughes and Cameron Crowe; the teen shows he likes are the quirkier ones — *Freaks and Geeks*, *My So-Called Life*, *Undeclared*. Quite astutely, Josh realized he couldn't pitch his show to a network as a "quirky character-driven show" like the ones he admired, none of which made it through a complete season. "You can't tell a network that's what you want to make because they'll just say, 'Those shows lasted 15 episodes and they're off the air and we don't want them.' But if instead you go to FOX and say, 'This is your new *90210'* — that's something they can get excited about. . . . And really what we hoped we had were these characters that were a little bit funnier and more soulful and different and specific than the kinds you usually see in that genre. They would be the soldiers inside our Trojan horse." It worked. *The O.C.* looked slick enough to be a descendant of *90210*, with a beautiful cast, beach parties, and serious soapy melodrama, but at the center of it was the Cohen family with Seth (Josh's partly autobiographical character), the outsider whose "moderately sarcastic point of view rings true for a lot of people who go through life guarded by their wits." Making the parents fully formed characters with their own plotlines, something Josh drew from Ang Lee's *The Ice Storm*, gave the show a complexity, heart, and a whole other demographic of viewers beyond their teenage years. "As much as our audience enjoys living vicariously in this wealthy world, I think the true wish fulfillment comes from wishing that they had a family like the Cohens — where the parents could be that cool and that grounded and that loving, but also real parents."

Describing the show as "highly ironic, but . . . highly optimistic," Josh's vision of *The O.C.* was picked up by FOX and he took on the day-to-day running of the show himself, writing episodes and earning praise from his network bosses. Said Marcy Ross, FOX senior VP of current programming, to the *New York Times*, "I have never seen anyone take to this medium as quickly as he has. I mean, sure, he's lost a lot of weight, he's falling apart, he does nothing but work. But he was born to do this." The pilot for *The O.C.* was nominated for a Writers Guild award; the show was a hit, pulling in an average of 10 million viewers a week, and it made a cultural impact — spawning MTV's "reality" show *Laguna Beach: The Real Orange County* (and its eventual spin-offs), Bravo's 2006 *The Real Housewives of Orange County*, and bringing to the mainstream the countless then-indie bands (Rooney, Phantom Planet, Modest Mouse, The Killers, The Thrills, Death Cab for Cutie) who were spotlighted in each episode, turning *The O.C.* into a powerful music tastemaker.

The O.C. ran for four seasons, losing some of its steam in its sophomore outing with audience criticism providing Josh a "real education. The second season is when a show defines its sustainability." Developing other TV projects as he turned over some of *The O.C.*'s day-to-day duties to his trusty co-producers, Josh signed a deal with Warner Bros. Television and writing and producing partner Chris Fedak to create *Chuck*, a smart action/comedy about a computer geek who gets tangled up with the CIA. It premiered on NBC in September 2007, the same month that other show he developed launched on the CW — *Gossip Girl.*

"When they sent me the [Gossip Girl] books, I said, 'I'll do this if Stephanie [Savage] does this,'" Schwartz said. "She's really tapped into young women and what's exciting for them. I knew the material was a little female-weighted for someone as ignorant of the female species as myself, and Stephanie would have great insight into it." Josh and Stephanie had worked closely together on *The O.C.*, which was produced by Wonderland Sound and Vision, the company Stephanie formed with McG in 2002.

Born in Ottawa in 1969 and growing up in Calgary, Canadian Stephanie Savage's upbringing was a far cry from the glossy, entitled world of *The O.C.* or *Gossip Girl.* "I grew up in a family where the thing that was valued most was being a hard worker, and if you commit to something, you follow through. And that may be considered a Canadian value, but it's definitely something that's served me well in my writing and my working in television. It's a hard, hard industry — there's so much work, so many details, and you just really have to commit to it."

Stephanie earned a BA in cinema studies and English at the University of Toronto and an MA in film history and theory at the University of Iowa before buckling down to get her PhD. While researching her dissertation (on late Hollywood star scandals) in 1995, she landed an internship at Flower Films, Drew Barrymore's production company, and immediately took to it, rising from intern to VP of development in a few short years. She ditched her dissertation and instead worked on *Never Been Kissed* and *Charlie's Angels*. "Stephanie always had an incredible motivation," Barrymore wrote in an email to the *LA Times*. "We used to tease her about it. She is so thorough and creative and has a wonderful determination to see every aspect of a job through." With McG (the director of *Charlie's Angels*), Stephanie founded Wonderland Sound and Vision where the wonder team developed *Supernatural*, *The O.C.*, *Fastlane*, and *The Mountain*, a short-lived series for the WB, which starred Penn Badgley. The *Hollywood Reporter* put her on their top 35 under 35 list in 2003, and *Glamour* listed her as a "power woman" in 2005.

The first episode of television Stephanie wrote was *The O.C.*'s season 1 classic "The Best Chrismukkah Ever," and she went on to write two episodes for *The Mountain* and 11 more episodes of *The O.C.* Forced to choose between developing Wonderland Sound and Vision and being a showrunner for *The O.C.*, Stephanie chose the latter. "That company [Wonderland] needed a full-time leader to manage personnel and chart a course for its future," Stephanie said. "There was no way I could do that job justice and also focus on growing as a writer." Her choice wasn't good news for everyone. "It was a little bit of a heartbreak for me because I invested so deeply in our partnership," McG said. "I'd always known she was a writer at heart. You have to support that move."

She moved to *The O.C.* "When I first found out what a showrunner was, I thought it was the strangest job I had heard of in my life. When someone's a writer, it's very creative and moody and you think of someone walking around the office in pajamas thinking of ideas. On the other hand, as a television producer, you have to be buttoned-up, organized and a feed-the-machine type of person. The idea that those two creatures were supposed to inhabit the same body was really a strange thing."

And when the opportunity came along to do it again on *Gossip Girl*, Stephanie jumped at the chance. "There was so much in the book. There were very bold characters, and I felt like there was a way to add humanity and dimensionality to them." Moving from one teen-centric show to another wasn't a problem for her. "I love telling teen stories where the characters are experiencing things for the first time — the stakes feel really high. I'll write teen stories as long as people will let me. I'll also be excited for the day when I'm told I can no longer write teen stories."

In August 2006, as *The O.C.* was moving into its last season, reports of the brand-new CW committing to a pilot of *Gossip Girl* marked the first major scripted project acquired by network head Dawn Ostroff. Taking its "C" and "W" from its two parent companies, CBS and Warner Bros., The CW Television Network was born from a merger of UPN and the WB; its freshman 2006 season featured existing shows like the WB's *Smallville*, *One Tree Hill*, and *Supernatural*, and UPN's *America's Next Top Model*, *Veronica Mars*, and *Everybody Hates Chris*. Dawn Ostroff worked to create an identity for the CW brand, focusing "intensely on finding shows that would finally define the CW as a net for young people, especially younger women."

Josh Schwartz and Stephanie Savage join a few beaming *Gossip Girl* cast members shortly after the premiere of season 1.

Josh and Stephanie put together a pitch package for the network, complete with a scrapbook of images that defined the look of the series — a lavish, "modern-day *Marie Antoinette*" décor to match the old-moneyed New York setting. The CW picked up on their passion for the project and the opportunity to have an *O.C.*-esque show in the fall 2007 line-up. From Dawn Ostroff's perspective, "There really hasn't been a show that has that opulence and that wealth and that setting since the days of *Dynasty* and *Dallas*. And of course, the generation we speak to [has] probably never heard of those."

A huge part of the look and feel of *Gossip Girl* would be created by shooting on location in New York, treating the city as if it were a character on the show. "There's no New York City on TV, or there wasn't when we started making the pilot, except what you could see in the background behind the dead bodies on cop shows. The *Sex and the City* fun, romantic world" was gone, said Savage to the *New York Times*. "We've never seen the city from the point of view of teenagers. It was very intriguing to see these young people — so sophisticated, so driven, so well traveled — feeling pressured to succeed more than their parents. It felt like a world with high stakes for young people." And the feeling was mutual; New York City was embracing film and TV crews. In 2004 New York Governor George Pataki had signed into law a program that gave a tax credit to production companies shooting in New York, and in 2005 Mayor Bloomberg ratified a companion program that would give an extra five percent, allowing shows like *30 Rock*, *Law & Order*, and *Gossip Girl* more access to location filming. "I was excited. It was this world that I loved and felt wasn't represented enough on TV," Stephanie said. "There was nothing that had that beautiful, romantic, Woody Allen version of New York."

And like the city itself, Stephanie and Josh "wanted fashion to be like a character in this show." They enlisted the help of Eric Daman, who had worked as an assistant stylist on *Sex and the City* and had "avant-garde, new New York" taste. He met with Stephanie, each with their own lookbook for the characters, and found an astonishing amount of overlap in the tearsheets they'd chosen. They developed individual looks for each of the six main characters. As music supervisor, *The O.C.*'s tastemaker Alexandra Patsavas was enlisted, whose other credits include *Without a Trace* and *Grey's Anatomy* (she's the one who used Snow Patrol's "Chasing Cars" to make that season 2 finale scene of Izzie and Denny so epic). After extensive discussions, the sound of *Gossip Girl* was created: "a musical soup of indie rock, New York–based projects, and poptronica."

The casting department saw 975 actors for the six lead roles, and Josh and Stephanie saw a few hundred of the most promising candidates before landing on the right cast. "The chemistry on *Gossip Girl* is similar to *Friends*. The first year of *Friends*, the cast really took off and was photographed everywhere. That's what happened on *Gossip Girl*. It's a one-in-a-million thing, like catching lightning in a bottle," said Dawn Ostroff of the show's impossibly good-looking sixsome. *Gossip Girl* became a part of the CW's sophomore schedule along with *Reaper* and *Aliens in America*. After only three episodes had aired, it was picked up for a full 22-episode season, surprising Stephanie and Josh. "We both got called to the phone together, which we assumed meant we were in trouble," she related to *Entertainment Weekly*. But Ostroff was completely behind the show, calling it the network's "crown jewel," despite the less-than-stellar Nielson ratings *Gossip Girl* pulled in.

"The show is a bigger deal than the ratings are reflecting," said Schwartz to *Entertainment Weekly* in November 2007. "I can honestly say I don't check the ratings after the show airs. We're more focused on the idea of cultural permeation." While viewers weren't necessarily tuning in for "appointment television," they were watching it on CWTV.com or downloading the show on iTunes. The audience, like the show's characters, is more tech-savvy than traditional, and wants to watch their shows when they want to, not when a network tells them to.

Ratings aside, people were talking about *Gossip Girl*: the Parents Television Council criticized it; *New York* magazine proclaimed it was the "Best. Show. Ever." The *LA Times* praised it because it "deftly intertwines irony with authenticity, poking fun at itself while also commenting on the voyeurism and sensationalism driving the culture right now." And for Stephanie Savage, the rampant discussion in print and online by critics and fans about plotlines, the cast, the fashion, and the music was proof positive that the show was hitting its mark. "For us, it's about how did you matter? Do people care and do they pay attention to what you're doing? I think the show is really succeeding in terms of getting people excited and giving them something to talk about." The cast graced the covers of magazines and, in a case of life imitating art imitating life, their private lives became the subject of gossip bloggers — are Chace and Ed lovers? Does Leighton hate Blake? Are Penn and Blake a real-life couple? *Gossip Girl* was nominated for six 2008 Teen Choice Awards and picked up Breakout Show and Choice Drama, Breakout Male (Chace Crawford), Breakout Female and Actress Drama (Blake Lively), and TV Villain (Ed Westwick). In 2009 the cast and show picked up another 10 nominations.

With another hit show on their hands, Josh Schwartz and Stephanie Savage had to ensure *Gossip Girl* lived up to the high bar it had set for itself. Said Josh, having learned a thing or two from *The O.C.*, "The key is not blowing through the great story lines right away. We worked really hard to pace ourselves this year." With Josh Schwartz producing two shows at once — his L.A. offices for *Chuck* and *Gossip Girl* are in the same building, with him running between them each day — and Stephanie Savage, the writing team, and postproduction also based in L.A., both showrunners pop by the New York set about once a month to, as Josh described it, "you know, hang out, high-five a few people and then leave."

What executive producer Bob Levy called the "balance between fantasy on the one hand and relatability on the other" in *Gossip Girl* has turned the show into a cultural phenomenon that drives trends and attracts a coveted 18–34 female audience to a network struggling to establish its own identity. "Older people come up to me," Blake Lively told *Entertainment Weekly*, "and whisper, 'I know I shouldn't be watching, but I have to. I'm addicted.'"

great adaptations

"I knew about [*The O.C.*], and that made me more worried that Nate's going to be a lifeguard, and it's going to be totally cheesy," said Cecily von Ziegesar about her pre-adaptation jitters (and inadvertently revealing that she'd never actually watched an episode of *The O.C.*). "I was worried they were going to ruin it, but then when I watched them filming the pilot and read the scripts, I got more and more hopeful, because it sounded like they wanted to stay close to the pilot [which was loyal to the books]," she said. "When I saw the pilot, I was thrilled, and I knew it was going to be big."

Before leaping into the task of translating the world and characters of *Gossip Girl* from page to screen, Stephanie Savage met with Cecily von Ziegesar in New York City, going for lunch at Barneys and then taking a tour around the Upper East Side. "We spent about four or five hours just talking about her world, because a lot of the stuff in the book is based on her own experience. . . . It's been really collaborative and really positive," said Stephanie Savage in an *Entertainment Weekly* interview.

In writing the pilot and adapting the characters, Josh Schwartz and Stephanie "started from a place of wanting to honor the characters and the world and the tone of the book, and then we had to ask ourselves as writers and working in a different medium, what changes we thought we had to make in order to make it a successful television show." And on television, you can't have teenagers smoking and swearing — goodbye, Gauloises. The key locations were made more TV-friendly both from a filming perspective and for the audience to keep track of. In the books, Chuck and Dan attend Riverside Prep on the Upper West Side, Nate goes to St. Jude's, and the girls go to Constance. For the show, Constance and St. Jude's were given a shared campus where all the students went to school. The Humphreys moved boroughs from Manhattan's Upper West Side to Brooklyn. "For the vast majority of Americans, the difference between the Upper East Side and the Upper West Side was a little bit too subtle to try to grasp," explained Savage, but an audience would instantly see the difference between Brooklyn and the UES. "From a social point of view, it contrasts the value of money, and fashion and beauty with that of family and being together," explained producer Amy Kaufman. A more difficult hurdle was moving Gossip Girl herself to a new medium. The solution? The all-knowing, editorializing narration by Kristen Bell.

Taking beloved characters and reinterpreting them for television required Josh and Stephanie to walk a fine line between staying true to their source material and creating something fresh that would work on TV, where "stories need to be more emotionally grounded" than they were in the Gossip Girl book series.

Not too much was changed in the central character of Blair Cornelia Waldorf, CvonZ's favorite. B may be the meanest, but "she also has this incredibly rich fantasy life and she makes the most mundane things into this wild romantic movie in her head. And she very much lives in her head. And she's hilarious." In the books, Blair is the prissy, straight-A student who is best frenemies with Serena and longtime girlfriend of Nate. Her parents' divorce happens shortly before the first novel; father Harold leaves wife Eleanor to live with a French man in a chateau. Blair loves her daddy and Yale (so much so that she names her baby half-sister Yale) and doesn't get along with her mother. She finds her completely and mortifyingly embarrassing. Eleanor's a socialite who falls in love with a far-from-classy Cyrus Rose and remarries him, bringing in to the picture Aaron Rose, the vegan, dreadlocked stepbrother who briefly dates Serena and then Vanessa, and whose dog, Mookie, terrorizes B's cat, Kitty Minky. Revamping the character of Eleanor Waldorf for the show by turning her into a fashion designer made her much more interesting and useful for storylines.

Blair also has a younger brother, Tyler, who doesn't do much but tag along on family vacations, and Blair doesn't think much of him either: "Blair had always identified herself as an only child, except for those rare occasions where she and Serena were getting along so well it felt like they were sisters." No wonder Josh and Stephanie just ditched him.

CvonZ's Blair is bulimic, and while everyone seems to know about it, nobody does anything. While the books don't take a very serious approach to a serious issue, the constant stomach gurgling and barfing do render B's disorder completely unappealing. Then there's B's obsession with Audrey Hepburn. Her love for *Breakfast at Tiffany's* and Audrey know no bounds in the books: she imitates her style, her haircuts; she writes her college admission essay as a screenplay of B as Audrey at Yale (it's diabolically bad and ill-advised). Keeping these kinds of details (like Blair's omnipresent ruby ring) were smart and simple ways for Josh and Stephanie to maintain the link between the original Blair and her re-imagined self. Said Stephanie, "Blair is probably a character the most like her character in the book. I think Blair in the book is really fun and she's kind of someone who's always scheming and always has a plan and always has something that she wants to achieve and it never quite works out no matter how hard she tries to manipulate the situation."

The TV version of blonde, beautiful Serena van der Woodsen is a dead-ringer to the one in the books, if only physically. The first *Gossip Girl* novel begins with S's return from boarding school, but unlike in the plot of the television pilot, she's not coming back because her younger brother Eric's in trouble — she got kicked out of boarding school for returning from Europe too late in the term (yawn). The creators wanted to raise the stakes for Serena and give her a more compelling reason to return to the Upper East Side. "We wanted her to be a sympathetic heroine, and having her help someone in her family felt like that was a good place to start," explained Savage. The original Serena doesn't return with a reformed bad girl persona; she's breezy and fun, flitting from boy to boy like a hummingbird goes from flower to flower, as she's described in *All I Want Is Everything*. CvonZ characterized S as "spacey, ethereal, the object of everyone's jealousy. She's the girl every girl wants to be and every boy wants. . . . Everyone is constantly making up stories about her but she's a little bit above it all and she rarely gossips about anyone else." Serena tries to stay out of the scheming that goes on around her onscreen as well. Like her book counterpart, S is a "veteran of half-truths and petty gossip. She knew the best way to handle it, too: ignore it."

Serena is the girl that everything good happens to, who can wear the inferior junior class uniform and look stunning in it, who rolls out of bed looking perfect. She's a simple creature looking for fun and attention. She models, she acts, she makes a film (about herself), rock stars fall in love with her. What Stephanie and Josh added to her character was depth and humanity and gave her a more fully developed family. "Serena is a character who we felt needed a bit of work because in the books she's a really fun main character but she's almost kind of Blair's foil. . . . Things just come to her so easily, nothing's ever a problem, she kind of treats people badly without really thinking about it, and things always go her way anyways," said Stephanie. In CvonZ's Gossip world, S's mother Lillian is a socialite, her father runs the Dutch shipping company his great-great-grandfather founded, and they live across from the Met in a glorious apartment. Her older brother Erik goes to Brown and is a sounding board for his sister's problems, when he isn't too busy recovering from a hangover or entertaining a lady friend (but S and E do share that same closeness the TV van der siblings have). Fleshing out her family along with her, Lily's backstory was created entirely from scratch, as was her relationship with Rufus Humphrey, with the dynamic between the two becoming a major focus of the show.

The first thing the creators needed to do with Dan Humphrey was to kick his chain-smoking habit. The original Daniel Jonah Humphrey smokes *all* the time. And he's usually drinking so much coffee that his hands are shaking. This guy is not in good shape. He's a poet (for a golden example of his work, check out "Sluts" in *All I Want Is Everything*) and has a brief period of fame — first as a literary star, then as the lead singer for a hipster band called The Raves. He's much less protective of Jenny and isn't the "moral compass" that Dan is on the show. His obsession with Serena in the first book parallels D's in the pilot episode; he admires the It girl from afar until he gets a chance with her. Josh and Stephanie took the brief romance between Dan and Serena and made it an epic series-long centerpiece — are they meant to be?

Little Jenny Tallulah Humphrey of the books can be described in one word: boobs. Her main physical characteristic and a lot of the plots she's involved in revolve around her absurdly large bosom. She goes bra shopping, boys stare at her, she considers a breast reduction. In the prequel (set in the pre-bust days), her entire story is about her wish to be bustier — oh, the irony. Short with frizzy brown hair, the book version of Jenny looks nothing like lanky blonde Taylor Momsen. "We made a point of not writing Jenny's large chest into the script because we just felt we would be saddling — quite literally — a young actress with something that would prove to be difficult over time," reasoned Stephanie. Jenny's artistic temperament was modified from a visual artist (she does a series of Nate portraits as well as some hymnal illustrations with S as an angel) to a budding fashion designer, helping the wardrobe department put her in fashionable outfits (and loads of them) while maintaining some sense of realism that Jenny could dress like that on a limited budget. CvonZ described Jenny as "always in the middle of the party and she doesn't really know how she got there but she's going with it." Giving her more agency and determination, Stephanie aimed for "a character that in this journey of trying to fit in at school might actually succeed in her goal and even triumph over the other girls at some point."

Vanessa Marigold Abrams is a hair different: in the books, V shaves her head, only wearing black and Doc Martens. She lives in Williamsburg with her sister Ruby, and her parents are artists living in Vermont. Josh and Stephanie took V out of Constance where she sticks out like a sore thumb in the books, but kept her ambition to be a filmmaker. Vanessa has a historic crush on Dan, her BFF, and he eventually realizes she may just be the girl for him. Stephanie anticipated that fans of the books would be most upset with the reimagining of Vanessa onscreen, and Cecily von Ziegesar said to MTV.com that she was most miffed at V's re-characterization. "I think Vanessa is one character they ruined," she said. "In the book, she's kick-ass and has a shaved head and wears lots of black. I think a lot of the readers who don't usually read teen fiction identify with Vanessa."

With Nate, the basics are the same: impossibly good-looking and sporty Nathanial Fitzwilliam Archibald, boyfriend to Blair Waldorf, who isn't sure he wants to do what she or his parents want him to do. This Nate loves smoking weed, sailing, and smoking weed. Von Ziegesar admitted, "In the books, Nate is pretty much stoned all the time. He's probably a little bit more complex in the show than in the books." Described as "like the dumbest Labrador retriever," he sleeps with Serena, makes up and breaks up with Blair, and dates big-boobed Jenny. His mother is French and dramatic, a far cry from prissy Anne Archibald of the show, and Captain Archibald has none of the failings Josh and Stephanie gave him. Chace Crawford described Book Nate as more "indifferent"; he could also be described as barely more than one-dimensional. His character was given more complexity.

When will TV Chuck Bass get a pet monkey? Von Ziegesar's Charles Bartholomew Bass is very much a secondary character in the original, described at every entrance as having "aftershave commercial good looks." He's a dandy; he's a perv; he goes a bit gay from *Because I'm Worth It* onward — only "a bit gay" as it's mostly Gossip Girl rumor (though he does steal Dan's sort-of boyfriend). He takes his pet monkey Sweetie with him wherever he goes and dresses it in outfits to match his own (like Kati and Is!). Very much a fringe character there for zaniness and color, the *Gossip Girl* team made him Nate's best friend, an antagonist to Dan, and a much more central and crucial role, which had a lot to do with Ed Westwick. Everyone fell in love with Ed's performance in the pilot episode, and agreed he should become a bigger part of the show. Making Bart Bass a widower gave an emotional depth to Chuck and opened the door to some inter-family romance for the parents. Another detail true to the books is Chuck's signature scarf. In the first book, S barfs on it after he tries to force himself on her. A fitting response.

It would be truly amazing (and a delight to fans of the books) if *Gossip Girl* had Dan and Jenny's crazy uncle — modeled exactly on Rufus of the books — come for a visit. What a special episode that would be. Cecily von Ziegesar's Rufus Humphrey is an "editor of the lesser known Beat poets" who's scrimped and saved and sent his kids to private school. The Humphrey household is in complete shambles, hairballs from Marx the cat tumble amidst piles of old newspapers. The kids are always eating cold takeout and drinking instant coffee; Rufus doesn't cook often, but when he does it's completely absurd and inedible. His sense of style is also mortifying: "His unruly hair was tied in a ponytail with a piece of the bright blue plastic bag the *New York Times* was delivered in every morning." And Momma Humphrey (Jeannette, not Alison) left the family when Jenny was little to live with a Count in the Czech Republic. Stephanie and Josh ditched the crazy and the unattractive, but kept the core of Rufus's character: he loves his kids, he values education and sacrificed so they could attend a high-quality school, and he is a total outsider to the privileged world of the Upper East Side, hindering his understanding of what his kids go through. He's a fairly liberal parent but when his kids cross the line, he puts his foot down, or at least tries to. (Like, for example, in *All I Want Is Everything*, when 15-year-old Jenny is in a semi-pornographic video on the internet. That is too much for Rufus.) And both Rufuses (Rufi?) like to cook: simple and delicious Italian food for TV Rufus, while Book Rufus makes lasagna by throwing in curry powder and rum and setting it on fire.

Kati Farkas and Isabel Coates have the same purpose in the books as on the show: gossiping background characters to play off B's Queen. The main difference is looks: Kati is a blonde and Isabel has brown hair while the show cast a Chinese-American actress for Kati and a West Indian–American actress for Is, presumably in an effort to make the show less than 100 percent WASPy.

After all their wholesale changes and tiny tweaks, Josh and Stephanie had an adaptation which not only satisfied themselves, their cast, and the network, but even Cecily von Ziegesar. "All the important details are there," CvonZ said to ABC News. "I think the show is so good. I am thrilled it's as loyal to the books as [it] is."

guide to the *gossip girl* books

1. *Gossip Girl* (2002)
Serena returns from boarding school to an icy reception, especially after Blair finds out that Nate and Serena slept together. Vanessa casts Dan in her short film, hoping to get closer to him, but he only has eyes for Serena. Jenny gets into trouble with Chuck at the Kiss on the Lips party.
Choice Line: "Jenny could hardly contain herself. Serena van der Woodsen! She was *there*, in the same room, only a few feet away. So *real.* And so mature-looking now. *I wonder how many times she's done it*, Jenny wondered to herself."

2. *You Know You Love Me* (2002)
Eleanor's upcoming wedding threatens to overshadow Blair's birthday. College interviews bring out the best and worst in the seniors, as B hangs out with her new stepbrother-to-be Aaron, and Dan finds out how just not into him Serena is. Nate starts hanging out with Jenny, and Blair steals cashmere pajamas for him. S and B finally become friends again.
Choice Line: "These sort of things didn't happen to her. They happened to losers with problems. . . . People with bad hair and skin problems and horrible clothes and no social skills. Blair touched the zit on her forehead once more. Oh God. What was she turning into?"

3. *All I Want Is Everything* (2003)
It's Christmastime in New York City and Serena moves from dating superstar Flow to vegan Aaron when they all end up on a Caribbean vacation with the Waldorfs. Jenny gets stalkerish with Nate. Dan writes a poem after a racy video of his sister, accidentally filmed by his girlfriend, hits the internet. *The New Yorker* decides to publish his poem! Blair finds out that her mother is pregnant and decides Nate isn't worthy of being her leading man.
Choice Line: "*Shaving your head and handling me (so delicately) / With satin and lace: / You're a whore.*"

4. *Because I'm Worth It* (2003)
Vanessa and Dan's romance comes to a halt when he turns into an overnight literary superstar. It's Fashion Week and Serena makes her modeling debut in the Les Best show, inadvertently pushing away her BF Aaron. Nate is sent to rehab where he meets Georgina Spark. Jenny lets Elise paint her in the nude and they kiss, but J is into Leo, the hot guy she spotted while shopping. Blair cuts her own hair and nearly sleeps with a man old enough to be her father.
Choice Line: "'Stress-induced regurgitation?' she answered tightly. She knew Jackie wanted her to say *bulimia*, but it was such a gross word, she refused to say it, especially in front of Nate."

5. *I Like it Like That* (2004)
Spring break arrives and so do Vanessa's weird arty parents. Serena, Blair, Nate, and Georgina are off to ski in Sun Valley where B nearly sleeps with S's brother Erik. Jenny finds out her boyfriend is keeping a secret from her (he's poor) and Dan interns at a pretentious literary magazine. Chuck gets a monkey.
Choice Line: "And after living with ['the biggest boobs in the entire school'] for fourteen years, she'd grown accustomed to people accidentally bumping into them because they stuck out so far."

6. *You're the One That I Want* (2004)
It's April and, for the seniors, that means college acceptance letters are arriving. Serena gets in everywhere she applied and Blair is waitlisted for dream school Yale. B spends a bizarre weekend at Georgetown, while S visits all her Ivy League choices and meets hot guys everywhere she goes. Jenny becomes a model with S's help. Dan and Vanessa live together for, like, a week. Blair names her new baby sister Yale and finally loses her virginity to Nate.
Choice Line: "Blair had a feeling her mother wouldn't look like she was twenty months pregnant instead of only seven if she'd stop eating so much."

7. *Nobody Does it Better* (2005)
Dan's poetic excellence lands him a short-lived gig as lead singer for It band The Raves. After briefly living at the Plaza, Blair moves in with weird, no-friends, no-hair Vanessa. Pictures of Jenny partying with The Raves get her in trouble at Constance, and she is desperate to attend boarding school. Nate steals his parents' yacht and misses the "Yale Loves New York" party. The boys crash the senior girls–only Hamptons spa weekend, where B catches S and N kissing.
Choice Line: "The Sunkist-orange ball that was the sun slid behind a horizontal wisp of cloud."

8. *Nothing Can Keep Us Together* (2005)
B moves out of V's apartment and into the Yale Club where she meets Lord Marcus. Filmmaker Ken Mogul is casting for a remake of *Breakfast at Tiffany's* and both B and S audition, while V is offered the job of cinematographer. As graduation approaches, Nate can't stop crying or taking Viagra. Jenny scouts boarding schools.
Choice Line: "It was sweet and sort of feminine of [Nate] to cry after they'd done it, and [Serena] suddenly realized she was the stronger, more 'masculine' one in their relationship. At least they'd finally done it."

9. *Only in Your Dreams* (2006)
Serena discovers acting is hard as she stars in *Breakfast at Fred's* and falls for her leading man (who secretly has a boyfriend). Blair tries to seduce Lord Marcus in London but he prefers his horse-faced cousin. Nate dates a Hamptons townie named Tawny and Dan two-times Vanessa with yoga-loving Bree. After being fired from the film, V gets a job as a nanny to two bratty rich boys. An unsatisfied B returns to New York and lives with Serena for, like, a week.
Choice Line: "'Uh yeah,' replied Dan nervously. *Bikram, Bikram, Bikram.* Not a movie. Maybe a restaurant? 'Right. Um, good, I'm, uh, starving.'"

10. *Would I Lie to You* (2006)
S and B plan to spend the summer after graduation playing muses to a fashion designer in the Hamptons, but get bored and ditch along with Nate, who was trying to earn his high school diploma working for the lacrosse coach. Blair and Nate get back together just as Serena realizes she's in love with him. Dan starts an experimental literary salon and thinks he's gay after making out with his male co-worker. Jenny's off in Europe with her crazy mother.
Choice Line: "Dear Jenny, I'm gay. Love, Dan."

11. *Don't You Forget About Me* (2007)
Summer's drawing to a close and the Waldorf–Roses throw a bash for B, who's just returned from a sailing trip with Nate to discover her family is relocating to California. She and Serena battle for Nate's affection, as S's movie career starts taking off. Vanessa's sister gets married and Dan finally figures out to whom his heart belongs, after his mother comes home to throw him a "Dan's gay — hooray" party. Nate is forced to choose between Blair and Yale, and Serena and the city, but he can't — so he hits the open water with Captain Chips to sail around the world.
Choice Line: "He'd loved her ever since he could remember, but he'd loved Blair too. And he wanted to be with both girls, always and forever. So why don't they all move to Utah?"

you know you love them: the cast

blake lively (serena van der woodsen)

Bringing the "bad girl gone good" character of Serena van der Woodsen to life is Blake Christina Lively, born August 25, 1987, in Tarzana, California. Though she never aspired to be an actress, it seemed a natural fit for the girl born into a family full of actors — her father Ernie is an actor/director, her mother Elaine an acting coach and manager, and her four older siblings have all worked as professional actors. Brother Jason played Rusty in *National Lampoon's European Vacation* and sister Robyn starred in *Teen Witch*. "My whole family's in the business," Blake told *Today* in 2005. "I never really went after it, just because it was already so much a part of my life" — even on the day she was born. "When I came home from the hospital, I literally didn't go to my house. I went to my sister's set." Her parents taught acting classes and would bring little Blake along. "I'm a naturally shy person, so it really helped. I would've just been hiding under the table, pulling on my mother's dress if I hadn't been in their classes. It forced me out of my shell."

After being homeschooled, she went to Burbank High School where she joined the show choir (despite professing not to be much of a singer), the cheerleading squad, and was the class president in her senior year. "I'm happy to say that I tried every sport and activity in high school, or just growing up. . . . It makes your school experience and memories just so much better. . . . If you get involved, you have this wonderful group of people that you have a class with during the day, you spend extracurricular time with — they become your friends, they become like your family."

Blake was on the path to applying to Stanford after high school graduation until her brother Eric stepped in. On a summer trip to Europe, he pestered his sister about what she wanted to do with her life; once back home, he asked his agents to start sending her out for auditions. "I didn't want to make him mad because he's such a good brother, so I just went on auditions to appease him. And then after a few months of auditioning, I got *Sisterhood*. . . . I knew that that's what I wanted to do, just because I had such a blast [filming]." Before landing that role, Blake had only one credit to her name: a bit part playing the tooth fairy in *Sandman*, a film directed by her father, when she was just 10 years old. Ernie Lively would be on set for her first major role as well, playing the father to Blake's character.

Cast as Bridget Vreeland in *The Sisterhood of the Traveling Pants*, Blake had to bring a beloved character from the young adult fiction series of the same name to the screen. The bestselling novels by Ann Brashares revolve around four BFFs who find a pair of jeans in a secondhand store that magically fit each differently shaped girl perfectly. Bridget spends the summer at a soccer camp in Mexico (where she falls for the hunky counselor), so Blake had to improve on her non-existent soccer skills before shooting began. But she didn't need any training in the being-a-bestie department. "I have a friend, my friend Jessica, who I've had since I was three years old and my friend Brittany who I've had since seventh grade. We can fight like [there's] no tomorrow and we can have these crazy times and prank, and go do nothing together and it's this great friendship because you have such a deep understanding of one another. We know each other so well, inside and out, that it's amazing." The first-time actress was up to the challenging role and received a 2005 Teen Choice Award nomination for Choice Movie

Breakout Female, along with her *Sister Pants* co-stars America Ferrera and Jenna Boyd.

With her newfound success, Blake decided to temporarily put her Stanford dreams on hold. As she told Radio Free Entertainment, "Everybody that was involved in my professional career said, 'This is the time. You have to do a movie back to back to back.' Whatever. I said, 'No, school is so important to me.' So [I compromised]. . . . What would be my first year of college, I'll just completely dedicate to acting." Her compromise paid off; in 2006, she filmed two movies, *Simon Says,* where she worked alongside her then-boyfriend Kelly Blatz, and *Accepted*, playing Justin Long's love interest in the fake-college comedy. Steve Pink, the film's director, said of Blake, "She has a great talent of looking at something both earnestly and satirically at the same time. . . . It shows her intelligence and her powers of irony. She really classed up the joint." Next up for the budding actress was the dark comedy *Elvis & Annabelle*. The film, about small-town Texas beauty queen Annabelle, who meets a young mortician (Max Minghella) when he brings her back from the dead with a kiss, premiered as the opening night gala at the South by Southwest Film Festival, and Blake went on to win the Newport Beach Film Festival Breakout Performance Achievement award. Despite its festival circuit tour, the film didn't get a theatrical release.

Moving from the big screen to the small screen wasn't the only daunting shift for Blake when she was cast as Serena in *Gossip Girl*. It was moving across the country from Burbank, California, to New York, New York. "At first, I was like, 'Oh, shoot, New York, I have to move — OK! Where's the plane ticket?' My whole base is in California, so to go off and have the experience of not knowing anyone in an unknown city and just living there is really, really thrilling to me." The city wasn't the only draw; Blake was happy to play a popular girl who wasn't a stereotypical mean girl. "I was really attracted to the role of Serena. It's good to portray the 'it' girl as a nice person because not all girls are mean." Comparing her own character to Serena's, then 20-year-old Blake told the Associated Press, "I think that I strive to do the right thing and not fall into the norm [like] so many young people in Hollywood who . . . get caught up in some of the nonsense. I really try to steer clear of that. So, you know, we're like that in the same way. We both giggle a lot. We look alike."

Her plans for Stanford were put on a much longer hold as she signed a multi-season contract for *Gossip Girl*, but she considered taking classes at Columbia one day a week while filming. Josh Schwartz claims the lure of the show wasn't the promise of an education: "I think the real carrot for Blake was the opportunity for clothing. I remember talking to her about that. She was like, 'Wait, so you're asking me to move to New York and wear the most incredible clothes, some of which you might actually let me keep?' So I think the wardrobe-reinvention carrot was stronger than the college-degree carrot."

Like the rest of her cast mates, Blake was soon the subject of gossip columns, with rumors flying that she and Leighton were real-life frenemies, that she'd had a nose job, and that her onscreen romance with Penn Badgley had moved off-screen. Of all the gossiping, Blake told *People*, "Everybody always tries to dig into your personal life or create things that aren't there. . . . It's silly. [I] just try not to listen to what people say. At least for me it's important — because I'm so close with my family and my friends — to keep core people around me that know the truth about everything." The press did get the love connection right. In May 2008, paparazzi photographed Blake and Penn kissing while on vacation in Cancun, and shortly thereafter the couple stopped hiding their romance. "I think she's incredible," said Penn of Blake. "She's an amazing person and she's beautiful — so there's not a lot to dislike." The two actors had actually met long before they worked together on *Gossip Girl*; they were homeschooled together when they were 11 years old.

The success of *Gossip Girl* and the popularity of her character put Blake on the covers of magazines and earned her another nomination at the Teen Choice Awards. This time she won, taking home surfboards for Choice TV Breakout Star Female and Choice TV Actress Drama. Audiences saw Blake return as Bridget in the sequel to *The Sisterhood of the Traveling Pants*. Lively was happy to revisit the role, as she told CNN. "These [films] are [about] four girls loving each other and supporting each other, and the friendship is really the most important thing. It's not the love interest or the cute, popular boy in school that you get."

Declared part of the New Wave of Hollywood by *Vanity Fair*, Blake seems to have her head on her shoulders and her feet on the ground — she doesn't drink, smoke, or do drugs, and she has a close family and the support of her dear friends. Blake revealed in her *Seventeen* cover story, "I come from a big family; there are five of us, and I'm the baby. I've just been so loved, and I'm used to really loving people and trusting them. So I don't have friends just to have friends. I have a small group of people I truly love with all my heart."

No hidden vices for Blake besides an addiction to Chanel ("I can't stand it: the security guards know me there") and an undying love for Guitar Hero ("The reason they wrote it in [to *Gossip Girl*] was because I'm such an amazing Guitar Hero player"). But just 'cause she's a good girl doesn't mean she doesn't know how to have fun — even if it's at her own expense doing an *SNL* skit playing a transvestite. With film roles in *New York, I Love You* and *The Private Lives of Pippa Lee* (playing the teenaged version of Robin Wright Penn), Blake Lively has proven she can still work in film and not just be known for her role as Serena. "You have to be willing to take a plunge now and then, because it's worth it. It's all about taking a risk."

leighton meester (blair waldorf)

Much fuss has been made about Leighton Marissa Claire Meester's family history, with tabloid headlines claiming the girl who would go on to play Upper East Side princess Blair Waldorf was born in jail. The truth behind the gossip is that Leighton was born at Baylor All Saints Medical Center in Fort Worth, Texas, on April 9, 1986; her mother Connie was allowed out of jail where she was serving a sentence for her involvement in a marijuana smuggling ring and stayed with newborn Leighton for three months in a halfway house. Connie served 16 months of her sentence and was then released, joining Leighton and her older brother Douglas, who were staying with their grandmother. (Her father Doug also served time.) "I wouldn't have volunteered that information but I've never kept it a secret either," said Leighton. "It's just that it's not my past; it's not my story to tell."

Growing up in Marco Island, Florida, Leighton had a "normal childhood." She and her mother have always been close and the actress calls her one of her best friends. "She's a very strong woman," Leighton said of her mother to *Rolling Stone*. "She was able to be there for me, and she shaped me into the person I am. She's been honest with me about everything." A self-described late bloomer, Leighton decided to become an actress early on, performing in a school production of *The Wizard of Oz*. The family spent some time in New York City, where Leighton's mother was supportive of her burgeoning career, but not pushy. "Every time I went to an audition, she always said, 'If you don't want to do this, we can leave right now,'" said Leighton. Signing with the Wilhelmina modeling agency, Leighton was in a Ralph Lauren campaign and photographed by Sofia Coppola before landing her first on-camera role in a 1999 episode of *Law & Order*. The family moved around Manhattan, living in some sketchy apartments while Connie made a living waitressing and writing screenplays. "I clearly wasn't an Upper East Side kid. It's hard for me to relate to people who were born with silver spoons in their mouths."

Moving from New York to L.A., Leighton attended Beverly Hills High School and felt like a fish out of water. "Most people there have a lot of money, and my family really didn't. They'd be making fun of my clothes or my bag or whatever." She was the target of the Blair Waldorfs of her school, as she told *Vanity Fair*, "There was always one little girl in each grade that was mean to me. But I was never mean to anyone. I was never like, 'Ew!'"

Leighton's career continued to build as she landed role after role on television series, most notably *Tarzan*, *7th Heaven*, *24*, *Veronica Mars*, *House*, *Shark*, and 12 episodes of the short-lived NBC sci-fi series *Surface*. In 2007, Leighton was in the movie *Drive-Thru* opposite future *Gossip Girl* co-star Penn Badgley. Playing a singer in that role, she got another chance to perform as Justine Chapin in season 1 of *Entourage*, a Britney Spears–inspired character who returned in season 5 and sang a duet with Tony Bennett. Leighton described that experience as "really awesome, to say the least. I don't even know if awesome is a word to describe it. It's incredible. I'm getting nervous just thinking about it, because back then I was like, 'Yeah, I can do this.' And then when the time came, I was like, 'Oh my god, I can't believe this!' But it was really, really great."

When Leighton first found out about the role of Blair on *Gossip Girl*, "I loved the character and the script, and I just *knew*." But Leighton was a blonde, and after auditioning multiple times, some of the producers couldn't get past the hair — Blair's a brunette. (Leighton's hair is naturally a dirty blonde/light brown color.) Stephanie Savage asked her to dye her hair and Leighton obliged — except she did it herself and it turned green. Her hairstylist roommate fixed it, Leighton did her final audition, and the part was hers. On playing a character who enjoys being vicious, "I actually really like it. I shouldn't enjoy it so much," she playfully told *Entertainment Weekly*. Her portrayal of Blair is successful because she not only does bitchy so well, but she also shows B's vulnerable side. "Leighton plays her with so much joy and she's so funny about it. . . . Leighton never misses a moment. She gets every color of the character," said Josh Schwartz. The actress remembers her initial direction from the producers on how to approach the role: "They were like, 'Be bitchy and nice, ugly and pretty, young and old, stupid and smart, innocent and slutty, blond and brunette. Can you be all those things?'" The character's complexity is what drew Leighton to Blair; it's not often a young woman on television is portrayed as more than one-dimensional.

With her celebrity gained from *Gossip Girl*, Leighton has not only graced several covers of magazines but landed endorsement deals, becoming the face of a Reebok ad campaign. She also uses her status to do charitable work, raising money for women's shelters and campaigning against domestic violence. While Leighton doesn't talk about her personal life in the press, the press loves to talk about her personal life. Leighton, who's been seen at various events and on set with Sebastian Stan (who plays Carter Baizen on *Gossip Girl* and starred in *Kings*) since July 2008, has described the type of man she's drawn to: "I think guys who are rebels and make their own rules are appealing. I don't want to tame anybody. I want them to be dark and bad."

Though she never wears hairbands, Leighton does take style clues from her onscreen counterpart, telling *Teen Vogue* she's realized she doesn't "have to be shy about dressing up." When she's not being Blair, Leighton is hard at work on her other passion: she's recording an album for Universal she describes as "very fun. It's edgy, like electropop rather than bubblegum, and you can dance to it." As she launches her music career, she is also keen to follow in the footsteps of accomplished actresses: "Cate Blanchett has a beautiful career that's inspiring, and she's a beautiful woman. She's never pigeonholed as one specific thing. She can go from being a hot schoolteacher to playing a very intense role, as in *Babel*. I think she's very versatile. I think Bette Davis was an incredible actress. And I look to her for a lot of inspiration, too." In between seasons of *Gossip Girl*, Leighton has a few film projects on the go.

She plays the babysitter for parents Steve Carell and Tina Fey in *Date Night*, she stars in a thriller called *The Roommate*, and she's reportedly in talks to star in *Beastly*, a retelling of *Beauty and the Beast*.

On the success of the show and the attention the cast is getting, Leighton has a theory: "People have a fascination with celebrity and they like to see rich, seemingly perfect people have real flaws and be all messed up." Not one for partying, Leighton aims to keep focused on her career and not on being a tabloid headline, saying to *Rolling Stone*, "I don't want to have to start over a million times. I want to have an abundance of good things in my life, and I want it to spread out evenly — I don't want it to just come and go."

penn badgley (dan humphrey)

Born November 1, 1986, in Baltimore, Maryland, Penn Dayton Badgley has perhaps the oddest story of how he was named. "My father was bouncing a Penn tennis ball for stress during my mom's pregnancy. When my mother got her first amnio . . . she just casually mentioned that the baby is the size of that tennis ball, and that's it. I'm glad it wasn't Dunlop or Wilson." Penn spent his childhood in Richmond, Virginia, and Seattle, Washington, attending Tacoma's Charles Wright Academy. By the age of 11, Penn had his heart set on being a performer and moved with his mother to California. (His parents divorced when he was 12.)

"I started with the Pine Nut Players in Monroe [Washington] and I went to Seattle Children's Theatre after that, which really sparked my interest. Through SCT I saw an ad on a bulletin board for an acting consultant [who could help] to get an agent, things like that. So I got an agent and after a few years I was in seventh grade and she said I should try going on to L.A. I came down and after a few years it looks like I'm going to be successful." Always a supporter, Penn's mother drove him 50 miles so he could be involved in a production of *The Music Man*. "I don't know if I loved acting at that point yet, but it was a happy accident and I do now. It's what I do best." In California, he was homeschooled before attending a public high school.

"My first day of high school one of my best friends got punched in the face by a senior. It was in the hall of a big public school. That was a rude awakening. I realized that kids just act so erratically. . . . The vulnerability of teens is universal and, sometimes, they'll act out like that guy acted out in an offensive way for no reason, hitting my best friend." At age 14, Penn decided to take the California High School Proficiency Exam, and then attended Santa Monica College, where he earned two years of credits before being accepted as a junior at the University of Southern California (he deferred admission).

Apart from his educational pursuits, Penn was working away at his acting career. After doing some voice work, he landed his first onscreen role on *Will & Grace*. Playing Phillip Chancellor IV, a guest role on *The Young and the Restless*, earned Penn a nomination for a 2001 Young Artist Award for Best Performance in a Daytime Series. Penn was cast in a lead role on the 2002 WB series *Do Over*, playing Joel Larsen, a 34-year-old man who gets to re-live his freshman year of high school. When the executive producer described him as an "old soul," Penn disagreed, "I don't think I'm really an old soul. . . . Somebody asked me if I'd been studying 34-year-olds, and I'm like, 'No.'" Penn filmed 15 episodes of the show, but it was canceled before the full season was finished. The *New York Times* gave him praise, saying the show was "made watchable by an engaging cast, especially Penn Badgley as Joel."

The WB felt Penn was an actor to hold on to and the network cast him in a new show. Penn played Sam Tunney in *The Mountain*, a drama set at a ski resort, but that show was canceled after its first season. The year after that, Penn was a lead in the WB's *The Bedford Diaries*, a show about college students in a sexuality seminar, along with future *Heroes* star Milo Ventimiglia. That show? Canceled in its first season. "It definitely felt like, 'What can we put Penn in this year because we want to keep him working with us?' There was a time when I felt a little cheesy, doing WB show after WB show — like it was repetitive," said Penn to the *New York Post*. But there was one more pilot in his future for the WB descendent, the brand-new CW.

"My agents sent [*Gossip Girl*] to me and, initially, I was hesitant because

I'd done so many WB shows playing the same guy; the nice guy with maybe a hard edge so, by the end of each show, I'd sort of transform the character into a cooler guy," said Penn with a laugh. "I actually worked with Stephanie Savage [on *The Mountain*]. I met Josh when they were trying to do a spin-off with Willa Holland, I think, for *The O.C.* I knew them both and I had a relationship with Stephanie and they sent me the script of *Gossip Girl* and they told me about the books. I knew nothing about them. It seemed like an amazing opportunity to work with them to be a part of something that could be big so I signed on. . . . Initially I wanted to play Chace's role, Nate. [Stephanie] said, 'I'm not sure you can play the floppy-haired, nerdy, sensitive guy anymore, but just take a look at this.' Eventually they found Chace, and once I saw him I was like, 'Nah, I'm not that guy. I definitely can't do that.'" As Dan, Penn is the "Josh Schwartz character" on the show, like Seth Cohen was on *The O.C.* "I am the Josh stand-in," Penn said. "I guess I know Josh will never write himself out."

Between all those TV shows for the WB, Penn made a few movies as well — *Drive Thru* with Leighton Meester and *John Tucker Must Die*. In its otherwise negative review of the flick, the *New York Times* again singled him out: "Penn Badgley is wildly charismatic in the role of John Tucker's younger brother. The entire picture could hang on his cheekbones alone." He hit the big screen again in 2008's *Forever Strong*, based on a true story of a rugby player's struggle. In 2009, he finished filming *The Stepfather*, a remake of the 1987 thriller of the same name. "I know that I, personally, did not watch the original. I believe in the original, my character was a girl. There are enough differences that I didn't want to have any predisposed ideas about it and anything that would mess with what I wanted to do with the character and the development and the arc. So I think, when we wrap, I might watch the original with a bottle of whiskey or something. I haven't had a drink in two months because I've been getting in shape, so I think it'll be nice."

Said Penn of his career path, "I want to do film. I want to be an actor — I don't want to be a celebrity. They are two different things, and people have forgotten that they are different. Because if you are one, you can be generally the other. Like if you are a celebrity, then anyone will let you be in a film or on a TV show, and if you're an actor, chances are if you are successful, you are becoming a celebrity."

With the success of *Gossip Girl*, Penn's personal life was dug into, in particular his relationship with Blake Lively. His TV dad, Matthew Settle, felt his TV son had the ability to handle the scrutiny. "In real life, Penn rolls with the punches better than anybody . . . I don't think he needs any advice. . . . They're a very hot couple. They look good together. And I think they're good for each other, so why not?"

Other than his work and ladylove, Penn's passions are music and soccer. "I love soccer. I kind of wish that I lived in Europe for that reason. I'd say my number one passion is music. I have started saying this and I like the sound of it. I think my job as an actor will fuel my music habit. So I spend a lot of time playing music and just like anything else, it comes in waves. Sometimes I won't play much, but you know, it can be really therapeutic. I listen to a lot of music and play a lot of soccer and go out just like anybody else." Said Penn in 2007, "Dan Byrd, who's on *Aliens in America*, . . . he and I have been producing songs together, where I sing on them. He raps, and I sing. I know everyone will be imagining, 'Yeah, right, I'm sure it's good.' But we're not doing it to sell it. . . . It's stuff that we just like to do. And it's really fulfilling, I have to say. . . . Music really is my passion."

When he was 12 years old, Penn recorded a pop song and had some other singing opportunities — some more successful than others. Penn names his most embarrassing moment as "singing the national anthem at a Tacoma Rainiers game. I didn't take it that seriously and I didn't think I'd forget the words, but I got up there and it was the line 'through the perilous fight' and I blanked at 'perilous.' I stopped and everyone was like, 'Perilous! Perilous!' And I turned around and just started over from there. . . . All the guys came out of the dugout and said, 'It's OK, man, everyone makes mistakes.'"

Comparing himself to his onscreen counterpart, Penn wagers, "I would like to think that I have the same integrity as his character. I am a little more socially confident. I am not the loner. . . . But I was very introverted as a kid. So there are more similarities in that way than people might at first think. But yeah, overall, I think we are very similar. And on a television show, over time, the character really becomes you or rather you become the character. You kind of switch into that mode very easily. As time goes on, you might see more similarities."

chace crawford (nate archibald)

Christopher Chace Crawford was born July 18, 1985, in Lubbock, Texas, to father Chris, a dermatologist, and mother Dana, a teacher. His upbringing wasn't very Upper East Side, growing up in the heart of Texas, but once he reached high school, he attended the private Trinity Christian Academy and found it could get gossipy. "I went to a really small high school so I learned about that whole 'bubble' thing going on there. The smaller it gets, the worse [the gossip] is." While Chace was mostly a good boy, he did get into a spot of trouble. "I went to juvenile detention when I was 15. It was all over a little misunderstanding with a pellet gun! I accidentally hit somebody on a golf course so I went to the center for the weekend. At the time my parents went ballistic, but it's a joke now." (No doubt the person Chace hit thinks it's *hilarious.*) Opting for painting and drawing over studying drama, Chace also played football and golf and had a part-time job. "I used to work as a 'greeter' at Abercrombie & Fitch, saying hello and welcoming the customers. I was never allowed to work as a cashier; I guess I was too good at smiling at people!"

After graduation, Chace moved to California to attend Pepperdine University, where he joined the Sigma Nu frat and studied broadcast journalism for a time. "Everyone else knew what they wanted to do," Chace told *Teen Vogue* in 2007. "But not me — I was the lone wolf." His mother encouraged him to pursue acting, and with some modeling experience under his belt, Chace was immediately signed by an agent. His first acting gig was in *Long Lost Son,* playing an abducted son who reunites with his mother. While filming *The Covenant*, a supernatural thriller about five rich prep school guys with superpowers, Chace met co-stars Sebastian Stan and Taylor Kitsch, with whom he remains friends.

With that relatively limited experience, Chace auditioned for the role of Nate Archibald in the *Gossip Girl* pilot. He auditioned "many times, I think I hit six times. The producers were always nice to me and kept calling me back. So I knew I had a chance." Said Josh Schwartz on first seeing Chace, "This guy is Nate." Though he was new to acting, there was a "sense of decency in Nate from Chace," said Josh, which made an audience want to follow him on his journey. "It's all new to me," said Chace when the cast began filming *Gossip Girl*. "The younger actors are sticking together — it's the only way to survive the craziness. Right now we can shoot in Central Park and nobody bothers us." Though Penn decided to live on his own, Chace and Ed Westwick got an apartment together in Chelsea.

On the show's racy content, Chace has mixed feelings. "Is that a weight on my conscience? Well, yes, I think it is. I come from a moral background, and I can see the power of the show, and imagine my old schoolteachers cringing, or my grandparents thinking 'Oh my God' when they see me, say, having sex on a barstool. But you have to remember, this is not a reality show. It's supposed to be pure entertainment." To the *Los Angeles Times*, he said, "I'm proud to be part of a show that's kind of redefining what it means to be a hit show with today's younger generation that is very media-savvy."

Chace appeared in two more films in 2008, *Loaded*, an action film starring Jesse Metcalfe, and *The Haunting of Molly Hartley*, a horror film with him in another private school uniform. After meeting Leona Lewis in London, she asked him to appear in her video, "I Will Be." For his work on *Gossip Girl*, Chace won the Teen Choice Award for Choice Breakout TV Star Male in the same year that his younger sister Candice won the Miss Missouri USA title. (Candice competed for the Missouri rather than Texas title because she was attending the University of Missouri and living in Columbia.) Chace was spotted with country singer Carrie Underwood and for a brief period, the gossip magazines made a big deal out of the new couple and their break-up, which reportedly was by text message. "It was mutual," said Chace of the break-up. "There's a lot more to it than that. The gossip magazines try to compartmentalize it by saying it was as simple as a text message — trust me it wasn't that simple." In addition to prying into his romance with Carrie, rumor had it that Chace and former *NSync member JC Chasez were lovers, and/or he and roommate Ed Westwick were. In a *Details* interview, Chace mocked the press's characterization of him: "Model turned actor, dime a dozen, eye candy, doesn't know what he's doing . . . and Perez Hilton says I have 'gayface.' So on top of everything else, I have to overcome gayface."

Taking a similar approach to the rumors printed about him as his co-stars, Chace said in *V Man*, "There's a lot of speculation with no reality to it, complete fabrications about my private life. It's just comical. I let it roll off my back." In the break between seasons 2 and 3 of filming *Gossip Girl*, Chace was cast in *Twelve*, a Joel Schumacher–directed adaptation of the Nick McDonell novel about drug use and decadence on the Upper East Side, co-starring Rory Culkin, Emma Roberts, and Curtis "50 Cent" Jackson. After Zac Efron dropped out of the *Footloose* remake, Chace was cast as his replacement. "Fame can be a double-edged sword," said Chace. "But right now I couldn't ask for more, and I certainly never complain about it. Actually, I genuinely like meeting people out and about, and making relationships. I find I have a natural affinity for people."

taylor momsen (jenny humphrey)

The youngest of the *Gossip Girl* cast, Taylor Michel Momsen was born in St. Louis, Missouri, on July 26, 1993. Her dad, a VP of an electronics company, and her mom Colette, a homemaker, had another daughter Sloane in 1996. Very early on, Taylor showed a talent for performing, landing a Shake 'N' Bake commercial when she was just three years old. Taylor enjoyed acting but doesn't have clear memories of her early work. "I don't remember what I did on set. I do remember a playroom with puzzles and coloring books." After a small role in the Dennis Hopper film *The Prophet's Game*, Taylor was cast as Cindy Lou Who in 2000's *How the Grinch Stole Christmas* and received a Young Artist Award nomination for her performance. *Grinch* director Ron Howard noted that Taylor once pointed out to him that he'd just cut a line of dialogue crucial to the story. "Nothing," he told *People*, "ever fazed Taylor." And the young actress seems unfazed by her success. "I've grown up acting. It's sort of all I've known. It's part of who I am now; I mean, I've been doing it since I was three, so . . ."

Her little sister Sloane had a cameo with Taylor in *The Grinch* as well as in 2002's *We Were Soldiers*. Taylor played Gretel in *Hansel & Gretel* and the president's daughter in *Spy Kids 2*. Like her TV big brother Penn, Taylor was cast in a failed WB show; hers was called *Misconceptions* and it never aired. In 2006, she played Samantha Wallace in the third *Shiloh* film, *Saving Shiloh*, an adaptation of the novel written by Phyllis Reynolds Naylor.

Taylor was cast in Gus Van Sant's 2007 film *Paranoid Park* as Jennifer, a popular cheerleader desperate to be accepted by her peers. "It was a really great experience for me to work with Gus. He's so brilliant and it was such a different thing from *Gossip Girl* or any other film that I've done. Just 'cause it was so laid-back and relaxed and there was a lot of improv. . . . It was so great as an actress — I really had to fully become my character. He would sit you down before a scene and say, 'This is what happened, this is what's going to happen.' He'd say, 'Go, be her.'"

That same year, Taylor landed another role as a Jennifer, *Gossip Girl*'s Jenny Humphrey. "When Josh and I met Taylor," said Stephanie Savage to the *Observer*, "she really had that great quality; on the one hand being Cindy Lou Who, really sweet and just sort of delightful and smiley and funny, and she can act her age. . . . But she also has that Gus Van Sant side to her — very grown-up, very self-aware. There is an intelligent, watchful darkness that she's got as well. Those two qualities flickering back and forth between the sweet and the innocent, and the more intelligent observer felt like that was really something that could be something magical for the role."

"With Jenny, there's that sense of a very intelligent, observant young girl looking around and going, 'You know, I'm not as rich as these girls, and I don't have that leg up because of my family, but I'm just as pretty and I think that I'm smarter, so if I play my cards right, I can win this game," said Stephanie.

On her very first day on set at *Gossip Girl*, Taylor made a memorable impression. "I came into the makeup trailer and it was the first time I was going to meet everyone! I had just put my wardrobe on, which included nylon tights, and when I walked into the room in my stocking feet, I went completely head over heels! Blake screamed because she thought I was seriously hurt and everyone else was just laughing. . . . Way to make an entrance, Taylor!"

It took her a while to get used to the crowds who gather to watch them film *Gossip Girl*, or to people recognizing her on the street. "It's funny because I forget that I look the same — you know, that I look the same all the time. I have two different modes: I have my on-set mode, and then I have my mode with my friends and family. My Taylor mode. And when I'm in my Taylor mode, I forget that people still see me as Jenny. It takes a minute." On her similarities to her character, Taylor said, "I think the cool thing is she has two sides to her, she has her Upper East Side role that she can fit into and her downtown life too. I have my uptown older group of friends and some of my downtown younger group of friends."

Managing work and school is made easier by attending the Professional Performing Arts High School along with Connor Paolo. "I go to a performing arts school so everyone's used to everyone working and leaving and stuff." Thirteen hundred kids auditioned for the freshman class of 100. "It's a tough school, it's rigorous, but it's really a great experience." Her life got even busier in June 2008 when she signed to IMG Models. "I love high fashion," Taylor told *Blackbook*. "It's been such a big part of my life, models and fashion, so it's really exciting to enter that world. It's a whole different ballgame." Addressing media concern that she's too skinny and may have an eating disorder, Taylor said, "I'm just kind of naturally thin. My mom's really thin, and I'm tall. Good genes . . . I just eat healthy. I walk a lot because I live in New York. So I try to walk a lot instead of taking cabs. I should probably start working out or something. I dance, so I guess that's a full workout. I've been dancing since I was three, so I guess that would be it."

Taylor's also been singing her whole life. She sang on the album *School's Out! Christmas* ("Rudolph the Red-Nosed Reindeer" and "One Small Voice") as well as in the *Grinch* movie. Her taste has matured with her, as she revealed to *ElleGirl* in 2007. "Music-wise, I love Paramore, they've been my favorite band for, like, three years. It's so cool, they're finally getting on the radio. I have such an eclectic mix, from The Beatles to Carly Simon to Paramore and Evanescence. Avril Lavigne, I still love Britney Spears. Top 100 chart stuff, random indie bands, so many different things; music is like my life. It makes everything right." Taylor's been working on an album (due out in fall '09 from Interscope) with her band, the Pretty Reckless, and has taught herself to play guitar. "I do write [the songs] all 100 percent myself. I'm the lead singer and I play guitar and I totally oversee it. It's a huge passion and totally important to me. It's really exciting and probably not what people are gonna expect. Kinda dark, a little bit heavier — but we have our lighter, fun stuff too."

Described by Chace Crawford as "pretty much perfect," Taylor now lives in the city with her family and her white Maltese dog Petal (who has black "punk rock" streaks on her head) and still wears a pink tutu every year on her birthday, a tradition since she was three. "It kind of chose me," she's said of her career. "I had the opportunity to say no, but I love it. I've grown up in it. It's kind of all I know."

ed westwick (chuck bass)

Playing the Upper East Side rogue Chuck Bass is Edward Gregory Westwick, a Brit born on June 27, 1987, in Stevenage, north of London, to parents Carole, an educational psychologist, and Peter, a business lecturer. The youngest of three boys, Ed attended St. Ippolyts Church of England Primary School and the Barclay School. When he was just six years old, Ed was in his first musical group. "My brother and I had a band, Fangs of Fury, for about five minutes. I just sat and watched him. So we were a two-man band, with one man doing something." His parents put him in piano lessons, but little Ed preferred playing soccer. And unlike his onscreen persona, Ed claims to have been the "nice one" of his brothers. "My brother Will was more of a devil," he said. "Though I was easily led astray."

Not sure what to do with himself, at age 18 Ed joined the National Youth Theatre. "After secondary school, I thought, 'What the fuck am I going to do with my life, man?' I was so frustrated with the idea that you had to figure it all out right away." His first film role came while he was a student at North Hertfordshire College — *Breaking and Entering*, directed by the late Anthony Minghella. Ed played a teenaged Bosnian criminal. The film turned out to be Minghella's last feature before passing away in 2008. "He was like a father to us on set," said Ed of his experience working with him. "He nurtured us and made us feel very secure, which was important because it was my first job. I had only worked as an amateur on stage and he taught me how to underplay things and make my gestures more subtle. I remember one lesson he gave me. I was going through my lines at the table and he told me to pour a glass of water to make my performance more natural. At the beginning I was very self-conscious and he used the glass of water as a distraction. He made me understand every last detail of a situation. And it wasn't just me. It was everybody, even Jude [Law]. He had a very clear vision, which he shared with everybody."

From there Ed appeared on British television shows *Doctors*, *Casualty*, and *Afterlife*. He played a bullying older brother in the 2007 Sundance Film Festival sensation *Son of Rambow*, and appeared in *Children of Men*. The young actor was in Los Angeles for pilot season when the *Gossip Girl* script came up. He first auditioned for the role of Nate, and then for the smaller role of Chuck, a part not originally slated as a lead. "He's not the kind of guy you normally see on TV, or a teen drama," said Josh Schwartz. Once Ed played Chuck with an American accent, rather than his native British, the producers decided the minor role should be made larger, so captivating was Ed's performance. But there were "massive immigration issues," and it looked like Ed's work visa wouldn't come through in time to shoot the pilot. Asked to recast the role, the *Gossip Girl* team held off, and at the very last minute, his visa arrived and Ed was able to play the part. "I learn so much every day, every week, every episode," Ed told *Teen Vogue* of his *Gossip Girl* experience. "And everyone on the show has created this great bond. We're like a family."

Asked to describe Chuck Bass, Ed told the U.K.'s *Daily Mail*, "He is completely diabolical but he is quick-witted and not intimidated by anyone. He goes after what he wants. It's just the nature of what he wants which is not good. But there are a lot more differences than similarities between Chuck and me. When I was 17, I had certain characteristics of Chuck's, but obviously the context was different. I didn't come from the Upper East Side and I didn't have the same desires. Oh, and I didn't have a string of lovers. I'm a good boy."

On the show's success, Ed seems unfazed. "I really don't think about it that much. I am who I am. . . . What will be, will be. I had no experience of being on an American TV show before, so I really didn't have any expectations. Basically, I was like, 'I'll stay focused on the work'; of course I'm aware of it, it's fantastic." To *Page Six Magazine*, he elaborated, "We were all thrown into this situation with a lot of attention on us, and you get a lot of free clothes and shit but that's no reason not to stay grounded. What am I really doing, baby? Saving the world? Nah, I'm on television."

His onscreen chemistry with Leighton Meester was an unexpected boon to the series, creating a whole legion of "Chair" fans. "You can't put a finger on what makes two characters connect. It's just chemistry. We have it. We feel it," said Ed on the Chuck–Blair sparks, a pairing original to the TV series. Leighton says of her co-star: "Ed is just incredible. He's got that kind of bad-boy edge to him, but he too has a real soft side. I find him to be the most down-to-earth, cool, and sweet guy. He gets into these funny moods where he's really silly. Ed's . . . great on stage. . . . He's really artistic and an amazing singer and dancer. He loves good rock, alternative music. . . . Girls just follow him. I have a feeling Ed would do OK even if he wasn't on a TV show."

Though he admitted to being the most flirtatious of the cast to *People*, Ed insists, "I'm not a player. I'm going to get a tattoo that reads, 'I heart romance.' I saw it on a bathroom wall in a bar. I'm the last of the romantics, so it's perfect for me." While filming season 2 of the show, Ed was spotted with co-star Jessica Szohr; photos of their Jamaican vacation made the tabloids and gossip sites. "I'm *all* for being in love," said Ed to *Teen Vogue*. "And whenever I like someone, I end up pretty much completely smitten." Other than being the subject of rumors, Ed has said the worst thing about being on *Gossip Girl* is "shaving every day. Chuck's supposed to be 17, so he can't have scruff yet. I get the makeup artist to shave me, because she just does it better. Poor Penn has to shave his chest — that's worse."

Other than acting, Ed's passion is music. With some friends in the U.K., he formed The Filthy Youth, a band he fronts. "I've always connected with music. Life's not always what you see; it's what's going on in your head. Music is what comes out of your subconscious." The band had a few songs featured in the season 1 episode of *Gossip Girl* "School Lies." "I read Jim Morrison's philosophy behind music. It wasn't just about the songs; it was about a show. Onstage, I'm a showman," he told *Cosmo Girl*. "I wouldn't say I'm a rock star, though. . . . All right, in my dream world, I am."

As if being Chuck Bass wasn't enough, Ed has kept busy with other onscreen work. "I'd love to do films, and I think it's important to stretch the acting muscle all the time, and meet new people that challenge and inspire you, people that force you to see things in a new way." In 2009's straight-to-DVD *Donnie Darko* sequel, Ed plays Randy. "We shot it in Utah. It's called *S. Darko*, and basically it takes place in 1995 and we're picking up with the younger sister, Samantha Darko. . . . It's got its own individuality, separate from *Donnie Darko*. It's got a lot of different things going on because it's about Samantha. It works on its own." Ed's also in the thriller *100 Feet*, playing a Brooklyn delivery boy seduced by Famke Janssen. Like Leighton and her Reebok deal, Ed's done an ad campaign with K-Swiss. After landing a part in season 3 of *Californication*, Ed got even better news — he was cast as Heathcliff in *Wuthering Heights*, an adaptation of his mom's favorite novel.

Winner of the 2008 Teen Choice Award for Choice TV Villain, Ed's proud of the work he does on *Gossip Girl* and of the show itself. "It's not just a show about teenagers, it's a show about fashion, lies and deceit, and all the things we all go through, or I should say, see on a television show. And it's a beautiful homage to one of the most beautiful cities in the world. I don't think anyone should feel guilty about watching it."

jessica szohr (vanessa abrams)

Born March 31, 1985, Jessica Karen Szohr raised in Menomonee Falls, Wisconsin, the oldest of six kids. One-half Hungarian, one-fourth African-American, and one-fourth Caucasian, Jessica's unique look brought her early success as a model. By age 16, she'd done ads for Crate & Barrel, Mountain Dew, Quaker Oats, Jockey, JanSport, and had a full-page ad in *Seventeen* magazine for Claire's Boutiques. Barely 5 feet 6 inches tall, Jessica's personality overcame her relatively short stature for a model. "[Clients] want a cool, edgy, fun kid and she has an explosive personality," said her then-agent. "She walks in a room and just takes over. . . . She beats out a lot of other talent because of that exotic look."

A cheerleader in high school, Jessica's teenage years were nothing like those portrayed on *Gossip Girl*. "It was very different from the world on the show, that's for sure. I'm from a very Midwest, family-oriented small town, and my friends were nothing like these kids that grew up on the Upper East Side. When I saw the pilot for *Gossip Girl*, I thought, 'There's no way anyone actually had lives like that in high school.' Now, I have friends who assure me that people certainly do."

She moved from Wisconsin to L.A. when she was 18. "I never thought acting was a realistic dream. But in my senior year of high school, my parents sat me down and asked if I really wanted to go to college, or was I just doing it for them. So with their blessing, I decided to go out to Los Angeles for pilot season." Starting in 2003, Jessica landed role after role, appearing on TV in *My Wife and Kids*, *What I Like About You*, *Drake & Josh*, *Joan of Arcadia*, *That's So Raven*, and *The Reading Room*; in the films *Uncle Nino*, *House at the End of the Drive*, and *Somebody Help Me*; and in Daughtry's video for "Over You." In 2007, Jessica landed a three-episode part on *CSI: Miami* and a series regular role as Laura on *What About Brian*. "I was a huge fan of *90210* so when I got to work with Tiffani Amber Thiessen, I was like, 'Oh my god!' . . . It was a lot of fun." *What About Brian* was canceled in May 2007 before her character's arc was resolved.

Jessica had seen the *Gossip Girl* pilot and heard about the upcoming three-episode role of Vanessa Abrams, Dan's BFF who returns to town. The way she landed the part was rather out of the ordinary. "I went to a barbeque with a friend of mine — [initially] I was sitting on the couch with my dog and was like, 'Go, just call me later.' They called back a little later and said it was only going to be 10 people. We show up and it ended up being at Josh Schwartz's house — I had no idea. We met Josh and Stephanie [Savage]. We were hanging out, eating by the pool, swimming. Two days later, I got a phone call from my manager saying apparently I had met the creator and executive producers of *Gossip Girl* and they wanted me to go in tomorrow and test at Warner Brothers. They'd send the tape to New York and [if they liked it], I'd leave on Friday. That is how it happened. I was coming out to do three episodes and then after a month and a half, they asked if I wanted to be a series regular."

Jessica moved across the country and took to New York City and her new castmates immediately, saying off screen she's closest with Ed. (The two began dating in 2008.) "I forget that I'm on a show people watch," said Jessica. "If people do recognize me, I usually think they need directions to the subway! There are a couple of fans that come to the set every day and stand around and watch. Which is a little weird. But we need the fans, so I think we all try our best when people are watching."

Her character is the most divisive among the fans — people love or hate Vanessa. But for Jessica, "Vanessa's such a caretaker and always trying to help people out and make sure everyone's OK, so I don't know why people wouldn't like her." Her hope for her character is that one day "Vanessa is going to stop being hurt by all these people and get a really cool rocker boyfriend that is in a band in Brooklyn."

In the break between seasons, Jessica worked on her first major roles in film. She's attacked by ravenous, evil fish in *Piranha 3-D*, due out in 2010. And alongside Brittany Snow, who played Lily in the season 2 *Gossip Girl* flashback episode, Jessica starred in the independent feature *Walks*, which takes place in the world of New York's underground street art, before returning to *Gossip Girl* for its third scandal-filled season. "Everyone has drama in their life," said Jessica, "so it's good to watch a show to be like, 'OK, my life's not so bad!'"

kelly rutherford (lily van der woodsen)

The woman behind Lily van der Woodsen is Kelly Deane Melissa Rutherford, born in Elizabethtown, Kentucky, on November 6, 1968. Her parents split up when she was just two years old, and Kelly lived with her mother, a model, as she traveled the country. "She was always very independent," Kelly's mother told *People* in 1997. "In first grade, she wanted to teach the class." When Kelly reached her teen years, the family settled in Newport Beach, California, where she attended Corona Del Mar High School.

Once she graduated, Kelly followed in her mother's footsteps, pursuing modeling and acting work in New York City, landing commercials and roles on soap operas. Her very first role was in a Mother's Cookie Ice Cream commercial with *Friends*' Matt LeBlanc. Playing Sam Whitmore on *Generations* was Kelly's first notable role, and she earned a nomination for a Soap Opera Digest Award for Outstanding Heroine (1989). Moving to Hollywood, Kelly continued to work on soaps and TV shows like *Homefront*, *The Adventures of Brisco County Jr.*, *Courthouse*, and *Kindred: The Embraced*. Kelly explained that an acting coach at the Beverly Hills Playhouse said to her, "'We need you to work on your sexuality.' She told me not to be afraid to be a woman. The work really liberated me." In more ways than one. In 1996, she was cast on the hit soap *Melrose Place* as call girl Megan Lewis, who has an affair with Dr. Michael Mancini as his wife Kimberly battles her brain tumor. Kelly stayed with the series until its end in 1999. "She has a smokiness, a film noir quality," said Thomas Calabro, who played Michael Mancini, "and that makes her different from everyone else on the show." Working in both film and television, Kelly acted in three short-lived but well-regarded series — *The District*, *Threat Matrix*, and *E-Ring* — before being cast on *Gossip Girl*.

In 2001, Kelly married Carlos Tarajano, a Venezuelan banker, but their marriage didn't last long enough for the *InStyle* issue featuring their nuptials to hit newsstands. She wed her second husband, Daniel Giersch, a German businessman, in 2006, and together they had a son, Hermés Gustaf Daniel Giersch, on October 18, 2006. But in 2008, while pregnant with their second child, Kelly filed for divorce, citing irreconcilable differences. Shuttling back and forth between L.A. where their home is and New York where *Gossip Girl* films, Kelly remained positive. "I get the best of both worlds. I get a little New York, I get a little Los Angeles and so does my son, which is fantastic. As long as there's a lot of love there, you can get through very tough times. . . . I'm doing so well because I know I'm making the right decision. I love my son so much and he's loved by both of us — his father and I — greatly. My greatest joy in life right now is being a mom." On June 8, daughter Helena was born.

Playing Lily van der Woodsen on *Gossip Girl* was a role Kelly was excited to take on, saying, "Oh she's so rich. And it's so fun. The clothes are so good. . . . It's such a fun world. The old-school New York, Upper East Side — it's not something we've seen much of recently." Asked about the similarities between the other successful nighttime soap she was on and this one, Kelly said, "I think it's a commentary on our culture and where we are. I think *Melrose Place* did that, I think *Gossip Girl* does that, and you get a view of a certain world." Though a new mother herself when she began playing Lily, Kelly was not used to playing the "mom" character. "I feel very fortunate the way they've written the series, because in the books our characters weren't as prominent and I think it's great that they have [brought them to the forefront]. Because it creates a different conversation between the parents, because a lot of parents watch the show too, and it sort of opens things up. You don't often see the parents on shows, so you don't understand why the kids are behaving the way they are. And on this show you really understand that the parents aren't perfect either." Kelly defended the show's risqué plotlines, saying *Gossip Girl* "shows a good example and a bad example and you learn from both." Playing Lily has also made her appreciate the challenges her own mother faced while raising her. "My mother and I are the exact age difference that Blake and I are. It is bizarre. I have a lot of questions to ask my mother — 'how did you do that?'"

matthew settle (rufus humphrey)

The youngest of six, Jeffrey Matthew Settle was born September 17, 1969, in Hickory, North Carolina, to Joan and Dr. Robert Settle, a Baptist minister. The family moved to Sevier County, Tennessee, when Matthew was 14, and he attended Seymour Community Christian Academy. After high school, Matthew moved to New York City to be a musician, and after some odd jobs, he found his way to Los Angeles. There he looked for acting work and landed a pilot, *Shaughnessy*, in 1996. His feature film debut was in the teen slasher *I Still Know What You Did Last Summer* playing Will Benson, Jennifer Love Hewitt's seemingly perfect college friend. The producers of that movie had nothing but praise for Matthew, saying, "There are very few actors that have star quality — that draw you in with something that separates them from the rest. . . . He jumped right out at us like a young Tom Cruise."

From there, Matthew's career continued to blossom with notable turns in award-winning miniseries, playing Captain Ronald Speirs in *Band of Brothers,* produced by Tom Hanks and Steven Spielberg, and as Jacob Wheeler in *Into the West,* another Steven Spielberg–produced project. It was through playing Captain Speirs that Matthew's father finally came around to his son's career choice. "My dad used to not like the fact that I wanted to be an actor, years ago, but then I did this miniseries called *Band of Brothers,*" he said on *Rachael Ray.* "My uncles were all in Normandy, two are passed away now . . . they were all war veterans of World War II so it kind of made him really proud and reversed his notion of what it could be. . . . It made him embrace the idea." From those successes Matthew also found himself all over network TV; he worked on *ER, The Practice, Law & Order: SVU,* and *Brothers & Sisters.* Matthew also hit the big screen in *U-571, Divine Secrets of the Ya-Ya Sisterhood, Rancid,* and *The Celestine Prophecy.*

Rufus Humphrey wasn't the first role Matthew played that required singing; in an Austrian film, he had to record a song, but being cast as the frontman of Lincoln Hawk did present some challenges. "I'm very musical, but didn't play guitar. It's been a fun ride improving. I'm really a novice, who can now pretend to make it work. I'm actually taking lessons right now. My special skill on my resumé was actually 'spoon.'"

On taking a "dad" role on *Gossip Girl,* Matthew said in 2007, "I'm married now with two dogs and a cat so I'm getting ready for a family in the next few years. I've learned a lot from playing Rufus, it's given me the opportunity to read a lot of parenting books." Timely preparation for his real-life role as father: on March 5, 2009, Matthew and his wife, actress Naama Nativ, welcomed 8-pound, 11-ounce, Aven Angelica. "I had a think tank of people helping me figure out what it's like to be a father," said Matthew of his education playing the head of the Humphrey household. "Nothing is ever too big a deal for Rufus. That made me strive for that." And his castmates were excited about the addition to the *Gossip Girl* family. "The kids were thrilled because they are going to be aunts and uncles. I won't have a shortage of babysitters."

Beyond the father connection, Matthew wagered that "Rufus is a little more clean-shaven than I am. I guess in every character you play there's a little bit of you in that character. But then you start reading *Rolling Stone,* which I didn't so much before, and you start adding things to yourself. Every character you play, you grow a little bit." Matthew is interested in trying his hand at directing, perhaps with an episode of *Gossip Girl* à la Jason Priestley and *90210*. "I'm kind of an idea guy and enjoy the steps involved in putting things together. Kelly [Rutherford] once told me, 'I can definitely see you directing, you just need a really good assistant!'" In the meantime, Matthew has continued to work outside of the *Gossip* world, playing President Kennedy in 2008's *The Express: The Ernie Davis Story* and playing a love interest to Heather Graham in the dark comedy *ExTerminators*, which premiered at 2009's South by Southwest Film Festival.

Matthew was unprepared for the reaction from *Gossip Girl* fans. "It's embarrassing at times. There are girls that come up and say, 'You're hot' in front of my wife." Fawning fans should keep in mind that Matthew's wife Naama used to be a drill sergeant in the Israeli army.

But Matthew's happy playing Rufus Humphrey. "He's the moral center of the show. He's a rock-solid dad. . . . People like Rufus so I'm hoping the producers don't change that. Because I don't want to get eggs thrown at me from across the street."

season one

Recurring cast: Robert John Burke (Bart Bass), Margaret Colin (Eleanor Waldorf), Emma Demar (Elise), Nicole Fiscella (Isabel Coates), Susie Misner (Alison Humphrey), Connor Paolo (Eric van der Woodsen), Sam Robards (Captain Howie Archibald), Amanda Setton (Penelope), Francie Swift (Anne Archibald), Zuzanna Szadkowski (Dorota), Michelle Trachtenberg (Georgina Sparks), Dreama Walker (Hazel), Nan Zhang (Kati Farkas)

"Has our bad girl really gone good?"

1.01 pilot

Original air date: September 19, 2007
Written by: Josh Schwartz, Stephanie Savage
Directed by: Mark Piznarski
Guest cast: Florencia Lozano (Eleanor Waldorf), Kimberly Herbert Gregory (Nurse), Andrew Stewart-Jones (Concierge), Lindsey Broad (Melanie91), Robert Stoeckle (High Society Man)

Serena returns to the Upper East Side after a year of unexplained absence to find her old BFF is not the welcoming committee she hoped for. Dan crosses the Brooklyn Bridge into S's life.

Bergdorf's and Bendel's, the Met and Central Park, parties and private school: welcome to the Upper East Side. Despite some first-time fumbling, the pilot episode of *Gossip Girl* gets the job done, introducing the characters, their world, and the major tensions for the series. With a plot pulled almost entirely from the first *Gossip Girl* book, Serena returns to a world in flux: Nate is pulling away from the life mapped out for him, Blair is desperate to lose her virginity and maintain her Queen B status, Eric attempted suicide and no one but the van der Woodsens know, the happy Humphrey family is short a mother, Jenny wants nothing more than to be cooler than her brother and is willing to work for it, and Dan can't resist the lure of the It girl.

Though we first meet Serena, it's Dan and Jenny who are the heart of the show, letting viewers see the UES through the eyes of the newbies whose middle-class Brooklyn life seems so humble in comparison to their Fifth Avenue classmates and their "heightened reality." The trust-fund kids may have the perks of privilege, but the Humphrey kids have a real family with a loving, anti-capitalist, breakfast-making dad. Even with a mother off in Hudson, the Humphreys are better off than the three wealthy families: the van der Woodsens — the son suicidal, the daughter glum and disengaged, and the mother desperate to keep up appearances; the Archibalds — the Captain using Nate to leverage a business opportunity and making him a prisoner in his own life; and the Waldorfs — the mother telling her teenaged daughter she'll never be happier, and a father who's left his family behind. With their strong foundation in Brooklyn, Dan and Jenny have the opportunity to make more of their station in life, a luxury not afforded to those already at the top.

And then there's creepy Chuck Bass. He loves the world he was born into and all the advantages it offers — and those it doesn't, he feels entitled to take by force. Serving as a foil to both Nathaniel and Lonely Boy, Chuck wholeheartedly embraces what Nate struggles with, and epitomizes the world that Dan abhors and is ostracized from. In the eyes of Chuck, Humphrey has no business on the Upper East Side; everything about Dan makes him unworthy — his social standing, address, clothes. And even though Dan thinks of himself in the same way to a certain degree — he tells the Palace concierge, "Nobody knows me" — it enrages him to hear it from Chuck.

Like *The O.C.* before it, *Gossip Girl* finds a tone in this pilot episode that combines dark realities — attempted suicide, attempted rape, broken families, and infidelity — with a light comic and self-aware touch. Josh Schwartz and Stephanie Savage find that difficult balance with a well-crafted script, a (mostly) capable cast, and a soundtrack that instantly sets the mood for each scene. Some of the "Isn't life hard when you're this fabulously wealthy and attractive?" lines fall flat with heavy-handedness, but it's only episode 1.

Not surprising in a show centered on a teenage gossip blogger, even fairy tales get a tech makeover with a Sidekick stepping in for the glass slipper in Dan and Serena's Cinderella story. The episode is chock-full of cell phones and texting (but could have done without that lame montage of girls reading the Gossip Girl blast). Rumors and reputations matter in this world, and the biggest secrets have no hope of staying unknown when the order of this mini-society is in turmoil and information travels at the speed of bytes. As the leader of the Constance girls, it's Blair's duty to uphold appearances, keeping prim as she puts S in her place on the Met steps. The social stratum there is crystal clear: B's at the center, Jenny is subject to dismissal, and S can't just come waltzing back and expect top step. Only in private does Blair reveal to S why she's upset: B was left out of the loop on S's departure and return, and had to deal with her parents' divorce alone. A valid reason to be pissed at your bestie. And then there's that thing about Serena and Nate and a drunken hook-up at the Shepherd wedding.

By the end of the episode, we're left with enough secrets, lies, and tensions to fuel plotlines for a few seasons: Rufus and Lily hiding their past relationship, Blair desperate to hold on to Nate and willing to ignore his indiscretion, the battleground laid out between Blair and Serena, the budding romance between Serena and Dan as both try to figure out their new identities, Jenny reeling from her first foray into Upper East Side society, and Chuck Bass with a taste for revenge and a new target (or two). . . .

"You're kinda not invited."
— B to S on the Met steps

JTLYK:

- The Kiss on the Lips party is on the 25th of September, a Tuesday. Apparently you can party on a school night on the Upper East Side.
- When Serena pops by the Ostroff Center to take Eric shopping, he is reading the issue of *Rolling Stone* that features Lincoln Hawk.
- So much can be revealed about a character in one tiny moment. Chuck spots Serena at the Palace bar and brushes through a group of women,

commanding them to "Move. Please." instead of simply walking around them.

- Nate's father tells him not to give up when things get hard. Reasonable advice except for the context: Captain Archibald considers Nate's relationship with Blair in terms of business and family obligations, not love or Nate's choosing.
- Rufus and Lily's banter at the art gallery reveals just how well these two know each other. Rufus opens with a dig at Lily's tendency to buy art to match her furniture, something she herself joked about at the Waldorf party.
- Blair just seems to *know* Chuck is standing behind her at the end of the episode. And that smirk she gets when he says he hopes Serena will show her face again? Spells trouble.

Secrets & Lies:

- Dan says Gossip Girl is "for chicks," denying that it's his one and only source on Serena.
- B pretends she knew that S was back to save face in front of Kati and Is.
- Lily hides Eric at the Ostroff Center, telling the world he's visiting his Aunt Carol in Miami.
- Chuck makes other people's business his business, holding on to S and N's secret until he can dangle his knowledge in front of Serena.
- Serena enlists Dan's help to lie to her mother.
- Lily doesn't react to the names "Lincoln Hawk" or "Humphrey" in front of Serena and Dan, keeping her past relationship with Rufus a secret.

Scrap!: Serena knees Chuck in the package after he tries to force himself on her. Dan punches Chuck after Chuck attacks Jenny, giving him a bloody nose.

Not a Girl, Not Yet a Queen Bee: J looks and acts every bit a freshman in this episode. She arrives at Grand Central Station looking like a kid, and is awkward and fawning around B and S. But J doesn't want to be "an anonymous loser who eats lunch alone and never gets invited to parties," and she's using what she has — excellent calligraphy skills, the ability to recreate designer dresses, and determination — to get what she wants: an invite to the party. Her naïveté and eagerness are quickly taken advantage of by Chuck, who destroys what Little J had envisioned as her society debut. Good thing she has Dan and Serena to lean on, because being sexually assaulted by a rich and powerful older guy is a terrible way to start your freshman year. As Gossip Girl says, Jenny's hoping for a "ticket to the inner circle," but her fate so far is to be a victim of its cruelty.

The Original Gossipverse: The plot of this episode is pulled from the first book, *Gossip Girl*, right down to Jenny's flustered introduction to Serena. But there are some notable revisions. Dan doesn't land a date with Serena after picking up her phone at the Palace, but instead meets up with her when she's hanging out with Vanessa at a bar in Brooklyn, the night of the Kiss on the Lips party. Chuck joins Jenny in a stall in the women's washroom, rather than taking her up to the roof; the scene in the book is less a clear-cut assault, but rather a dicey situation where a guy is moving too fast for a girl too overwhelmed to stop him. Nate and Serena didn't hook up at a wedding, but at Nate's house during summer vacation before 11th grade, and it was the first time for both of them. And the Constance Billard yogurt flavor of choice is lemon.

That's How It's Done in *The O.C.*: Serena steals Ryan Atwood's pilot episode move, wistfully staring out the window as she travels from one world to another. Overbearing socialite mom Eleanor Waldorf tells Blair what to wear and how to wear it, just like Julie Cooper tells Marissa early in season 1. The flicker of romance between rich girl and poor boy, while not particularly original to the Schwartz & Savage universe, was played out with Marissa and Ryan. Dan definitely has a Seth Cohen vibe to him with his rambling, his quick wit, and his standing as a social pariah.

Welcome to the Real World:

- "I don't care if it's Murakami, it clashes with my sofa," says Lily to the tittering UES society ladies. Takashi Murakami is a Japanese artist whose Superflat style is a mix of high and pop culture, and whose admirers include noted blogger/rapper Kanye West.
- When D is reading Gossip Girl, the links at the top read: "Reason #643 Why We Love the Tischs," referring to the family who owns Loews Hotels, and "Brearley's New Uniforms Are Fugly," the Brearley School being a K–12 all-girls private school on the Upper East Side.
- Lily and Rufus trade barbs about the good old days (the '90s) with Rufus

referencing Lily's past dalliances with "Trent" Reznor of Nine Inch Nails, "Layne" Staley of Alice in Chains, and "Perry" Farrell of Jane's Addiction and Porno for Pyros.

- Eric is staying at the Ostroff Center, a fictional treatment facility named after real-life CW exec Dawn Ostroff.
- Spotted on the side of the bus D almost misses: an ad for the CW's *Smallville.*
- Nate pines for USC, not Dartmouth; his college aspirations may spring from show creator Josh Schwartz, who went to the University of Southern California.

Locations:

- With the Metropolitan Museum of Art (1000 Fifth Ave) as a key location for *Gossip Girl*, the museum gets some bonus exposure. Banners for the Samuel Palmer exhibit (which ran from March to May 2006) and the Venice and the Islamic World exhibit (March to July) are in the background as the girls vie for steps dominance.
- The Constance girls get their morning coffees from Sant Ambroeus (1000 Madison Ave).
- The address J texts to D — 712 Fifth Avenue — is the address of Bendel's.
- Serena meets Blair at Gilt in the Palace Hotel (455 Madison Ave).
- S fondly remembers "dancing on tables at Bungalow" with B, a bar in Chelsea where celebrities and celebrity gawkers go, if they can get past the doorman (515 W 27th St).
- Serena prances on the bar at the Campbell Apartment (Grand Central Terminal, 15 Vanderbilt Ave), before she and Nate do it.
- Nate and Blair have make-up sashimi at Geisha (33 E 61st St).
- The Kiss on the Lips party is held at The Foundry, 42–38 9th Street in Queens.

Oops: Taylor Momsen puts the same envelope into the box of invitations twice over breakfast at the Humphrey loft. As Dan leaves Rufus postering, the sign behind Rufus has one poster, but in the reverse shot, it has two.

The Look: With distinct looks for each character, costume designer Eric Daman gives a character a backstory with just one outfit. Serena's first outfit

Only the best for *Gossip Girl:* its iconic opening scenes were filmed at NYC landmarks Grand Central Station and the Met.

of the series, at Grand Central Station, captures her mix of expensive designer pieces suited to a girl of her wealth (and a daughter to Lily van der Woodsen) with a dressed-down, edgier, urban twist: the cognac vintage leather jacket; Cheap Monday jeans; Petit Bateau black-and-white striped T-shirt; Ralph Lauren scarf, belt, and Kyle calfskin boots; a Coach Hamptons vintage leather hobo bag and vintage Vuitton suitcase. For her date with Dan, in a

gossip girl, version 1.1

As valiant of a kickoff as the pilot episode was, certain aspects of the show got a revamp as it moved into its full season.

- Gossip Girl's website got a design overhaul from the tacky pink layout with the lady's silhouette to the way sleeker design we know and love.
- The Humphrey loft was remodeled and the cat (sitting on D's desk as he reads Gossip Girl) is never to be seen again.
- Recast! Eleanor Waldorf is played by a different actress (Margaret Colin) for the rest of the series. The Waldorf apartment also gets a revamp.
- Chuck makes a reference to his mother's Paxil and the hotel his parents (plural) own. He must have been high, because we soon find out that Bart Bass is a widower.
- Chuck Bass and Nate Archibald taking public transit to school? Never again.
- The hair department steps up their game: settling on Nate's brushed-forward look, trimming down Dan's oversized sideburns, and sorting out the mess that was B's hair at the Kiss on the Lips party.
- Penn Badgley must have watched the pilot and realized how unappealing that tongue-sticking-out thing was that Dan does when S says they're going out. It doesn't (and should never) happen again. Thank you, Penn.
- In the pilot, the Humphrey loft is said to be in Williamsburg, but the exterior of the building is actually in Dumbo, a discrepancy that irked New Yorkers. In an email to *New York* magazine's Daily Intel blog, Stephanie Savage explained, "The interior of the Humphrey loft was shot at a private residence at The Foundry, in Long Island City, so that wouldn't work for the exterior shot. We were never able to find a satisfying exterior location in Williamsburg that seemed right for the loft (matched the shape of the windows, height of ceiling, brick on the walls, etc.), but it matches perfectly with the beautiful building at the foot of the Manhattan Bridge in DUMBO. By the time we realized this, we had already shot Jenny and Dan in the cab in 'The Wild Brunch,' where Williamsburg is mentioned for the last time, ever. Since then, we have mentioned neither DUMBO nor WILLIAMSBURG by name, referring to where the Humphreys live only as 'Brooklyn.' . . . Since committing to our new location, we are really trying to be consistent!!"

gold Tory Burch mini dress and black Wolford tights, she may be overdressed for a Lincoln Hawk show but looks the part of golden girl. Blair's look is all about precision and appropriateness, topped with a hairband and a few bows — her signature pieces. On the Met steps, Blair makes her Constance Billard uniform unique with an ivory Alice + Olivia blouse, yellow hairband, white tights, and black-and-red patent Anne Klein Paleo flats, complete with elegant bows. Kati and Is dress both to match each other and to set off Blair and make her pop — they're in white knee socks with peep-toe shoes (green for Kati, purple for Is) and textured, patterned coats that set off B in navy. Jenny has on cute polka-dot flats and green cabled tights paired with a pink floral Lilly Pulitzer coat; a very different look from when she arrived at Grand Central in the Humphrey Uniform (plaid shirt and jeans). Dan's a plaid shirt man like his father; his idea of dressing up is throwing on a vest for his date with Serena. Compare that to Chuck Bass in ascot and pink shirt at the Waldorf party, and at Kiss on the Lips, in a bow tie and his signature J. Press silk patchwork scarf.

Music: Music supervisor Alex Patsavas crammed 20 songs into the pilot, an all-time record for her.

- "Young Folks" (Peter, Bjorn and John): Serena arrives at Grand Central and we meet the Humphreys
- "If It's Lovin' That You Want" (Rihanna): the Waldorf party soundtrack
- "What Goes Around" (Justin Timberlake): Serena arrives at the Waldorfs
- "The Gift" (Angels & Airwaves): S visits Eric at the Ostroff Center; Jenny, Dan, and Serena leave the Kiss on the Lips party
- "Diamond Hipster Boy" (Washington Social Club): good-morning music at the Humphrey loft
- "Concerto in G" (Vivaldi): D runs for the bus and listens in on Chuck and Nate's conversation about Serena
- "99%" (The Mooney Suzuki): Rufus posts flyers and Dan educates him in the ways of MySpace
- "Bounce With Me" (Kreesha Turner): Jenny, Serena, and Eric cross paths at Bendel's while Dan hides behind cocktail dresses
- "Back to Black" (Amy Winehouse): B and S make nice at the Palace bar
- "Space for Rent" (WhoMadeWho): J convinces D to go after S
- "Send You Back" (Matthew Dear): Chuck keeps Serena company at the Palace bar

- "Photograph" (Air): Serena and Nate hook up at the Shepherd wedding
- "Joyful Waltz" (Zdeněk Barták): D returns S's Sidekick to the hotel concierge
- "Hang Me Up to Dry" (Cold War Kids): Blair and Nate have lunch
- "Time Won't Let Me Go" (The Bravery): Lily confronts Rufus at his gallery, and Dan and Jenny marvel at how cool they've become
- "Hard to Live in the City" (Albert Hammond Jr.): Limo party! Blair, Nate, Chuck, and the girls en route to Kiss on the Lips; Dan picks up Serena at the Palace
- "The Way I Are" (Timbaland featuring Keri Hilson and D.O.E.): the DJ at the Kiss on the Lips party likes his hip hop
- "Go" (Hanson): Dan and Serena chat with Rufus outside the Lincoln Hawk gig while another forgotten band from the '90s provides the soundtrack
- "Don't Matter" (Akon): Jenny tries to deflect Chuck's advances when they move somewhere quieter to "talk"
- "Knock, Knock" (Lyrics Born): Dan and Serena look for Jenny at the party

Connor Paolo as Eric van der Woodsen

The only actor playing a teenager on the show who is a New Yorker born and raised, Connor was born on July 11, 1990, to a musician mother and writer father. Training at the Professional Performing Arts School, he got a role on *All My Children* when he was just nine years old. Playing two memorable (and somewhat creepy) roles on *Law & Order: Special Victims Unit* helped him land film roles in *Mystic River*, *Alexander* (as the Young Alexander), *World Trade Center*, *Snow Angels*, and 2009's *Camp Hope* and *Favorite Son*. Connor has a love for theater, appearing in the Broadway production of *The Full Monty* and off-Broadway and community theater productions of *Richard III* and *A Midsummer Night's Dream*. In a case of real life imitating his onscreen role as Eric van der Woodsen, Connor and friend Taylor Momsen attended high school together during season 1. On the show's success, Connor said, "It's really permeated all walks of life. You've got eight-year-old girls who watch it and really shady old men who watch it and all seem to love it equally."

"It looks like the ultimate insider has become a total outsider."

1.02 the wild brunch

Original air date: September 26, 2007
Written by: Josh Schwartz, Stephanie Savage
Directed by: Mark Piznarski
Guest cast: Andrew Stewart-Jones (Concierge), Jessica Jade Andres (Girl #1)

Blair declares war on Serena, and Dan unwittingly enters the battlefield: a posh brunch at the Palace Hotel.

Fustercluck, indeed. Last episode, Dan, Jenny, and Serena helped introduce us to the world of the Upper East Side, and now we learn who governs it and how. Blair and Chuck act as gatekeepers to this *very* exclusive society, and everyone has to follow its rules: no scotch before noon; if you sleep with your best friend's boyfriend, at least have the decency not to lie about it; hiding from society will only make people gossip about you more; destroying your former BFF's budding romance is totally acceptable but annoyingly unsatisfying; mothers can boss you around in absentia; and, most importantly, there is a price to pay for admission into this not-so-perfect world.

Chuck and Blair don't take kindly to rules being broken, particularly when they are the ones who end up humiliated, and neither hesitates to destroy Serena or Dan. Even without the vengeance seekers, Serena was having a hard enough time on her own, trying to leave behind her past self and become the person she wants to be. And everywhere she turned her two suitors, Nate and Dan, were waiting for her. I'd agree with Rufus on this one: "a kid like Dan is exactly what Serena needs."

By the end of the episode, Dan moves from being the guy desperate for a second chance — to atone for The Wave — to being the kind of guy you only get one chance with. His crash course in Serena's crazy world — where you can't trust anyone, any secret will be used to someone's advantage, and hurting people is a sport — leaves him resolved that it's not for him. Dan is used as a pawn in B's eye-for-an-eye revenge on Serena: S stole B's boyfriend so B will take S's new love interest away. Blair has a certain sexual competitiveness with S; taking Nate upstairs for a quickie in Chuck's room has nothing to do with him or their relationship, but with evening the playing field between her and Serena. Twisted. What Blair needs is a new blonde friend, one that's a subordinate, not an equal, and Jenny Humphrey seems more than happy to be that minion.

Two episodes in, *Gossip Girl* is, so far, a great guide in how *not* to parent. Howie "The Captain" Archibald is disgustingly self-interested; luckily Nate knows better than his own father. Lily seems to have reasons to hide her past relationship with Rufus and her current one with Bart, but with a mother like that, it's not surprising Serena isn't more forthcoming and relies on fibbing to get out of her obligations. Chuck's boozing and womanizing is an effort to emulate and impress his father, but Bart reprimands his son while failing to model better behavior. And while single-dad-of-the-year Rufus seems to be doing everything right, his kids are keeping secrets from him too — neither Jenny nor Dan tells him what happened at the Kiss on the Lips party.

The series hits its stride with this episode, confidently complicating a web of relationships that rivals any teen soap and keeping up *The O.C.*–style tone of overwrought emotion and saucy one-liners. The end montage, set beautifully to The Bravery's "Believe," lays the foundation for the next episodes: Nate and Blair making a tentative peace on her bed; J proudly looking at herself; Lonely Boy . . . uh, lonely; Chuck reading Gossip Girl in bed with

a model; and Serena in a wash of gray, wind in her hair, pain in her heart, and totally alone.

"Just saying, death by scarf? Not that intimidating."
— Nathaniel mocks Chuck's signature

JTLYK:

- Nate waited for months and months before telling Blair about him and S hooking up. He's a liar too, B. Just because he finally told you the truth doesn't mean you should forgive him.
- Nate has a special "talking to adults" tone of voice; he uses it when he runs into Lily at the Palace.
- Blair says to Jenny that Chuck likes to brag about his "conquests, not his victims." Does that mean Chuck routinely assaults girls and everyone just shrugs it off with "Oh, that Chuck is disgusting"?
- Someone should teach Serena how to delete images from her phone. You don't have to throw the whole thing in the trash!

Secrets & Lies:

- Nate fibs to Blair about already being awake when she calls him on the morning of brunch.
- Kati and Is have no idea what it is Serena did to make Blair so upset with her.
- Blair tells Serena she knows that S had sex with her boyfriend and icily calls her a whore and a liar.
- Blair sees through Jenny's excuse to pop by — the urgent return of calligraphy pens — to the real reason for her visit.
- Nate halfheartedly lies to Dan, saying he's "just in the neighborhood" and doesn't have anything in particular to talk to Serena about. Dan doesn't bother with an excuse of his own.
- Nate lies to Chuck, saying he was waiting for him, not for Serena or with Dan.
- S can't tell her mother, or Dan, the real reason going to the Bass brunch is a bad idea, so she uses D as an excuse again. Dan plays along with S's fib, likely assuming her reluctance to attend has to do with the altercation at Kiss on the Lips.
- Serena lies to Dan to have a secret talk with Nate.

- Nate has broken his promise to never talk to Serena again. B thinks S can't be trusted, but can Nate?
- Dan overhears Lily's conversation with Bart and keeps it from Serena.
- Dan reveals to a pissed-off Blair and Chuck that Nate was waiting for Serena at the Palace.
- Blair pretends she is telling Dan about S's sordid past to protect him from future harm, not owning up to her real motivation: revenge.

Scrap!: After promising to give Chuck a matching shiner, Dan instead gives him a good shove. But it's the innocent waiter who gets the brunt of it.

Not a Girl, Not Yet Queen Bee: After admitting she feels dumb for thinking Chuck's intentions were innocent, Jenny chooses a consult with the Queen over a heart-to-heart with her big bro, providing him with more advice than he gives her. Serena being on the outs with Blair works in Little J's favor. As she watches B get ready for the Bass brunch, Jenny plays the role of the wide-eyed sycophant, swooning over the beautiful house, flowers, and clothes, and passes B's test of her mettle: negotiating Blair's barbed question about J's friendship with Serena, then revealing TMI about Cedric the Cabbage Patch Kid. Blair rewards J with a Blair's Army uniform (an Eleanor Waldorf original). Jenny misleads her dad into thinking she wants to spend quality time with him when really she wants to Waldorfize their loft. Her echo of B's "They're hydrangeas" is frighteningly spot-on. Looks like Little J has her eye on the Upper East Side, and but will she heed Blair's forewarning? "If you want to be part of this world, Jenny, people will talk. Eventually. You need to decide if all this is worth it."

The Original Gossipverse: The brunch is pulled from the first book, but in that version, it's at the Met and Dan's not there. The statue models appear in *Don't You Forget About Me*, at another Met party; Bartholomew Bass does a bit of skeezing out, peering down Is's mom's dress. Believe it or not, Chuck isn't the one to insult Serena and Jenny in the books; it's Dan who writes a whole poem about how Jenny and his girlfriend (Vanessa, not Serena) are sluts.

That's How It's Done in *The O.C.*: The morning talk about The Wave is a very Seth and Ryan conversation. And there's nothing like a beloved

eleanor waldorf designs by abigail lorick

Call it an Eleanor Waldorf original on *Gossip Girl,* but if you want the dresses Jenny, Blair, and Serena wear this season, track down Abigail Lorick. The designer behind Eleanor's fashion line was launching her own line around the same time the *Gossip Girl* wardrobe department was looking for a stand-in, and Lorick knew Meredith Markworth-Pollack, assistant costume designer. "I showed them Lorick and they thought it would be a good fit for the line behind Eleanor Waldorf," Lorick told Stylelist.com. Her dresses are the centerpiece of "Bad News Blair," and the designer herself made a cameo appearance as one of Eleanor's assistants. Working with the show has been huge for promoting her line. "After the episode with the backless dresses we had 20 girls a day calling wanting that dress. I couldn't believe that everyone was so influenced by it. They didn't even want to try it on — they just wanted it!" It's no wonder Lorick was chosen; the concept behind the line is completely in sync with *Gossip Girl* style: "a contemporary, preppy chic classic line . . . bringing this modern elegance back to my generation of women. It's finding that line — keeping that timelessness but being sexy, fun, and quirky at the same time."

childhood toy still cherished by a teenage boy to make him endearing. Captain Oats, meet Cedric the Cabbage Patch Kid.

The Wild Bunch (dir. Sam Peckinpah, 1969): An extremely violent and critically acclaimed Western, *The Wild Bunch* is about a group of outlaws, led by a weathered guy named Pike Bishop (William Holden), who go from town to town robbing banks and raising hell. Bounty hunters are on their tail and with them is Deke Thornton (Robert Ryan). Thornton and Pike were once besties but they had a falling out: Pike took off on Thornton when the law caught up with them at a whorehouse (I hate it when *that* happens). Now Thornton has to find Pike and turn him over or he'll be thrown back in jail.

Pike knows he did wrong by his friend and urges loyalty to the new members of the bunch: "When you side with a man, you stay with him. Otherwise you're finished." If one part of the group falters, they are all destroyed. These hardened criminals dream of the happier, simpler time when they were children, and the film ends (after a *serious* fustercluck shootout) with a montage of good times gone by — but now the bunch is disbanded and most are dead. Thornton moves along with a new gang while wistfully recalling his days with the old.

While the 1913 Texas–Mexico border is a far cry from today's Upper

East Side, and dusty chaps the antithesis of B's prissy hairbands, at the heart of both *The Wild Bunch* and "The Wild Brunch" are friendship, loyalty, betrayal, and abandonment. Blair cannot forgive Serena — not because S slept with Nate but because she betrayed the one person she was supposed to be loyal to, B. In the final scene, Serena looks at pictures of her very own wild bunch: Blair, Chuck, Nate, and S having a laugh in a more innocent time. Like Thornton, S realizes that part of her life is over and tosses her phone. She needs a new bunch to ride with.

Welcome to the Real World:

- More '90s rock references from Rufus: the Warped Tour started in 1994 combining skateboarding and punk/alt-rock bands. It's still alive and kicking . . . kinda like that chemistry between Rufus and Lily.

Locations:

- The Waldorfs live at 1136 Fifth Avenue.

Oops:

- As blog ManhattanOffender.com pointed out, Serena gets out of the cab into oncoming traffic without so much as a look out the window or over her shoulder. That's more awkward than Dan's wave. Cab etiquette dictates that everyone pile out curbside to avoid S getting run over, or at least honked at.
- The concierge tells Dan that one time Serena left and was gone for six months. How would he know that? The van der Woodsens haven't always lived at the hotel; their actual home is being renovated, as S told Nate in the pilot and mentioned to her mother in this episode.
- Chuck has a black eye from Dan hitting him, but in the previous episode he had a bloody nose. Powerful punch, Humphrey.
- The note from Blair's mom on her garment bag says that brunch is at 2 p.m., but Bart Bass scolds Chuck for drinking scotch when it's barely noon. Is Eleanor on Parisian time?

The Look: Just because the show's known for its cutting-edge fashion doesn't mean there's never a fugly outfit. Witness what Serena puts on to visit B on the morning of the brunch. The Roberto Collina crochet sweater, Vena Cavi cami, 7 For All Mankind cut-off jean shorts, Minnetonka black lace-up boots, and Coach bag make this beautiful girl look trashy enough to be dressed down by B (lounging in Sophie B "In Love Again" lingerie, as one does) for sleeping with her boyfriend. Luckily she classes it up for brunch with the embroidered Blumarine flower dress. Blair is in a virginal white Thread Social (summer 2007 collection) dress with a black bow headband at the brunch, and fans of the original book series get a close-up of her other signature piece: the heart-shaped ruby ring. Jenny has a Freddy&Ma clutch with her when B gives her the so-last-season-blue Eleanor Waldorf original, which is actually the Lorick GG strapless dress (see sidebar).

Music: The brunch prep montage of chopping and tossing is to the tune of "Hit Me Up" (Gia Farrell). Phone play: N tries to track down S, S tries to talk to B, B ignores message from S to Rihanna's "Shut Up and Drive." S ransacks her hotel room and bickers with Lily to "When Did Your Heart Go Missing" by Rooney. Dan paces the courtyard of the Palace until S arrives to "The Ballad of Gus and Sam" (Ferraby Lionheart). Serena and Dan hesitate outside the Bass brunch to Joss Stone's "Tell Me 'Bout It." The brunch soundtrack is "The Queen and I" by Gym Class Heroes. More "Shut Up and Drive" as S and N chase after B. Gossip Girl narrates the end of the episode with some help from The Bravery's lyrics to "Believe."

Robert John Burke as Bart Bass

If Chuck's dad looks familiar, that's because Robert John Burke has been working nonstop in film and television for the past 20 years. But *Gossip Girl* is his first teen drama: "I'm a peripheral — I'm the old guy, which I blinked and became. But that's fine, though. You know, there's a place for that. I think it was brave of them to cast me because I don't usually play, uh, billionaires." Having played recurring characters on TV shows such as *Law & Order: Special Victims Unit*, *Oz*, and (concurrently with *GG*) *Rescue Me*, Burke has also worked extensively in film with directors Oliver Stone, Spike Lee, George Clooney, and Steven Spielberg. A New Yorker, Burke aided in the search and rescue after 9/11 and has since become a certified New York State volunteer firefighter. He's also a third-degree karate black belt, so let's hope Dan keeps mum on Bart's relationship with Lily. . . .

"World War Three just broke out. And it's wearing knee socks."

1.03 poison ivy

Original air date: October 2, 2007
Written by: Felicia D. Henderson
Directed by: J. Miller Tobin
Guest cast: Jenna Stern (Constance Headmistress), Reed Birney (St. Jude's Headmaster), Darren Pettie (Jed Hall), John-Paul Lavoisier (Field Hockey Coach), Yetta Gottesman (Faculty Member), Cherise Boothe (Dr. Miller)

It's Ivy Week and that means our UESers need to be on their best behavior . . . at least in front of the grownups.

What more could you want from an episode of *Gossip Girl?* The battle between B and S explodes into a full-on fight, Dan provides us with secondary embarrassment galore (from shaving mishaps to misunderstanding S's "Is it over?"), and hard knocks are doled out for rich and "poor" alike. The campy fun of Blair and Serena's feud gets Mean Girlsian when S decides to play along. But after Downer Dan brings in the judgment and Blair takes things too far, the episode crescendos to the series' first truly emotionally honest scene: Blair reading the letter she never sent to Serena.

The first episode not written by the Schwartz/Savage team starts with a great montage of the students getting ready for school under the enormous pressures to live up to the overachievements of their parents, a pressure that Dan, as an outsider, belittles again and again. Not from a legacy, Dan feels as if he's the only one who has to strive to make his parents' sacrifice worthwhile (by getting into the school of his choice). What he doesn't understand is how suffocating being part of a legacy can be. N's desire to choose his own path in life — to go to USC — is squashed by his father at all turns. If Captain Howie gets his way, Nate will go to Dartmouth, then law school, and will marry Blair Waldorf. Way to make something as unappealing as possible, Pops. Pitting Dan and Nate against each other — as would-be suitors to Serena and as potential Dartmouth students — draws into contrast the difficulty both sons face in the wake of their fathers' convictions. Rufus staunchly believes in meritocracy, that Dan's success is inevitable because of his hard work and smarts, while the Captain happily adheres to the oligarchy of the

Upper East Side. Dan and Nate are discovering that things are less clear-cut from where they stand.

For Blair, things are more complicated than they first seemed, too. Her single-mindedness to ruin Serena in every possible way stems not just from S's deception and infidelity, but from how utterly devastated she was to be abandoned by her best and only real friend. Blair truly is alone, with the only constant in her life her housekeeper Dorota. From the Ivy Week morning scene with Blair reminiscing as one would with a parent to the raw loneliness of her unsent letter to Serena, this episode showed us the heart hiding beneath that manipulative exterior. Her father left her family, Serena ditched and betrayed her; it's too much for her to handle when the rest of her world is so empty. No wonder she's holding on to Nate, not punishing him for cheating — she can't afford to lose him. It's too bad the easy friendship she has with Chuck is based on being the best team of social destruction. Those two search for secrets and destroy lives well together.

A fast-paced, zippy episode with new combinations of characters interacting — including a budding friendship between Jenny and Eric that looks promising.

"Didn't see that coming? Yeah. Well, it must be a shock for someone who thinks she knows everything."
— Eric brings the war to an end by throwing himself into it

JTLYK:

- After tossing her phone in the garbage in the previous episode, Serena has upgraded to an iPhone.

Secrets & Lies:

- Blair fibs to Kati and Is to get them out of the room, so she can speak to Chuck privately.
- To plot against Serena, Blair enlists Chuck, who loves to be "in on the ground floor of a scandal."
- B lies to Nate, pretending that a call from Chuck is her mother phoning from Paris.
- Serena tries to sabotage Blair's chances at Yale by scooping up the rep at the mixer.
- Lily and Bart Bass pretend to be nothing more than acquaintances,

hiding their romance, while Eric awkwardly pretends to have just returned from Florida.
- Blair puts on a show of being charitable and sincere as she announces the Ostroff Center and puts Serena on the spot. (Like a private Manhattan rehab center needs the help.)
- J, not much of a secret keeper, tells D that S is lying to protect her little brother. Protecting a younger sibling is something Dan can respect.

Scrap!: Serena and Blair have it out on the field hockey pitch. Blair fakes an injury.

Not a Girl, Not Yet a Queen Bee: Looks like J is leaning toward Serena's side over B's — imitating her style, befriending her brother, and defending S's character to D. So not a Waldorf move. But she does wear her Eleanor Waldorf dress to the mixer.

The Original Gossipverse: Serena of the Books is also late for assembly, on her first day back to school in book #1, *Gossip Girl.* Most of the college aspirations stem from the books: Serena is headed for Brown. Blair's love for Yale is limitless. In *You Know You Love Me,* Nate is destined for Brown (not

upper east side 101

A quick guide to the neighborhood the Waldorfs, Archibalds, van der Woodsens, and Basses hail from.

- The Upper East Side stretches from Central Park to the East River, from 59th to 96th Streets.
- It was mostly undeveloped until after the end of the Civil War; it took its first step toward becoming Manhattan's "Gold Coast" in 1896 when Caroline Schermerhorn Astor moved to a mansion at Fifth and 65th Street, making it a fashionable area for the elite.
- The UES is home to America's wealthiest zip code, 10021.
- The area also has the highest percentage of Republicans in Manhattan.
- It is known for its prestigious private schools: there are 23 of them.
- Museum Mile (Fifth Avenue from 82nd to 104th) is home to 10 museums (with an 11th to join in 2010).
- Known for its world-class shopping on Madison Avenue, the Upper East Side is also full of luxury hotels.

Dartmouth) but contemplates taking a year off to sail. In the books, Nate is passed up for the position of LAX captain until another kid gets busted and N is made captain (*I Like it Like That*). Nate, not Chuck, hooks up with a hot college rep in *You're the One That I Want.*

That's How It's Done in *The O.C.*: Though polar opposites, Chuck Bass echoes Seth Cohen with his "I'm Chuck Bass" in the Ivy interview. The name somehow provides a complete portrait of the man, in the same way that *The O.C.*'s oft-repeated "Seth Cohen" did.

Poison Ivy (dir. Katt Shea, 1992): Drew Barrymore stars as Ivy, the sexy bad girl from a broken home with platinum blonde hair and red lipstick on every day of the week. She befriends rich girl Sylvia Cooper (Sara Gilbert), a loner who, despite being clever and accomplished, is trapped in a giant, claustrophobic house with her dying mother (Cheryl Ladd) and her distant richie-pants father (Tom Skerritt). Sylvia constantly lies to make herself sound more interesting than she is (she has a black father! she tried to kill herself!) but Ivy changes *everything* and likes Sylvia just as she is. Everyone in the Cooper house falls for Ivy (including the dog): Ivy comforts the mother and then starts stealing her identity, she seduces the father, and she has a pseudo-lesbian thing going with Sylvia. But one little push takes everything from creepy to violent, and Ivy's insidious plot to become part of the Cooper family comes to a crashing halt.

The friendship between hot blonde Ivy and dowdy brunette Sylvia isn't exactly a Serena–Blair dynamic (Blair would kill me for making the comparison), but both Sylvia and Blair feel the betrayal of their besties. Ivy goes for the father rather than the boyfriend, but the result is the same: Blair feels like Serena destroyed her life and she will take an eye for an eye. Good thing there's no unrailed third-story balcony at that Ivy Week mixer. . . .

Welcome to the Real World:

- The fictional J.L. Hall's *The Petting Zoo*, a.k.a. D's favorite book, is inspired by Dr. Seuss's *The Lorax* (1971), a fable about environmentalism and consumerism. Theodor "Dr. Seuss" Geisel did go to Dartmouth (class of 1925), and it was there that he first started writing under the pen name "Seuss."
- Nate and Blair are hanging at her house: he's reading *The Petting Zoo*

and she's reading *InStyle*. A bit lowbrow for a Waldorf? The magazine's website has a "Get the Look" feature on *Gossip Girl* style, so maybe this is the show's way of saying thanks.

Locations:

- Lily spends her Saturdays at Bliss. The chain of spas has three Manhattan locations: Bliss Soho (568 Broadway), Bliss 57 (12 W 57th St), and Bliss 49 (541 Lexington Ave).
- The field hockey scene was filmed at Cadman Plaza park in Brooklyn.
- Blair comes to make peace with Serena while she is reading at the Bethesda Terrace Arcade in Central Park.

Oops: A poster on the bulletin board in the St. Jude's hallway lists Ivy Week as September 10–14, but the earlier Kiss on the Lips party was on the 25th.

The Look: Best outfits of the episode go to Kati and Is for their souped-up field hockey uniforms: neon knee socks, visors, and accessories galore. A classic Serena just-rolled-out-of-bed look when she arrives to school late: gray knee-high Chinese Laundry Strate tall suede boots (which promptly sold out everywhere after this episode aired), a Magaschoni cashmere vest over a white

Note to *Gossip Girl* fans looking to brood where Serena does:
the bench S sits on at the Bethesda Terrace Arcade isn't normally there.

Petit Bateau long-sleeve Henley shirt, French Toast plaid skirt and tie, and (it's all in the details) a Black Sheep and Prodigal Sons tie pin. She dresses it up for the Ivy mixer in a Vena Cava cream embroidered chiffon and caramel silk charmeuse dress (from the spring/summer 2007 collection) with a scarf in her hair. Nate's wardrobe in this episode also epitomizes his style: the loose tie with his school uniform, a navy V-neck cable-knit sweater over a blue Oxford shirt with jeans when he's reading *The Petting Zoo*, and an appropriate but dull suit for the Ivy mixer with his hair brushed back off his face (his go-to look for dressier events).

Music: Maybe one of the best songs to open any episode of a television show ever? Fergie's "Glamorous" as sung by the Constance Billard choir featuring our dear Little J. Not that I wasn't already in love with you, *Gossip Girl*, but this moment made it for keeps. (The song is a bonus track on the show's soundtrack, *OMFGG*.) The field hockey B vs. S throwdown soundtrack is will.i.am's "I Got It From My Mama." When D has his "melodramatic entrance" to the Humphrey loft, the appropriately titled "Can't Be Happening" by The Marlows is playing. S is listening to "Raise Your Hand" (Lifeblood Remix) by The Lights as she walks to the Ostroff Center and Chuck tails her in the limo. As Rufus returns to Casa Humphrey with his good news, D and J are chilling on the couch listening to Feist's "I Feel It All." Lincoln Hawk, unplugged, provides the music for the Ivy Week mixer, playing songs a far cry from "early '90s post-punk meth rock." And when Rufus and the boys need a break? Ladyhawke's "Dusk Till Dawn" picks up the pace for them.

Sam Robards as Captain Howie Archibald

Born in New York City to actor parents Lauren Bacall and Jason Robards, Sam followed in their footsteps. Beginning work as a professional actor in his twenties, he found success in television roles *(The West Wing, Spin City, Sex and the City, Law & Order)* as well as in film *(American Beauty, Prêt-à-Porter, Artificial Intelligence: AI, The Rebound)* and was nominated for a Tony in 2002. He had the opportunity to act alongside both his mother, in *Prêt-à-Porter*, and his father, who died in 2000, in 1988's *Bright Lights, Big City*.

"As much as a BFF can make you go WTF, there's no denying we'd all be a little less rich without them."

1.04 bad news blair

Original air date: October 10, 2007
Written by: Joshua Safran
Directed by: Patrick Norris
Guest cast: Peter O'Brien (Photographer), Sebastian Stan (Carter Baizen), Michelle Hurd (Laurel), Jill Flint (Bex), Chase Coleman (Boy), Jeff Mantel (High Stakes Poker Dealer), Gerardo Rodriguez (Player), Jaron Vesely (Ticket Clerk), Lucas van Engen (Doorman)

Nate ruins the fun on Chuck's "lost weekend" of manly misbehavior, while Blair vies with Serena to be the apple of Eleanor Waldorf's eye. Dan leaps to conclusions. Again.

What does your choice of friends say about who you are? In this episode of *Gossip Girl* we learn that despite the shortcomings of our besties, they always have our back — even when family doesn't.

The return of Eleanor Waldorf (with a different face from the pilot episode) further exposes what lurks beneath Blair's façade of absolute control: insecurity and vulnerability. As much as she strives to have a perfect appearance, boyfriend, and control of the social scene, Blair is still wholly susceptible to her mother's waxing and waning affections, doubting that her mother's love is unconditional — and with good reason. Eleanor chastises Blair about food, sees her as an opportunity and then an obstacle in her company's success, manipulates Serena into betrayal, and expects all to be understood despite some "mishandling." Her first words in the episode are to scold Blair. Maybe B was better off with Dorota raising her.

When Blair speaks up to her mother and sabotages the photo shoot by stealing the clothes, she's taking a step in the same direction as Nate. Blair refuses to be treated as an afterthought and her mother's last priority. Both Blair and Nate are beginning to realize you don't have to accept the hand your parents deal you. And when your family fails you, your best friend picks up the slack.

Chuck watches out for Nate even as Nate questions "all that is holy" to him. Resisting the life plotted out by his parents, Nate is susceptible to the hilariously and fraudulently self-righteous Carter Baizen and the freedom of the "real world." Chuck unapologetically embraces the role of the idle, rich teenage boy (boozing, over-indulgence, twins) and resents that one of his ilk (Carter *invented* the lost weekend) has rejected his values. When the Anti-Chuck turns out to be a swindler, Nate still has Chuck standing by him.

Chuck may believe that "everyone wants to be us," but if Dan Humphrey ever did envy the lifestyle of his classmates, his exposure to Blair and Serena's world has made him run for the modest but stable comforts of Brooklyn.

"She's everything I hate about the Upper East Side distilled into one 95-pound, doe-eyed, bon mot–tossing, label-whoring package of girly evil."
— Lonely Boy on Queen B

JTLYK:

- No Little J in this episode. She's off in Hudson with her absentee mommy.
- Those dudes who check out Serena (and Blair) are *way* too old to be ogling 16-year-olds. Totally skeezy . . . and totally accurate.
- The dresses B and S are holding when Eleanor and Laurel first think of using Blair as the model are the same ones the girls later wear in their photo shoot.
- Serena is actually, though temporarily, happy: running into Dan while shopping, goofing around with Blair and the girls. A far cry from her melancholy state in the previous three episodes.
- On top of the wardrobe in Blair's room are Care Bears, a Cabbage Patch Kid, and some dolls.
- Rufus describes "girls like Serena" exactly how Bex describes Alison's painting: complicated and enigmatic.
- When S calls Dan and he's brushing his teeth before beddy-byes (at 10 p.m.), he has a worn Lincoln Hawk T-shirt on. Aw, what a supportive son.
- Blair and Serena are once again positioned as competitors. Blair worries that Serena is going to usurp her position — in her dream, with her mother, in the spotlight, and with her boyfriend.
- Is Captain Archibald sketchier than we already knew? Why did he empty Nate's trust fund and not mention it?

Secrets & Lies:

- Rufus continues to hide his past with Lily when he tells Dan he once dated a girl "a lot like Serena." Understatement of the century.
- Chuck knew that Carter wasn't truly Nate's friend and that he couldn't be trusted, but Carter succeeded in hoodwinking Nate into the rigged poker game.
- Carter steals the baseball and the watch — sorry, Chuck, the *Piaget* — from the Palace suite.
- Blair pretends not to mind when Eleanor tells her she's been replaced for the photo shoot.

breakfast at bendel's

Based on the 1958 Truman Capote novella, *Breakfast at Tiffany's* (dir. Blake Edwards, 1961) is the story of Holly Golightly, a seemingly carefree girl living on the Upper East Side who thinks she should marry rich so she can take care of her brother Fred. The film opens with the iconic scene of Holly having breakfast outside Tiffany's, her solution to getting "a case of the mean reds," when suddenly "you're afraid and you don't know what you're afraid of." Her life keeps slipping out of her control and into it she draws her neighbor, a writer, whom she calls Fred after her brother. Both rely on generous companions of the opposite sex to support them financially (though neither is explicitly prostituting themselves), and the two unlikely friends fall in love over the course of the film. Audrey Hepburn (1929–1993) wasn't the first choice for the role; Truman Capote wanted Marilyn Monroe to play the part, and Hepburn later said she wasn't sure if she was the right choice for it. But it's hard to imagine anyone but her as the now-iconic character. Hailed as a style icon, Hepburn influenced fashion both on- and off-screen wearing clothes by leading designers like Givenchy, Ferragamo, and Valentino. She projected an image of grace, elegance, and stylishness borne from her background as a ballet dancer, and is responsible for popularizing enduring wardrobe staples like the little black dress, oversized sunglasses, pearls, Capri pants, and ballet flats.

"Bad News Blair" opens with Blair dressed as Holly Golightly, stepping out of a 1960s-era cab in front of Henri Bendel, her substitute for Tiffany & Co. (and where her mother's new clothing line will be available). Blair thinking of herself as Audrey Hepburn is a character trait taken straight from Cecily von Ziegesar's book series, where B's obsession doesn't border on but dives deep into the absurd. The show toned down the Audrey references to a dream here and there, a portrait of the actress in B's room, and an inspiration for her personal style. Blair's desire to emulate Audrey Hepburn is not without irony; as much as Hepburn was stylish, she was a humanitarian known for her generosity and kindness toward others. Not B's strongest points.

- Eleanor tricks Serena into modeling in Blair's stead, but B doesn't believe it was an honest mistake on S's part. Her trust in Serena is still shaky.
- Dan tells Blair how he really feels about his mother's absence from the family, something he hasn't told Alison, Rufus, or Jenny.

Scrap!: Nate starts a tussle with Carter when he realizes the poker game's a setup.

The Original Gossipverse: Blair's Audrey Hepburn fantasies are pulled from the book series, where Blair is completely obsessed.

That's How It's Done in *The O.C.*: In the season 1 episode "The Strip," Ryan gets roped into an illegal poker game in Las Vegas to help Seth pay off his hooker debts.

Bad News Bears (dir. Richard Linklater, 2005): The original was made in '76, but let's focus on the somewhat more palatable remake. Billy Bob Thornton stars as a former MLB player (albeit with a *very* brief career) who coaches the Bears, a ragtag Little League team. Estranged from his own teenage daughter, Coach Billy Bob offers advice to a kid on the team: tell your parents what they want to hear instead of the truth, that way everyone's happier. Competitiveness nearly drives the Bears apart, until they realize — until we *all* realize — that winning the championship doesn't matter. What matters is having fun, being a part of something, and being . . . loved. Switch baseball for high fashion, Billy Bob for Eleanor Waldorf, the Bears for Blair-Bear and S, and you'll see that an impromptu photo shoot in Central Park is just as good as having a non-alcoholic beer fight on the baseball diamond after losing the championship.

Welcome to the Real World:

- The baseball that Carter steals from Chuck's suite is Babe Ruth's "called shot." Legend has it that in game 3 of the 1932 World Series, Babe Ruth pointed out to the centerfield bleachers and in his next at-bat, hit a homerun precisely where he said he would. That ball would be more valuable than Chuck's Piaget.
- The girls are reading *InStyle* and *Elle* on B's bed.

- Bex the Sexy Art Buyer compares Alison's work to Julian Schnabel, a fellow Brooklynite who rose to prominence with his Neo-Expressionist paintings in the early '80s, and to early Francis Bacon, whose work in the 1930s was characterized by boldly colored and haunting images.
- Serena and Blair would have been precocious nine-year-olds when they danced around to Christina Aguilera's 1999 hit "Genie in a Bottle."
- Serena makes a few 2007 pop culture references trying to get B to loosen up: the much-besieged Britney Spears attacked a paparazzo's vehicle with an umbrella in February, and "Cyborg Spice" documented her move from London to L.A. with a special called *Victoria Beckham: Coming to America*, which aired in July. It was *may-jah*.
- Whilst chilling at the Humphrey loft, Dan reads the Best of 2006 issue of *Cool'eh* magazine. Must've been a keeper.
- B suggests her mom's campaign deserves an Alessandra Ambrosio rather than an amateur. Ambrosio is a Brazilian supermodel who has worked with all the major designers and magazines, is a Victoria's Secret Angel, and one of the top-earning models in the world. She's just a bit more experienced than Blair.
- To be fair Jessica Simpson's film acting career lasted longer than B's modeling career: *The Dukes of Hazzard*, *Employee of the Month*, *Blonde Ambition*, and *Major Movie Star*. You haven't heard of those last two because they were major flops (everywhere but in the Ukraine).

Locations:

- Chuck and the boys play b-ball at the Sara D. Roosevelt Park at East Houston and Chrystie streets.
- American designer and socialite Tory Burch's flagship store is in NoLita at 257 Elizabeth Street. And Dan likely picked up his Cubans at Café Habana (17 Prince St).
- When Serena cancels on him, Dan is in line to buy tickets at The Sunshine (143 E Houston St), the "hippest theater in NYC," according to the *Village Voice*.
- Blair catches Serena doing the photo shoot on the roof of Silvercup Studios (42-22 22nd St, Queens), where the *Gossip Girl* sets are housed on the lot formerly occupied by *The Sopranos*.
- Eleanor tries to soften the blow of kicking B off the Bendel's campaign with the promise of dinner at Café des Artistes (1 W 67th St), which

overlooks Central Park. The grilled steak frites: $39. Crushing your daughter's dreams: priceless.

- B and S pose in front of the Plaza Hotel fountain (768 5th Ave).

The Look: Serena and Blair's day-of-shopping outfits are so S and B: Serena's in a BCBG denim vest, Wrangler jeans, carrying a Gucci Indy bag

Like many a tourist before them, Serena and Blair pose by the Pulitzer Fountain in front of the Plaza Hotel.

with long metallic knotted necklaces while Blair's prissed up in a Milly dress paired with a wide cream hairband. All the Eleanor Waldorf dresses the girls wear are Lorick (see page 65). At the test shoot, Serena is in a modified-for-the-show Vena Cava silk charmeuse dress with a Havasu print. When Blair catches S modeling, she's stunning in a green Catherine Malandrino dress. S has a Carrie Valentine relaxed chic bag when she leaves the photo shoot. Only Chuck Bass would wear (or could wear) that ensemble he put together to play basketball. Otherwise the boys keep up their signature styles: Chuck in pink striped shirts and bow ties, Nate in blues with vaguely nautical detailing, and Dan back in a vest to go to the movies with S.

Music: As B's vintage cab pulls up to Bendel's in the opening dream sequence, Henry Mancini's "Moon River," the signature song from *Breakfast at Tiffany's*, plays, and again when Blair arrives at the rooftop photo shoot and sees Serena modeling. B wakes up to find Eleanor and Serena having brunch to "Make It Bounce" by Invisible Men. X5's "The Focus" kicks off the boys' lost weekend. Eve's "Tambourine" starts as Serena walks away from

Dan. Kati, Is, and Serena hang out in Blair's room to "Candy Store" by Miss Eighty 6. More from Miss Eighty 6 ("Till the Sun Comes Up") when Chuck and his boys arrive at the basketball court. Blair does her test shoot to "Until You Can't" by Alana D. Chuck leads the boys on a bar crawl to "Bounce Back" by Early Earl (featuring Miss Eighty 6). Just before B gets the bad news from her mom, there's a snippet from "Habanera" from Georges Bizet's *Carmen.* The appropriately titled "Beautiful Girls" by Sean Kingston provides the soundtrack to B and S's carefree photo shoot.

Sebastian Stan as Carter Baizen

Born in Romania on August 13, 1983, Sebastian Stan lived there and in Austria before moving to New York State at the age of 12. He performed in theater productions as a teen and studied acting at college as well as at the Globe Theatre in London. His first television role was in *Law & Order;* he also appeared in *Tony and Tina's Wedding, The Architect,* and 2006's *The Covenant,* opposite Chace Crawford and Taylor Kitsch. Sebastian appeared on Broadway in *Talk Radio* in 2007, and starred in 2009's NBC series *Kings.* And if you've had the opportunity to see the terrible video for "Wake Up Call" by *Heroes* star Hayden Panettiere, Sebastian is the object of her affection. Hope that didn't make his real-life girlfriend, Leighton Meester, jealous!

"You can't save a damsel if she loves her distress."

1.05 dare devil

Original air date: October 17, 2007
Written by: Lenn K. Rosenfeld
Directed by: Jamie Babbit
Guest cast: Halley Wegryn Gross (Harper), Kaitlyn Ashley Benson (Maya), Jed Orlemann (Club Stockbroker), Kim Shaw (Amanda), Marcella Lowery (Ostroff Nurse), James Lorenzo (Car Service Driver), David Arden Engel (Fancy Restaurant Waiter), Rob Falcone (Police Officer #1), Jaymes Hodges (Club Manager), Sean Ringgold (Club Security Guard), Peterson Townsend (Club Stockbroker's Friend)

What Dan thinks Serena wants and what she actually wants for a first date prove to be two very different things. And it's makeover week for Little Jenny Humphrey as she is initiated by Queen B and her minions at the annual sleepover.

Is there anything more simultaneously unwelcome and endearing than an older sibling who fancies themselves a parent to their little brother or sister? Jenny and Eric would argue no. As Serena and Dan and Lily and Rufus worry, the two 14-year-olds get to enjoy an adventurous, rule-breaking, boundary-pushing night on the town.

After Serena stands her ground and goes on the date with Dan as promised, rather than to B's event-of-the-season sleepover, Blair simply has no choice (in Blair world) but to find entertainment elsewhere: initiating Little Humphrey with a no-holds-barred game of truth or dare. But in the same way that Serena isn't subservient like Kati, Is, and the no-name girls, Jenny proves herself to be a willful protégé. J proves she can think on her feet (and in her heels), but her assertion that she knows who she is and won't compromise her character is less than believable. She has gone along with all of B's suggestions and is keen to impress and emulate her classmates.

And as Lily and Rufus talk about the wall between a parent and their teenage child, the 20-year-old wall between the former lovers starts coming down. Thank god Alison is busy showering in Hudson while her "friend" answers her phone; that means Rufus doesn't have to feel (too) guilty if the sparks between him and Lily lead to more than pasta making.

And in that other budding Humphrey–van der Woodsen romance, Dan and Serena's first official date is gloriously awkward. The mismatched outfits, Serena's over-the-top assumption that the Vespa is Dan's, Dan's desperate attempts to appear comfortable at the posh restaurant, and his nickel-and-diming make dating seem like the Worst. Idea. Ever. Of course, once D and S level with each other about their expectations, things get way, way less awkward. (But a bit boring for Serena. She had to hang around while Dan played pool with the dive bar dude.)

With the exception of Absentee Alison, things are looking pretty rosy: Dan and Serena are making out, Jenny's gained acceptance with the popular girls, Blair and Serena are pals, Rufus and Lily have become friends again, and Eric finally gets to go home to his family. What could *possibly* go wrong?

"Either 'Dan Humphrey' is an alias or your son is not very popular."
— Lily tells it like it is to Rufus

JTLYK:

- Last week Jenny was away and in this episode there's no Nate or Chuck.
- Dan could not get cuter. First, Cedric the Cabbage Patch Kid, now a Teenage Mutant Ninja Turtles piggybank?
- Alison earned $2,650 for the sale of her painting.
- "Her? Really?" — Kati and Is with their matching outfits and in-stereo commentary are just too hilarious.

- Serena makes a bit of money on her date with Dan. She pays for the dinner on her mom's credit card, but takes the 75 bucks Dan wins playing pool to cover dinner. I'm guessing she won't be handing that cash over to Mommy Dearest.
- The magazine Dan was reading in the previous episode is still sitting on the coffee table at the Humphrey Loft.
- Take note of B's exceptionally direct rebuff of Hedge Fund Mafia Guy's slimy come-on: "Well, my answer is usually never say never. But for you I'll make an exception." Please re-use whenever appropriate.
- Dan is supposed to be a pool wizard but he calls the cue a "stick."
- The "no offense"/"none taken" exchange between Serena and Jenny is echoed at the end of the episode with Eric and Blair. Those van der Woodsens don't want to offend anybody.
- The Lincoln Hawk record Rufus is listening to has a Parental Advisory warning on it, and is called *Acid Re*–something (Rufus's thumb partially obscures the title). *Acid Reign*? *Acid Reflux*?
- "Done and done" is the catchphrase of B's soiree; it's said by Harper, Blair, and Jenny.

Secrets & Lies:

- Blair pretends to be high on every drug under the sun to distract the nurse while Jenny busts Eric out of the Ostroff Center.
- Lily lies to Rufus when he questions her concern about Eric being AWOL, providing the weak cover story that he's missing from his room at the Palace rather than reveal to Rufus that E's staying at a treatment center.
- Jenny calls Hedge Fund Guy's girlfriend and pretends to be a girl named Claire.
- Lily tells Rufus that Eric tried to kill himself. Other than Serena, Rufus is likely the only person she has told. Must be a relief for Lily to share that with a sympathetic person, and much more effective than retail therapy.
- Blair tricks Jenny into stealing the jacket from Eleanor Waldorf Designs knowing full well that the alarm will go off and J will be trapped.
- Jenny lies to the NYPD and pretends to be Blair Waldorf.

Scrap!: For our weekly scuffle, things get physical when Hedge Fund calls D's little sister "jailbait."

best frenemies forever

Much of the drama and intrigue comes from what the *New York Times* called the "unnavigability of friendship" on *Gossip Girl*: "the ruling passion is power: the pride that comes with connecting with one's ilk and asserting control, as well as the scorching pain of rejection and ridicule. Sex is easy; it's the cliques that take time and solicitude." Jenny doesn't want to be like her big brother was in his freshman and sophomore years (a friendless nobody who ate lunch by himself), but trying to be friends with Blair and her circle has less to do with traditional ideas of friendship (enjoying each other's company, being there for each other) than paying her dues and being initiated into an exclusive club. Blair and her back-up bitches are unkind to girls they deem subordinates, putting on a show of friendliness to play games with their unsuspecting, but rather willing, victims. While Jenny can be naïve, she also shows a talent for navigating the tricky shark-infested waters of frenemies. She and Serena may get along just fine, but if B is pissed at S, as she was in "The Wild Brunch," taking the wrong side is a surefire path to social suicide. But Jenny sees the trap: "I don't have a problem with [Serena], but if someone did have a problem with her, I wouldn't have a problem with that either."

The centerpiece friendship is between Blair and Serena, who have been BFFs since childhood. That friendship is rife with tension. Blair already felt like second fiddle to Serena (less attractive, less sexually experienced, second best in her mother's eyes), but Serena abandoning her and sleeping with Nate destroyed a precarious trust and pushed Blair into fight mode. As much as Serena tries to apologize and remove the "enemy" from their "frenemy" status, B has a hard time seeing S as anything but a competitor. The best thing about friends, how well they know and understand each other, can quickly flip into the worst thing when that knowledge is used to hurt rather than help.

Depictions of female friendship as treacherous territory are nothing new in pop culture; before there was Serena and Blair, there was Regina George and Cady, Kelly and Brenda, the Heathers and Veronica, Betty and Veronica, Hermia and Helena. . . . Nor is it (sadly) just the stuff of fiction. "There are some catty fights in our grade, not only for power, but for very stupid reasons. Like if you're wearing the same shoes," said a 13-year-old student at Spence interviewed by the *New York Times* about how realistic *Gossip Girl* is to the life of an actual Upper East Side teenager. "At an all-girl school, you fight over who has the most guy friends. Knowing lots of boys makes you the alpha girl, the girl who goes everywhere, who knows everyone, who is the captain of the in crowd," said another 13-year-old Spence girl. "Behind your back, your friends will call you a slut," said a 16-year-old Hewitt student. And affluence does matter: "We have this friend on the Upper West Side. She left our school because everyone else was on the Upper East Side and really, really rich. She felt disincluded," a 19-year-old Hewitt graduate said. And the ratings for the show, high among female viewers and split almost equally between urban and suburban/rural areas, reveal the frenemy problem isn't confined to the Upper East or Upper West Side.

The Original Gossipverse: Gossip Girl informs us that Nate is closing up the family yacht; he shares his sailing passion with Book Nate who loves nothing more than the open water. In *You're the One That I Want*, Dan is worried about his little sis, and his girlfriend Vanessa reassures him like Serena does in this episode, "She's more together than you think."

That's How It's Done in *The O.C.*: Ryan and the gang were routinely kicked out of places for fighting. Season 3 Kaitlin Cooper is the best role model for being a bad-ass 14-year-old. Like Serena and her love of classic rock, Marissa shocked and impressed Seth and company with her taste in music.

Daredevil (dir. Mark Steven Johnson, 2003): Like every superhero movie, this one starts with the requisite origin story: little Matty Murdock is a New York kid who gets beat up because his dad is a washed-up boxer who works for the neighborhood kingpin. Matthew discovers his dad roughing someone up, gets some biohazard juice in his eyes, and is blinded, but *also* gets super senses, which kind of evens things out. Until Pops is murdered. Vengeance will be Matt's. The kid grows up to be Ben Affleck, a lawyer who represents innocent people by day and fights crime in a leather outfit by night, calling himself Daredevil. He falls in love with martial arts expert Elektra (Jennifer Garner). Her daddy is murdered by Bullseye (Colin Farrell) but she thinks Daredevil did it and she gets stabby. About a third of the movie is devoted to the final battle scenes, which feature nonstop shoddy special effects and Bullseye throwing a church collection plate at Daredevil before disabling him by ringing church bells.

Throughout the movie, Matt Murdock tries to convince himself that he's not a bad guy (despite killing *loads* of people). Little J makes a similar argument that is just as unconvincing: she isn't one of the mean girls, she just hangs out with them, lets them dress her up, and does what they dare her to. This episode is the origin story of the new Jenny Humphrey. That last slow-mo shot of her getting into B's elevator is a sign she may turn out to be an even more morally ambiguous character than Daredevil — and definitely a more entertaining one.

Locations:

- S wonders if her mystery date with Dan will be a "guerrilla art exhibit in Dumbo," the Brooklyn neighborhood where the exterior of the Humphreys' building is located (on Water Street, at the foot of the Manhattan Bridge).

- Dan and Serena play pool at the now-closed Hog Pit (22 Ninth Ave).
- The fictional club where B and the girls go is Visconti, but the scenes were filmed at Marquee (289 Tenth Ave).
- The shop standing in for Eleanor Waldorf Designs is Rubin Chapelle (410 W 14th St).

Oops: When J sneaks into Eric's room at the Ostroff Center, Connor Paolo flips his *Spin* magazine shut twice.

The Look: Blair, Kati, and Is reach new heights of glory with their school uniforms: B is in a navy L.A.M.B. sequin argyle cardigan over a ruffled shirt with a champagne headband with side bow, while Kati and Is help the audience at home remember who is who with "K" and "I" monogrammed ascots on otherwise matching outfits. Lily's black leather jacket is perfect for her trip over to Brooklyn, where she reminisces with Rufus about their rock 'n' roll past together, but she keeps it uptown with her cognac Hermès ostrich bag with gold hardware. Jenny arrives at the sleepover in 3GR jeans and an Alex & Chloe golden key pendant and is met by Blair in a black Stretsis ruffle silk dress crowned by a diamante 3.1 Phillip Lim headband. The wardrobe department was clearly having fun with the makeover montage, creating perfect Beyoncé, Mary Kate Olsen, and Hannah Montana outfits for Little J. Her new look, as styled by Blair, is a Jasmine Di Milo yellow dress with a Milly Peter Pan collar coat and an Alex Woo Little Letter J necklace, while Blair changes into a black 3.1 Phillip Lim lantern-sleeve gamine dress. The jacket Jenny steals from Eleanor Waldorf Designs was made by Lorick specially for the episode. Serena wears a Catherine Malandrino nailhead bead dress for her date with Dan.

Music: The lavish setup for Blair's soiree is to the tune of The Little Ones' "There's a Pot A Brewin'." (Music supervisor Alexandra Patsavas heard The Little Ones play at South by Southwest in March 2007, licensed this song, and signed them to Chop Shop Records, her Atlantic imprint.) A little of Bach's "Brandenburg Concerto No. 3 in G Major" sets the stuffy scene at the restaurant where Dan takes Serena. Little J finds the perfect outfit with the help of B and "Rock Star" by Prima J. "Came to Dance" by Cadence Blaze plays when Little J gets the text from Eric. The real Dan Humphrey date at the dive bar starts off with "Jezebel" by Two Hours Traffic. The background actors dance with unconvincing enthusiasm to "Whine Up" (Kat Deluna featuring Elephant Man) at the club. D teaches S to play pool to "Deals" by All Wrong and the Plans Change. Serena's jukebox choice is Ozzy Osbourne's "Mama I'm Coming Home." Serena and Dan arrive at Visconti to "Get Ur Party On" by Zooland. Dan and Serena kiss for the very first time to "Something Like That" by Song and Wager, which stands in as a Lincoln Hawk track.

"The other part we love about a masquerade? When the mask finally comes off and the truth is revealed to all."

1.06 the handmaiden's tale

Original air date: October 24, 2007
Written by: Jessica Queller
Directed by: Norman Buckley
Guest cast: Ward Horton (Edward Abbot a.k.a. RichBoyIV), Chase Coleman (Rich Kid), Mark H. Dold (The Dapper Clerk), Caridee English (Karissa)

Dan's old friend, and flame, Vanessa comes back into town just in time for the masked ball, where nothing goes as planned. The parents have a party of their own to attend, complete with costumes and manipulation.

You can *always* tell who it is hiding behind the mask but fiction asks us to suspend our disbelief, and masquerades have long served writers as a way to complicate relationships: mistaken identity, the freedom to misbehave when you're anonymous, and the ability for the uninvited to easily gain access to a party like Romeo sneaking into the Capulets' masked ball. The Humphrey kids follow in that grand tradition, playing the role of the unwelcome masqueraders who cause a ruckus.

The "overprivileged, underparented trust-fund brats" are royalty on the Upper East Side; these society functions, their courtly balls. Serena, who lives at the *Palace*, is framed as a princess who's betrayed by her white knight, while Jenny plays Cinderella to Blair's wicked stepsister. While B's totally condescending "Your time will come" fits her stepsister role perfectly, Jenny won't wait and, with the help of fairy godmother Vanessa, gets to the ball. And while Blair may have both ladies-in-waiting and a handmaiden, she's short a prince: Nate is too distracted by real-life worries to play a role in her fairy tale. Blair, so wrapped up with the idea of a grand romantic gesture, doesn't realize that Nate actually needs her, especially since his best friend just wanted to "bump" the Captain's cocaine. His past affection for Serena catches up to him, but when he spills his feelings, it is to, as it must be at a masked ball, the wrong girl. Oops.

The past has also caught up to Dan, who finds himself in his own love triangle and deceiving the two girls he cares about most. In the parallel universe of Oldsville, Rufus and Lily and Bart do the same dance of deception, hiding their affection behind half-successful ruses. The post-kiss "I need a drink" moment is hilarious, but Rufus is obviously harboring some real old-flame feelings for Lily. No wonder he had such insight for Vanessa about her feelings for Dan.

"I'm sorry. I'm sorry. Case of mistaken identity! Ironically, not involving masks."
— Dan after grabbing a stranger he mistook for Vanessa

JTLYK:

- This is the first episode to open with a new story on Gossip Girl's homepage related to the end of the previous episode. This week's story: "*Macking in the Meat Packing.* Spotted: S and Lonely Boy, macking in the Meat Packing. Opposites do attract, but for how long?"
- Serena and Dan know exactly what the other is thinking for the second time with the "masked balls are pretentious" thing. The first time was in the wake of Dan's wave in "The Wild Brunch."
- B has a picture of a bulldog on the bulletin board in her room. She truly does love Yale.
- Serena and Lily are getting along better now that Eric is back at home.
- The van der Woodsens live in suite 1510 at the Palace.
- In Serena's IM friend list are "n8" and "chucktastic."
- Even though the party at Eleanor's has a Moroccan theme, Anne Archibald is too conservative to dress up even a teensy bit.

- Chuck likes his women "beautiful and mean." Anyone we know who fits that bill?
- It had to hurt for V to hear Dan say he past-tense loved her, in a pre-shaving 16-year-old way. Ouch.
- Lily puts her hand on Bart the same way she did with Rufus in the previous episode. Rufus takes it as his cue to leave.
- This is the second episode in a row where Jenny is mistaken for Serena.
- Of course, Chuck Bass wears red socks to match his red devil outfit.
- If Dan has been obsessed with Serena since 9th grade, that means there was a year of overlap where he was in love with Vanessa and admiring Serena from afar. Does Dan have room in his heart for both ladies at once?

Secrets & Lies:

- On the phone, D lies to S about who she hears talking in the background, saying it's J, not Vanessa.
- Lily fibs to Serena: "Who would I be dating?" Um, Bart Bass and/or Rufus Humphrey? Take your pick, Lil!
- D lies to Vanessa, saying he has an American history paper to write when really he's headed to the ball. (Which, Dan, BTW, is totally a lie, not "merely refraining from sharing the truth.")
- Rufus figures out that Lily brought him to the party to make Bart Bass jealous. And it works.
- Dan tells the doorman at the ball that he's Jack Altman (the drunk dude headed uptown) to get in.
- Despite the no-freshmen-allowed rule, Jenny sneaks into the masked ball. She deceives Chuck in order to get some measure of revenge.
- Dan is totally busted by Serena and by Vanessa for both his lies.
- Vanessa masks her true feelings for Dan by saying them with a heavy layer of sarcasm. Dan doesn't realize that she really means what she said.
- Case of mistaken identity involving masks! After the mask switcheroo in the ladies room, Nate thinks J is Serena and tells her he isn't over her, then kisses her. Dan also thinks J is Serena and calls after her, apologizing. Luckily he doesn't kiss her. Ew.
- Captain A-hole doesn't admit the drugs are his, and instead pins the blame on Nate.
- D promises to lie less to V (and to eat more Ukrainian food).
- Dan and Serena are keeping secrets from each other. In "The Wild

Brunch," Lily asks Dan not to tell Serena about L's relationship with Bart Bass. And in this episode, Jenny asks Serena not to tell anyone about her sneaking into the ball.

Not a Girl, Not Yet a Queen Bee: After spilling a few secrets early on, Little J is turning into quite the secret keeper. You can bet that she hasn't told anyone about her run-in with the cops ("Dare Devil"), and now she's sneaked into the ball and doesn't tell Dan. If Blair hadn't caught her bracelet, her secret would have been safe. But Jenny has an even bigger secret: Nate is in love with Serena, not with Blair.

The Original Gossipverse: Dan and Vanessa haven't known each other since childhood in the books; they meet when they're locked out on a roof together at a party (like Chuck in this episode). From that day forward, Vanessa has a crush on Dan, but hides her feelings from him.

That's How It's Done in *The O.C.*: Seth lies to Summer when she overhears a girl talking in the background ("The Game Plan"), but he pretends it's *This American Life*, not a sibling.

The Handmaid's Tale (dir. Volker Schlöndorff, 1990): Based on the 1985 novel by Margaret Atwood, *The Handmaid's Tale* is set in the not-so-distant future. The human race is plagued by widespread sterility and in the Republic of Gilead, a fascist state, women who can reproduce are captured and forced to become "handmaids." Placed in a wealthy household, the handmaid is made to have sex with the husband, hoping to provide a child for the wife (who's in the room during the "ceremony"), all in service of God and country. The story follows Kate (Natasha Richardson), a handmaid placed in the not-so-warm-or-loving house of Serena Joy (Faye Dunaway) and the Commandant (Robert Duvall). Luckily, there's a hot driver (Aidan Quinn) who she can have sex with. The Commandant is sterile, and if she doesn't become pregnant, it's off to the Colonies (which is worse than it sounds). Religious fundamentalism, violence, the stripping of human rights, and complete gender inequality are the cornerstones of this society, which rebel forces strive to overthrow. It's a doozy. To boil down a complex film (and a more complex novel) into one sentence: things go terribly awry when people are deprived of personal freedom.

And so it goes on the Upper East Side: Nate is trapped in a life he doesn't want, Blair is making her little minion J work for no reward, Serena tries to change her life but keeps bumping against the society she was born into. Fortunately for our handmaiden, Little J doesn't endure the same torture Kate does as she navigates a world governed by strict rules and punishments, and becomes privy to its secrets and deception. Like Kate, Jenny breaks the rules knowing what the consequences could be if she's caught. She won't relinquish control to Blair or to Chuck, humiliating him for his act of sexual violence with a considerably less aggressive punishment than Kate has for the Commandant. Blair, like Serena Joy, is controlling, trying to make Nate the boyfriend she wants him to be, but his eyes, like the Commandant's, are on another lady.

Welcome to the Real World:

- Vanessa surprises Dan by asking about a borrowed copy of *The Crying of Lot 49*, Thomas Pynchon's excellent 1966 novel.
- Vanessa jokes that Vin Diesel's 2005 family comedy *The Pacifier* played for a year at the one theater in Woodbury, Vermont.
- When Nate finds the cocaine in his father's study, Chuck says, "Chi Chi, get the *yeyo*," a Tony Montana line from *Scarface*.
- RichBoyIV's MySpace profile says he goes to Dalton, a real-life UES private school. Also, he wants to meet Angelina, LiLo, and Halle Berry. His profile picture couldn't look more like an actor's headshot.
- J's ball gown is borrowed from Vanessa's friend who works in the costume department at BAM (the Brooklyn Academy of Music), a cultural center and performing arts venue that's been around since the turn of the 20th century.
- When Chuck asks who the disguised J is, B guesses that she's from Chapin, another UES private school.
- The family ring was given to Mrs. Archibald's great-grandmother by Cornelius Vanderbilt (1794–1877), who was one of the wealthiest men in the world thanks to his shipping and railroad empires.

Locations:

- An art-house cinema in Soho, the Angelika Film Center (18 W Houston at Mercer) would never screen *The Pacifier*.

- The masked ball takes place at the Prince George Hotel ballroom (14 E 28th St).
- Vanessa picks up pierogi from Veselka (144 Second Ave at 9th), "Ukrainian soul food in the heart of the East Village." (It's also where Nick meets up with Norah in *Nick and Norah's Infinite Playlist*.)

Oops: The receipt Jenny signs for Blair at the beginning of the episode is for $16,145.04. But the addition is wrong: the subtotal and tax add up to $16,137.04. What's a measly $8 when you're spending that much on one night? And why haven't Dan and Vanessa spoken in over a year? Seems a little unlikely that they would be *completely* out of touch for a whole year after being besties for life. And if they haven't spoken, how does V know about Alison's sojourn in Hudson?

Spotted: Cycle 7 *America's Next Top Model* winner Caridee English overacts in her one scene as Bart Bass's "attractive 25-year-old mannequin" at Eleanor's party. She also appeared in an episode of the CW's *One Tree Hill*. One of *ANTM*'s most charming winners, Caridee is set to host a show on Oxygen in 2009 and is a spokesperson for the National Psoriasis Foundation.

The Look: Blair Pants Watch! For the first time on the show, Blair is not in a dress or skirt but wearing shorts at home on the morning of the masquerade ball. Jenny runs B's errands in a KensieGirl polka-dot dress, Marc by Marc Jacobs camel blazer, and carries a Magical Pegasus Yak Pak bag. Serena is in an Elle Macpherson Intimates flame chemise in pink in B's room, and is lounging in a burnt orange Natori Beijing Labyrinth robe, which she leaves open to answer the hotel-room door (as one does) and finds Nate standing there. Lily's Moroccan-themed outfit is Matthew Williamson's Kandi beaded kimono dress. For the ball, costume designer Eric Daman drew inspiration from masquerades in the tradition of the Venetian court. Serena's canary yellow gown has an empire waist, chiffon layers, and is paired with a marabou shrug, rhinestone belt, big bow, and diamond necklace. Jenny's vintage gown is similar enough to S's to be mistaken for it, but hers is layers of tulle in yellows with a lace insert on the bust and a full crinoline skirt with matching tulle flowers. Topped with a tiara, Blair's masked ball look is black-on-black in a "Marie Antoinette style"; the rose-embroidered dress is shorter in the front to show off her Max Studio Zulli boots (which sold out after this episode aired). Her outfit is finished with a sequin star capelet. On the complete other side of the fashion spectrum is Vanessa Abrams, a girl with Brooklyn street style wearing bright, bold colors, animal prints, shimmering leggings, and statement jewelry (like her CC Skye hoop earrings) to create a casual, playful look.

Music: Dan and Vanessa make plans to see a movie to "Central Park" by Goodmornings. "Kiss Kiss" by the Yeah Yeah Yeahs sets the pace for the masked ball. As Jenny explores the ball, Nekta's "Guess Who" is the

Nan Zhang as Kati Farkas and Nicole Fiscella as Isabel Coates

Born on November 1, 1986, in China, Nan Zhang moved with her family to New Orleans when she was six years old. Ten years later, she won Chanel/*Seventeen* magazine's New Model of the Year and considered modeling instead of the academic career she'd been preparing for. She attended Johns Hopkins, where she studied medicine with a specialty in neuroscience, before leaving her studies behind to pursue modeling and acting. While getting a manicure on the Upper East Side, she was spotted by a casting director and got a bit part in *The Shanghai Hotel* followed by a role in *West 32nd.* Her first major role is as Kati Farkas.

Of Indian and St. Lucian background, Nicole Fiscella was born in Rochester on September 15, 1979. She landed her first acting role, on *Gossip Girl*, after achieving success as a model. She's appeared in *Cosmo*, *Elle*, *Lucky*, *Cosmo Girl*, in campaigns for Pantene and Gap Body, and she's the girl who makes LL Cool J tingle in his video for "Baby." Nicole has a BA in anthropology from Tufts and is pursuing an MS in human nutrition, taking online courses from Bridgeport University. Like Nan, she's also the daughter of two doctors, which inspired her choice of studies. "We were always the health-nut family. I think I always wanted to do something in the medical field a little bit, but not as far as being a doctor, so this is a good median," she told the *New York Observer*. To help her play someone significantly younger than she is, she gets "some inspiration from my younger brother, who's 19, so it's around that age, and he'll tell me what all his little girls say and everything like that. So that helps. It's fun. I like it, and hell, if I can live young forever, why not?"

soundtrack. Vanessa comes back to give J her keys and Chuck asks J to dance to "Take It to the Top" (5 Alarm Music). Dan cuts in on Serena and Rich Boy IV while they dance to "A Taste (The La La Song)" by Sofia J. Serena confronts Dan about his lie to "Nasty Funky Crazy" (Becca Styles). And Dan tries to explain his other lie to Vanessa with Miss Eighty 6's "Ring a Ling" in the background. Nate is on a mission to find Serena to Beck's "Timebomb." Anne Archibald confronts Nate about the cocaine she thinks is his to "Happy Ending" by Mika.

"Prohibition never stood a chance against exhibition. It's human nature to be free. And no matter how long you try to be good, you can't keep a bad girl down."

1.07 victor, victrola

Original air date: November 7, 2007
Written by: K.J. Steinberg
Directed by: Tony Wharmby
Guest cast: Shaun Earl (Maxie Mae), Jessalyn Wanlim (Pauletta Cho), Gregory Northrop (Policeman)

As their parents push them together, Nate and Blair drift further apart. Dan and Serena find themselves at a crossroads in their relationship. Chuck Bass shows some admirable initiative with his new burlesque club, and is rewarded for his efforts.

Remember back at the Bass brunch when Chuck told Blair he was "honored to play even a small role in [her] deflowering"? Well, OMFG. What an ending. While it was clear from the first little flashforward scene that the dancing girl Chuck found so mesmerizing was Blair, it was completely unexpected that Serena and Dan would be the ones who wait while Blair would finally lose her virginity . . . and to Chuck! Fabulous.

Nothing like finding out the guy you thought you were going to marry is still in love with your best friend to make a girl freak the eff out. With such tight restrictions on our favorite Upper East Siders, even the most goody-goody are bound to break the rules and find some escape — whether it be in Brooklyn, at Victrola, in the back of a limo, or in cocaine and embezzlement. The Captain relentlessly mixes business with family interests, working with Eleanor and his wife to commit Nate to Blair. When both Archibald parents push Nate away when he tries to speak truthfully with them — his mother audaciously blaming him for his dad's drug problem, his father eager to pimp out his son to secure his deal with Eleanor — Nate turns Howie over to the police. He is a more responsible and moral person than his parents. The other dysfunctional father–son dynamic centers on responsibility too: Chuck wants to impress his father with his initiative, but Bart sees only the worst in his son. After being chastised by his father, Chuck gets loaded to live down to the low expectations Bart has for him, and leads Lily to believe Bart has been unfaithful.

Do you come back from that kind of betrayal, real or rumored? Jenny sees her parents' marriage falling apart, as well as Nate and Blair's relationship. Like Nate, no one in her family will speak honestly with her, so she too decides to step in for her parents: asking Alison to return to the city.

Love is a tricky business (especially on teen soap operas) as Serena discovers when she and Dan finally have the opportunity and the romantic, no football sheets setup, to consummate their lurve. Serena has had sex, sure, but she's a true-feelings virgin and isn't ready. A sweet moment between Dan and Serena, and no doubt Vanessa will be relieved. (She was probably perched on the fire escape watching, waiting to burst in at the crucial moment.) In another touchingly honest moment, Nate can't tell Blair he loves her and she realizes she doesn't need him. What she needs is an escape. You go, baby vamp.

"You sure?"
— Chuck Bass finally asks a girl before pouncing on her

JTLYK:

- Top story on GG: "*Who was that masked girl?* Spotted: Cinderella making an escape from the masked ball. Seemed like the mystery girl even left behind her very own glass slipper: a diamond bracelet. Meanwhile, Chuck Bass was spotted pulling a Britney. He was walking barefoot down 27th street. Um, gross." (And that's why you can't trust gossip sites, people. Chuck was wearing socks.)
- This is the first time Chuck has been earnestly excited, and his dad is initially pleased to see C interested in something other than partying.
- The *New York Observer* article that Chuck holds up is dated September

17, 2007, and reads in part "Mega-Mogul Bart Bass Rose Up from Nowhere."

- Like father, like son. In "The Wild Brunch," Chuck tells Bart he thought he threw the party as an excuse for booze and models. Bart says nearly the exact thing to Chuck at Victrola.
- Bart talks about "going public" with his relationship with Lily, the same way a company goes public. Does every Upper East Side dad equate romance with commerce?
- Dan falls asleep reading the *Kama Sutra*.
- Captain A expects Nate to understand that a client comes before him, much like Eleanor chose business over family in "Bad News Blair" and expected B to understand.
- Bart puts his hand on Pauletta Cho's leg, hip, and back as he directs her into the limo. No wonder Chuck didn't think it was a business meeting.
- Vanessa clearly is not over Dan: she pokes her head back in the Humphrey front door for a wistful last look, and she lists off Serena's supposed conquests (boarding school professors, bullfighters, and Nate). Has she been reading Gossip Girl or is this what Dan has told her? Either way, not very sisterly, V.
- Dan's dream sequence of Nate and Serena making out and giving him pointers is a recreation of the scene from the pilot where N and S do it at the Shepherd wedding, but here the Humphrey kitchen stands in for the hotel's abandoned ballroom.
- The first thing B takes off on the Victrola stage is her signature hairband. Saucepot!

Secrets & Lies:

- Captain Archibald plays down his drug problem, saying it was a one-time thing.
- Jenny is desperate to find the bracelet, knowing that Blair will kill her if she finds out either that she's lost it or that she went to the ball.
- Nate talks to Jenny to make sure she keeps his secret, and tries to bribe her with chocolates — before giving them to Blair and pretending they were for her all along.
- B calls Jenny out for sneaking into the ball, telling her she hates secrets "more than anything." But later, B has a secret to tell J: she thinks Nate is giving her his family ring.

- Bart commands Chuck to stay quiet about catching Lily and Bart together.
- Jenny overhears her dad and brother talking about her mom having an affair, but pretends not to. Rufus then lies to her and tells her nothing's up.
- Captain A lies to Nate, telling him he has to work late when he's actually at the club buying drugs (standing on a stairway in plain sight — complete sneakiness fail).
- Eleanor leads Blair to believe that Nate is the one who wants her to have the family ring, when really it's just the meddling and selfish parents.
- Chuck tells Lily what he thinks he saw between Bart and Pauletta Cho.
- Nate spills the beans about the Captain and the coke to his mother, who can't accept the truth.
- Little J tries to hide the truth from B but Blair sees through her. Jenny reveals that Nate's not over S and is punished for it with a permanent dismissal.
- At the celebration at the Waldorfs, both Blair and Nate pretend that there's nothing they should be saying to each other.
- Nate bribes Blair's doorman to conceal his father's arrest.
- Captain A is not only arrested for the drugs on him, but is charged with embezzlement and fraud.

Scrap!: Howie Archibald punches his son in the face.

Not a Girl, Not Yet a Queen Bee: "Game recognizes game," says Blair to Jenny, but Little J needs some lessons in respecting her superiors. Jenny is in a tight spot: she has information that will hurt B, but is desperate to keep on her good side. In this episode, Little J is surrounded by people lying to her (Dan and Rufus) or implicating her in their lies (Nate). What's an ingénue to do? The right thing — being honest — may get her kicked out of the inner circle, but Jenny isn't devious enough to hide the truth from Blair Waldorf, who has an uncanny ability to see through her lies. Jenny hurts Blair by revealing her secret and sees Blair's vulnerability, which she is punished for.

The Original Gossipverse: Vanessa quotes Dan on his philosophy regarding sex: "Sex is meaningful, like art. And you don't rush art." Not too far off from Book Dan, who feels pressure from his more experienced girlfriend (V) to go all the way: "[Sex] *was* a poem. Probably the most important poem he would ever write." Blair loses her virginity to Nate, not Chuck, in *You're the One That I Want*. And it ain't in the back of a limo.

That's How It's Done in *The O.C.*: Captain Archibald is charged with embezzlement and fraud, much like Marissa's dad Jimmy in season 1. The director of this episode, Tony Wharmby, also worked on 10 episodes of *The O.C.*

Victor Victoria (dir. Blake Edwards, 1982): Julie Andrews stars in this musical comedy, set in 1934 Paris, as a destitute singer, Victoria, who meets up with a recently fired cabaret performer, Toddy (Robert Preston). The fast friends cook up a plan to launch Victoria's career as a female impersonator: she pretends to be a man performing dressed as a woman. "Count Victor Grasinzky" is the toast of gay Paris, but gangster King Marchand (James Garner) has his doubts that Victor really is a man. The two bicker in that particular way that means they are smitten with each other. In a long comedy-of-errors sequence, Marchand spies Victoria getting in the bath and confirms his suspicions. Marchand and Victoria try to be a couple: he pretends to be a gay man, she continues as Count Victor, but two pretenders is "not a good basis for a relationship." As the lies unravel, Victoria decides she would rather be herself and sacrifices her success as Victor, confident that her true love has always been able to see through her façade and love her for who she truly is.

The old-style cabaret lounge setting of *Victor Victoria* is not the only echo in "Victor, Victrola": Blair and Nate have been keeping up appearances, holding on to a relationship that wasn't working for either of them. Like Victoria, Blair puts on a disguise, playing the part of the prissy good girl, but beneath the façade she is scheming. And the one person who sees and appreciates that side of her is Chuck Bass. Since his first schemes with Blair, Chuck has recognized her for who she really is: clever, witty, devious, manipulative, insecure, beautiful, and his second-toughest critic. Their banter, like Victoria and Marchand's, was a telltale sign of an illicit hook-up on the horizon.

Welcome to the Real World:

- B thinks the dress her mother suggests she wear would be perfect if she were sailing up on the *Mayflower*, which brought the pilgrims over to the New World in 1620.

- Vanessa catches Dan watching *I Am Curious (Yellow)*, a 1967 Swedish art film with lots of sex and nudity in it.

Locations:

- The Box (189 Chrystie St, pictured below) provides the venue for Chuck's new venture, Victrola.
- The interior of Rufus's gallery is shot in-studio, but the exterior shots are of the Front Room Gallery (147 Roebling St, Brooklyn).

Oops: Not only is the *Observer* article dated the 17th, but the day planner on the Captain's desk is also open to September. What a long and excitement-filled month it's been.

The Look: Blair looks fantastically preppy at Constance in a navy Balenciaga fall/winter 2007 collection blazer with yellow-and-blue-striped trim over

a ruffled white-and-blue striped button-up shirt with oversized collar and navy tie, accessorized with a black Valentino couture bag, red bow headband, and white tights. Top marks to B. She actually wears casual clothes (!) when talking to her mom about what to wear to dinner: watch the mirror reflection for a glimpse of red lounge pants with her green-striped polo shirt. She drops her pale green Marc by Marc Jacobs Mia lace dress and throws off her Stacey Lapidus three-row crystal headband on the stage of Victrola to reveal a Valentino spring 2007 slip. Chuck dresses up for his business pitch in a pinstripe suit with purple accents (he is still Chuck Bass after all) but he's back to the bow tie for the final Victrola scene.

Music: The episode opens with "Stripper" by Soho Dolls and it plays again as Blair walks into Victrola after breaking up with Nate. Barely audible is Classic's "So They Say" in the scene where Chuck shows Victrola to B before school. Nate asks Jenny not to tell to "Ballad of an Easy" (David McConnel). Bart gives Chuck a piece of his mind after catching him with the Cherry Stem Tying Burlesque Girl to "Release" by Miss Eighty 6. Dan and Serena make out in D's room to John Ralston's "Second Hand Lovers." The Archibalds arrive at the Waldorfs to "Just Love" (Harry Warren). In Dan's amazingly factually accurate dream sequence of Nate and Serena making out, "Photograph" by Air is once again the soundtrack. The girls of Victrola dance to "Girl I Told Ya" by Valeria (featuring Aria). Howie overdoes the toast to Eleanor while Vivaldi's "Winter" from *The Four Seasons* plays. Dan has "Whatever (Folk Song in C)" by Elliott Smith playing (and skipping) in his sexed-up bedroom. "With Me" by Sum 41 plays during the final montage where Rufus and Lily watch the installation, Jenny arrives in Hudson, Dan and Serena cuddle, and Chuck and Blair hook up in the limo.

Francie Swift as Anne Archibald

Playing the humorless mother to Nate is Francie Swift, a Texas-born actress. With a long list of roles on her resumé, Francie has appeared on *Law & Order* and *A Nero Wolfe Mystery*, and plays Holly Frobisher, the wife to Ted Danson's character on the critically acclaimed FX drama *Damages*.

"Whoever thought monarchy was dead didn't realize it just changed zip codes."

1.08 seventeen candles

Original air date: November 14, 2007
Teleplay by: Felicia D. Henderson and Joshua Safran
Story by: Felicia D. Henderson
Directed by: Lee Shallat Chemel
Guest cast: Peter Maloney (Priest), Zoe Winters (Waitress), Dan Ziskie (The Archibald Lawyer), Leah Johnston (Cellphone Camera Girl)

What will B get for her 17th birthday? A Japanese-themed party, a diamond necklace, a broken heart, or all of the above? Serena and Vanessa bond over Guitar Hero.

After weeks of bad fathering on *Gossip Girl*, the bad mothers finally get the spotlight. Eleanor Waldorf doesn't give a hoot about her friend, the recently indicted Captain Archibald, just about her business deal souring; Alison Humphrey doesn't realize her wrongdoing goes beyond simple adultery; and Anne Archibald, the worst of the bunch this episode, continues to blame Nate for the family's problems while emotionally blackmailing him to give Blair the Vanderbilt ring. Nate is, once again, shot down for being rational and levelheaded with his mom's condescending "This is a conversation for adults." Dan, like his UES counterpart, has to spell out to his mother what is so wrong with her behavior (abandoning family = bad). Aren't parents supposed to, you know, parent?

To be fair to Alison, when she and Rufus have it out (before getting it on), we finally understand her: she's not just a flaky mother but a woman whose entire adult life was in support of her husband's. From that perspective, Alison being selfish for the first time and pursuing her artistic aspirations seems way less unreasonable. (But cheating? On Rufus? Still not cool.)

Vanessa and Serena become literal competitors in their Guitar Hero showdown, but the girls have been competing for the number one spot in Dan's affections since V returned to town. Dan breaks the Rules According to Blair: when a girl gets a boyfriend, she becomes the best friend and the best friend becomes the second best friend. Dan talks to Vanessa, his BFF, about his mother's return, not to Serena, his GF, and that is a problem for her. Seriously? Serena's reaction was completely selfish, stomping off because she feels slighted rather than asking Dan how he's doing with the *major* family drama he just went through. Maybe save the rules of being a boyfriend for part 2 of the conversation. Dan's problem is more important than who he tells first.

Once again Chuck gives Nate advice that's both selfish and sound-minded, telling him to put an end to the control his parents have over him (a sentiment echoed by Jenny). But Chuck doesn't have Nate's back when he doles out his words of wisdom. When Nate stands up to his parents, refusing to pimp himself out, he unwittingly steers Blair into the arms of his best friend, a move Chuck helps orchestrate.

But all is forgiven from where I stand, because the chemistry between Blair's sharp-tongued no-longer-a-Virgin Mary and Chuck's smarmy devil makes this episode. From the opening scene of Blair at confession to the Nate wager to the tender moment when Chuck gives B her birthday present, Leighton Meester and Ed Westwick turn those other plotlines into background action.

Chuck: "I feel sick. Like there's something in my stomach. Fluttering."
Blair: "*Butterflies*?"

JTLYK:

- The headline on Gossip Girl is "Blair Bares All."
- B changes her mind about not needing Nate pretty quickly; by the next morning she's asking God to send her boyfriend back to her.
- The coffee shop where Vanessa works is the same place where Rufus and Lily grabbed an Americano back in "The Wild Brunch."
- Blair calls her mother "Eleanor," not Mom or even Mother.
- Jenny has the same ribbon-crossed bulletin board that Blair has in her bedroom (and the *O.C.* girls had in their rooms).
- The headline on the *New York Journal* reads "Archibald Indicted: Multiple Charges, Firm Missing Millions."
- Dan describes Constance–St. Jude's as a school populated by mean girls and date rapists, i.e. Blair and Chuck.
- Vanessa keeps bringing the awkward. Maybe don't say to Dan "You didn't tell her?" right in front of Serena if you're trying to make nice.

- Jenny is the subject of a Gossip Girl post, but once again only as a mystery girl. When will she properly debut? Poor Little J.
- Alison is in the Humphrey Uniform, wearing Rufus's blue plaid shirt, when Jenny comes home and finds them all snuggly.

Secrets & Lies:

- Blair wants to pretend that she and Chuck never had sex.
- Dan snarkily suggests that if the Humphreys want to keep secrets, they should move somewhere with more walls than the loft.
- B lies to S about telling Nate to focus on his family and not on her birthday party. Later she tells Serena that she couldn't tell her about the break-up because if she didn't say it out loud, it wouldn't feel real.
- B hates secrets but is harboring a big one.
- Anne Archibald tries to use her son to fix her husband's shattered career, and Nate calls shenanigans on it.
- Serena was right: when she and Nate talked about his dad's drug problem in "The Handmaiden's Tale," she said the Captain was probably scared, and Mrs. Archibald says the same thing to Nate here.
- Blair plays it coy on the phone with Nate, telling him he'll really have to work hard on the relationship if they're going to try again. Pretty rich, B.
- Chuck lies to Nate saying Blair grilled him about the break-up. (Or is that what the kids are calling it these days?)
- Blair and Chuck realize that he actually likes her, and after she rebuffs him, he insults her by telling her the sex wasn't that good anyway. Obvs not true, since C's desperate for more, but no one wants to hear that after their first time.
- Nate is quick to forgive Jenny for telling Blair about the masked ball incident. He wants to make sure she doesn't feel guilty for something that isn't her fault. His parents have made him particularly sensitive about that.
- Chuck reveals to Blair what Nate told him in confidence: that he is courting her again only to get to Eleanor and help his family.
- When Dan interrupts Serena and Vanessa's bonding session, he jokes that the girls share secrets. Secret keeping: the first sign of friendship?
- Serena catches Chuck and Blair fooling around.

Not a Girl, Not Yet a Queen Bee: Being kicked out of the inner circle seems to be turning out just fine for Jenny. She orchestrated her parents back into each other's arms, and found a (hot) friend in Nate Archibald.

The Original Gossipverse: Jenny and Nate hugging is the subject of a Gossip Girl blast; in *All I Want Is Everything*, it's way worse: Jenny and Nate are dating and a video of them fooling around in Central Park gets on the internet. B's birthday in the books is around the same time of year, but just after Thanksgiving rather than just before.

That's How It's Done in *The O.C.*: Waffles are to the Humphreys what bagels were to the Cohens. On *The O.C.* and *Gossip Girl*, breakfast is definitely the most important meal of the day.

Sixteen Candles (dir. John Hughes, 1984): A quintessential '80s teen film, Molly Ringwald plays Samantha, a girl whose entire family forgets her 16th birthday since it happens to fall the day before her older sister Jenny is getting married. Sam is in love with Jake Ryan (Michael Schoeffling), a senior who's dating the prom queen and who doesn't even know she exists. Or so she thinks. She fills out a "sex survey" in independent study, saying she'd most like to do it with Jake, and it accidentally falls into his hands. A freshman geek, Farmer Ted (Anthony Michael Hall), is trying to win her affections with awkward attempt after awkward attempt — on the bus, at the school dance, in the auto workshop at school — until they become friends. After some misinformation from exchange student Long Duk Dong, Jake finds Sam, and they celebrate her birthday in that classic scene — sitting on the dining room table, b-day cake between them, sharing their first kiss.

Like Sam, Blair's birthday is overshadowed by larger events — the Captain's indictment, her tryst with Chuck, and her break-up with Nate — making it her "worst birthday ever." Jenny and Nate have a nice Sam–Jake Ryan thing going — younger outcast girl and hot guy who's dating the queen of the school — as their unlikely friendship grows when they avoid B's party. Now that Chuck realizes he has actual feelings for Blair, he could use the words of wisdom Sam's dad gives her: they're called crushes because they hurt.

Welcome to the Real World:

- Blair suggests to the priest that she'll subject herself to the "thing with the

teeth around my thigh like Silas"; clearly her knowledge of Catholicism comes straight from *The Da Vinci Code*.
- Blake Lively is a real-life Guitar Hero addict.
- Ugh, pop-culture reference fail. Nicole Fiscella's awkward delivery of Isabel's insult is almost as lame as Britney's "Gimme More" performance at the 2007 VMAs.

Oops: A few little continuity errors in this episode. Taylor Momsen's hair hops back and forth over her shoulder as Jenny and Nate talk outside B's party. Susie Misner pulls the blanket down over her legs twice when Jenny comes home to the Humphrey loft.

Locations:
- B goes to confession at the Church of St. Ignatius Loyola (980 Park Ave).
- Communitea, where Vanessa works, is actually in Queens (47-02 Vernon Blvd), not Brooklyn.

The Look: After taking it all off, Blair's back to being all buttoned-up for her appointment with the Man Upstairs in a gorgeous high-waisted skirt. Serena wears a gray Alexander Wang T-shirt dress with gold grommets, Wolford Versailles tights, and Jimmy Choo Reba leather ankle boots to B's birthday. Blair deliberately leaves her neck bare and her hair up with her black dress from Valentino's fall 2006 ready-to-wear collection, ready to display the

Susie Misner as Alison Humphrey

If you want to see Dan and Jenny's mom do the "Cell Block Tango," rent 2002's *Chicago* and watch for Liz. New Jersey–born Susan "Susie" Misner began her performing career as a dancer on Broadway and in music videos. She had her first major acting role on *One Life to Live* (her character drowned underneath the summerhouse), and has since appeared on all three *Law & Order* series, *CSI* and *CSI: Miami*, as well as *Fringe*, *New Amsterdam*, *Life on Mars*, and *Rescue Me*. Stepping into a tough role as the Humphrey kids' absentee mother, Susie tries her best to make us understand why Rufus loves Alison and why Alison would cheat on him.

Trying on Catholicism at St. Ignatius Loyola, a short walk away from her Fifth Avenue home, Blair discovers that priests do not grant wishes like genies.

necklace she thinks Nate will be giving her. But it's Chuck who gives Blair the gorgeous diamond Erickson Beamon necklace.

Music: Alexandra Patasavas put The Virgins' entire five-song EP in this episode. "One Week of Danger" by The Virgins plays when B has a quick flashback to her night of passion with Chuck, when she leaves the cathedral, and again when Serena catches B and Chuck at it. "Birthday Song" by The Shapes is on during the extremely awkward Vanessa/Dan/Serena chat. Blair explains the rules of boyfriends and best friends to Serena with "Love Is Colder Than Death" (The Virgins). Nate is listening to The Virgins' "Rich Girls" when his mother interrupts him. Dan tells his mother how it is to "Whenever We Finish" (Two Hours Traffic). B's party kicks off with Puffy

you know you love me. (you do, don't you?)

More than real estate prices separate Brooklyn from the Upper East Side on *Gossip Girl*; wealth, class, value systems, and ambition divide the two worlds. Dan wants to be a writer; his ambition is to attend Dartmouth where the best English department is. Jenny, just 14, is industrious, recreating designer dresses, and her talent matures as she does. Vanessa is already very focused; not only does she know what she wants to be, a filmmaker, she's already doing it, like Dan with his writing and Jenny with her clothing design. The Upper East Side kids have more vague ambitions. Blair wants to go to Yale because her father, whom she idolizes, did; she wants to replicate his path, but what she wants to study or eventually have as a career is anyone's guess. Serena's keenness to go to college is primarily as an escape from the tortures of high school. Nate's parents lay out his ambitions for him (Dartmouth, law school, Blair), and while he knows he doesn't want that, he doesn't know what he *does* want. Chuck doesn't care about his education, just the results (see "Desperately Seeking Serena"), but like Blair, he does want to impress his father by mimicking Daddy's interest in business and entrepreneurship. The Upper East Siders are all striving to succeed, but how or at what eludes them.

This lack of direction could simply be because these characters are teenagers, and not everyone knows what their calling is by age 17. But the clear line between the Brooklyn and UES characters suggests maybe, just maybe, there's something to their lifestyle and upbringing that's hindering their development. In Madeline Levine's book *The Price of Privilege*, she outlines what characterizes her affluent teenaged patients. Reading the descriptions you'd swear Nate, Chuck, Blair, and Serena were sitting in her office: easily frustrated; impulsive; have trouble anticipating consequences of actions; overly dependent on adult approval and on peers; feeling of emptiness derived from a stunted ability to develop a sense of self; lack of independence, autonomy, competence, and ability to make healthy moral decisions, in part due to parents who are "alternately emotionally unavailable or intrusive." These materially privileged teenagers routinely present a "false self" that appears to be well-adjusted and overachieving in school and extracurricular activities, and throw their parents for a loop when they finally exhibit "troubled" behavior.

In a culture that values materialism over philanthropy, individualism over empathy, perfectionism over perspective, and competition over cooperation, affluent parents tend to emphasize how their children "do" — perform in school, their appearance, the type of friends they have — rather than who the kids "are." The result could be a Blair Waldorf type: groomed to perfection, a model student who had the perfect boyfriend, bulimic, cruel, competitive, striving, manipulative, and on antidepressants but still unhappy. Or someone like Old Serena who gained popularity with her "rule-breaking behavior" (substance abuse, promiscuity, defiance at school); Nate, who withdraws from his life, smoking up so he can stop thinking about how trapped he is in his own life; Eric, who seems to be well-adjusted until he tries to kill himself; or Chuck, another rule-breaker, a sensation seeker with little impulse control or empathy for others.

Gossip Girl's world of the Upper East Side places top value on external motivators — like wealth, status, collecting rare commodities (art, designer clothing), and grades — rather than on personal relationships or values like integrity, conscience, generosity, or community. (Gotta go to Brooklyn for that.) The old saying "money can't buy happiness" has been proven true; there's no correlation between income and personal happiness. What has been documented is "silver spoon syndrome," an inverse relationship between income and a child's closeness to their parents. Someone like Blair or Nate or Chuck experiences their parents' love as conditional and doesn't have positive role models to mimic. They don't see adults routinely behaving with respect, compassion, or integrity. The UES kids may be materially advantaged, but they find themselves struggling to choose between self-destructive behavior and becoming autonomous, some with more success (Serena, Nate) than others (Chuck, Blair).

The Brooklyn kids aren't perfectly happy and adjusted either, but their struggles and failings mimic the "traditional trajectory of adolescence," Jenny's character arc in particular: "withdrawal, irritability, defiance, rejection of parental values, trying on and discarding different identities, and finally, a development of a stable identity." So buck up, Little J: you may be miserable now, but those people you envy just might be miserable their entire lives. For the Upper East Siders, the path to contentment is so rarely followed it may as well not even exist. As Chuck says to Nate in the pilot: what they're "entitled to is a trust fund, maybe a house in the Hamptons, a prescription drug problem, but happiness does not seem to be on the menu."

AmiYumi's "Nice Buddy." Nate loiters outside B's party and runs into Jenny to "How We Breathe" by Pinback. "Fernando Pando" by The Virgins is on when Serena talks to Dan about Vanessa being at the party. In a scene that eats up way too much valuable *Gossip Girl* time, Serena rocks out on Guitar Hero to Lynyrd Skynyrd's "Free Bird." Dan and Serena have a talk about talking to "Inside Out" (Miss Eighty 6). Nate and Jenny sit on the steps to Eskimo Joe's "How Does It Feel?" and Blair realizes she's spending this birthday without him. Rufus and Alison cuddle post-coital to "Kissing Song" by Dawn Landes. "Radio Christine" by favorite-band-of-the-week The Virgins is on when Serena and Vanessa make nice.

"When the cat's away, the mice will play. Have fun, little rodents."

1.09 blair waldorf must pie!

Original air date: November 28, 2007
Teleplay by: K.J. Steinberg, Jessica Queller
Story by: Lenn K. Rosenfeld
Directed by: Mark Piznarski
Guest cast: Michelle Hurd (Laurel), John Shea (Harold Waldorf), Luz Alexandra Ramos (Nurse)

Thanksgiving — a time for tradition, turkey, flashbacks, and secrets from the '80s.

The first *Gossip Girl* holiday episode ditches its narrator and, taking a page from the *Lost* handbook, uses a flashback to last year's Thanksgiving to give us a taste of how our beloved Upper East Siders got to be so delightfully dysfunctional.

The way they were in 2006? Effed up. The glimpse into the married life of the Archibalds is frightening. Anne strips the Captain of any pride in his work by flippantly offering him a check. Why bother trying to prove himself? The Captain has so little self-worth by this Thanksgiving that he tries to kill himself. No wonder Nate doesn't want to follow the path his parents set out for him; he has a shining example in front of him that privilege doesn't bring happiness.

Last year Serena was the one who needed taking care of, but now that she's got her boozing under wraps she can return the favor and take care of Blair. Taking a holiday centered on feasting, the writers capture that too-much-turkey feeling and push it to its full pathological extent. No surprise to readers of the book series, Blair battles bulimia and it comes back full force when she feels completely overwhelmed: she's fighting with Serena, her father didn't come home for Thanksgiving, she and Nate have broken up, she's slept with Chuck and regretted it and done it again, and her mother is still a selfish pill. Flashing back to all the moments of Blair eating — sushi with Nate in the pilot, a berry at Dorota's insistence the morning of Ivy Week, a bite of fruit after her mother chastised her ("Bad News Blair") — we then see a moment we haven't before. B goes into the bathroom of the sushi restaurant and makes herself throw up, as present-day B scarfs the entire,

enormous pie. Presumably the writers knew from the get-go that Blair would be bulimic, but in the pilot episode, Eleanor says to her, "You'll never be more beautiful or thin or happy than you are right now." Would any mother of a daughter with an eating disorder say that? Would she direct her daughter toward the low-fat yogurt instead of the croissant, implying B needs to watch her figure, as Eleanor did in "Bad News Blair"? It's difficult to reconcile that with the obvious concern that Eleanor has for her daughter in the flashback scenes, whispering to Harold and monitoring B's canapé intake.

Alison's failures became more understandable last episode, and now it's Eleanor's turn. She is still mourning her failed marriage and trying to hold on to Blair, who she knows loves her father more. Eleanor's otherwise controlling and selfish character is softened in those final scenes.

Since the almost-all-knowing audience at home already knew about the secretive past of Rufus and Lily, the fun here was all about the awkward. How many times did Jenny mention that the van der Woodsens and Humphreys are *not* related? Still, the ick factor is there, and judging by that wistful look in Rufus's eye, he won't be able to stay away from Lily.

"Raise your hand if you're over 30 and acting really weird right now."
— Dan, moments before the Lily/Rufus/Alison triangle is revealed to the kids

JTLYK:

- No sign of Vanessa or Chuck Bass this episode.
- Top story on Gossip Girl: "*What did Serena see?* In a world where so much happens behind closed doors, you'd think people would learn to shut them. We're dying to find out what Serena saw behind the door at Blair's Birthday Party. You can be sure Gossip Girl will stop at nothing to make sure what goes on behind closed doors definitely does not stay behind closed doors."
- Of course Blair was dismissive of Dan last year too. Hilarious.
- How quickly things turn between Blair and Serena. When Blair feels judged by S, she responds viciously and cruelly in the way only a best friend can.
- In the flashback, Eleanor talks to Dorota like she's new (or doesn't speak English?) but Blair shared childhood memories with Dorota in "Poison Ivy," so she's been working at the Waldorf house for years. Add "bitchy to the help" to the list of Eleanor's charms.

- Like mother, like daughter. Blair lied to Serena to avoid the reality of her break-up with Nate. Eleanor lies to keep Harold away and protect herself from the pain of their divorce.
- Dorota, whose name means "God's gift," is awesome. Not only does she make sure Blair knows the truth behind Eleanor's machinations, she also ensures Blair is properly accessorized. When B leaves the Thanksgiving table upset, Dorota clears the staff out of the kitchen so B can have her meltdown in private.
- Uninvited or disinvited? Blair prefers the former; Anne Archibald, the latter.
- *In vino veritas.* In her drunken state, Serena provides a perfect description of her BFF: "Blair's a bossy genius."
- Nate holds a joint but doesn't light it when he sits wondering whether to call B or S. He seems less interested in weed now that his dad has a debilitating drug problem.

Secrets & Lies:

- Dan doesn't bother telling Serena that he kinda saved her life on Thanksgiving last year.
- Serena gives Blair an opportunity to tell her about Chuck; B doesn't take it.
- Serena describes Dan's dad as "really cool," not knowing her mom is well aware of how cool (and how hot) Rufus is.
- Lily pretends she's not feeling well to avoid an awkward dinner at the Humphreys'.
- Lily and Alison pretend to have never met before.
- Jenny, Dan, Serena, and Eric don't know much about their parents' histories.
- Eleanor denies she lied to Harold about B not wanting to see or talk to him.
- Alison learns that "Rosewood" wasn't about her; it was about Lily's horse. Ouch.
- Rufus won't tell Lily how he feels about her. Alison overhears that L and R kissed, something she probably wouldn't have found out otherwise.
- Eleanor admits to lying to Blair about her father.
- Nate won't let his parents lie to him anymore. He calls them out on every lie they try to tell.

That's How It's Done in *The O.C.*: Marissa, daughter to the dad who's a shady businessman, ODs in Mexico but insists she wasn't trying to kill herself.

John Tucker Must Die (dir. Betty Thomas, 2006): The *Gossip Girl* hair stylist didn't get Dan's hair right in the flashback scenes: in 2006, Penn Badgley's hair was really, really bad. Penn plays little brother to John Tucker (Jesse Metcalfe) in this teen revenge comedy. Tucker is the big man on campus who dates three ladies (Ashanti, Sophia Bush, and Arielle Kebbel) at the same time without their knowing. The girls find out and team up for revenge under the unlikely leadership of the formerly invisible Kate (Brittany Snow, Lily Rhodes in "Valley Girls"). With a taste of popularity, Kate goes from a friendless nobody to a lying, social-climbing mean girl before she learns that pretending to be someone you're not sucks and can destroy everything and alienate everyone you value.

Kate's character arc is more Jenny Humphrey than Serena or Blair, though B does know a thing or two about putting on a front to the world to hide who you really are. The main point of *John Tucker Must Die* (other than an unsuccessful attempt to recreate *Mean Girls*' teen comedy awesomeness) is that honesty is totes the best policy when it comes to romance, friendship, and family. And that's a lesson our *Gossip Girl* characters learn over and over again. (But let's hope it never sticks, or else this show will be dullsville.)

Welcome to the Real World:

- Harold Waldorf's pumpkin pie recipe is stolen from Bobby Flay, celebrity chef and restaurateur.
- B is on Lexapro, a brand name for escitalopram, used to treat depression and anxiety by inhibiting serotonin reuptake.
- Surprisingly, Dan doesn't make a dig at Lily's reading material, *At First Sight* by Nicholas Sparks.
- Lily grew up on a ranch in Montecito, California, near Santa Barbara; it's one of the richest communities in all of America.

Locations:

- Serena is stumbling out of Barrio Chino (253 Broome St) as Dan picks up pumpkin pie at Babycakes (248 Broome St) in the flashback.
- The Archibald Thanksgiving dinner is from Citarella (Upper East Side

location, 1313 Third Ave), the gourmet food market serving NYC and the Hamptons.
- The Happy Humphreys play football in Fulton Ferry Park (26 New Dock St, Brooklyn).

Oops: Some of the background actors in the Chinatown scene are clearly wearing summer clothes, not appropriate for Thanksgiving in New York.

The Look: Flashback fashion! Serena's hair is straight and long, and her style is more garish in a green Alice + Olivia Marilyn pleat mini dress, Forever21 Vogue faux leopard coat, and Payless Shiloh cuff-low boots. Blair's hair is shorter, straighter, and her style is less sophisticated, but her plaid Fremont Capulet coat is lovely. Eric doesn't have those godforsaken highlights yet. Dan is wearing the Lincoln Hawk T-shirt he was wearing in "Bad News Blair." (I love when "poor" characters on TV shows have to wear the same costume twice. It's so *realistic*.) Flashforward to 2007 and Dorota has a special Thanksgiving-themed maid uniform. Blair finds out her father isn't coming home wearing an orange patterned Lorick dress, which her mother tells her to change out of (but it's your design, Eleanor, you should find it more "fetching"). B opts for a Dita Marc by Marc Jacobs lace and metallic dress, adding a Trina Turk espresso capelet crop jacket when she leaves the Waldorf apartment. Serena's dressed down for the holidays in Rich & Skinny Sleek jeans, BCB Girls Pauline boots, and a Kooba Natasha bag. J plays football with the Humphreys in a plum Tocca Amelinda wool puff sleeve coat.

Music: Nelly Furtado's 2006 hit "Promiscuous" accompanies Blair as she pulls a drunken Serena out of a bar. "Recurring" (Bonobo) plays as Serena smashes mashed potatoes into her face. "Here It Goes Again" by OK GO was very cool 'round Thanksgiving 2006, when Dan returns home with stories of rescuing Serena. This year's Waldorf dinner features Vivaldi's Mandolin Concerto in C Major. To the tune of "Grand Opening" (Will Dailey), Serena's dinner at the Humphreys is interrupted with a phone call. Nate and Serena and Blair have a water fight (way more fun than a bath) to "La Ritounelle (Mr. Dan's Magic Wand Mix)" by Sebastian Tellier. 2006's Thanksgiving at the Waldorfs also had Vivaldi playing, "Autumn" from *The Four Seasons*. "Today" by Stickboy is playing when Lily arrives at the restaurant for an endless supply of French fries. The final montage is to Vanessa Carlton's "Nolita Fairytale."

don't i know you from somewhere? the bloodlines of *gossip girl*'s characters

Drawing not just from Cecily von Ziegesar's characterizations, the writers of *Gossip Girl* pull inspiration from a multitude of sources to create a cultural mash-up that resonates so well in Blair, Serena, Chuck, Nate, Dan, Jenny, and company. Stephanie Savage and Josh Schwartz have pointed to some: the novels of Edith Wharton (an inspiration also for CvZ's novels) and Evelyn Waugh, Sofia Coppola's *Marie Antoinette*, Douglas Sirk's 1950s movie melodramas (acclaimed as subversive sudsers), and the main man himself, Shakespeare. *New York*'s Daily Intel blog added to that list some literary precedents for the rogue Chuck Bass: Alex Rex from Nabokov's *Laughter in the Dark*, Wilde's Dorian Gray, and Alexei Vronsky from Tolstoy's *Anna Karenina*.

soap operas

From the long-running prime time soaps of the 1980s like *Dynasty* (1981–1989) and *Dallas* (1978–1991) to the teen dramas like *Beverly Hills, 90210* and *Dawson's Creek*, *Gossip Girl* ain't ashamed of where it comes from. The melodrama, conniving, intrigue, and romance are a huge part of the show's appeal, but it's saved from the fate of daytime cheesiness with a dryness, wit, and self-awareness that didn't exist in its entirely earnest teen predecessors of the '90s. The original teen drama about a middle-class brother and sister trying to navigate a wealthy zip code and the challenges of high school at the same time, *90210* (1990–2000) moralized in a way that a show can't get away with today (unless it's on the Disney Channel). The Serena/Blair dynamic descends from Kelly and Brenda's — a reformed bad girl blonde and a bitchy brunette who have a tenuous friendship, which is stretched past its limit when they fight over Dylan. *Dawson's Creek* (1998–2003) changed the genre by making its characters smart *and* angsty; the fast dialogue may not have sounded like real teenagers talking but it made for an intelligent show full of cultural allusions. Those very same qualities were a crucial part of Josh Schwartz's first teen drama, *The O.C.* (2003–2007), and its successes helped reshape the *Gossip* characters from their book counterparts: Seth's wry humor and Ryan's outsider qualities went into Dan, Summer's eye-rolling flippancy and Taylor's determination into Blair, Sandy Cohen's hard-working moral compass father figure into Rufus, and Kirsten Cohen's WASP princess with a heart into Lily. *Gossip Girl* also follows in the footsteps of *Sex and the City*, a cheekily narrated dramedy set in Manhattan known as much for its fashion as for its frank sexual content and focus on female characters.

teen films

Josh Schwartz has called Chuck Bass a "throwback to the James Spader type of villains of the '80s," and he certainly looks the part in "School Lies." John Hughes' 1986 film *Pretty in Pink* has Spader playing Steff, a "richie" who taunts wrong-side-of-the-tracks Andie (Molly Ringwald), keeping the lines between cliques clear. Like our Jenny, Andie dresses fashionably because she can create her own clothes, and she lives with her dad, her mother having recently left the family. Hughes' *The Breakfast Club* gets a name check in "Woman on the Verge" and the season 2 episode "Summer, Kind of Wonderful" nods to *Some Kind of Wonderful*. Teen films of more recent years influenced *Gossip Girl* too, like 1999's *Cruel Intentions* (see page 227) and 2004's *Mean Girls*.

all about eve

From Joseph L. Mankiewicz's 1950 film *All About Eve*, the uneasy relationship between aging Broadway star Margo Channing and the oh-so-helpful but conniving upstart Eve Harrington provides inspiration for Blair and Jenny's relationship. Eve is a deceptively innocent young woman who ingratiates herself into Margo's life only to slowly take it away from her — her love interest, her career, her fame, and her friends — making Margo seem jealous and irrational while she's at it. Margo sees what Eve is up to in her "feverish little brain" but convincing Karen, a good-natured Serena type, is difficult. She doesn't know what it's like to use people and betray their loyalty for one's own advantage. Addison DeWitt, a theater columnist, is the one man who sees Eve for what she is; he knows her secrets and still wants her, like Chuck admiring Blair's scheming and cruelty.

becky sharp

From William Thackeray's *Vanity Fair* sprung the character of Becky Sharp; so captivating was she that her story was turned into a play (by Langdon Mitchell) and then a 1935 film (both called *Becky Sharp*). Becky's social climbing and relentlessness now find their way into Little Jenny Humphrey. Whip-smart Becky is a poor girl who befriends the upper-class Amelia and tries to get a marriage proposal out of her brother, but his father would never approve of him marrying such a low-class girl. Our heroine takes her charms elsewhere, landing an officer and becoming Mrs. Rawdon Crawley. That's not enough for Becky, who's eager to live a life of luxury beyond her and her husband's means; she takes things too far, and ends up abandoned and in poverty but still striving. Becky lies, manipulates people, cheats, and is concerned almost solely with social climbing, status, and material goods. With no heed to the feelings or wellbeing of others, Becky takes advantage of and ruins those who show her the most kindness. Luckily, Jenny Humphrey was given a heart and a conscience to make her character more troubled and ambiguous than plain old conniving Becky Sharp.

Margaret Colin as Eleanor Waldorf

Playing the mum to Queen B is Brooklyn-born Margaret Colin. She studied at Hofstra University but didn't quite earn her degree, instead focusing on her professional acting career. Her early work included a few roles on soap operas, *The Edge of the Night* and *As the World Turns*, and since the mid 1980s, Margaret has worked in film, television, and on stage, and won a Saturn Award for her role as Lisa Wiseman on *Now and Again*. In between episodes of *Gossip Girl*, Margaret played a supporting role in the modern-day noir *The Missing Person*, which debuted at Sundance in 2009.

"Spotted: Chuck Bass losing something no one knew he had to begin with. His heart."

1.10 hi, society

Original air date: December 5, 2007
Written by: Joshua Safran
Directed by: Patrick Norris
Guest cast: Caroline Lagerfelt (Celia "Cece" Rhodes), Sebastian Stan (Carter Baizen), Zander Gladish (Prince Theodore), Beth Fowler (Mistress of Ceremonies), Paul Niebanck (Tailor), Andre Blake (John Maybury, *New York Times* Journalist), Edward J. Hyland (Chuck's Driver)

At the debutante ball, the Upper East Siders prove true the old saying that it's not who you arrive with, it's who you leave with that matters.

The Annual Dispensary Cotillion and Debutante Ball: gorgeous, formal, totally legendary, for charity, and full of young women with good graces? Or out of touch, totally classist, antiquated, where young women are auctioned off to the highest bidder?

Whether you side with "My ice doesn't like to get lonely" Cece or "It's Dan" Humphrey, debutante balls are a mainstay of high society. Back in the olden times (18th-century France), the meaning of the word "cotillion" evolved from an underskirt to a name for a country dance (because so many underskirts were seen when the women were dancing). From there it morphed into an upper-class-only event where young women were officially introduced to society, having reached "marrying" age. Traditionally debutantes wear white gowns, gloves, and are presented by their fathers and curtsy after being introduced. While the traditions are a bit different at the *Gossip Girl* cotillion, the game's the same and it's just as important: lead deb Blair wants a ball "to die for," committee woman Lily wants to make her mother happy, and former chairwoman Cece cares enough about debuting Serena properly to risk the love her granddaughter has for her.

The girls are charged with representing themselves well at the society function, but who is the right escort? Nate, the brooding gentleman; Chuck, the sexy rogue; Carter, the fraud; or Dan, the lovable outsider. As awful and manipulative as Grandma Cece's speech is to Dan, she's right: he is out of place, he doesn't like high society, and he feels (and looks) awkward. What she isn't right about is the choices Serena will make. Assuming that Serena will follow in her own and in her mother's footsteps is Cece's miscalculation. S rejects Cece's traditional, classist views and the idea that every girl inevitably turns into her mother. Serena's defiance rouses Lily as it echoes the same sentiments she felt toward her own mother 20 years ago — "all you care about is what people think of you when they look at me." Even if she wasn't strong enough when Cece gave her the Rufus-or-the-inheritance ultimatum, Lily proves that she can choose love over money by giving her blessing to the formal debut of Dan and Serena as a class- and borough-bridging couple.

"I shouldn't have let you let me go."
— Rufus, after learning why Lily left him so many years ago. *Swoon.*

JTLYK:

- No Vanessa again this ep, and Eric van der Woodsen is MIA too. Doesn't Cece love her grandson enough to manipulate him?
- Top story on Gossip Girl: "*B and N: It's Over!* Witherspoon and Phillippe. Then McAdams and Gosling. Now Waldorf and Archibald? Say it isn't so. Blair and Nate have been together for like ever and now they're finally over. Blair was spotted in tears at her 17th Birthday over the breakup. It's Blair's party and she can cry if she wants to. And she totally did in front of all to see."

- The deb ball is on Sunday, December 17th, 2007.
- Chuck should heed his own advice — "don't eff with an effer" — and not try to manipulate Blair.
- Carter's description of his posh trip sounds hella different from when he was telling Nate about it in "Bad News Blair" — cleaning up after Hurricane Katrina *and* pheasant hunting with the sheik?
- When Cece says to Dan that people will wonder if he's Serena's charity case, she's right on the money. In "Bad News Blair," Blair referred to Serena talking to Dan as "charity work."
- Serena's original statement for the ball said she wants to take a year off school and teach English in South Asia. How plebian of her, but it's the first indication of any aspirations she has.
- Lily corrects Dan when he calls her "Mrs. van der Woodsen" the same way he kept correcting Cece when she called him "Daniel."
- How much can one girl's chin wobble before she bursts into tears? Little J's gets a workout as her mother gives her a talking-to.
- Blair is wearing the necklace Chuck gave her when she and Nate have sex.
- Hats off to the writers for making us cheer for the Blair–Nate hook-up mere weeks after getting us behind Blair and Chuck. Both seem so right, so how can it be wrong to have both?

Secrets & Lies:

- B hides her relationship with Chuck from Nate, lying about why she's late to meet him and saying it's Serena who keeps texting her, not Chuck.
- Jenny lies to Lily and tells her she's allowed to go to the ball. Alison catches her shoe shopping with Lily, but doesn't out her lie.
- When Nate turns to Chuck for help with Blair, Chuck manages to not actually lie, but he definitely deceives Nate by turning suspicion on Carter Baizen.
- Cece shows the schemers how it's done: she manipulates Lily and Serena to get S to debut: she tries to play on Dan's insecurities, she attempts to bribe Rufus, she gets Lily to rewrite Serena's statement for the ball, she lies to Serena about not having cancer, and she had called Carter a week prior to the cotillion, knowing that she would get Serena to debut. It's awful, but impressive.
- Cece reveals a secret kept from Rufus for close to 20 years: Lily chose her inheritance over Rufus, not another man over him.

- Blair can see in C's smug expression that he plotted against her and pieces together his scheme. It backfires just like Grandma Cece's did.

Scrap!: Nate punches Carter Baizen.

Not a Girl, Not Yet a Queen Bee: Choosing re-admittance to the inner circle over Alison's gallery opening, Jenny proves she may not be as sure of herself as she said she was back in "Dare Devil." She knows she's doing wrong: her reaction to seeing the shoes her mom was about to buy her is as telling as that wobbly chin trying to hold back tears. Alison, the very same mother Jenny herself dragged back from Hudson two short episodes ago, gives her the best "I'm not mad, I'm disappointed" speech TV has seen in a while: "Every choice that you make defines who you're going to turn into . . . Ask if you like the person you're becoming." Who you gonna be, Little J?

The Original Gossipverse: The Green Cashmere Sweater with the Gold Heart on the Sleeve pops up a lot in the books: B gives it to N and he later discovers the pendant sewn in so N would "always be wearing her heart on his sleeve." At a graduation party, Nate gives her the sweater back and she takes it (*Nothing Can Keep Us Together*), though TV Blair makes him hold on to it. Mrs. Lillian van der Woodsen, in one of her very few lines in the entire book series, tells her daughter how she used to organize cotillions. *So* not the Lil we know.

That's How It's Done in *The O.C.*: In the fourth episode of *The O.C.*, Marissa and Ryan flirt at the cotillion dance rehearsal; she changes her mind about attending (and then back again) and finally she and Summer debut. But guess what else happens? A fight breaks out! In "The Nana," Seth's grandmother shows up and is strangely pleasant, hiding the fact that she has terminal cancer. Ryan's dad shows up in "The My Two Dads," faking a terminal illness so his son will talk to him.

High Society (dir. Charles Walters, 1956): In *High Society*, a remake of *The Philadelphia Story* with music by Cole Porter, rich blonde goddess Tracy Lord (Grace Kelly) lacks "an understanding heart." No one knows her father cheated on her mother and left the family, and now Tracy demands perfection from her boring fiancé George (John Lund). But hounding her is her rich ex-husband

Dexter (Bing Crosby) and an everyman reporter Mike Connor (Frank Sinatra). She struggles to keep up appearances in front of the reporter, hiding the truth of her family's situation by putting on a perfect show. Mike and Tracy fall for each other after too much to drink at her swellegant engagement party. In the haze of her champagne hangover the next morning, Tracy sees that a slip-up now and then is good for you, especially if you learn something, and that the safe choice isn't necessarily the right choice. Dexter, a man who has had wealth handed to him, admits that kind of instant prosperity causes people to have strange ideas about things — like how to behave and what one's entitled to.

Like Dexter, Chuck Bass mistakenly thinks that amusing games of subterfuge will win back his girl's heart, but unwittingly he pushes her into someone else's arms. Like Tracy, Serena is adamant she won't turn into her mother, but it's Lily who realizes keeping up appearances isn't worth the price of happiness.

Welcome to the Real World:

- Blair is chosen for "A Night Out With," a real column in the *New York Times*.
- Blair asks Carter if he stayed at the Burj al Arab in Dubai, a luxury hotel shaped like a boat's sail and situated on an artificial island; it was once the second tallest hotel in the world, and the room rates range from $1,000 to roughly $20,000 a night. But no, he stayed on Palm Island, artificial islands grouped in the shape of a palm tree and chock-a-block with posh resorts for the Carter Baizens of the world.
- B threatens to go Naomi Campbell on her assistant at the ball. And if anyone could channel the model as famous for throwing phones and tantrums and abusing her staff as she is for modeling, Blair could.
- Kati wants to major in neuroscience. Nan Zhang, who plays Kati, studied neuroscience at Johns Hopkins.

Locations:

- Blair imagines a security detail and a high-speed chase back to the Pierre Hotel (2 E 61st St) after the ball.
- The Manhattan Penthouse (80 Fifth Ave) stands in for Prescott Dance Studios.
- Jenny goes shoe shopping with Lily, and Nate gets fitted for his tux at Saks Fifth Avenue (611 Fifth Ave).

- Nate gets Laurent-Perrier for the car ride over to the cotillion, and suggests going to B's favorite, the Modern (9 W 53rd St), for dessert.

The Look: On her way to meet her grandmother, Serena's in a gray Nanette Lepore symphony sequin cardigan with a Botkier weekender bag and Moschino T-strap inspired booties. Blair Pants Watch! She's in red shorts at dance rehearsal, along with a Zara blazer, and wears jeans to see Nate for his tux fitting (with red, black, and gray Zara pumps). No wonder Nate thought she wasn't herself; she was wearing denim! Jenny's pink dress for the deb ball is D&G. Instead of opting for the traditional white gowns and gloves for the debutantes, Eric Daman put his leading ladies in metallic shades, "umbrae of fog and champagne, silvers and gold." Serena is in gold, to play off B's dress, with an Asian-inspired embroidered fabric, a long sweeping train (with

The home of the Basses and van der Woodsens and host to brunches and balls, the Palace Hotel gets more screen time than Vanessa.

a finger hook) and detailed with rosettes and chain mail along the bust line to create a "sun goddess" look. Blair's luxurious gown is inspired by a Marie Antoinette/Louis XIV style with five layers of train, a bust line almost like a corset, and embroidered fabric finished with B's signature bow on the shoulder. Blair wears her diamond necklace from "Seventeen Candles." Nate's tux matches B's dress; all Chuck has is the sparkliest tuxedo shirt man has ever seen. And what do you wear when your heart is broken and you need to skip town? If you're Chuck, a red turtleneck and a trench coat, collar flipped up. Oh Chuck.

Music: The episode kicks off with "Comin' Home Baby" (Mel Torme). Dance practice for the ball is to Daniel May's "The Speakeasy." Blair and Chuck make out to "You're a Wolf" by High Society. "Pretty Please" by Lissa plays as Jenny is busted shoe-shopping with Lily by Alison. More Vivaldi at the Waldorf tea party, the Largo section of "Winter" from *The Four Seasons*. Dan arrives at his mother's show opening to Rooney's "What For," which is still playing when he gets the phone call from Lily. The Pierces perform at the ball, playing "Secret" (when Nate punches Carter) and "Three Wishes" (when Chuck and Blair dance). Dan carries Serena and twirls her out of the ball, and Blair and Nate finally consummate their epic relationship to "Apologize" by OneRepublic (featuring Timbaland).

Caroline Lagerfelt as Celia Rhodes

That air of nobility that Grandma Cece has? Caroline Lagerfelt is a descendant of Swedish royalty and was raised there, the daughter of an ambassador. Caroline began her career as a stage actress in the 1970s, and focused on television roles through the 1980s and '90s, most notably playing Inger Dominguez on *Nash Bridges*. Her role on *Gossip Girl* isn't the first time she's played a messed-up grandmother on a teen soap: she played Sheila Silver, David's grandma, on the original *90210*.

"Looks like daddy's little girl isn't sugar and spice and everything nice after all."

1.11 roman holiday

Original air date: December 19, 2007
Written by: Jessica Queller
Directed by: Michael Fields
Guest cast: William Abadie (Roman), John Dossett (Jack Roth), John Shea (Harold Waldorf), Derek Cecel (Alex), Austin Lysy (Freddy Parnes)

There's nothing like Christmastime in New York City, but for the Waldorfs, Humphreys, and van der Woodsens, this season promises to destroy old traditions and create a few new ones, for better or worse.

The problem with Christmas in your teenage years is it never seems as awesome as it was when you were a kid. Especially when family traditions and harmony are disrupted by a parent's interloping new love interest: Roman, Bart Bass, and Alex the Hudson Neighbor. Blair and Jenny, in particular, and Dan, Serena, and Eric want things to be the way they used to be, but now their family circumstances are in flux, changing in ways they don't like. So is it better to live in a fantasy and try to force things into the old way, or to accept that things have changed and create new traditions? Even Vanessa has to accept the new normal between her and Dan, helping Serena with the gift for D and (after a warning from Blair) not taking any credit for it.

Before Blair decides to accept Roman, we get a glimpse at how totally batty B can be. She calls Roman a French fox parading as an innocent lamb, but that is precisely what she is (well, an American fox). She has her daddy fooled; he's astounded Blair could be so cruel as to execute the Freddy ruse (and he doesn't even know about the Tonya Harding incident). While B is right to be angry with her father — he left her family, moved across an ocean, and came home for only two days — she tries to compete with Roman and destroy her father's relationship, rather than telling her dad how she feels. It's like Harold and Eleanor completely forgot to teach their daughter how to communicate her feelings and only taught her how to scheme and dream.

The Humphrey kids also resolve that it's better to face reality — Alison is going back to Hudson (good riddance!) — than to live in a fantasy. And the siblings will always be there for each other: Dan and Jenny, and Eric and Serena . . . and maybe, one day soon, Chuck.

"A single entrée at a mid-priced restaurant. Three-quarters of a DVD box set. Maybe a pair of Wolford stockings."
— Blair's not-so-helpful ideas of what S can buy Dan for $50

JTLYK:

- Gossip Girl's top story: "*Where is Chuck Bass?* Spotted: Chuck Bass getting into the back of a limo with his luggage in tow. Word has it he's heading for the airport. But why the sudden fast getaway? Is there something you're running away from C? Let's hope you're not gone for good. What will the people of the Upper East Side do without our resident schemer? Our world might become a lot safer, but it's also become a lot less fun."
- In the opening scene, Serena has a little bow in her hair made out of her hair. It's like her head is a present all wrapped up.
- Vanessa is quick to reassure Serena that Dan didn't let her read his story either. A sweet thing to say considering their past conflicts over who is closest with Dan. But then Dan ruins it by calling V's present the best ever.
- Serena is multi-lingual — in "Seventeen Candles," she speaks a tiny bit of Japanese, and hurrying Blair to a cab S shows off her French. (Well, *Franglais*, but we'll count it.)
- Roman compares Blair to a *macaron*, a traditional French pastry which is (presumably) what's in the box he hands her.
- Like mother, like daughter. Eleanor pulls a total Blair move when she whacks Roman with her purse. And she likes to gossip, spilling to Blair about Roman's ex-lover Freddy.
- Rufus and Alison try ever so hard to fix their marriage — for a whopping month — before calling it quits. The fact that they are both so quick to agree that it isn't working shows that neither of them really wants to be together anymore.
- Dan can be a pretty good big bro. He lovingly pesters Jenny to talk about their mom's infidelity the same way he made sure she knew he was there for her after Chuck attacked her at the Kiss on the Lips party.
- Vanessa's shift at Communitea happens to finish the very second that

Serena shows up to ask for help. It's a Christmas miracle!
- The same portrait of Audrey Hepburn that hangs in B's bedroom is above the bed in her new room in Harold's chateau. The cat named Cat is from *Breakfast at Tiffany's*.
- Looks like Serena had Lily pegged: considering Bart's proposal at the end of the episode, Serena's remark that she'll just meet Lily's new beau at the wedding could be prophetic.
- Dan first met Serena at a birthday party on October 8, 2005.
- If Nate went to Monaco and Anne Archibald is spending Christmas in Connecticut, does that mean the Captain is with her or still in the hospital . . . alone?
- What is Vanessa doing for Christmas? Her parents are in Vermont, and there's no mention of her sister in this ep. Maybe the Abrams family is atheist!

Secrets & Lies:

- Lily is working to trust Bart again and doesn't want to tell people about their relationship for fear that he will be unfaithful and she will be humiliated.
- Blair thinks her father only left New York to "ride out the scandal" of him coming out and leaving Eleanor.
- Opening Christmas cards, Dan comes across a letter from Alison's beau Alex, asking her to meet up with him. (A hook-up note sent by post to the family home? Sneakiness fail.) Rufus asks the family to pretend it never happened so Christmas isn't ruined.
- Eleanor pretends to be okay with Roman's presence at their Christmas, refusing to show her true feelings and act like a "pathetic scorned wife."
- Alex reveals to Rufus that Alison is still talking to him and hasn't told him it's over, which is what Alison led Rufus to believe.
- Blair pretends her laces are undone but really she's checking texts from Chuck, who knows that she and Nate had sex. And then she trips *pauvre Roman*, but her sabotage backfires when her dad spends hours with him at the hospital instead of with her.
- B bribes Freddy to show up at the Christmas Eve party in an effort to break up her father and Roman.
- When Rufus can't tell Lily how he feels about her, Lily lies to him and says she is going with Bart to Anguilla. And looks baffled at her own fibbing.

- Blair suspects that Vanessa still has feelings for Dan and ulterior motives for helping Serena. B's little talk seems to do the trick.
- Roman is upset with Harold for trusting appearances and not him. Eleanor recognizes Blair's scheming and tricks Freddy into telling her the truth.
- Lily helps Dan sneak the Chrimbo tree into the suite at the Palace.
- Dan reveals to Rufus that Lily lied about going away with Bart.
- Rufus finally gets the courage to tell Lily the truth about how he feels.

Scrap!: Blair intentionally trips Roman and he ends up on crutches.

Not a Girl, Not Yet a Queen Bee: Jenny's quest for social acceptance is put on hold as she spends the holidays with family. This episode, she's a kid who wants to pretend her family is as solid as it was last Christmas.

The Original Gossipverse: V's Christmas present to Dan is that his story, "10-8-05," will be published in the *New Yorker* summer fiction "20 Under 20" issue. In *All I Want Is Everything*, Dan writes a poem about how Vanessa and Jenny are total sluts (it's so bad it's worth reading the whole book), emails it to V, and she submits it to the *New Yorker*. About two days later and over Christmastime (i.e., when most businesses are closed), he gets a letter from the submissions editor saying his poem, "Sluts," will be published in the Valentine's Day issue! Dan loses his virginity to Vanessa after she reads one line of a story he's written about her (in *Because I'm Worth It*). That schtick works, apparently?

Blair is the one with a new and unwelcome stepdad and stepbrother; Eleanor gets engaged in *You Know You Love Me*. Blair of the books shares her TV counterpart's feelings about her dad, for the most part: "Blair didn't really mind that her father was gay, but she wished he'd find a boyfriend to live with in New York instead of France so he could take her shopping more often."

That's How It's Done in *The O.C.*: Holiday episodes were an important part of the *O.C.* world. One word: Chrismukkah. William Abadie, who plays Roman, appeared in a season 4 episode, "The Metamorphosis," as Taylor's French husband's lawyer.

Roman Holiday (dir. William Wyler, 1953): Filmed on location in Rome, *Roman Holiday* is a charming film about Princess Anne (Audrey Hepburn, who won an Oscar for the role), a young woman on a diplomatic tour, whose every moment is watched over and scheduled. On a stop in Rome, she has a total bore of a day and that night, has a minor meltdown, and is medicated. A little bit high and feeling free, she sneaks out and ends up staying the night, innocently enough, with Mr. Bradley (Gregory Peck), an American journalist. In the morning, he realizes who he has in his room and convinces her to spend the day with him doing whatever she pleases. He lies to her, using her for a tell-all story that will make him a good chunk of change, and she lies to him, pretending to be a school girl, not a princess. After a lovely day around Rome that ends with a brawl on a boat and a kiss under a bridge, the two have fallen in love but must return to their separate worlds. Anne and Mr. Bradley realize they must make do with their lot in life, that life isn't always what you like. Having had a taste of freedom, Anne asserts herself and takes her life out of the hands of her handlers. No more milk and crackers at bedtime for this girl.

While it seems like Blair always does as she pleases, she could use a break from her overly structured life like her idol Audrey gets in *Roman Holiday*. She does learn that she must make the most of her new family situation, embracing Roman and realizing her father does still love her.

Welcome to the Real World:

- Figure skating champ Tonya Harding was involved in the cover-up of her ex-husband's 1994 attack on fellow competitor Nancy Kerrigan to take her out of the U.S. championships with a leg injury. Like for B, the result was more attention for her competitor.
- Serena did one print ad for Gap when she was 12, and the *Gossip Girl* cast did a whole campaign during this Christmas season.
- One of the present-for-Dan ideas: an original poster of Truffaut's *The 400 Blows*, a 1959 classic French New Wave film. Dan would *so* be into that.
- Blair has the March 2007 copy of *Jane* magazine in her bedroom, with Drew Barrymore on the cover. Stephanie Savage worked for Barrymore's company Flower Films, and there are a few nods to the actress in *Gossip Girl* (episodes "Poison Ivy" and season 2's "Never Been Marcused" are plays on Drew B films).
- Roman and Eleanor have known each other since before Marc Jacobs

went into rehab (so about eight years). Marc went back into rehab in March 2007 after having been sober for seven years.
- Roman tells Blair that in the Zac Posen cape she got for Christmas, she looks like a brunette Catherine Deneuve, the French film star who has been called the most elegant woman in the world.

Locations:

- Roman crashes Blair and Harold's annual ice-skating outing at Wollman Rink in Central Park (pictured on opposite page).
- Harold misses out on tea at The Gallery in The Carlyle (35 E 76th St).
- Rufus keeps Alison's date with Alex at the LIC Bar (45-58 Vernon Blvd, Queens).

Oops: The shots of Central Park are impossibly autumnal for December 24, even when you factor in global warming. Why does Alison say "Eleanor's?" like she's never heard about that party? She overheard Lily say that Rufus kissed her at Eleanor's party in the Thanksgiving episode. Roman says to Eleanor that they've been friends since before Marc Jacobs went to rehab, but Harold and Roman met for the first time at last year's Thanksgiving ("Blair Waldorf Must Pie!"). Isn't it a bit odd that Roman and Eleanor have known each other for ages but Harold hadn't previously met him?

The prop department only made the first bit of Dan's "10-8-05" story coherent. After a few sentences (the ones Dan says to Serena), things get trippy. Behold: "I was accidentally invited to a birthday party. I met a girl there. She said two sentences to me, and I never forgot her. Her name was Serena and she was the most beutiful [sic] girl I ever saw. She spoke to me. She was ~~tremendously~~ excited and keen about the whole thing. She could ~~never~~ have got started again if it hadn't been for her enthusiasm and hard work. He was an enormous help to her. She was detailed by the committee to live on a farm. He showed me a card which stated he was a communicant of the church I replied I should make inquiries as to weather [sic] the paras need him. Her home was situated in the middle of the plantation on the slope of a hill. . . ." I guess Dan writes experimental fiction?

The Look: After her choir performance wearing red-and-white knee socks to die for, Little J dresses down for the holidays, putting away her wannabe prep style and pulling out her casual Brooklyn look, helping Dan with the

Tree Project wearing a plaid Alice Ritter shirt, brown print Min-k wool sparkle leggings, a brown Tocca Alessandra Windowpane coat (altered to fit Taylor Momsen just so), and brown Frye Veronica lace-up boots. Blair spices up her school uniform with bright blue tights, black Boutique 9 Sarah boots, and a red Valentino patent signature satchel (and giant candy canes). Serena's present is rejected by Dan, but her white-and-red striped Alexander Wang sweater dress — paired with wine-colored Nine West Naso shoes, a Vena Cava purple coat, and metallic Moschino tote — was quick to sell out. Blair's skating outfit is a Zara cape and skirt, Victoria's Secret cashmere turtleneck, ivory Lara Kazan floppy beret, and Urban Outfitters sparkle and fade opaque tights. Keeping up her holiday tradition, Dorota has a special Christmas-trim maid's uniform. Serena wears a cocoa sequin dress from Henri Bendel while B opts for a Tibi St. Honore pleated dress at the Christmas Eve party. For Christmas morning, Blair dons a white-and-red polka-dot babydoll from Victoria's Secret.

Music: *Gossip Girl*'s Christmas episode fittingly opens with the most materialistic of all carols, "Santa Baby," sung by the Constance Billard choir. "O Christmas Tree" by The Plush Interiors is playing at Communitea when

Serena meets up with Dan. Rufus keeps Alison's date with Alex to "Stuck for the Summer" by Two Hours Traffic. The McGuire Sisters' "Christmas Alphabet" provides a cheery soundtrack as Harold helps Roman skate and ignores his daughter. Jenny and Dan brainstorm gifts for Serena to "Christmaskwanakah" (The Dan Band). "Deck the Halls" by The Republic Tigers is playing when Serena asks Vanessa for help. Poppa Waldorf gives his Blair Bear one of her gifts to "The General Specific" by Band of Horses. The Christmas morning montage wraps up the episode with "All That I Want" by The Weepies.

John Shea as Harold Waldorf

How fitting: the actor who plays father to Yale-obsessed Blair actually attended Yale himself. John Shea earned his MFA in directing from the School of Drama in 1973. Best known for his portrayal of Lex Luthor in the 1990s TV show *Lois & Clark*, John's nonstop acting career didn't prevent him from writing and directing 1998's *Southie*, a critically acclaimed independent feature starring Donnie Wahlberg. The Emmy-winning John Shea lives in New York City with his two children and second wife. No hot male model or *chateau en France* for him.

"One thing about being on the inside: once you're there you don't always get to choose where you stand."

1.12 school lies

Original air date: January 2, 2008
Written by: Lenn K. Rosenfeld
Directed by: Tony Wharmby
Guest cast: Linda Emond (Headmistress Queller), Reed Birney (Mr. Prescott), Kyle Gilbert-Gregory (Andrew Collins), Joe Hickey (Serena's Driver)

With the fate of the junior class hanging in the balance after an illegal pool party, Dan finds himself thick as thieves with his least favorite UESers.

It's conundrums and grand gestures week on *Gossip Girl!* The code among the students is the old pack mentality of nobody says nuthin', nobody gets in trouble. But Dan knows (and Chuck emphasizes) that as an outsider he lacks the security that comes with being filthy rich; there is an "upstairs/downstairs thing." It's an issue in Lily and Rufus's relationship too. Whenever they bicker, he tries to make her feel guilty about wanting to keep her life of privilege. And (tragically) Rufus thinks that's why she chooses to marry Bart and not run away with him. Lily makes a huge sacrifice for her daughter in this episode. But why does she have to marry Bart? Can't she, like the inimitable Kelly Taylor once did when faced with the choice of Brandon or Dylan, choose to be single? And while it would be awkward if your mom dated your boyfriend's dad, it doesn't turn your boyfriend into your stepbrother — that's just what the gossips would say. It would seem Serena *does* care what society thinks of her, no matter how often she says she just wants to be herself.

S's talk with her mom makes her realize she has to tell the hardass headmistress the truth to protect Dan, at whatever cost to herself. Nate tries to make a similar self-sacrifice, thinking he's protecting Blair and her future, and wins Blair back. Vanessa pulls a "do the right thing" move too, protecting Blair by giving her the tape and a blank to Chuck. But the safe money is on Bass finding some other way to torture his ladylove.

"Going to blackball me from eating yogurt on the Met steps? You have nothing I need."
— Vanessa to Blair

JTLYK:

- No sign of Jenny this week.
- Top story on Gossip Girl: "*What is B Hiding?* Has anyone else noticed Blair has not been acting like her usual self? She has been behaving all secretive as she goes off into corners texting away to an unknown source. Does she have a secret lover? Or did Nate just hump and dump her? Maybe she's having some girl problems with Serena? Luckily for us, on the UES, secrets always end up being revealed, whether you like it or not."
- "Ah, incest, the universal taboo." S's comment is directed at Chuck at the pool party, but it's Lily's relationship with Rufus, not Bart, that freaks Serena out with its potential pseudo-incestuous side effects for her and Dan.
- Getting the students to write a 10,000-word essay on "What the Hell

Were You Thinking" is a total Principal Vernon move. In *The Breakfast Club*, the detainees had to write an essay on "Who You Think You Are."

- Blair has a funny tendency of confessing to adults in positions of authority, telling Headmistress Queller about having done a "stupid thing" with Chuck and then Nate, the same way she confessed to the priest in "Seventeen Candles."
- Chuck's face when Nate tells him how "worth it" it is to work for Blair's affection is priceless.
- Chuck takes a page from the Grandma Cece playbook when he dresses down Dan at B's "study group" party.
- Lily's estimate of the "way we were over a decade ago" is a bit short; it would be more like two decades ago. Dan and Serena are 16-going-on-17 in 2007, which means Rufus and Alison were together by 1990. Rufus and Lily had their epic romance sometime in the mid-to-late '80s. If they are 40ish now, they would have been 20ish then.
- Is Chuck really interested in sleeping with Serena (or bathing with her) or is he just trying to annoy the hell out of her?
- Nate tells Blair that nothing can tear them apart. But if Nate finds out about her and Chuck, will he forgive Blair as she did when he slept with her BFF?
- In "Roman Holiday," Lily says she's not asking her kids' permission to date Bart, waving off their protests over her choice of suitor. But when Serena begs her not to date Rufus, Lily takes her seriously. Guess she knows how it feels to have a Humphrey man be the most important thing in her world.
- Now that B and S are friendly and S and V are friendly, the requisite girl-fighting positions are occupied by polar opposites Blair and Vanessa.
- Blair tells Nate she loves him — "always have, always will" — just like she did in the very first episode.

Secrets & Lies:

- B brings the awkward when she brushes off Nate in the pool ("good catching up"), but she has to be distant with him or else Chuck will tell.
- B thinks everyone is always scheming and sees Vanessa's film as her way to get closer to Dan.
- Wily Headmistress Queller sees through Nate's lie and knows he wasn't the one who broke into the pool. Nate is a terrible liar for a guy who spends

spotted

"That nonchalant look is hard to do. You don't want it to feel 'styled.'"
— costume designer Eric Daman on S

chuck bass
urban dandy

"I always make sure I mix some of the higher-end looks with something from a less expensive brand. . . . That's how people dress today anyway."

"Peacock is the operative word."
— Josh Schwartz on Chuck

"Fashion knows not of comfort.
All that matters is the face you show the world." — Blair

Jenny's two sides: "the downtown, at home kind of look and the Upper East Side, dressing up, going to see Blair look."

headban
for a cro
own
ead

“[Serena] is like French *Vogue* and Blair is American *Vogue*.”

no slouch

"Dan's no slouch even though he's supposed to be poor and from Brooklyn. They say he wears L.L. Bean now; they've said that at least several times, which is offensive to our costumer because I wear a lot of Marc Jacobs."
— Penn Badgley

so much time with the King and Queen of Upper East Scheming.
- Chuck pays off Vanessa for the tape, but she dupes him with a blank.
- Lily arranges to meet Rufus and go away for the weekend, while Bart is standing mere feet away on a business call.
- S admits to D that she broke into the pool but kept it from him so he wouldn't judge her or be faced with protecting either his future or hers.
- Blair tells Nate that she doesn't want to be with him when she so totally does.
- Lily lies to Serena, saying she is going on a "spa trip" for the weekend.
- Lily doesn't tell Rufus the real reason she won't go away with him.

Scrap!: Two guys at the pool party are play-fighting when one cracks his head and falls into the pool.

The Original Gossipverse: V makes a film about Dan in *Because I'm Worth It*, and that one goes badly too. *Making Poetry*, as her film is called, starts with her filming him writing poetry, shirtless, and ends with her catching him making out with literary star and yellow-toothed Mystery Craze (actual name of character) at a surprisingly well-attended poetry reading.

That's How It's Done in *The O.C.*: In the season 2 episode "The Rager," a party gets way out of control and a girl ODs and ends up in the pool, bringing the party to an early end. Things get pseudo-incesty when Ryan is dating Lindsay and she turns out to be his adopted mother's sister, a.k.a. his sorta-kinda aunt. Marissa's mother, Julie Cooper, gets engaged to Caleb Nichol, the stern billionaire who's a terrible father and only has one facial expression; that relationship, like Lily and Bart's, is more about security than romance. (And if Marissa and Ryan had been dating, she would have been his adopted-step-aunt, if such a thing exists.) In season 3, the private school gets a new tough dean who makes life difficult for Marissa and Ryan.

School Ties (dir. Robert Mandel, 1992): A private school, an honor code, secrets, and lies. Need I say more? David Green (Brendan Fraser) is scouted by boys prep school St. Matthews in his senior year of high school; they need a star quarterback, and graduating from the prestigious school will help him get into Harvard. Green is from Union Hill, a working-class neighborhood, and he's Jewish; it's 1950-something, so his dad and his coach tell him to

"mindblowingly inappropriate": *gossip girl*'s been bad

Since its debut episode where teenagers were drinking, smoking weed, having sex (or at least trying to), and, in Chuck's case, committing sexual assault, *Gossip Girl* has come under fire for showing age-inappropriate behavior irresponsibly. "We take the message the show is sending incredibly seriously. These are flawed characters," said Josh Schwartz while doing pre-publicity for the show in July 2007. "We're not presenting this as a perfect world." Stephanie Savage defended the show in the *LA Times*: "When people say the show glamorizes teen drinking and sex, they aren't really watching the episodes. Not all the characters drink or have sex, and when they do, it's always put in a context. Behaviors are rooted in character. There's decision-making, regret, and consequences involved." Dan, Jenny, Vanessa, Eric, and New Serena don't (or rarely) drink while Chuck, Blair, Kati, Is, Old Serena, and the countless teenaged extras do. Nate is a bit of a fence sitter, with his marijuana habit tempered by his father's drug problem. Serena's former life of promiscuity (whatever portion rumor and reality) is outdone only by Chuck's unapologetic taste for debauchery, and he's portrayed as the villain impossible not to love.

Speaking to NPR News, Stephanie talked about the show's approach to "bad behavior": "The consequences may not happen in the same episode as the activity. It feels like, if you're doing activity-consequences in the same episode, that's starting to feel like an after-school special. It's starting to feel very preachy. And honestly, life isn't like that." And those consequences come from the peer group rather than a parent for the most part. Serena is temporarily ostracized for sleeping with Nate; Dan, Serena, and Jenny loathe Chuck for his behavior; Dan scolds Jenny for drinking at the club with Blair and company. The only time a character has been reprimanded by a parent for drinking was when Bart Bass told Chuck to lose the scotch at the brunch. And in that case, switching to champagne was socially acceptable, underage or not. Lily has referenced how difficult and wild Serena used to be; Rufus has had the sex talk with Dan.

"School Lies" was the first "activity-consequences" episode for the show, with a party getting way out of control and the school administration clamping down on the students. And the consequences would have been major for a character like Dan, but Serena, part of the moneyed elite, got a slap on the wrist. When it comes to issues of glamorizing sex, drinking, drug use, and wealth, *Gossip Girl* doesn't make pronouncements of good or bad, right or wrong, but lets the characters navigate the gray, ambiguous moral landscape of adolescence on the Upper East Side. As Penn Badgley put it to the *Seattle Post-Intelligencer*, "[*Gossip Girl*] doesn't encourage it in a way where it's like, 'Look at these kids drinking, and smoking pot and having sex, and look at the great lives they lead!' They're all really unhappy. They're all really screwed up."

keep that detail quiet. He complies: taking off his Star of David and not punching his new friends in the face when they make anti-Semitic comments; he even chooses to play in the football game instead of observing Rosh Hashanah. The über-privileged bigot Charlie Dillon (Matt Damon) grows jealous when David not only outshines him on the field but steals "his girl" (Amy Locane); then he learns that David is Jewish. After a fistfight in the showers, David is ostracized and tormented, then accused of cheating on a history exam. He knows it was Charlie who cheated, but his fate lies in the hands of his classmates who have to decide who will be expelled. The school has a system of self-regulation. Says the headmaster, "We judge ourselves by the highest standards . . . [and strive to be] an elite that care more for honor than advantage, service than for personal gain."

Like David Green, Dan Humphrey is a fish out of water whose presence in the elite world raises the hackles of rich boy and resident prick Chuck Bass. Dan is dating golden girl Serena, calling into question the way things are done, and threatening to disrupt their carefully guarded society. Charlie tells David Green that he envies him: "If you get what you want, you'll deserve it, and if you don't, you'll manage." Beneath that roguish exterior, Chuck envies that same quality in Dan, and like Charlie Dillon, turns that envy into torment.

Welcome to the Real World:

- The new headmistress is named after *Gossip Girl* producer and writer Jessica Queller.
- Dan asks if the Skull and Bones stuff is a bit much, referring to the secret society at Yale that boasts some very powerful alumni.

Locations:

- The address Serena gives Dan for school, 719 East 82nd Street, would put you somewhere in the East River. One of the buildings that stands in for Constance–St. Jude's is the Synod of Bishops of the Russian Orthodox Church, at 75 East 93rd Street.
- Kati and Is met (and made out with) a guy from the Cornell ethics department at Bilboquet (25 E 63rd St).

Oops: Good on Nate for responding so quickly to the emergency, but he clearly isn't a lifeguard; if someone might have a spinal injury, you don't drag

Inside the Synod of Bishops of the Russian Orthodox Church building (one of the Constance–St. Jude's exterior locations) is a ballroom wing on the west side and a two-story garage on the east.

them out of the pool like that. And Andrew Collins has a head injury, not cardiac arrest: he likely needs mouth-to-mouth resuscitation, but not CPR. The photos of the party from the cell phone possess that *CSI* power of limitless resolution — they look so much sharper on the school's giant TV screen than they do on the cell's tiny screen.

The Look: Chuck looks so totally '80s with his Ray-Bans on at the pool party, saluting his bad-boy teen-flick predecessors, and Blair's in a red polka-dot Harajuku halter bikini. On the steps at Constance, Serena's in brown Coach Weslyn boots and a Charlotte Ronson leather jacket with her uniform (and black tights). For the study group, Blair's in a Marc by Marc Jacobs navy skirt with white piping, Brooks Brothers fitted blue striped shirt, argyle J. Crew vest, and an ivory satin Camila headband. The boys keep their looks consistent: Dan in another shirt in the plaid parade, Chuck in a brown turtleneck under a deeper brown jacket, and Nate in a navy-and-white striped sweater. B's in a Catherine Holstein tuxedo bib dress (yuck) when she gets a visit from V. Serena's wearing a Marc by Marc Jacobs wool felt coat over her uniform and has a 7 For All Mankind black ruffle tote with a gold chain after she gets a light punishment from Queller. At her mother's engagement party, Serena wears a black studded Diane von Furstenberg Everly embellished dress and tops it with a gray Rebecca Taylor fur-trimmed coat when she makes her escape to Brooklyn.

Music: "School Lies" opens with "Oh Yeah" (Moby). The party continues with LCD Soundsystem's "Someone Great." Ed Westwick's band, The Filthy Youth, get some play as Dan and Vanessa enter Blair Waldorf's evil lair with "Come Flash All Your Ladies," and "Orange" as Dan tells S Chuck has a point, and Chuck and Blair are caught on tape. Blair shows up at V's work to clear her debt to "Breakfast in NYC" (Oppenheimer). Bart toasts Lily's acceptance of his proposal and Lily tells Rufus she won't be going away with him to "Come Home" by OneRepublic. Bart and Lily's engagement celebration continues with Antonín Dvořák's "Four Romantic Pieces." Serena learns Bart helped her out of her trouble at school to Mozart's "Piano Quartet No. 1 in G Minor." Serena crosses the river and arrives at the Humphrey loft to La Rocca's "Cross the River."

"Looks like the Virgin Queen isn't as pure as she pretended to be."

1.13 the thin line between chuck and nate

Original air date: January 9, 2008
Written by: Felicia D. Henderson
Directed by: Norman Buckley
Guest cast: Jill Flint (Bex), Veronica Taylor (Bryn)

A pregnancy rumor makes Brooklyn's Prince Charming desperate to tell Serena that he loves her, and Queen B is viciously dethroned.

The queen has fallen, but did Blair deserve what she got? Her reputation is arguably the thing she values most: she'll mistreat her family, her friends, her boyfriend, she'll lie and destroy, but always maintains her innocent lamb façade. With Gossip Girl's target focused on B, her classmates whisper about her fall from grace and she's labeled a hypocritical slut. Her clique, Chuck, and Nate all shun her. She loses more than she wagered in the game she was playing with Chuck, and she can't pretend her life is perfect any longer. In the Thanksgiving episode, Blair says to Serena, "What? Nate gets the free pass and I'm the slut?" and here it's proved true. The old double standard of a woman being judged for her promiscuity while a man is congratulated is alive and well at Constance–St. Jude's, where Chuck Bass can do as he pleases and Nate Archibald's infidelity didn't even get a Gossip Girl post — the photo of him with Jenny was to humiliate Blair rather than punish Nate. And while Blair tried to forgive Nate for sleeping with her best friend, he shows no sign that he'll do the same for her.

How many times has Lily van der Woodsen been married? Clearly enough times to program her daughter into having trust issues. After Serena balks when Dan says "I love you," the definitely-smarter-than-his-sister Eric explains to S that their mother's pattern of marrying anyone who declares his love (anyone but Rufus, I guess) has conditioned Serena to think love will fail the test of time. And while Dan has no right to freak out when she doesn't immediately return the "I love you," he is right to love Serena for never giving up on Blair. Especially since those epic friendship moments between the two are some of the best scenes of the series. Double especially when Blair is wearing such a fabulous travel outfit.

"I'll try to be more succinct. You held a certain fascination when you were beautiful, delicate, and untouched. But now you're like one of the Arabians my father used to own: rode hard and put away wet. I don't want you anymore. And I can't see why anyone else would."
— Chuck Bass utters the cruelest combination of words known to humanity

JTLYK:

- No Vanessa this week.
- Top story on Gossip Girl: "*King N and Queen B Rule Again.* We all knew their break up couldn't be for good. What's Blair without Nate? He's the Jimmy to her Choo. The Dom to her Pérignon. One cannot happily exist without the other. We're thrilled to have our happy couple back. They're the epitome of UES high school royalty. Long live the King and Queen, happy together and so in love."
- Jenny's shriek in the first scene was glorious. Taylor Momsen needs to do a horror movie.
- The montage of random UES high schoolers reading Gossip Girl hasn't happened since the pilot. We didn't miss it.
- Art galleries are the place to be for newly single men. Two offers of a date

in less than two minutes. Well played, Poppa Humphrey. But like Blair, Rufus sees that juggling two love interests gets complicated fast. Also? Smug Bex is no replacement for Lily or for Alison.

- Penelope says, "The boyfriend and the best friend," and Hazel chips in, "Pretty classy." In the pilot, Chuck says, "The best friend and the boyfriend. Pretty classy," to Serena.
- After Chuck viciously insults Blair, for the first time ever she has no retort. She is absolutely crushed.
- Blair is wearing the cape she got for Christmas at the heliport.
- The helicopter guys had *just* finished loading all of B's luggage when she tells them she's not going.
- Since B isn't pregnant, why did her mom hear her puking? Was it nerves? Is she bulimic again?

Secrets & Lies:

- B lies to herself, pretending the negative parts of her life don't exist. She tried this strategy after she found out Nate slept with Serena (pretending like it never happened and like S didn't exist), and it didn't work then either.
- Serena confides in Dan about B's predicament and Jenny eavesdrops.
- Serena finds out Blair had sex with Nate from Chuck. B's been keeping secrets from her bestie.
- Serena says to Eleanor that Blair's version of the story is always better than the truth.
- Blair kept the truth from Serena because she didn't want to be judged for sleeping with Nate, the way she felt for sleeping with Chuck.
- Secret is out: Chuck sends a tip to Gossip Girl about B doing two guys in one week. Gossip Girl was right: hell hath no fury like Chuck Bass scorned.
- Jenny spills to Nate about Chuck and Blair.
- Blair tries calling Chuck a liar, but Nate reveals Jenny was the one who told him.
- Nate is the most cut-to-the-chase, honest character: he tells Chuck and Blair exactly how he feels and cuts them out of his life for their betrayal, the same way he refuses to listen to lies from his parents.
- Penelope, Hazel, Kati, and Is ostracize Blair now that she's been outed as a judgmental hypocrite.

- Blair blames Serena for telling her "low-rent boyfriend" who told his "social-climbing sister." In her anger, Blair alienates her friend by insulting her and her soiled reputation. Blair should now know how it feels to be judged and talked about and lay off Serena.

Scrap!: Nate and Chuck do battle in front of the whole school.

Not a Girl, Not Yet a Queen Bee: Just when Jenny thought all her social-climbing efforts were for naught, a secret falls in her lap and she uses it to get back at Blair. Now she's on the higher step, part of the inner circle, and has her own protégé to run errands for her and a bitchy expression to prove just how well B trained her. Jenny's made her choice and I'm guessing her mother would not be proud.

The Original Gossipverse: In the books, Blair has a plan for her life, "a script she wanted to follow exactly," and, like TV B, creates a perfect movie of her life in her head and then is disappointed by reality. Elise is also pulled from the books but is Jenny's friend, not her servant girl.

That's How It's Done in *The O.C.*: In the season 4 episode "The Earth Girls Are Easy," Taylor finds out that Summer's period is late and tries to get her to take a pregnancy test. There's a zany mix-up and Ryan believes it's his

strike out for K

The Writers Guild of America went on strike on November 5, 2007, when the writers' negotiations with film and television producers failed to come to an acceptable agreement, and the strike lasted until February 12, 2008, when production started up again for some shows, while others called it a season. After "The Thin Line . . ." aired in January, there were no new episodes of *Gossip Girl* left to air. Instead, the CW ran a special called *Gossip Girl Revealed,* with the cast talking about the show, then re-ran the episodes from the beginning. With 13 episodes already aired and a season slated for 22, the CW announced *Gossip Girl* would be getting five episodes post-strike. The truncated season wasn't the only change to the show. After production wrapped for the strike, Nan Zhang (who plays Kati) decided to return to school; as Josh Schwartz explained, she enrolled at Brown but "didn't tell anyone on the show." Ack! Education's important and everything, but who will wear matching outfits with Is?

girlfriend who might be preggers, not Seth's. At the end of season 1, Ryan deals with an actual pregnancy when Theresa may be carrying his kid.

A Thin Line Between Love and Hate: It's a movie; it's a song. The movie (dir. Martin Lawrence, 1996) is one of the worst ways to spend 108 minutes. Ladies' man Darnell (Martin Lawrence) and his buddy Tee (Bobby Brown) have a system: don't fall in love, don't be faithful, just play women and give them enough attention so they don't get pissed off. But in walks Brandi (Lynn Whitfield), a hard-to-get woman whom Darnell seduces. After telling her he loves her, he finds out she is super crazy (she talks to herself in the mirror *and* wears too much lip liner). Meanwhile Darnell falls in (real) love with sweet and sassy girl-from-the-neighborhood Mia (Regina King). Darnell breaks up with all his other ladies to prove his love to Mia. So Crazy Brandi puts an orange in a stocking and beats herself with it. Then she tries to kill him. He pushes Mia away to protect her, there's a big battle, and the crazy lady goes to jail. Darnell learns the real meaning of "I love you" and not to ever, ever misuse those words again.

There's not much worth gleaning from *A Thin Line . . .*, but as B knows, it sure is tricky juggling multiple love interests and keeping secrets — almost as tricky as trusting that the person saying "I love you" means it, right S?

Locations:

- Kati and Is are going shopping at Barneys (660 Madison Ave) and then to Decibel (240 E 9th St).
- Dan and Serena have a chilly picnic in Stuyvesant Park (2nd Ave and 15th St).
- Chuck is having a drink at Butai (15 E 18th St) when Blair stops by for some psychological torment.
- Serena stops Blair from leaving at the downtown heliport (Pier 81, W 41st St and 12th Ave).

The Look: Love the Met steps outfits: Kati is in a black-and-white Paul & Joe Sister You Win poncho, red-and-white striped Dollhouse Cruiser flats, gray tights, and navy shorts. Over a green cardigan and her uniform, Jenny wears Lauren Moffatt's hooded toggle jacket in blue, plus purple tights and a Hat Attack plaid cap. B gets her bitch on in a navy Tory Burch Mercedes trench, gorgeous Sam Edelman Rita tri-color patent ankle boots, and a

Be&D Twiggy patent tote. Serena tries to reason with her bestie wearing Ever's Los Feliz leather hoodie in red (don't try to find it in that color; it was made only for *Gossip Girl*), Chanel boots, and a large top handle Gucci Indy bag. More Be&D bags later in the episode: Blair's got the Kan Kan ruffle tote in black when she asks her mom to let her go to Paris, and Serena has the Annie tote in saddle when B tells her she's not pregnant. In his most unappealing outfit since the basketball disaster in "Bad News Blair," Chuck lounges in his Palace suite in a yellow turtleneck, green Adidas tear-aways, and a cardigan. Awesome. Blair Pants Watch! She's wearing jeans at home when Serena comes by to pressure her into taking a pregnancy test. Blair's

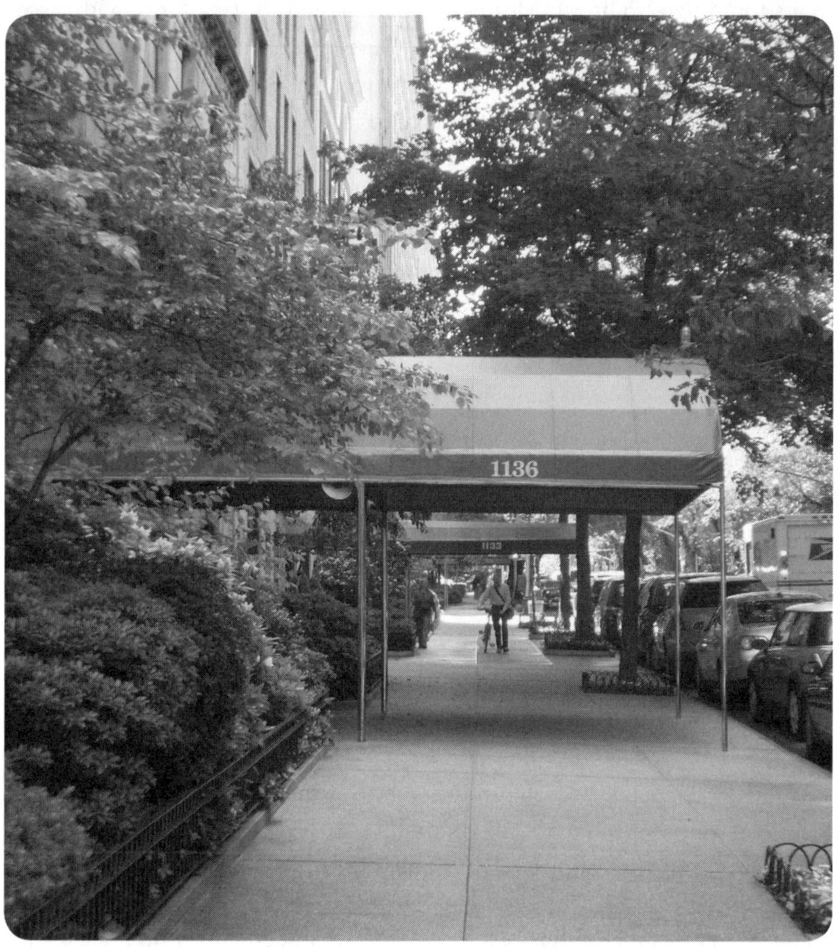

Blair runs home to her Fifth Avenue penthouse when her life falls apart.

multicolored Jennifer Ouellette turban headband cannot protect her when the girls of the steps reject her. Serena's wearing a purple Elie Tahari Georgia coat when she stops B (in her Zac Posen cape) from leaving NYC. But most importantly, if Serena's dissing Eric's terrible highlights, does that mean the poor boy will have better hair color soon?

Music: Serena is spotted buying a pregnancy test to "Got Your Number" by Nadia Oh. Serena tells Dan she's not pregnant to "The Dark Side of Indoor Track Meets" (Falling Up). Nate and Blair kiss in the courtyard while Chuck Bass lurks in a corner to "You'll Change" by Machine Translations. Bryn leaves and Bex arrives at the Bedford Gallery to "Where There's Gold" (Dashboard Confessional). Dan stalks off after professing his love to Serena to "The Air We Breathe" by Figurines and it continues as Blair wanders alone. "Good Morning.Goodbye" by Dan Cray Trio plays at Butai when Blair congratulates Chuck on winning. Serena convinces Blair to stay and fight to "Happily Never After" (Nicole Scherzinger).

Zuzanna Szadkowski as Dorota

Dorota! The much-loved and much-abused Dorota is brought to life by Zuzanna Szadkowski. Born in Warsaw, Poland, Zuzanna grew up in Indiana before moving to New York City to study acting at Barnard College, then earned an MFA at The A.R.T. Institute for Advanced Theater Training at Harvard University/MXAT. She appeared in two episodes of *The Sopranos* as Elzbieta, the Polish maid, before being cast on *Gossip Girl* as Dorota, the Polish maid, and appears in *Where is Joel Baum?* as . . . um . . . a Polish maid. But it is as Dorota, the best Polish maid of all, that Zuzanna has developed a hardcore fanbase who love her every moment on screen, a role that she described to *Daily Intel*: "As Dorota I bustle around, eavesdrop, disapprove, approve, and get really excited about all things Miss Blair. . . ." In an MTV interview, Zuzanna said, "I was born in Poland, so I am able to identify with her in that way. Certainly the accent is modeled after people in my own family, so hopefully I am doing it justice. My family loves it and I know that in Poland *Gossip Girl* has a lot of fans. We have Poland represented on the Upper East Side!"

"The price of fitting in may have gotten a little steeper."

1.14 the blair bitch project

Original air date: April 21, 2008
Written by: K.J. Steinberg
Directed by: J. Miller Tobin
Guest cast: Karla Mosley (Waitress), Audrie Neenan (Betty), Ryan Woodle (Delivery Man)

It's Little J's 15th birthday and she's desperate to fit in with her new social circle. Rufus thinks Jenny Cake is a good idea. Serena receives naughty packages and blames Chuck.

The game of scrambling for acceptance at Constance reaches new heights now that Jenny is in and B is out. Jenny and Blair are both acting like big old fakers in their own way: Blair duping Rufus to get J kicked out of the inner circle, and Jenny lying at every turn as she navigates a world way too expensive for her. Serena is naïve to think that "nature will take its course" and Blair will be queen again by being nice. After all, S has been on her best behavior for the better part of a year and Lily *still* thinks of her as a troublemaker. And while Chuck was impossibly cruel to Blair in the last episode, he's nothing but a gentleman to his new family — and his father thinks the worst of him. Bart tries to bribe Chuck into behaving (when he hasn't actually been misbehaving), not believing Chuck when he says it wasn't him behind the packages. Having lost Nate and kicked aside Blair, Chuck goes from looking pleased to have a sister to torment and toasting his new family to skulking back to his old suite. Bart has no faith in Chuck, Lily has no faith in Serena, and both are wrong about their kids. What a pair.

It's one thing to be wrong about your kids when they turn out to be better behaved than you assumed, but poor Rufus finds out how Jenny has been keeping up with her new group of friends. As manipulative as Blair is, she's right when she tells Rufus that Jenny's "trying to reconcile who [she's] becoming with who [she] used to be." And how do you that when you're obsessed with what you're going to wear and how you're going to pay for $120 brunches? If only Jenny was like Dan: content to be friendless at school.

"Dad, you think that you can just send me off to school with a plaid skirt and a MetroCard and everything will be OK."
— Jenny realizes that parents just don't understand

JTLYK:

- Top story on Gossip Girl: "*B Missing in Action!* Blair Waldorf was last spotted at the downtown helipad trying to make a quick getaway from the scandal that turned the Upper East Side upside down. She hasn't been seen since. Where did B go? Did she enroll in Spence under an alias? Or did she actually skip town for destination: unknown? We're just dying to find out where our former princess could be hiding. Come out come out wherever you are. We want to play, B."
- The episode opens in widescreen for the *Breakfast at Tiffany's* dream sequence. In the film, Holly turns around to find Fred holding Cat, the two creatures she cares most about in the world. Poor B's dream turns nightmarish when the exceptionally handsome Nate as Fred shows up Cat-less and calling her Jenny. Ew is right.
- Nate continues his Tells It Like It Is parade and warns Jenny about the new crowd she's hanging out with, saying she's not like those other girls.
- Chuck is actually considerate to Dan, having a place set for him for the tasting with the wedding caterer.
- The taglines on the porn in the mysterious package Serena gets: "What do you give the girl who has everything? A contract," and "Smile, you're on carnal camera!"
- B disses Jenny's borough even to a stranger when she calls 411 and asks for a listing in Brooklyn: "I think that's in New York."
- Like mother, like daughter. In "Dare Devil," Dan reminds Rufus how unsuccessful the surprise party that he threw for Alison's 30th birthday was. And Jenny's was a fail too. Why wasn't Dan around to warn Rufus? Weird (read: convenient for the writers) that he didn't talk to his dad or sister on her birthday.
- The girls are holding their birthday hats at J's surprise party. Can't ruin the hair with cardboard.
- Since when does everyone know that Eric was in the Ostroff Center?
- Wouldn't Penelope, Hazel, and Is already know that Jenny is "low rent"? They would know she lives in Brooklyn, who her dad is, and how her family name means nothing on the Upper East Side.

- Serena isn't wearing a jacket when she calls on Chuck at the end of the episode because they live in the same hotel, just different suites.
- Who is G? Why are Serena and Chuck so scared about her return?

Secrets & Lies:

- Chuck smokes up in Serena's bathroom so their parents would think it was S, not him. No wonder Serena is convinced it's Chuck sending her the packages to make her look bad.
- Jenny tells the girls that she has a few dresses on hold at Bendel's for her birthday. Lie!
- J invites Blair to have dinner with the girls at Butter, planning to stand her up. This way she avoids an expensive meal out and humiliates Blair. Win-win.
- J steals a Valentino dress from Hazel's, and the blame falls on the maid. Then she steals it again from the consignment store.
- Rufus gets played by Blair into throwing the cheesiest, girliest bday party ever. Icing on the cake for B? J's wearing stolen goods.
- Jenny keeps lying even when she's caught wearing the dress.
- J has been keeping up appearances with her friends by pretending she's not hungry and eating her brown-bag lunch in the bathroom.
- Like Blair, even when J's down, she's not out. She uses Nate to win back her place with Penelope and co., who decide to forget about the whole dress-stealing thing.
- S apologizes to Chuck once she finds out it wasn't him sending the packages.

Scrap!: Jenny assaults Blair with yogurt.

The Original Gossipverse: In *All I Want Is Everything*, J keeps borrowing money from her dad to keep up with Nate (she's dating him), and she sneaks out of the apartment to a party to see Nate when she's grounded. In *Because I'm Worth It*, B realizes S is the "absolute queen of comebacks": "If anyone could help Blair shimmy her way back to the top and make everyone fall in love with her again, Serena could."

That's How It's Done in *The O.C.*: Both Cooper girls do a bit of stealing: Marissa shoplifts in the very first Chrismukkah episode. Fourteen-year-old

Kaitlin returns from boarding school in "The Sister Act" with frat boys on her tail looking for a bag of cash she stole. Kaitlin's 15th birthday party sucks too, and she ditches it to hang out with an older guy in "The Pot Stirrer."

The Blair Witch Project (dir. Daniel Myrick and Eduardo Sánchez, 1999): Groundbreaking at the time and much spoofed since its release, *The Blair Witch Project* is a horror film that purports to be found documentary footage of three student filmmakers who went into the woods in 1994 and were never seen again. Heather, Josh, and Mike were making a documentary about the legend of the Blair witch, and there's lots of creepy local stories to kick off the story — a man who kidnapped and murdered seven children in 1940, five men found dead and bound together at Coffin Rock, and a witch who haunts the woods. After the filmmakers head into the woods, the spooky factor of the film comes mostly from an unseen threat — weird things happen, strange noises at night, of course they get lost, and then one of the three disappears in the night. The other two can hear their friend being tortured in some unimaginable way but can't find or help him. (And if that doesn't freak you out, at least the handheld camera work will make you nauseous.)

Jenny's been living in constant fear herself — of rejection, ridicule, and of being outed as a fraud. And that moment comes with her very own Blair witch proving to be a real danger.

Welcome to the Real World:

- Chuck calls his soon-to-be stepmother "Lily von Bülow." American heiress Sunny von Bülow's husband Claus was accused of the attempted murder of his wife by administering insulin that put her in a vegetative state. He was convicted of the crime, but the decision was overturned on appeal when evidence showed Sunny's symptoms were the result of a prescription drug overdose.
- To make B feel better, S dishes that Maya (one of the girls in "Dare Devil") finally made it into Brody Jenner's cell phone. In an episode of *The Hills*, Lauren looked through Brody's cell contact list and found such charming entries as "Brittany-Canada-Whore." Ugh is right.
- Hazel's mom's one-of-a-kind Valentino was made for her in 1968, the same year Jacqueline Kennedy married Aristotle Onassis.

Locations:

- Jenny's birthday party was originally going to be at Socialista (505 West St).
- Blair spends two nights in a row at Butter (415 Lafayette St, pictured below).

The Look: Blair even dreams designer: she's wearing Christian Louboutin Ernesta plateau sandals as Audrey. First day back to school after spring break and the girls are decked out: S in Uggs, a Just Cavalli leather jacket, and a Valentino bag; B opting for a Ralph Lauren large sporting tote, Bulgari BV8020B sunglasses, and a wide blue Decolette satin belt over her jacket. The effect of Jenny, Hazel, Penelope, Is, and Elise walking down the street in their spring prep look is pure *Gossip Girl* gold. Jenny's outfit is way unrealistically posh, but nicely nods to the Valentino, the key outfit of the episode. She has a $2,495 Valentino Maison studded bag in purple, a Valentino coat, Moschino shoes with Juicy Couture navy and white polka-dot socks, white stockings, and a purple headband. Lily wears a Tory Burch Thila beaded dress at the tasting. Jenny shows up at Butter in a purple Dolce & Gabbana dress. The red one-of-a-kind Valentino really is a one-of-a-kind Valentino; the designer lent it to the show for this plotline. But forget all that: never has there been an article of clothing better suited to a person than Chuck's knit shark sweater at the end of the episode. Inspired.

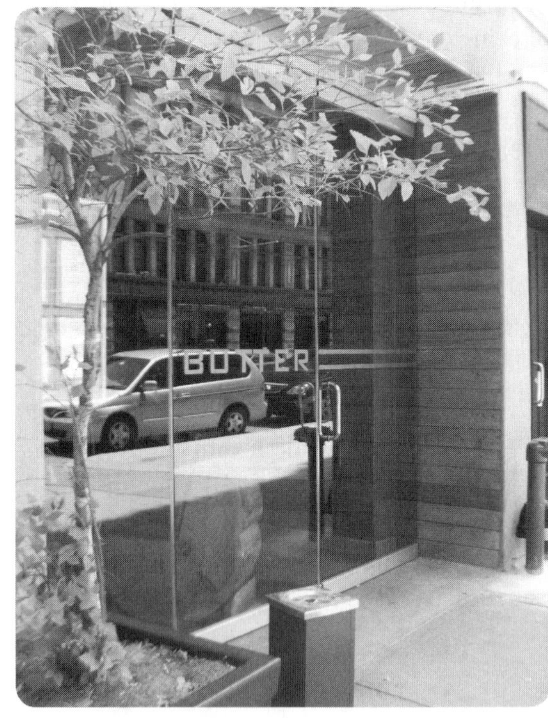

Music: "Moon River" (Henry Mancini) plays in the *Breakfast at Tiffany's* dream sequence. A quick breakfast at the Humphrey loft features

"Eucalyptus" by The Deadly Syndrome. "Feeling Better" by The Teenagers is on when Serena and Dan's make-out is interrupted by Chuck. Jenny hangs out with her new besties at Hazel's to "Back Seat Taxi" (Silver Money). Blair realizes she's been stood up and orders the seared squab to "Drive Me Crazy" (Miss Eighty 6). The Upper East Cyborgs show up at Butter after Jenny's failure of a birthday party while Classic's "On the Run" plays. Blair and Is head for the bar and inadvertently open up some seats at the table to Kylie Minogue's "Rippin' Up the Disco." Penelope is won over with an Archibald to "Sour Cherry" by The Kills.

"Guess big brother's been teaching little sis how to snag the ones with the trust funds."

1.15 desperately seeking serena

Original air date: April 28, 2008
Written by: Felicia D. Henderson
Directed by: Michael Fields
Guest cast: Yin Chang (Nelly Yuki), Jesse Swensen (Asher Hornsby), Jolly Abraham (Waiter), Erica Knight (Serena's SAT Replacement), Jeffrey Omura (Todd Jansen), Jake Silbermann (Guy #1), Jasmin M. Tavarez (Hostess)

It's SAT time and the world's upside down: Serena's confiding in Chuck, Nate's with Vanessa, and Blair's been demoted to a subplot. Maybe it's because of the new bad girl in town, Georgina Sparks.

The SATs and a new villain in one week? The worst comes out in just about everyone as they cheat, lie, steal, manipulate, drug, obsess, and do a little bit of studying. While the looming test brings out Blair's manipulative best, Georgina brings out the self-destructing worst in Serena. S makes "huge mistakes" when she's with Georgina; it's clear that they love to party together — booze, drugs, guys — but what is the big secret from last year that could bring them both down? Something so bad she can't even tell Chuck . . . the ramp-up to the big season finale has officially begun.

There's nothing more fun than watching a perfect relationship fall apart. Serena and Dan have weathered the crazy friends, the weird Rufly connection, the judging and trust issues, the "we're from different worlds" challenges, and the first times having sex and saying "I love you." The only thing left for them to deal with is Serena's crazy-ass past. And S is dead set against confiding in Dan about who she used to be. As S turns away from goody-two-shoes Dan, she relies on the assistance of resident evil-doer Chuck to deal with her Georgie problems, and other than some quintessentially Chuck lines (asking Serena to beg for his help, taunting Dan on the phone), he steps up and plays the role of big brother.

While one romance crumbles, another is ignited. Guess when Vanessa told Blair that Nate was "one of the good ones" back in "School Lies," she meant one of the ones she would totally make out with.

"Hey S, I'm just sipping on a gingko-biloba blended and wondering how your stomach migraine is."
— Blair takes a break from the destruction of Nelly Yuki to check in on her bestie

JTLYK:

- The top story on Gossip Girl doesn't quite fit its headline: "*Why is Serena so worried?* Anyone else notice Serena's been acting like her old self? She was spotted at Constance with a case of champagne in tow. Thirsty much? Pop open a bottle and let's toast to old Serena's return. Welcome back, S! We sure have missed you."
- Vanessa is *so* rude to Nate when he offers Dan his prep books. Hopefully she'll lose the "venomous without provocation" and realize that everybody's got a story, not just Nate. There's no need to be bitchy.
- The Upper East Cyborgs are more accomplished than they appear: Penelope is a National Merit scholar and Isabel is a concert pianist.
- Rufus rewards Jenny's hard work with a new sewing machine, but his refusal to let her date or lift the grounding sentence turns her smile into a scowl.
- In an episode where everyone is so mean to everyone else, Nate taking Vanessa to write her SATs comes off as especially sweet. Except to Blair and Dan, who share a WTF moment.
- How many hot dogs does Asher think two people can eat? Is he secretly a competitive eater?
- Where did Georgina get the dog from? How did she find Dan in Central Park? And wasn't Dan a little bit too flirty with "Sarah"?

Secrets & Lies:

- Serena gets Chuck to do some investigating on her behalf to find out where Georgina is.
- Chuck pays someone to take the SATs for him. And then, to "help" Serena, he gets someone to take them for her too.
- G pretends not to be into drugs anymore but is busted when her dealer calls.
- Chuck lies to Dan for Serena, telling him she has food poisoning. C and S need to work on their lying tag-team, because she doesn't get the story straight. Lying 101: always best to be vague if you don't know the details of the fib.
- Blair tricks Nelly Yuki into trusting her, bribes Todd into her plan (by offering up Isabel), then steals the batteries to Nelly's calculator. That's one way to prep for the SATs.
- Blair's plot against Nelly Yuki looks like child's play next to Georgina,

who tells New Serena her turnaround is inspiring, and then drugs her to get her Old Serena back.

- Dan gives Serena every opportunity to open up to him, and she keeps pushing him away. Even Chuck encourages S to tell D the truth about G. *Chuck!*
- Georgina pretends to be Sarah (with a dog named Georgie) to Dan. What is this girl up to?

Not a Girl, Not Yet a Queen Bee: Not satisfied with just being a part of the inner circle, Jenny is vying for queen status and just may have found her king. Jenny clearly hasn't learned her lesson despite telling Rufus she has; she's just found a new strategy to get to top step.

The Original Gossipverse: Michelle Trachtenberg's G fits the description of the character from the book series. Georgina Spark (not Sparks) arrives at a group rehab session Nate is in and is described as a "coked-up version of Snow White." In *I Like it Like That*, Jenny picks up a boy she spots at Bendel's, then stalks him with Elise, and sees him walking dogs. Book Vanessa has college aspirations, even though her parents and sister didn't go; she wants to go to NYU for film. Vanessa's sister Ruby is in a band — punk yes, lesbian no (sorry, Nate). Dan says the Humphreys had a cat named Iggy; in the books, it's Marx.

Desperately Seeking Susan (dir. Susan Seidelman, 1985): Roberta (Rosanna Arquette), a housewife with a boring life and a self-important hot-tub-salesman husband, loves reading personal ads, particularly the "Desperately Seeking Susan" ads placed by a lovelorn Jimmy. Susan (Madonna) is a hardscrabble New York City girl who steals and makes her way in the world the best she can, and has fun while she's at it. About to leave her latest beau behind in a New Jersey hotel room, Susan steals some stuff, including a pair of earrings she finds in the guy's jacket. Those earrings turn out to be stolen ancient Egyptian artifacts, the guy's a mobster, and he's about to be murdered. The murderer sees Susan leaving, wearing her signature jacket. At a store in the East Village, Roberta buys that jacket after Susan exchanges it for a pair of sparkly boots (which are *way* better than the jacket, let's be honest). The murderer accosts Roberta, thinking she is Susan; Roberta bonks her head and wakes up in the arms of Des (Aidan Quinn), a friend of Jimmy's. Roberta doesn't remember a thing and spends the bulk of the movie living life as "Susan," while the real Susan tries to track her down and the murderer tries to get the earrings back and kill her. In the end, Roberta remembers who she is but rejects her old life, opting to leave her housewife days behind and stay in the city with the way-hotter-than-her-husband Des. Roll credits to "Get Into the Groove."

Moving from the grungier Lower to the posh Upper East Side, "Desperately Seeking Serena" also centers on false identity — a hired "Chuck" and "Serena" to write the SATs, Blair pretending to be kind to Nelly Yuki, "Savannah" and "Svetlana," Georgina faking out Serena and then pretending to be Sarah, and Dan desperate to get the truth out of Serena while she battles to stay true to her new self. Madge's Susan is Roberta's other wilder half — who Roberta would be if she was free and followed her heart instead of being stuck in her dullsville life — while Georgina is the wilder half of Serena better left bottled up.

Welcome to the Real World:

- Georgina may be rumored to be dating the Prince of Belfort but he's not a real prince. A small Swiss mountain town's effort to revive its economy resulted in naming a Zurich resident "prince" of the castle (named Belfort) for at least a year beginning in March 2007.
- Jenny scopes out the boys at Dalton and Collegiate, both real private schools.
- Nelly Yuki got her first violin from Itzhak Perlman, the violin virtuoso.
- When Penelope grills Nelly Yuki to discover her weakness, she is holding *Pretty Is What Changes*, a memoir by *Gossip Girl* producer/writer Jessica Queller.

Locations:

- Georgina and Serena meet for a no-drinks, one-hour dinner at Spice Market (403 W 13th St).
- The SATs are held at Hunter College (695 Park Ave).

The Look: The bright, bold spring colors continue to be front and center. Chuck and Blair may say they hate each other, but their matchy-matchy outfits scream "we're meant to be." Echoing Chuck's orange trench in a yellow Ralph Lauren trench, Blair has on a Zara sweater over a Valentino Red

Cotton Jacquard blouse, a Ralph Lauren belt, her uniform skirt, H&M red tights, and a Brooks Brothers wool quilted quarter flap bag. Serena's carrying a Burberry Prorsum Mason Warrior bag in beige and wearing a Mike & Chris Jude lambskin leather trench. Blair Pants Watch! She's wearing red pants in

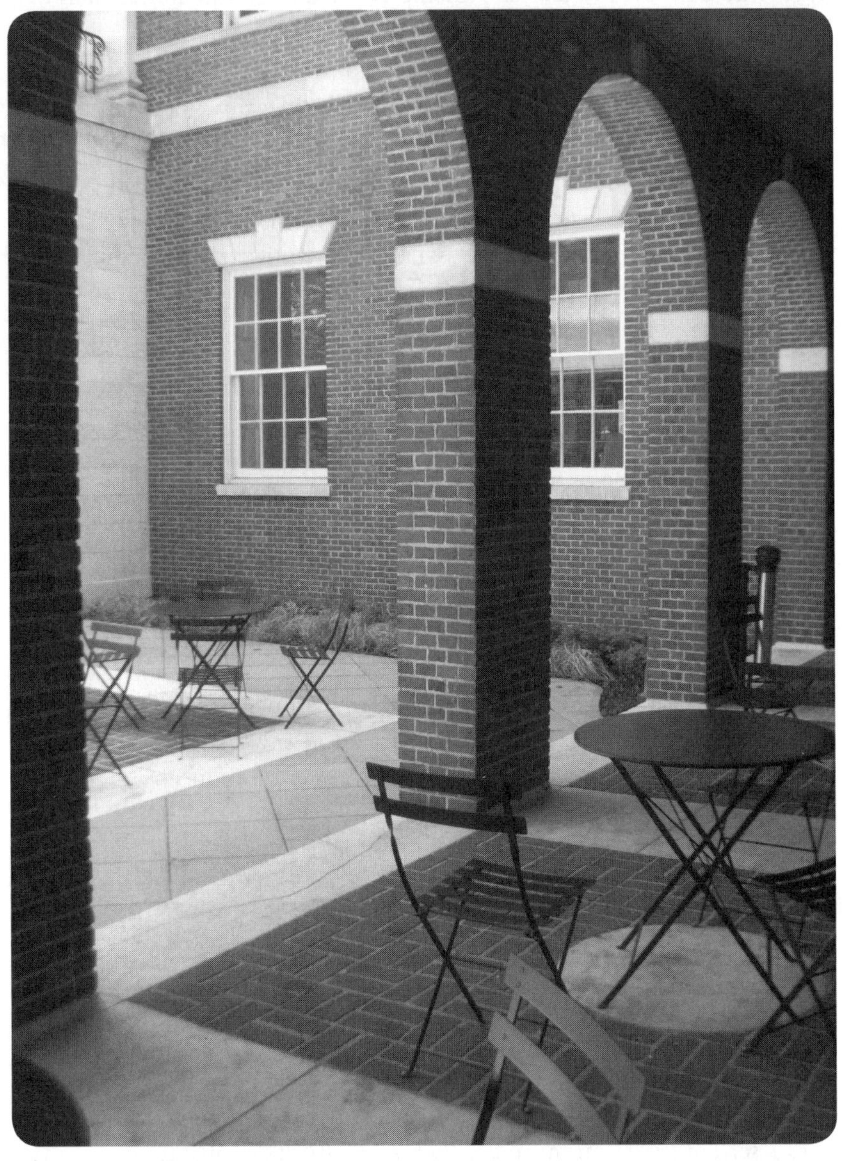

The Museum of the City of New York is used for the school's front courtyard, where Georgina makes her unexpected appearance.

G roofies S at the Spice Market in the Meatpacking District.

the opening study montage and shorts at home when she first schemes to get Nelly Yuki. Blair tricks Nelly Yuki at school wearing a Brooks Brothers Mackintosh cape in navy and holding a red Valentino couture braided tote. Georgina Sparks makes her debut in Tom Ford Camilla sunglasses, J Brand "The Doll" 22" bell leg jeans in tar, and a Gucci Hysteria python bag. She gets drunk with Serena wearing a LaROK Rock Star tunic and red Aldo Atlantic City high heels. Jenny goes boyfriend hunting in a navy Priorities Angelina belted trench and H&M scarf with a Marc Jacobs bag. Serena lies to Dan about her food poisoning wearing black Barneys NY Becca boots and holding a Botkier Nicole tote in champagne.

Music: "Do the Panic" by Phantom Planet provides the soundtrack for the opening SAT studying montage. At Communitea, "Campus" by Vampire Weekend is playing when Nate drops off the SAT prep books for Dan. Georgina and Serena catch up to "Crimewave" (Crystal Castles vs. Health). The reminiscing turns ugly when G's dealer calls to "Nice Sweet Sexy" (Difx featuring Imperio and Cru). Blair downloads "Elevator" by Flo Rida featuring Timbaland, and then plays it as she walks by Nelly Yuki in the hall. Dinner without cocktails is to The Ting Tings' "We Started Nothing."

Michelle Trachtenberg as Georgina Sparks

Born in New York City in 1985, Michelle Christine Trachtenberg brings a whole new dimension to girly evil on the Upper East Side as Georgina Sparks. Michelle started acting as a child in commercials, before graduating to television with *All My Children*, and then to film with the title role in 1996's *Harriet the Spy* and Penny in *Inspector Gadget*. In season 5 of the show, Michelle joined the cast of *Buffy the Vampire Slayer* as Buffy's little sister Dawn and by the end of the series in 2003 had convinced its loyal audience to love her character. Since then she's appeared in *Ice Princess*, *Euro-Trip*, *Six Feet Under*, *House*, and *17 Again*. Michelle is fluent in Russian, thanks to her Russian-born mother, so that "Svetlana" accent? Totally authentic. Michelle added some of her own flair to Georgina's style: the bad girl sports some pieces from the actress's jewelry line, Bella Veritas.

"The only thing more shocking than the truth
are the lies people tell to cover it up."

1.16 all about my brother

Original air date: May 5, 2008
Written by: Paul Sciarrotta
Directed by: Janice Cooke
Guest cast: Yin Chang (Nelly Yuki), Jesse Swensen (Asher Hornsby)

Sex, lies, and memory cards. Serena and Eric's big secrets are finally revealed.

Information is power and the winning strategy to the games people play with each other in the *Gossip Girl* world. But when secrets kept from family and friends and the lies told to cover up the truth are coming out, the stakes get too high for Little J or Serena to keep playing. The battle between Blair and Jenny for Queen Bee continues on the Met steps with each girl's micro-army — Hazel, Penelope, and Elise on Team J; Is, Nelly Yuki, and absentee S on Team B — and it seems like Jenny's winning. After trading barbs via Gossip Girl (J's poor, B's a slut, yawn), Blair takes aim at the new and powerful accessory Jenny can't help showing off: her boyfriend. Comparing Asher to an ugly patchwork Louis Vuitton bag, Blair makes a point Serena agrees with: boyfriends are just like handbags or any other commodity. And while that's a vile idea in the regular world, in the *Gossip* world she's totally right. Jenny intentionally sought out a rich guy to date so she could parade him about as a status symbol. And it was working.

But the pathetic part is that Jenny believes her own lie and likes Asher . . . or at least what he provides: "status, access, resources." Gay or straight, who cares: Asher's a prick and he mistreats Jenny and Eric. For a 14-year-old who was suicidal mere months ago, Eric is admirably (if a little unrealistically) resilient — he deals with his mother's less than understanding reaction to his sexuality and confronts Asher and Jenny in front of the whole world (since everything ends up on Gossip Girl). That Eric has a better chance at happiness if he's honest is a lesson he teaches his mother, whose heartfelt apology and concern for him makes forgivable her craptastic reaction at the dinner table.

Lily's apology was just one of many in this episode. Serena apologizes to Eric for being distant after returning for his sake, and she apologizes to Blair for not being available to her either. And after pulling the classic "how are you going to stop me?" move and taking off to Asher's party, Jenny returns home, dreams crushed, social life ruined, with the realization that what she wanted so badly wasn't worth the cost. Her apology to Rufus is touching, but the scene that takes the emotional cake is saved for last.

"All About My Brother" has the best ending since Chuck and Blair hooked up in the limo. Serena's big reveal — the heartfelt sister talk from B; the overly lined, full of tears eyes on S; the music kicking in after S's "I killed someone" — never fails to bring on the shivers. A great TV moment and a perfect set-up for the final two episodes of the season. Who the eff did S kill? And will the people who love Serena stand by her side when they find out she *killed* someone? An epic episode.

"Even you should know that jealousy clashes with L.L. Bean pants."
— Little J directs her vemon at Dan

JTLYK:

- Upper East Side hot guy count is low this week with both Nate and Chuck MIA.
- Top story on Gossip Girl: "*Is the Bad Girl Back?* Serena van der Woodsen was seen throwing back so many drinks she'd make Amy Winehouse proud. Word has it S even missed her SAT's because she was too hungover to take the test! WTF is up with that? Well, Gossip Girl isn't going to lie. We're kind of excited to see old Serena back. Because let's face it, the new Serena was getting to be a bit of a yawn."
- Serena still calls Chuck one of her "monsters," but it's sweet that he calls to check up on her and she seems happy to get the call. Chuck has also been playing the good brother to Eric, who turns to him after he's forced out of the closet and tells his sister the "guy's got his faults but he's never judged me."
- Oh, the busy life of a bride-to-be. Check out Lily's schedule: breakfast meeting with Bart and his lawyers about the pre-nup; mani/pedi at Red Door Spa; Mark Ingram Atelier for final dress fitting and jewelry selection; coffee with Louise; Preston Bailey for flowers and table settings final approval; conference call with *House & Garden* about the article; meet Jill at Barneys to get honeymoon and getaway outfits; Sylvia Weinstock for cake tasting; Godiva for gift-bag chocolates; and Jacques Louis for

game over?

All season long, our Upper East Siders have treated each other like pawns and playthings, but in "All About My Brother," the outright references to games were numerous.

- "Cheating, drinking, drugs. It's all fair game, but outing your sister's boyfriend is dark." (Blair)
- "Motive is irrelevant as long as our endgame is the same." (Blair)
- "This is not a game to me." (Dan)
- "The minute you start sending tips to Gossip Girl, you're in the game with the rest of us." (Jenny)
- "This is not a game. . . . I'm not playing with you this time." (Serena)
- "It's just a friendly game." (Georgina)
- "You win." (Jenny)
- "Sweetie, we just started to play." (Blair)

dinner with William and Charlie, drinks after. (Guess that dinner was canceled for the quiet van der Woodsen family supper.)

- When G shows up for dinner at the van der Woodsens' suite, Lily says she always loves when Georgina visits. In "Desperately Seeking Serena," S tells Chuck that her mom doesn't like G. Guess this comment is courtesy of those good social graces of the Upper East Side.
- The rest of the Gossip Girl blast about Jenny swiping her "V card at A's register": "Didn't anyone teach you, J? You shouldn't give away the ending if you want him to pick up the book again."
- Little J pushes Dan out of her bedroom, kind of a pointless move since the garage door that separates their rooms is open. He'll go into his room and still pretty much be in her room.
- Let's hope that J's actual first time is better than Hazel's and Penelope's. Neither has fond memories of losing their virginity. But Jenny's track record with boys — Chuck and Asher — isn't promising.
- Just like when she kept quiet about his stay at the Ostroff Center, B cares about Eric so doesn't use Asher's cell phone evidence to destroy Jenny . . . until she gets permission.
- Lily doesn't call Bart Bass to talk about Eric, she calls Rufus. Hmmm.
- Serena reassures Eric by saying, "I'm your sister. We're us. You can tell me anything." Later B uses the same strategy, saying, "We're sisters. You're my family. What is you is me. There's nothing you could ever say to make me let go," harkening back to the first honest conversation we ever

saw between S and B at the Palace bar in the pilot when S referred to them as sisters.

- Blair hits Asher on the back with his cell phone like she's knocking on a door. Such a Waldorf move and completely hilarious.
- About Little J, now ruined, Blair says "looks like someone needs a semester in France." So glib, even though it was she who was completely gutted and desperate to leave NYC just before spring break.
- The post–gay bomb story on Gossip Girl: "*J's Dream Night Ends in Disaster*: Little Jenny Humphrey definitely had a night she'll never forget. Poor girl is only fifteen and is already a full-blown beard. With Jenny's humiliation soaring off the charts, we're sure she's going to be flying under the radar for a bit. I mean, how can you show your face after your boyfriend was outed and you were too blind to even see he was gay?"
- Dan is left-handed (and better than Rufus at Scrabble).

Secrets & Lies:

- The Gossip Girl blasts are full of ludicrous rumors until she makes evidence a requirement for tipsters. (So what proof did Dan send of boy-on-boy action?)
- J lies to B and the girls, saying her phone call is from the party planner. Then she lies to Rufus about Asher's party.
- Rufus snoops in his daughter's email because he doesn't trust her, despite her recent good behavior. Lily brushes off the privacy invasion, reasoning that if J's "well-being is at stake" it's fair game. Um, how was her well-being at stake?
- Jenny mistakes Eric's concern about Asher for him having a crush on her, when really he has a crush on Asher. But he keeps his secret.
- When Dan confronts Asher, Asher denies the kiss by getting crude fast, and then covers it up with another lie to J.
- Serena lies to Dan about the call from the concierge and won't tell D why he can't trust Sarah.
- Blair enlists Nelly Yuki and Is to steal Asher's phone.
- Georgina recorded "that night" without S's knowledge and threatens to show Dan and Vanessa if S doesn't play along with the Sarah game.
- Jenny lies to her girlfriends about Asher going to third, and about losing her virginity to him. While she admits to Dan that she didn't sleep with Asher, she pretends she knew all along that he was gay.

- Penelope spells out what Jenny's unforgivable offence is: lying to her girlfriends about sex.
- Serena has been keeping a *very* big secret from everyone.

Scrap!: Dan is ready to beat Asher up when he talks smack about Jenny.

Not a Girl, Not Yet a Queen Bee: From "Lost your taste for yogurt?" to total social suicide at her "coming out" party, this episode gives us a glimpse of Jenny as Queen Bee — and it ain't pretty. Luckily Jenny doesn't like what she sees in herself — nothing but lying, stealing, manipulating, and desperate clawing — and gives Blair her formal resignation from being solely obsessed with the four Gs: guys, girlfriends, and Gossip Girl. Back home at the Humphrey loft, Rufus and D will always let her back into the fold. Hopefully Little J can find some middle ground at Constance so she won't have to stay who she is now, the very person she said she didn't want to be in the very first episode: a girl without any friends.

The Original Gossipverse: After saying Jenny is just infatuated with Asher and not in love, Vanessa calls Dan out for falling in love with Serena after "one glance at a ninth grade birthday party." In the books, Dan also falls in love with Serena after she attends the only party he's ever thrown, in the ninth grade. (In the first book and the prequel, the party was in eighth grade, but most of the books call it ninth. Consistency, conschmistency.) In *Only in Your Dreams*, Serena falls for the leading man in the remake of *Breakfast at Tiffany's*. (S plays the Audrey role. For real.) They go on a date but then she finds out he's gay and was using her as a very public cover-up. Unlike J, there's no humiliation and S has the self-confidence not to be too upset. In *I Like it Like That*, Jenny's boyfriend is hiding a secret from her: he's not gay, he led her to believe he was rich when really he's poor, his parents are elderly, he's an *actual* dog-walker, and his house smells like popcorn. Ew. The Sparks family backstory is a bit more depressing in the books: Georgina's father is dead and her mother lives in Barbados, but G lives in a big old empty house in Connecticut.

That's How It's Done in *The O.C.*: In "The Secret" in season 1, Luke's dad is outed.

All About My Mother (*Todo sobre mi madre*, dir. Pedro Almodóvor, 1999): The mother is Manuela (Cecilia Roth) whose son Esteban dies on his 18th birthday, the night they see a production of *A Streetcar Named Desire* starring Huma Rojo (Marisa Paredes). In mourning, Manuela goes looking for the boy's father, a transvestite whom he never knew, but she only finds that the father has impregnated a young nun Hermana (Penélope Cruz), so she takes her under her wing. Working for Huma as she plays Blanche DuBois, Manuela mimics the actions of Eve Harrington of *All About Eve*, but without malice or self-interest, before giving her assistant role over to Agrado (Antonia San Juan), an old friend and transvestite prostitute. The film draws heavily on the culturally ingrained characters of Margo Channing, Eve Harrington, Blanche DuBois, and Stella Kowalski, but inverts them, toying with traditional ideas of gender, motherhood, and friendships between women.

Cleverly tying together the Blair vs. Jenny plot with Eric being pushed out of the closet, "All About My Brother" also inverts the Margo/Eve dynamic, with Jenny giving up her battle to be queen, something Eve Harrington would never do. And as both Serena and Eric lay bare a huge secret they have been harboring, they are buoyed by the unwavering support of those closest to them, like Manuela, Huma, Hermana, and Agrado have for each other.

Welcome to the Real World:

- In the opening Met steps scene, there's a big banner for the Gustave Courbet exhibit, which ran until May 18, just shortly after this episode aired.
- Little J as the next Brooke Astor? The thrice-married New York City aristocrat (1902–2007) wrote four books about her life and marriages and was known for her philanthropy, famously quipping, "Money is like manure. It should be spread around."
- The book "Sarah" is reading at Communitea is *NFT (Not For Tourists)*, a guide to New York City for all kinds of city dwellers: the newly arrived, the long-time residents, and the up-to-no-good fakers.
- Naturally, Lily would use all the top wedding people in Manhattan: Mark Ingram (who makes a cameo) at the atelier, Sylvia Weinstock for the cake, and Preston Bailey as the event designer.
- Lily instructs her assistant to seat Eliot Spitzer, recently disgraced former Governor of New York, as far away from Serena as possible. Spitzer resigned from office after being linked to a prostitution ring in March 2007.

- Vanessa Hudgens and Katie Holmes are both subjected to rumors that their relationships with Zac Efron and Tom Cruise, respectively, are covers and that their boys are gay.
- Dan doesn't know of one of the most famous Manhattan socialites: he looks bewildered when Blair makes a Tinsley Mortimer reference.
- Madonna and Britney locked lips at the 2003 MTV VMAs during a performance of "Like a Virgin," causing a bigger ruckus than the news of Asher and Eric's kiss.

Locations:

- After destroying Jenny's party, B suggests plans to the girls for the next night: dinner at Graydon Carter's The Waverly Inn (16 Bank St) and drinks at 151 (151 Rivington St).

Oops: Wouldn't Gossip Girl's minions have spotted the Return of Georgina Sparks and tipped her off? And since Dan reads Gossip Girl, he would know that sweet Sarah is actually evil Georgie. Seems like Gossip Girl is only all-knowing when it's convenient for the plot. (Unless Georgina *is* Gossip Girl. . . .)

The Look: For the showdown on the steps, Jenny opts for a yellow Michael Kors trench (like B's yellow trench last episode; biting her style much, Little J?), blue glitter Stacey Lapidus headband, Hue fishnets, dulled silver flats, and a fuchsia Foley + Corinna mid city tote. Blair is armed with a Foley + Corinna Jetsetter Jr. bag in Riverstone, Tory Burch Kitty Wedge shoes, a navy-and-white Rag & Bone exclusive cropped Mac trench, and red Zephyr tights to match her candy-cane-striped headband. Serena comes to school in a Tory Burch shrunken Sgt Pepper jacket and Marc by Marc Jacobs sweater vest with nude Loeffler Randall Olivia D-Ring flat boots and Katherine Kwei Donna knotted lambskin tote. At Asher's party, the fashion is totally lacking — Unity boys apparently only wear ugly plaid patchwork shirts. Jenny looks lovely in lavender wearing a Blugirl spring 2008 dress and Stacey Lapidus silk headband with a vintage clover brooch. She admits defeat with a Marc by Marc Jacobs building block hoodie and a Foley + Corinna glazed leather city tote along for moral support. Blair crashes (and destroys) J's party looking classic in a rhinestone-collared black Foley + Corinna dress. Serena's wearing a silver

Gryphon mini-tent jacket and Gemma Redux Lariat necklace when she finds out Sarah is Georgina.

Music: "Good to Be Alive" by Joey Sykes is playing at Communitea when Vanessa and Sarah chat. Lily is on her way out of the Palace and bumps into Rufus to "Cheap and Cheerful" by The Kills. At Mark Ingram Atelier, the Allegro from Beethoven's "Sonata No. 5 in F Major" is playing. The van der Woodsen dinner discussion is to OneRepublic's "Say (All I Need)." Asher's party kicks off with "Paralyzer" (Finger Eleven). Serena goes to talk to Dan and meets Georgina-as-Sarah to "U.R.A. Fever" by The Kills. Penelope and Hazel talk to J about losing her virginity to "Shut Up and Let Me Go" (The Ting Tings).

Jesse Swenson as Asher Hornsby

An ensemble member of the Broadway production of *Spring Awakening*, Jesse was the understudy for the lead role of Melchior Gabor and studied theater at the Boston Conservatory. His band, Bubble & Squeak, released its first album in February 2008, *Dansing Is an Emotion*. *Gossip Girl* was his first onscreen role, but coming up are roles in *Army Wives* and the film *Fade to White*.

"Just because you tell the truth doesn't mean there won't be consequences."

1.17 woman on the verge

Original air date: May 12, 2008
Written by: Joshua Safran
Directed by: Tony Wharmby
Guest cast: Stephen Kunken (Journalist), Elan Moss-Bachrach (Pete Fairman), Robert Sella (Claude), Craig Walker (Roadie), Rachelle Wintzen (Girl)

With Serena in crisis, Blair enlists the help of Nate, Chuck, and even Lily. Rufus's Spotlight on the '90s concert provides a venue for Georgina to dupe Dan and for Lily to sow her wild oats one last time before her wedding.

Turns out the answer to why Serena left Manhattan was way darker than simply sleeping with her best friend's boyfriend. After the incredible "I killed someone" moment at the end of the last episode, Serena's definition of "kill" turns out to be more than a bit liberal. Witnessing a guy overdose and then seeing his corpse taken out of the hotel would be totally traumatic. Feeling in some way responsible, completely understandable. But only on TV would someone think of what happened as Serena killing Pete Fairman. The plot point highlights how much of a soap opera *Gossip Girl* is, but at least it's only Serena who sees her actions as murderous. Even with the leeway of Serena's flair for the dramatic and the fact that she's been sitting on this secret for a year, stewing in her guilt, *and* is only 17, the reveal was a letdown.

Last episode Jenny was kicked out of the inner circle, and this week Dan gets the boot, with the old gang (the non-judging Breakfast Club) keeping him away. But only Serena herself can make him stop asking questions, and she opts for a lie over the truth. No matter what the problem, or who is pissed with whom, Blair, Nate, Chuck, and Serena will stick by each other. And the same goes for Lily with Serena. Lily chooses being a mother over being a bride and helps her daughter overcome her worst problem yet, recognizing that S has been living her life with "care, compassion, and respect." It's about time, Lil! The advice she gives Serena in the limo — that you can either smash into a problem or adjust and go around it to move forward in life — becomes a literal choice for her when Rufus stands in her way. Her choice to smash into Rufus and make out with him? Awesome.

Less than awesome is Dan's inability to recognize that Georgina is all kinds of bad news. C'mon Humphrey, she is wearing way too much dark eye makeup and black nail polish. That spells evil on the Upper East Side.

"I'm Chuck Bass."
— C doesn't bother to detail his wrongdoings when three words say so very, very much

JTLYK:

- Off in Hudson this week: Little J. She can't do a semester in France but she can get out of town.
- Top story on Gossip Girl: "*Trouble In Paradise?* Is the honeymoon over for our famous lovebirds? They've recently been spotted arguing on several occasions. What's the deal? Did Serena finally wake up and realize she was dating Lonely Boy? Is Dan totally fed up with Serena's recent wild girl actions? We hope they'll bounce back from this rough patch because, surprisingly, Gossip Girl thinks they're a pretty cute couple (even though he's from, ugh, Brooklyn.)"
- Rufus and Dan mention a few Lincoln Hawk songs: "Track Me Down," "Something Like That" (which was in "Dare Devil"), and of course "Everytime."
- The elevator ride was as awkward as it was full of Gossip Boy hotness. Oh Chuck and Nate, when will you be besties again?
- The *New York Post* story Rufus didn't want to see: "*Beauty Bags Bass: Wedding of the Year Tomorrow.*"
- The housecoat Serena is wearing at Blair's is the same one that B was wearing when they planned the masked ball in "The Handmaiden's Tale."
- Blair tells Serena they're the non-judging Breakfast Club. John Hughes' 1985 *The Breakfast Club* is about five teenagers stuck in Saturday detention who realize there's more to a person than a stereotype.
- If S left the Shepherd wedding wearing Nate's tuxedo shirt, WTF was *he* wearing?
- Like mother, like daughter. Lily is keeping secrets from Bart and being elusive like Serena is with Dan. Both van der Woodsen women enlist the help of Chuck Bass when they need some recon done.
- Lily needs a Pam Beasley to her Michael Scott to screen her conversations

with her children: her second take is always better. With Eric in "All About My Brother" and with Serena in this episode.

Secrets & Lies:

- Rufus tells Dan that the reason why Serena won't tell him the "whole truth" may be because he can be so judgmental.
- That *Rolling Stone* journalist has done his research. He knows about the Rufly relationship that she'd kept secret, at least from her children.
- S lies to Dan about sleeping with random dudes instead of telling him the truth.
- Serena finally tells Blair, Chuck, and Nate the secret she's been carrying with her for the past year.

"and who am i?"

While it may be the one secret she'll never tell, the question "Who is Gossip Girl?" is asked at the beginning of every episode. Her identity was never revealed in the book series, with Cecily von Ziegesar commenting, "Originally the books were going to be this unfolding mystery about figuring out who Gossip Girl is, but then the characters' stories took over. And that became a behind-the-scenes mystery that didn't really matter anymore." Stephanie Savage gave an equally vague response to the question, saying with a laugh, "We are all 'Gossip Girl.' We all feed that chain, participating in that circle and circus of information, whether we want to admit it or not." From the first episode of the show, it became clear that while Gossip Girl has agency in the plot and affects the lives of these characters (spreading information, encouraging characters to take action, ruining Blair's birthday party), she's a narrative device. Period. She has the omniscient ability to see and know things no army of cell-phones-in-hands gossipmongers could tell her.

Exhibit A: in the pilot episode, Gossip Girl instantly knows that Blair and Serena have had a falling out before the girls have even talked to each other — Nate's told Blair about the Shepherd wedding, and Chuck has confronted S, but the rest of the world has no way of knowing. Ah, but what if one of *them* is Gossip Girl? On to exhibit B: when Blair and Chuck start making out at the end of "Seventeen Candles," Gossip Girl calls Chuck "the gift that keeps on giving." (Ha ha! Ew.) How does she know they've hooked up before and are hooking up again? In the next episode's home page story, she's back to not knowing ("What did Serena see?"). Gossip Girl is used well and to the writers' convenience to provide snarky commentary and truisms, to drive the plot, and to raise the stakes, but let's all cross our fingers that her identity is never revealed. It would be like asking the audience to pay no attention to the writers behind the curtain.

- Lily only watches half of the video and judges S harshly, despite hearing Georgina say Serena won't know she's being filmed.
- Straight-shooter Nate reveals to Vanessa that Sarah is not to be trusted and is actually Georgina.
- Vanessa — "not a big fan of liars" — gives Georgina the opportunity to tell the truth, but G passes.
- Georgina lies to Dan, telling him a would-be-moving-if-it-were-true story about a stalking, abusive ex-boyfriend.
- When S asks B why she's at the '90s concert, she halfheartedly lies, "I'm a big Leaky Hawk fan?"
- Georgina pretends that her threatening call to Serena was actually her checking in with her mom, and then takes the battery out of D's phone so they won't be interrupted by his pesky girlfriend. Evil!

The Original Gossipverse: Chuck lost his virginity to Georgina in the sixth grade, but hasn't been avoiding her in the Bookverse. In fact, he's happy to sit naked in a hot tub with her in *I Like it Like That.*

That's How It's Done in *The O.C.*: In season 1's "The Secret," Ryan, Marissa, and Seth arrive at school with Luke after the entire community learns that his dad is gay. Trying to convince him not to bail on school, each character runs through their misdeeds — Ryan's the kid from Chino who burnt down the house, Marissa's the girl who OD'd in Mexico, and Seth? "I'm Seth Cohen." Just like Serena, Marissa struggles with the guilt of not-really-killing someone, actually two someones: she puts Ryan's brother in a coma and she feels responsible for Johnny's death in season 3.

Women on the Verge of a Nervous Breakdown (*Mujeres al borde de un ataque de nervios*, dir. Pedro Almodóvor, 1988): The second Almodóvor film in a row to inspire an episode's title, *Women on the Verge . . .* is just as its name suggests — it follows Pepa (Carmen Maura) and the women around her on one particularly bad day in Madrid as they inch closer to total freakouts. Pepa's lover Ivan is leaving her; his literally crazy ex-wife Lucia is out to get Pepa; and Pepa's friend Candela is tangentially involved in a terrorist plot to take down a flight to Sweden that night. There's barbiturate-spiked gazpacho, a young and buttoned-up Antonio Banderes, a bed on fire, a few rides in the Mambo Taxi (you must see it to understand its glory), a feminist lawyer who needs to reread the definition of feminism, and more boldly colored outfits than hairbands at Constance. The film is about the crazy things done in the name of love.

Like Pepa seeking Ivan, Dan tries to find Serena while Serena, at the end of her rope, will do whatever she can to salvage her relationship with Dan — even if that means telling him a lesser-of-two-evils lie. The main parallel between the film and the episode it lends its title to lies in Blair, Chuck, and Nate rallying to help Serena when she is in crisis mode. Like their counterparts in the film, these UESers are willing to do whatever is necessary to protect each other.

Locations:

- Serena left her phone at 1Oak (453 W 17th St).
- Serena's bad girl past includes making out with investment bankers at P.J. Clarke's (915 Third Ave).
- Not surprisingly, the writers chose a fictional hotel, the Eastview, for the setting of the teenage-sex-tape-drug-overdose scene.

Spotted: Queen of Cakes Sylvia Weinstock, the cake designer for the Bass–van der Woodsen wedding, is welcomed to the rehearsal dinner by Bart Bass. Lisa Loeb is host and performer at the VH1 Classics concert. Best known for the 1994 hit "Stay," Lisa continues to record and tour, has had two reality shows, *Dweezil & Lisa* and *#1 Single*, and voiced Mary Jane in MTV's *Spider-Man: The Animated Series.*

Oops: When Lily bails on her engagement party, Kelly Rutherford puts her hand on Robert John Burke's shoulder twice. As Georgina tells her tall tale of an abusive ex to Dan, Michelle Trachtenberg's hair keeps popping back and forth from behind her ear.

The Look: Blair enlists the help of C and N wearing a yellow Marc by Marc Jacobs dress from the spring/summer 2007 collection and a Jennifer Behr large bubble stud headwrap. Vanessa's concert outfit is so right for this character: a leopard print H&M sweater over a Truly Madly Deeply printed babydoll shirt, a bracelet from Forever21 along with her signature chunky gold jewelry, and her hot pink Doc Martens (which she also wore in "Desperately Seeking Serena"). At the rehearsal dinner, the bride-to-be is in a black Alberta Ferretti dress and Van Cleef & Arpels jewels. Chuck pairs an Etro bow tie with a Gianfranco Ferré suit. Both B and S wear Foley + Corinna dresses (perhaps as a sign of their solidarity?), Blair's with pearls and Jennifer Behr's Victorian crystal and silk satin headwrap and Serena's with a Burberry London gold single-breasted trench over her navy Hollywood dress.

Music: "Cities in Dust" by Junkie XL opens the episode and plays again when Lily ransacks Serena's bedroom. "Hook and Line" by The Kills plays when Pete and Serena make out, and again when Georgina kisses Dan. The Republic Tigers' "Fight Song" opens the rehearsal dinner scene. Lisa Loeb performs "Stay (I Missed You)." Rufus and the rest of Lincoln Hawk perform their awesomesauce song, "Everytime" (which is a bonus track on the official *Gossip Girl* soundtrack, *OMFGG*).

"Dearly beloved, we are gathered here today to watch this man and this woman totally eff things up."

1.18 much 'i do' about nothing

Original air date: May 19, 2008
Written by: Josh Schwartz, Stephanie Savage
Directed by: Norman Buckley
Guest cast: Lydia Hearst (Amelia), Candy Buckley (Mrs. Sparks), Mark La Mura (Mr. Sparks), Chad Brigockas (Shady-Looking Guy), Zack Conroy (Ben Simmons), Charles Gemmill (Justice of the Peace), Robert Sella (Claude)

Time for the wedding of the season, but Lily has a choice to make — Bart or Rufus? Serena and Dan are left in the wake of Georgina Sparks.

Ah, nothing like waking up on the day of your wedding in bed with a person you're not marrying. The morning of the Bass–van der Woodsen wedding is the Morning After, not just for Lily and Rufus but Georgina and Dan (who, I'm assuming, went to third) and Blair and Chuck (who just cuddled).

Who among our beloved GGers can let past wrongs or past loves go and who can't get past the past? Using an extended real estate metaphor like only a real estate mogul would, Bart asks Lily to let go of Rufus, a relic from her youth. She agrees, choosing to move on instead of rebuilding the past. Serena wants to hold on to what she has with Dan, but he can't get over the insanity of the past few months and lets her go. In a moment of rare insight, Captain Archibald gives good advice to his son and Chuck: life's too short not to forgive each other. The Captain's bad behavior ends up bringing the boys back together. And Chuck's two for two: his speech about perseverance and forgiveness wins back Blair, who forgives (but doesn't forget) the Arabian horse comparison. But the glee of seeing Chuck and Blair happy is short-lived (of course): Bartholomew "Buzzkill" Bass has to put a damper on Chuck's hots

for B with a speech about his son learning responsibility, sacrifice, faithfulness, and compassion from Blair. Bart is officially the cooler of lust on the Upper East Side, taking out Rufly and Chair in one day.

A satisfying season ender, but one that had no real hope of living up to the excitement of "All About My Brother" or "Woman on the Verge." The summer ahead promises new flames and foes: Vanessa has her eye on Dan, Nate and Serena are summering together, Chuck's ditched B for Amelia, B's already found a friend in the Bass Industries marketing department, Rufus is on the road, Lily's a newlywed, and Jenny will be spending the summer interning with Eleanor Waldorf.

"Haven't you heard? I'm the crazy bitch around here."
— Blair Waldorf FTW!

JTLYK:

- Top story on Gossip Girl: "*That isn't Serena!!* Um, do I need to get my eyes checked because that totally doesn't look like Serena. If I didn't know any better I'd say the mystery girl Dan is kissing looks like, dare I say it, Georgina Sparks? WTF is Dan doing? And where the hell is Serena? Well, I wouldn't put something like this past Georgina. She is totally crazy."
- When Rufus wakes up in bed with Lily, check out his tattoos. On one arm the bird is carrying a banner that reads "Jenny," and on the other, "Daniel." Aw.
- Even if frenemies are in enemy mode, they help each other when it really matters. Chuck makes sure Nate knows Captain A is being sketchy, just like the gang rallied around Serena in "Woman on the Verge."
- Chuck tells Blair that she doesn't belong with Nate, "never have, never will," distorting her love-for-Nate catchphrase, "always have, always will."
- Note to Dan and Vanessa: maybe move the original works of art a few feet away from where you're repainting the gallery walls.

Secrets & Lies:

- On the phone with Bart, Lily doesn't mention she's in bed with Rufus. But Bart seems to know about her lingering affection for Rufus.
- Captain A tells Nate his lawyers are positive about the trial's outcome

(not true) and that the phone call is from his sponsor (also not true).

- Serena finally tells Dan everything. But she won't let Dan tell her what happened with Georgina, feeding him a cover story instead.
- Dan and Blair plot against Georgina, and B declares, "Humphrey, you are a born liar!"
- Dan can't not tell Serena about what he did with Georgina. Points for being honest, Dan. But dude, choose your moment. Seconds before she walks down the aisle in her mother's wedding is *not the right time*.
- Captain A tells Nate he was hiding the truth to protect him.
- Dan can't forgive Serena's lies and omissions.
- Chuck lies to Blair about why he's missing the flight.

Scrap!: Serena is totally ready to kick Georgina's ass, but Dan steps in. Nate finally gets to punch Captain A-hole, getting him back for the totally undeserved clocking in "Victor, Victrola." (Thank you, Josh and Stephanie.) Blair kicks Chuck in the shins with her rather pointy shoes. Ouch.

by any other name . . .

Gossip Girl hearts nicknames, but she isn't the only one. The *GG*ers were also known as:

Dan: Lonely Boy (Gossip Girl), The Invisible Man (Jenny), Cabbage Patch (Blair), Brooklyn (Gossip Girl), Global-Warming Grinch (Serena), Humphrey Dumpty (Chuck), Squeaky-clean Humphrey (Blair), Virgin (Blair)
Jenny: Little J (Gossip Girl), Little Humphrey (Blair), Jen (Dan), Cinderella (Blair), Queen Wannabe (Gossip Girl)
Serena: It Girl (Gossip Girl), Uptown Express (Gossip Girl), Princess (Chuck), Serena Second Edition (Georgina)
Blair: Queen B (Gossip Girl), Blair Bear (Harold), Virgin Queen (Gossip Girl), Snow White (Georgina), Snow-Not-So-White (Eric)
Eric: Blond Mini Chuck (Blair)
Lily: Lily von Bülow (Chuck)
Carter Baizen: Sasquatch (Chuck), Matthew McConaughey Between Movies (Chuck)
Georgina: Whore-gina (Chuck)
Vanessa: Michael Moore (Blair), Docu-Girl (Chuck), Punky Brewster (Chuck)
Chuck: Charles (Lily), Mistake So Far in My Past I Barely Remember (Blair)
Nate: Nathaniel (Chuck), Socrates (Chuck), Man Bangs (Dan)

The Original Gossipverse: We learn that Georgie sold her prized show jumper, Guns'n'Roses, for coke in *Because I'm Worth It*.

That's How It's Done in *The O.C.*: In "The Anger Management," resident schemer Julie Cooper-Nichol shuts down Charlotte and her season 3 con, telling her there's only room for one manipulative bitch in Newport. Julie Cooper gives us two wedding inspirations for Lily and Bart's nuptials: she married Caleb, the proto-Bart, in the season 1 finale, and she has to choose between stability and wealth (Bullit) and love (Frank) in the series finale. The CW marketing team had a bit of cheeky crossover fun: on the wedding website created for Lily and Bart, one of the guest RSVP notes was from Kirsten Cohen promising she and Sandy would be in attendance.

Much Ado About Nothing (dir. Kenneth Branagh, 1993): The *Gossip Girl* writers couldn't have picked a better finale title for an episode that serves for the season as the final scenes of a Shakespearian comedy do for the play — villains punished, ruses revealed, matches made. Shakespeare's turn-of-the-17th-century comedy about love, marriage, jealousy, and scheming was adapted for the screen by Kenneth Branagh right around the peak of Lincoln Hawk's popularity. After the prince, Don Pedro (Denzel Washington), and his men arrive at Leonato's place in Sicily, Claudio (Robert Sean Leonard) falls for Hero (Kate Beckinsale), daughter to Leonato (Richard Briers), and Don Pedro agrees to woo her on Claudio's behalf at the masked dance. The evil brother of the prince, Don John (Keanu Reeves), first tricks Claudio into thinking Don Pedro is taking Hero for himself, and after that fails, he deceives Claudio and Don Pedro into thinking virginal Hero is a fornicator! Claudio completely loses it at his wedding to Hero, cruelly accusing and rejecting her. A plot is hatched to pretend Hero has died of shame while her father, priest, and cousin try to clear her good name. That's just one of the plotlines. Another concerns cousin Beatrice (Emma Thompson), a sharp-witted unmarried woman who is determined to stay a maiden, and Benedick (Kenneth Branagh), a man who has no use for love but only for making merry and trading barbs with Beatrice. Don Pedro schemes with the rest of the characters to trick Beatrice and Benedick into thinking each loves the other, hoping they will marry when Hero and Claudio do. And as with all Shakespearian comedies, *Much Ado About Nothing* ends with a wedding (make that two), a song, and a dance.

Chuck and Blair are the direct descendants of Benedick and Beatrice: barbed dialogue, sparking chemistry, and an audience rooting for the unlikely couple to realize they love each other. And just as Beatrice asks Benedick to kill Claudio for destroying Hero (her BFF), Blair wants punishment for Georgina, the person who wronged Serena (but in our modern times, a woman can destroy her enemy herself). By the end of "Much 'I Do,'" Nate and Chuck are pals once again, like the once-estranged Claudio and Don Pedro. If only the boys had read their Shakespeare, they would know: "Friendship is constant in all other things / Save in the office and affairs of love."

Welcome to the Real World:

- Lincoln Hawk is hitting the road with The Breeders, who released *Mountain Battles* in 2008; Luscious Jackson announced in 2006 that they were getting back together after a six-year break, and released a greatest hits album in 2007.
- Captain A promises to watch the Yankees game with Nate; on May 21, 2008, pitcher Joba Chamberlain helped land an 8–0 victory. It's off by two days but we can pretend this is the game the Captain meant.

The production team brought in hanging wisteria, ficus trees, and, of course, lilies to the Design Museum's garden to make everything perfect for Lily's fourth wedding.

the devil's in the details: season 1 stats

- 7 of 12 parents are AWOL.
- Characters make unexpected pop-bys 34 times.
- Breakfast at the Humphreys is shown 8 times.
- Blair rolls her eyes 11 times (but you know she's rolling them off-camera too).
- There are 7 must-attend events of the season.
- Serena and Lily have 6 arguments.
- Chuck wears 9 bow ties.
- Dan wears 5 vests.
- The students are shown in class zero times. (Assembly and field hockey practice don't count!)
- Chuck has sex with 6 ladies (that we know about).
- Not including when she talks about herself, "Gossip Girl" is said 22 times.
- Blair wears 36 different hairbands.

- Georgina says she lasted longer in rehab than Lohan. Lindsay stayed at the Cirque Lodge Treatment Center in Utah from August to October 2007, after a six-week stint at Promises led to a relapse and an arrest in July.
- Jenny's internship with Eleanor Waldorf Designs is through Parsons The New School for Design, which runs a Pre-College Academy program for high school aged students.
- As B packs for her trip, she has a Bluefly bag on her bed. Bluefly.com offers a "shop their closet" feature for *Gossip Girl* characters.
- Chuck calls Vanessa "Punky Brewster," the title character from the '80s sitcom about a spirited, hardscrabble brunette orphan.

Locations:
- Bart Bass meets Lily at the first building he ever bought, 105 Chambers Street.
- The van der Woodsen–Bass nuptials take place at Cooper-Hewitt, National Design Museum (2 E 91st St).
- In case you want to send Lonely Boy or Little J a postcard, their mailing address is 455 Water St., #6, Brooklyn, NY, 11211.

Spotted: Sylvia Weinstock is a guest at the wedding. Lydia Hearst plays Amelia, Lily's interior decorating assistant. Great-granddaughter to William

Randolph Heart, Lydia is a model/heiress/actor/fashion designer/former *Page Six Magazine* columnist. "I am all business, I am all work," Lydia told *The Observer*. "You have to take it seriously — this is a world that will eat you up and spit you out faster than you know what hit you, and you need to stay ahead of the game and you need to understand that it's not all about the parties."

The Look: The last outfit on Georgina Sparks is a Marc by Marc Jacobs demi sheer gray blouse, black Urban Outfitters lux pleated bustle back skirt, a black YaYa Aflalo Dallas leather jacket with an ASOS beaded rosary necklace. (For rosaries on bad girls precedent, please see *Cruel Intentions*.) Blair's hair and outfit when she takes down Georgina are magnificent: Marc by Marc Jacobs Flock of Hearts print top with Diane von Furstenberg's Bitiri jacket in Island Clover green, a yellow Gucci Hysteria bag (which Georgina has in python), and Stuart Weitzman Loopy pumps. On to the main event: the wedding of the season. Lily wears a Vera Wang gown; her maid of honor S is in a yellow tiered floral Fillipa dress from Ralph Lauren's spring 2008 collection set off by black accents; B's Collette Dinnigan peony print silk lam halter dress perfectly accompanies her bestie's outfit without getting too

Kristen Bell as Gossip Girl

We may never find out Gossip Girl's identity, but we know who adds that sassy narration to the show as the voice of the blogger: Kristen Bell. After a string of smallish roles in TV shows, films, and movies-of-the-week, Kristen came into mainstream popularity playing the titular character on *Veronica Mars*, which she starred in (and narrated) for three seasons. After our favorite girl detective was taken from our screens prematurely (I am still angry with you, CW), Kristen starred in 2008's *Forgetting Sarah Marshall* as Sarah Marshall, and played Elle in seasons 2 and 3 of *Heroes*. With talk of a *Veronica Mars* movie and other projects on the go, Kristen has no shortage of work but that likely won't include an onscreen turn on *Gossip Girl*. She told the *CW Source*, "I'll leave everything up to Mr. Schwartz, but I doubt it." And while Kristen admits that like everyone, she gossips, she doesn't delight in it the same way that her "gossipy internet voice" does: if you gossip, "hopefully you feel guilty about it."

matchy-matchy. Blair finishes her look, as always, with a Jennifer Behr patent orchid on a skinny headband and Lover shoes by Stuart Weitzman. Then there's the unfortunate Vanessa wearing J's latest creation, which can only be described as a poofy orange Creamsicle mess. (And did Little J also make hair extensions for Vanessa? Thankfully V's hair is back to normal in the coda scenes.) At the end of the episode, Serena and Nate run into each other and S is in a Christian Cota capelet, Alexander Wang gray tank, Wrangler jeans, and has a Chanel executive bag. Blair arrives at the heliport wearing the Captain dress by Bettie Page Clothing, Yves Saint Laurent Escarpen shoes, an Eric Javits squishee cap in natural/black, and a red vintage Louis Vuitton Cannes bag. The one style note to keep with you over the break between seasons: Chuck wears his signature scarf during sex. Of course he does. He's Chuck Bass.

Music: The episode opens with "Beautiful World" by Carolina Liar. Georgina is trapped by Dan, Blair, and her mean parents to The Kooks' "Do You Wanna," and the song plays again at the end of the episode. The final wedding preparations are to "Time to Pretend" (MGMT). A traditionalist for her fourth wedding, Lily walks down the aisle to Wagner's "Bridal Chorus." Serena and Dan have their last dance to "The Ice Is Getting Thinner" by Death Cab for Cutie.

Questions for Season 2:

- What's the story on Serena and Eric's dad? Will the elusive Mr. van der Woodsen be illuminated in season 2? Ditto for Chuck's mother — when and how did Bart Bass become a widower?
- Now that Lily has made her choice and married Bart, will Rufus find a new true love? Will he and Alison try again?
- Blair didn't take too kindly to Nate dating Vanessa. And now that that's over and Chuck is misbehaving, will the old flame reignite between Queen B and King N? Or will Serena once again stand between them? They looked mighty friendly heading into the summer break.
- Will Dan and Vanessa finally hook up?
- Has Little J learned her lesson? Is she done vying for Queen B status at Constance? Will she find a real boyfriend? Or a best friend? Or, like, *any* friends?
- Will the *Gossip* kids ever actually be seen in class?

- September will be the start of senior year for Serena, Dan, Blair, Chuck, and Nate. College decision time . . . Since Nate got Vanessa to write the SATs, does that mean she'll be tagging along to college in season 3?
- Have we seen the last of Georgina Sparks? Captain Archibald?
- Will Vanessa's sister ever make an appearance, or will we see Vanessa's apartment? Her parents or other friends? That girl is a mystery wrapped in an enigma.

season two

Recurring cast: John Patrick Amedori (Aaron Rose), Mädchen Amick (Catherine Beaton), Laura Breckenridge (Rachel Carr), Robert John Burke (Bart Bass), Yin Chang (Nelly Yuki), Margaret Colin (Eleanor Waldorf), Matt Doyle (Jonathan Henry), Tamara Feldman (Poppy Lifton), Nicole Fiscella (Isabel Coates), Armie Hammer (Gabriel Edwards), Desmond Harrington (Jack Bass), Patrick Heusinger (Marcus Beaton), Michelle Hurd (Laurel), Caroline Lagerfelt (Celia "Cece" Rhodes), Connor Paolo (Eric van der Woodsen), Amanda Setton (Penelope Shafai), Wallace Shawn (Cyrus Rose), Sebastian Stan (Carter Baizen), Zuzanna Szadkowski (Dorota), Michelle Trachtenberg (Georgina Sparks), Dreama Walker (Hazel Williams)

"Tans fade, highlights go dark, and we all get sick of sand in our shoes. But the end of summer is the beginning of a new season. So we find ourselves looking to the future . . . you ain't seen nothing yet."

2.01 summer, kind of wonderful

Original air date: September 1, 2008
Directed by: J. Miller Tobin
Written by: Joshua Safran

Guest cast: Jay McInerney (Jeremiah Harris), Paloma Guzmán (First Girl with Dan), Catherine Haena Kim (Second Girl with Dan), James Duer (Lifeguard), Ashley Cook (Chuck's Beach Girl)

As summer draws to a close, the too-exclusive-for-Jack Johnson White Party draws our lovely Upper East Siders (and Brooklynites) back together for some make-outs and fake-outs.

Like *Gossip Girl*'s freshman season, its sophomore year has a shaky start with a lot of action crammed in. Why the CW gave two-hour premieres to cycle 97 of *America's Next Top Model* and the *90210* reboot but not its "crown jewel" is a mystery. The final scenes of season 1 suggested certain characters would find themselves in love by summer's end but it was all misdirection: Nate is with a married woman, not Serena; Vanessa is in Vermont; Dan is serial dating; and Blair and the Helicopter Hottie's only ride together was on that flight. Though the show returns with the same quickfire exchanges, incredible clothes, and heartbreaking moments, this episode packs more tired or unrealistic plot devices than normal: Chuck has upgraded from twins to triplets — and they have a special nudity-allowed beach pass? Nate leaps out of a window and runs half-naked in the street *just* as Serena and the

At a real-life Vitamin Water party in the Hamptons to celebrate the premiere of season 2, it looks like Taylor Momsen needs to switch flavors from Energy to Tranquilo.

Camaro-honking townie drive by? Cece helps former enemy Dan because her entire belief system and personality went into remission with her cancer? Dan catches Serena and Nate kissing for the first time in two years? Two of the girls Dan's seeing happen to be at the same party, talk to each other about *Dan*, and confront him at the precise moment when he's judging Serena? Convenient!

But what saved "Summer, Kind of Wonderful" was the two epic relationships. From an outsider's perspective, Dan and Serena getting back together is a terrible idea: they haven't worked through any of their issues and he's still leaping to judgments without realizing his own hypocrisy. When they broke up in "Much 'I Do,'" Dan said he didn't know how to make things go back to the way they were. Well, by not dealing with any of their issues, they'll be sure to go back to the way things were when they were bad. But for now who cares if they're doomed to repeat relationship history — Serena's had a long lonely summer, they have amazing chemistry, and the two of them look impossibly hot in their White Party outfits. (Once Dan's jacket is off. Ahem.)

As the summer ends, the *Gossip* characters are keen to make amends for the wrongs of the past year. Jenny apologizes to Eric for being awful to him last spring. Cece's actions to help Dan win back Serena show her remorse for her "Hi, Society" sabotage. At the Jitney with a bouquet of yellow roses as a peace offering, Chuck is ready to apologize for abandoning Blair. Blair is making apologies of her own to James/Marcus for using him, and he pledges honesty in return. And Chuck's appeal to Blair to stay with him and not go with Marcus is heartbreaking. But not enough.

"Three words. Eight letters. Say it and I'm yours."
— Blair gives Chuck one more chance

JTLYK:

- MIA for the season premiere: Vanessa escaped to Vermont to hang with her parents. Lily and Bart Bass are apparently still honeymooning.
- The opening scene of Nate and Catherine making out in the car evokes Nate and Serena's epic session at the Shepherd wedding.
- Gossip Girl's blast about B's return reads: "SPOTTED: Blair Waldorf at CDG, claiming her premiere space in L'Espace Parisien a whole week early. Now what could make Queen B abandon her two dads and come

home une minute before Labor Day? I have a million questions, but I bet Chuck Bass is the answer to all of them . . ."

- The passage Jeremiah Harris reads from *Pacific Standard Time* may be Dan's favorite, but it's actually from Jay McInerney's *Bright Lights, Big City*: "'Things happen, people change,' is what Amanda said. For her that covered it. You wanted an explanation, an ending that would assign blame and dish up justice. You considered violence and you considered reconciliation. But what you are left with is a premonition of the way your life will fade behind you, like a book you have read too quickly, leaving a dwindling trail of images and emotions, until all you can remember is a name." The central character of the book cannot overcome the end of his marriage, much like Dan, floundering in the wake of his breakup with S, unsuccessfully tries to distract himself.
- D's unwritten story is titled "5.19.08," the day he and Serena broke up (also the air date of season 1's finale).
- At the beginning of last season, in the kitchen at the Palace, Chuck told Serena how they were more alike than she'd care to admit. In this episode, he says the same thing to Blair. Both girls are repulsed by the suggestion, but more than a little scared it's true.
- Chuck has been hurt by the "heart on the sleeve" pendant before. In "Hi, Society," he overhears Blair refusing to take it back from Nate.
- Serena takes a page from the Rufus School of Manipulation. He pulled the same make-'em-jealous strategy in "The Handmaiden's Tale," kissing Lily to help her win back Bart Bass.

Secrets & Lies:

- Serena and Nate pretend they're dating to cover up his affair with a mystery woman.
- Catherine is cheating on her husband.
- Serena catches Nate fleeing a rendezvous and discovers he's seeing Catherine.
- Dan lies to Jeremiah Harris, saying his story is done and just needs a polish when he doesn't have anything more than a title.
- D is at least a two-timer; according to his little sister, he's dating a new girl every night.
- Blair uses James to make Chuck jealous. Though Chuck sees through her ruse, he's still hurt by it.

- Blair lies to Chuck, telling him she gave James her heart pendant.
- Chuck can tell when Blair is lying because her eyes do "that thing where they don't match [her] mouth."
- Cece tells Dan that Serena has just been pretending to be over him, but she really still loves him.
- Serena kisses Nate to make Catherine jealous.
- James figures out Blair's charade before revealing that he too has been lying. He pretended to be someone else because girls always want him for his title, not for him.

Scrap!: Dan gets a double shot of Vitamin Water on Grandpa Rhodes' suit when his two-timing ways are revealed.

You'll B a Woman Soon: Blair comes home from her vacation with one goal in mind: prove to Chuck Bass that she's moved on. Of course, in truth she hasn't. From the moment she steps off the Jitney and sees Chuck waiting for her, Blair uses James as a prop in her play of contentment. Hurt and humiliated when he stood her up at the beginning of the summer, she tries to hurt him in the same way. Haven't you heard, B? An eye for an eye makes the whole world blind.

The Original Gossipverse: Blair dates Lord Marcus in *Nothing Can Keep Us Together*, and he gives her a Bulgari "B" necklace like the one Blair describes to Serena in this episode (but actually got from her father). Dan has a literary internship that he sucks at in *I Like it Like That* and is a two-timer (with Bree and Vanessa) in *Only in Your Dreams. Would I Lie to You* takes place in the Hamptons — Nate is the one who dates a townie, but he's also avoiding the advances of an older woman (his coach's wife). Serena and Blair throw colorful cocktails on their doppelgänger at an all-white party. There's another all-white party, thrown by the lead singer of The Raves, in *Nobody Does it Better.*

Some Kind of Wonderful (dir. Howard Deutch, 1987): Written and produced by John Hughes, this teen flick covers a lot of the same territory as the earlier *Pretty in Pink* — romance that crosses the class and clique divide, a pair of quirky outsider besties (one of whom loves the other), and the realization that not all popular kids are jerks (just most of them). Aspiring artist

Keith (Eric Stoltz) comes from a working-class family; has a part-time job at the gas station; a best friend, Watts (Mary Stuart Masterson), who's a drum-playing tomboy; and a crush on hot girl Amanda Jones (Lea Thompson), who's dating a rich popular jerk Hardy Jenns (Craig Sheffer). Secretly in love with Keith herself, Watts warns him to stay away from the "big money, cruel-heart society that spits on" everyone else, but Keith asks Amanda out anyway, and she agrees. (Her boyfriend is cheating on her.) Amanda may hang out with the rich crowd but she's not wealthy herself, and when she dumps Jenns, her friends dump her. After Keith's little sister overhears Jenns planning to beat Keith up at his party on Saturday night, the little sis tells Keith that Amanda's in on the "joke," that the date is just a setup to humiliate him and beat him up. With the help of Watts and the school's tough guys, Keith takes Amanda on an elaborate, romantic date (including an awkward scene in a posh restaurant like the one with Dan and Serena in "Dare Devil") to prove he's not a "nothing," and he gives her a pair of diamond earrings bought with his life savings. After a confrontation at Jenns' party where the nice guy dresses down the prick, Keith and Amanda leave triumphant. But he's realized he loves Watts, not Amanda. Seeing that, Amanda gives him back the earrings and says she's going to stand on her own instead of leaning on a boy. Keith chases after Watts and gives her the earrings, saying she looks good wearing "his future."

Like the film's trio, Chuck, Blair, and Marcus find themselves in a love triangle. Like Watts watching Keith on his date with Amanda but keeping painfully quiet about her feelings, Chuck knows he's the right one for Blair but is too scared to tell her that he loves her. When Keith confronts Amanda about being in on the joke, she justly calls him a hypocrite right back. They mislead and use each other just as Blair and Marcus do, building their relationship on half-truths and full-on lies.

Welcome to the Real World:

- Serena has spent her summer watching *The Closer*, the award-winning TNT crime drama starring Kyra Sedgwick. Its fourth season premiered on July 14, 2008.
- Noah Shapiro (not a real person) from the long-running literary magazine *The Paris Review* looks forward to receiving Dan's story. Jay McInerney's first published story was in *The Paris Review,* and that story later became the opening chapter of *Bright Lights, Big City*.

- "What's a Jitney?" asks Chuck Bass. The Hampton Jitney, which Blair arrives on, has been shuttling New Yorkers out to the Hamptons since the '70s.
- Blair's favorite movies all star Audrey Hepburn: 1961's *Breakfast at Tiffany's*, 1953's *Roman Holiday*, and 1957's *Funny Face*. But B has no love for 1963's *Charade.*

Locations:

- The Upper East Siders are summering in East Hampton, but the Hamptons scenes were filmed in Roslyn, New York.
- Jeremiah Harris is reading at the Housing Works Bookstore and Café (1126 Crosby St).
- One of Dan's girls said she attended a symposium at the 92nd Street Y on the Upper East Side.

- Chuck tells Serena he's going to the Lily Pond (44 Three Mile Harbor Rd) with the Beach Triplets.
- Serena's been ordering in from Della Femina (99 North Main St, East Hampton), not Nick and Toni's (136 North Main St, East Hampton).
- Blair tells Serena she could only think of the Chuck Basstard while staying at the Hotel du Cap, the famous hotel on the French Riveira.
- Dan gets fired by Harris, who's drinking and writing at Puck Fair (298 LaFayette St).
- The White Party was held at The Villa at Chestnut Hill in Upper Brookville, New York; it neighbors the Planting Fields Arboretum State Historical Park in Oyster Bay where other Hamptons scenes were filmed.
- Nate and Catherine will continue their affair back in the city at the Mercer Hotel (147 Mercer St).

Spotted: Jay McInerney plays Jeremiah Harris, Dan's favorite author and his boss for the summer. After the publication of *Bright Lights, Big City* in 1984, McInerney was named by the *Village Voice* as one of a "literary brat pack," which also included Bret Easton Ellis. McInerney has published 12 books. Of *Gossip Girl*, McInerney told *New York*'s Daily Intel, "It's my daughter Maisie's favorite show, and I got kind of hooked myself last season. In fact, I'd actually read a couple of the novels when they came out years ago." Tinsley Mortimer, a guest at the Vitamin Water White Party, loves Little J's dress and is pals with Lily van der Woodsen. A regular on society pages, Mortimer is a famous Manhattan socialite who designs handbags and clothing for Samantha Thavasa.

The Look: Catherine makes out with Nate in a Diane von Furstenberg Pelego tie-dye wrap dress. Serena hits the beach in an unflattering YaYa Aflalo Sparrow tunic, Kate Spade Anguilla Venice Basket bag, and a red coral Ronni Simon crochet bracelet. With summer blonde highlights, Blair steps off the Jitney with green Salvatore Ferragamo bag in hand wearing a Lorick floral print blouse, Vera Wang silk shorts, teal L. Erickson headband, red Gabriela de la Vega bracelet, and Delman Sacha heels in navy. Lounging by the pool, B's swimsuit is Ferragamo, her flip-flops are Te Casan, and her bracelet is CC Skye. Serena goes on her date with a townie wearing a Blumarine animal-print halter dress (shortened for the show), Chanel purse, and Te Casan sandals. At the van der Woodsen supper, Blair and Chuck show their connection through color, both in green. B's in a Milly green-leaf print silk dress with a green JoomiNYC printed headband with flower. Blair has Alice + Olivia's Garden Party dress on when she bumps into Chuck, and Serena gives Nate a talking-to while wearing a Vena Cava geometric tank dress. At the White Party, Blair wears a Marc by Marc Jacobs Joelle halter-style dress with a Jennifer Behr headband and white Chloe Paddington pumps. The dress Jenny designed is actually an Eric Daman original paired with a Ferragamo purse and Natalie Portman for Te Casan vegan shoes. Tinsley Mortimer, in a Thread Social tiered mini dress, has a clutch from her own fall/winter collection for Samantha Thavasa. Serena is the showstopper in a white chiffon gown from Oscar de la Renta's spring/summer 2008 collection; her metallic hairband is stunning. And Chuck Bass in his black-accented white suit? Three words, eight letters: he is hott.

Music: The recap of season 1 is to The Windupdeads' "Reverse of Shade." Nate and Catherine make out in the car to Shwayze's "Buzzin'." Blair arrives to see Chuck waiting for her to an acoustic version of Motion City Soundtrack's "Fell in Love Without You"; it plays again when Dan and Serena watch the fireworks on the beach. Blair and Serena catch up poolside to "Crazy" by Jem. Nate and Catherine fool around at her house to "Break it Down" by Alana D. The White Party starts with Teyana Taylor's "Google Me." Serena kisses Nate to Lady Gaga's "Paparazzi." S tries to talk to Dan to "Not Your Gurl" by Amy Correa Bell.

Mädchen Amick as Catherine

Mädchen Amick, who will, in the heart of *Twin Peaks* fans, always be Shelly Johnson, guest stars as Catherine, the married woman Nate is having an affair with. Mädchen is no stranger to shows centered on Manhattan's elite (she played Carrie Fairchild on Darren Star's short-lived series *Central Park West*) or to CW teen dramas (she had recurring roles on both *Dawson's Creek* and *Gilmore Girls*). In the 2008/2009 TV season, she was on *Gossip Girl*, *Californication* (playing Janie Jones), and *My Own Worst Enemy*.

"Chuck's date and Blair's date are mother and son? And Nate and Blair are exes. And Nate and the mother are in a *book club*? Now there's a novel plot twist."

2.02 never been marcused

Original air date: September 8, 2008
Directed by: Michael Fields
Written by: Stephanie Savage
Guest cast: Francie Swift (Anne Archibald)

Blair throws a Welcome Back to the City party to impress Lord Marcus and his evil stepmother while Dan and Serena find the end-of-summer heat irresistible. Rufus returns.

The last weekend of the summer brings its romances to a head: will Blair be more than a summer fling? Can Dan and Serena actually work this time? Will Catherine and Nate keep their affair going? Serena and Dan try their best to keep their hands off each other, but can't. They ignore their own misgivings as well as the warnings Blair and Rufus give them. Nate also finds himself in a purely physical relationship with Catherine, but unlike D and S, he is desperate for advice and assistance. His family is in financial ruin, his mother has kept the truth from him (again), and his best friend has lied to him (again). Last season, the Captain and Mrs. Archibald tried to pimp out Nate to Blair to secure Eleanor's favor, but he refused. Now Nate is choosing that path for himself in an effort to save his mother from further social disgrace. A noble but terribly misguided act. He chastises his mother for keeping the family's bankruptcy from him, but Nate does the exact same thing — keeping his situation a secret from Chuck, Serena, and Blair. The non-judging Breakfast Club rallies when a member is in trouble, but Nate is too proud to ask for help.

Like his BFF, Chuck's goal is noble — to provide Mrs. Archibald with financial assistance — but his methods are sketchy. Lying to Nate only serves to anger and alienate him. Chuck's powers of deceit fail to achieve his less-than-honorable goal as well. His attempt to use the Duchess to destroy Blair's relationship with Marcus is nearly successful, but Blair foils him again (with her far-from-honorable blackmail of the Duchess).

After a summer in Vermont with her parents, Vanessa finds not much has changed back in the city: Dan is still girl-crazy, though focused on just one; Jenny is working all the time; and Nate is too busy to spend time with her. She's back in the role of resident advisor and lonely girl, providing a kind ear to both Nate and Rufus. Rufus confides in her but not in his children, as he makes the decision to be a father rather than a rock star. Having the happy Humphreys together again is a bittersweet moment, which marks the end of Rufus's much-deserved summer break from the stresses of parenting and the heartbreak of watching the woman he loves marry another man. Since Alison decided it was her turn to pursue her career rather than be the primary caregiver, Rufus has to sacrifice the passion he has for performing so his kids' own passions can develop. It's back to the kitchen for Rufie.

"I have to present myself as a crown jewel surrounded by other, smaller, slightly flawed gems, but quality stones nonetheless."
— Blair explains to Dorota why the guest list just won't work

JTLYK:

- Lily and Bart are still out of town, and Eric's only action is off-screen.
- Top story on Gossip Girl: "*Serena and Dan 2.0.* Looks like these former lovebirds couldn't stay separated for too long. Are S&D going to unbreakup? Or was this makeout session just a casual encounter? Like I've said before, the heart makes people do crazy things. . . ."
- Blair explains the James/Marcus situation to Serena by referencing one of her favorite movies. In *Roman Holiday*, Audrey Hepburn's character pretends to be a commoner to an American journalist (Gregory Peck), but she's actually a princess.
- Gossip Girl wonders if Chuck and Catherine's secret meeting is "risky business," referring to the 1983 Tom Cruise film about a high school student who gets involved with a more mature call girl.
- The iconic photo of Rufus performing that Lily took back in the olden days is on the wall of the Humphrey loft once again. Rufus took it down in "School Lies" after Lily got engaged to Bart.

Secrets & Lies:

- Marcus is reluctant to introduce Blair to the Duchess, but doesn't tell her why.

- Chuck pretends to be friendly with Marcus but is conniving against him. Chuck plots to break up Blair and Marcus.
- Blair lies to Marcus, telling him she needs a ride home to New York, and then invents a party so she can spend more time with him. All part of her plot to prove she's worthy of a long-term commitment.
- Anne Archibald has been hiding the truth from Nate again.
- Catherine sees that Blair's display of sophistication is false, and a failed attempt to impress her and Marcus.
- Serena tries to avoid a scene at the party by quickly explaining how Blair, Nate, and Catherine know each other, adding in a fib about Nate in a book club. Not the most believable cover story.
- Chuck secretly helps Anne Archibald, but alienates Nate by lying to him about why he's selling his shares in Victrola. Like Blair, Chuck's intentions are good but his methods are duplicitous.
- Serena tells Dan that Catherine is Nate's mom's friend, not Nate's secret lover.
- Catherine offers to help Nate out financially in return for a continued sexual relationship. Hmm, is there a word for exchanging sex for money?
- Rufus tells only Vanessa that he wants to keep touring; to his kids, he just says, "There's no place like home."
- Vanessa pretends not to care that Nate canceled their plans.

You'll B a Woman Soon: It's not often that Blair Waldorf feels that she isn't classy enough, but dating British royalty puts her in a spin. She tells Serena that she loves Marcus but she is more in love with the idea of dating the perfect gentlemen. Unlike with Chuck in "Summer, Kind of Wonderful," Blair schemes to impress rather than destroy. But when a secret lands in her lap, she can't help but use it to her advantage.

The Original Gossipverse: Blair is desperate to hold on to Lord Marcus in *Nothing Can Keep Us Together;* she meets Lord Marcus's cousin in *Only in Your Dreams* and gets a chilly reception.

That's How It's Done in *The O.C.*: In season 1, Julie Cooper hooks up with Marissa's teenaged ex-boyfriend Luke.

Never Been Kissed (dir. Raja Gosnell, 1999): Drew Barrymore stars in this romantic comedy about Josie, a copy editor at the *Chicago Sun-Times* who's assigned her first undercover feature story and given a chance for a high school do-over. Her first time 'round, "Josie Grossie" was awkward, unpopular, and cruelly tormented. Her return to high school promises more of the same — misguided fashion choices, nerdy friends, and derision from the trio of mean popular girls. In her English class, taught by super foxy teacher Sam (Michael Vartan), she studies Shakespeare's *As You Like It*. Josie identifies with the character of Rosalind, who disguises her real identity and through putting on another's persona finds the opportunity for real love in her life. Her boss orders her to befriend the popular crowd, which she can only do once her brother (David Arquette) enrolls and paves the way with his instant coolness. Though she ends up winning prom queen (in a Rosalind costume), it's at the cost of her friendship with math geek Aldys (Leelee Sobieski). Getting a "great story" means betraying Sam and cooling the spark of attraction between them. Putting herself completely out there, she writes a different story for the paper and waits for Sam to show up at the high school's championship baseball game to give her her first real kiss.

Blair's attempt to be something she's not is just as much of a failure as Josie's (but with better clothes). Desperate to impress the Duchess and hold on to her boyfriend, Blair puts on a show of pretension and sophistication. Despite her fumbling, Josie's intentions are always good, just like Blair's. As B says to Serena, she just wants Marcus to approve of her and then she'll stop scheming. Josie is faced with a decision — write a story that would destroy her love interest's reputation or take a giant leap and risk losing her job — and she chooses to take the leap. Nate, on the other hand, knows that sleeping with Catherine for money is wrong, but he doesn't have the courage to find an honest way out.

Welcome to the Real World:

- Blair stayed up reading *Debrett's Peerage & Baronetage*, a genealogical guide to British aristocracy that has been published since 1769, and watched Stephen Frears' 2006 film *The Queen*, which starred Dame Helen Mirren as Queen Elizabeth II.
- Tom Hanks, who gave Marcus a tissue according to B, was indeed at the funeral for Diana, Princess of Wales, in 1997. Blair calls her "Lady Di,"

a commonly used name referring to her maiden name and title of Lady Diana Spencer.

- Serena hands Dan the June/July 2008 issue of *Nylon* with Scarlett Johanssen on the cover. One of the headlines is "The Original Gossip Girl: Beth Ditto." Blake Lively and Leighton Meester each had a cover for the May 2008 issue of the magazine.
- The exhibit at the Bedford Avenue Gallery is of Nathan Nedorostek's artwork. In 2008, Nedorostek published a 52-page book of photography entitled *Eulogy for Marissa Cooper* — yes, *The O.C.*'s Marissa Cooper — in an effort to channel "the grief and emotion of a heartbroken television viewer." (Nedorostek's work pops up again in "Prêt-a-Poor J.")
- Serena asks Dan to come to B's party to display his knowledge of Premier League Football, England's professional league. And B hopes D "knows his arse from his Arsenal," the famous North London football club (and subject of Nick Hornby's fandom in *Fever Pitch*). Like his character, Penn Badgley is a soccer fan.
- After Catherine tells B that Marcus will never end up with a "lowly Waldorf," Blair disses Britney in her distress. Ms. Spears "forgot" to wear knickers a few times in 2007 and loves Nyla's Burger Basket, a Mississippi burger joint near her hometown of Kentwood, Louisiana.

Locations:

- Chuck interrupts Blair and Marcus's last Hamptons breakfast at Citron (62 Main St).
- The Chuck and Marcus squash game was filmed at the Eastern Athletic Club (43 Clark St, Brooklyn).
- Blair throws her party at the Hudson Hotel (356 W 58th St) on the Sky Terrace.
- When B awkwardly tries to start a conversation with a reference to England's Chelsea Football Club, Serena cracks an even more awkward joke about loving the Balenciaga boutique in Chelsea (542 W 22nd St).

Oops: So did Vanessa spend her summer with her parents in Vermont or at the gallery converting a storage space into a café? It would take more than a long weekend to put the Bedford Avenue Gallery Café together.

The Look: Serena boards the bus home in a Dream Society Delicate tank in smoke and 7 For All Mankind denim shorty shorts. Blair plans her party in a Marc by Marc Jacobs custard and red Alessandra bow dress, Rachel Leigh satin rope peace bracelet, and Unisa Adeline wedges. Serena arrives at the Waldorfs in an ivory Wayne shoulder-zip top and white 7 For All Mankind Ginger jeans. At her Welcome Back to the City party, Blair has a Garland Collection large signature pendant (which reads "Waldorf") on with her strapless black-and-white rose print dress and Forever21 pearl bead headband. Serena's in a Starry Night halter dress by Adam with a long Margo Morrison moonstone chain necklace. Jenny arrives home from the Hamptons in an orange and blue Tova Celine dress. At the end of the episode, Serena is wearing a Diab'less nightgown and B is in Elizabeth and James Priscilla dress.

Music: Dan and Serena wake up to "Boy in a Rock 'n' Roll Band" by The Pierces, who performed at the debutante ball. Serena eats chocolate-covered strawberries to The Fratellis' "Tell Me a Lie." Rufus checks out the new café at the gallery to "Spent Nights" by Magic Bullets. Blair mistakes Boccherini's *Minuet* for Mozart at her party. Vanessa agrees to look after the gallery should Rufus go back on tour to Wes Hutchinson's "Move On." Rufus looks around the Humphrey loft to "Cat Piano" by Seabear. Blair catches Nate and Catherine going at it in the library to "Creator" by Santogold. The episode finishes with "New York, I Love You But You're Bringing Me Down" by LCD Soundsystem.

Patrick Heusinger as Marcus Beaton

Born in 1981 on Valentine's Day and raised in Jacksonville, Florida, Patrick Heusinger decided to be an actor at age 13 after appearing in an amateur production of *Annie Get Your Gun*. After graduating from Juilliard, he made his film debut in 2005's *Sweet Land*, and has since appeared in *The Nanny Diaries* and *Tie a Yellow Ribbon*. In 2007, he toured the U.S. with *Spamalot* (as Lancelot) before being cast as Lord Marcus on *Gossip Girl*. On *30 Rock*, he played a former Wall Streeter now working as a party-hard intern at NBC. Of his varied roles, Patrick said, "I look on everything I do, every part I play, as a learning process. It just doesn't stop."

"Sorry to break it to you, B, but this party just went over to the dark side."

2.03 the dark night

Original air date: September 15, 2008
Written by: John Stephens
Directed by: Janice Cooke
Guest cast: Purva Bedi (Clare), Alexandra Carl (Laurel's Assistant), Gonzalo Escudero (Buckman), Amy Evinger (Atelier Model), Annalaina Marks (Chuck's Fling Girl), Michaela Annette (Mini Serena), Ellie Pettit (Mini Blair), Lydia Grace Jordan (Mini Mean Girl)

A citywide blackout brings hidden feelings and secrets to light. Jenny proves to be a helpful little bird at Eleanor's atelier.

With Chuck off his game, Dan and Serena forced into public with their relationship, and Nate unhappy in his role as gigolo, the buildup to the blackout is rife with tension and potential. The pressure on Dan and Serena to talk through their problems — from family, friends, and hilariously well-informed and sharp-tongued 12-year-olds — is enough to cool their attraction in the heat wave. As soon as they're literally trapped in a conversation, they see the inherent and seemingly insurmountable flaws in their relationship. Dan and Serena's breakup scene was devastatingly fantastic — they love each other so much but it isn't enough to keep them together. Their earlier frustration with each other softens into sadness. Never in the history of television has there been a more touching line spoken to an elevator door than Serena's "I love you."

The Nate and Vanessa Are Meant to Be plot came a little bit out of left field; at the end of last season, she ditched Nate for just the possibility of spending the summer at Dan's side. But combine a long lonely summer, the irresistibility of Nate Archibald, and V realizing that flirting with Rufus is a bad idea (c'mon, you saw that chemistry), and it starts to make sense. Vanessa tries to encourage the best in her friends, and tells Nate that he deserves more than a twisted relationship with Catherine. But V's moral standing is useless when the Duchess pulls the rug out from under her, threatening to turn in the Captain.

The Duchess sees her own sexual frustrations with her husband mirrored in Blair's with Marcus. What Catherine says, B already knows. Blair doesn't feel alive with Marcus like she does when she's with Chuck. Chuck knows it too and tries to use his sexuality to drive Blair crazy and into his arms. It almost succeeds in ending Blair and Marcus. But Chuck and Vanessa are both left the losers with the Beatons winning the round: Nate stays with Catherine, Blair stays with Marcus. The only new pairing, besides Rufus and his date Clare (!), is Little Jenny Humphrey and Eleanor Waldorf. Last season J was Blair's protégé; now she's Eleanor's. Just like her daughter, Eleanor mocks Jenny and bosses her around to comedic effect. And as Blair learned quickly, so does Eleanor: Little J has game. (She was bang-on about the neckline looking like a pilgrim at a funeral.) Let's hope this Humphrey–Waldorf dynamic is more peaceful than the last.

"You're not using Blair as sexual Drano."
— Serena is once again repulsed by her stepbrother

JTLYK:

- Lily is still MIA, but calls from Shanghai.
- Top story on Gossip Girl: "*B Lands Lord.* Lordy lord lord. B snagged royalty. It only makes sense that Queen B would find her Prince Charming. And we couldn't be happier for the new couple. Lord is a definite upgrade from Chuck Bass. He has something Chuck is totally lacking: Class."
- *Little Lord Fauntleroy* (1886) by Frances Hodgson Burnett is the story of good-natured Cedric, a poor Brooklyn boy who finds out he is actually a lord. He teaches his grandfather, the Earl, compassion and charity, while Gramps teaches him how to behave like a member of the aristocracy. The name is now used mostly with derision to mean a spoiled, pompous brat — more of a Chuck type than a Marcus.
- Chuck calls his Japanese flight attendant "Madame Butterfly" after the title character of the Puccini opera about a Japanese woman, a geisha, who marries and falls in love with an American man who thinks of her as entertainment rather than as a wife.
- Marcus says Blair is nothing like that tart who starred in 2007's *Atonement.* Cecilia (Keira Knightley) and Robbie (James McAvoy) are caught in a passionate encounter in the library in a crucial scene early in the film. Leighton Meester can do a spot-on Keira Knightley impression,

which she did on *Tyra* in 2007 while promoting season 1 of *Gossip Girl.*

- Chuck calls Marcus "Bertie Wooster," a character from P.G. Wodehouse's comic *Jeeves* novels. Wooster is a gentleman but, as Jeeves describes him, "mentally negligible."
- *The Graduate*'s Mrs. Robinson (Anne Bancroft) is the older woman who seduces college-age Benjamin (Dustin Hoffman). Benjamin ends up falling in love with her daughter, Elaine (Katharine Ross), against Mrs. Robinson's wishes.
- Not uncharacteristically, Eleanor doesn't acknowledge that she's met Rufus before. Lily brought him to the Waldorfs in "The Handmaiden's Tale."
- When Serena asks Dan why he loves her in "The Thin Line," he says, "I love you because you make no apologies for being exactly who you are." That reason for loving her has turned into a reason he can no longer be with her.

Secrets & Lies:

- Idiotically, Nate revealed to Catherine where his father was hiding.
- Nate lies to Catherine by telling her he was talking to his mother, not Vanessa.
- Dan fibs to Rufus that he and S have their issues "all squared away."
- Catherine spies Nate and Vanessa having a romantic moment outside his house.
- Blair tells Serena that she is fooling herself about Dan, and while she's right, Blair doesn't admit that she's fooling herself about Marcus.
- Blair lies to Vanessa, saying she's inviting her to the party to keep Nate company. Blair tells a different story to Nate. The truth is she's arranging it for Catherine.
- Nate lies to Vanessa and cancels their date when he finds out from Marcus that Catherine is going to the party.
- Jenny is caught bad-mouthing Eleanor's designs and fired for it. Eleanor needs trustworthy interns.
- Vanessa decides to go with the immature option Rufus offers and pretends not to receive N's "don't come" message.
- Blair unconvincingly tells Chuck that her sex life with Marcus is satisfying.
- Nate wises up to Blair and Catherine's plan.

- Vanessa catches Nate and Catherine together.
- Blair halfheartedly lies to Marcus, saying she thought she was making out with him. Neither Marcus nor Chuck believes it.
- Vanessa lies to Nate to protect him and his family, saying that Catherine loves him.
- Vanessa tells Nate's secret to Dan.

Scrap!: Marcus clocks Chuck.

You'll B a Woman Soon: Blair is chronically unwilling to admit when she has a problem. A passionate person, B finds she can't get no satisfaction with the stuffy British lord. But she pretends everything's perfect with Marcus and is increasingly frustrated. Being caught in her somewhat accidental kiss with Chuck forces her to be honest with Marcus. And the result of her honesty? A passionate embrace from him.

The Original Gossipverse: Blair is puzzled by Marcus's lack of sexual interest in her in *Only in Your Dreams*.

The Dark Knight (dir. Christopher Nolan, 2008): The second Batman movie with Christian Bale as the Caped Crusader, *The Dark Knight* introduces the Joker (Heath Ledger), a new breed of criminal in Gotham, and Harvey Dent (Aaron Eckhart), the rising star District Attorney, a white knight to save the city by battling its criminals through the justice system. The Joker brings chaos to Gotham's consortium of criminals and taunts Batman, goading him to reveal his true identity. Harvey Dent and Bruce Wayne are two sides of the proverbial coin, representing different ways to serve their city. Says Dent, "You either die a hero or live long enough to see yourself become the villain." The Joker forces Batman's hand and makes him choose who lives — the woman he loves or Dent — and his choice turns the disfigured but surviving Dent into Two-Face. In a moment of great self-sacrifice, Batman makes another impossible choice — shouldering the blame for Two-Face's crimes — and he becomes a villain in the public's hearts. He protects Gotham without the city realizing he's their dark knight.

The Upper East Side's agent of chaos, Chuck, plays the Joker in Blair's life, upsetting the careful balance she's building with Marcus. Betrayal is as rampant at B's party as it is in the Gotham police department: Marcus discovers Blair with Chuck, and Vanessa discovers Nate with Catherine. Like Batman forced to choose between saving the woman he loves or the man who could save Gotham, Vanessa must make an impossible decision: to be with Nate and destroy his family or push him away to protect him. At the end of *The Dark Knight*, Batman keeps secret Harvey's crimes and shoulders the blame all alone. Vanessa keeps Catherine's blackmail under wraps, but at least she has Dan's shoulder to cry on.

Welcome to the Real World:

- Serena says Dan isn't the "twenty-second Lord of Westmorlandshire," but neither is Marcus, or anyone else, as the title doesn't exist. The closest thing Marcus could be is Earl of Westmorland, a county in northwest England.
- Blair can't help showing off her anglophilia at her party: Balmoral Castle and Estate in Aberdeenshire is the Scottish home to the British Royal Family and has been since 1848. Prince Harry is third in the line of succession to the throne.

Locations:

- The Duchess takes Nate shopping at Ralph Lauren (867 Madison Ave).

Oops: When Marcus runs into Nate outside Central Park, Nate's earphones go back and forth from around his neck to his hands.

The Look: Blair is wearing a peacock blue Nanette Lepore Ambiance top when Marcus calls her a delicate flower. When she gets the call from the Duchess, she has on a beige Dice Kayek blouse, a modified Anna Sui skirt, and Susan Daniels headband. For her party, she puts on a yellow silk 3.1 Phillip Lim Grecian pleated dress. Duchess Catherine likes her DvF. Shopping with Nate she has a Diane von Furstenberg Bennett jersey wrap dress on, and at B's party she wears a fuchsia Diane von Furstenberg blouse and Catherine Malandrino skirt with a Gemma Redux necklace, Ferragamo clutch, and gold Giuseppi Zanotti pumps. Vanessa is dressing above her income bracket this episode. When she works up the courage to call Nate, she's in the brightly colored and striped Marc by Marc Jacobs Spectrum top, and for B's party, she's in a Jovovich-Hawk dress accessorized with Verre New York necklace and Nine West bracelet. Serena is spotted with Dan (who's in Levi's and a

Ted Baker striped T) wearing a Young Fabulous & Broke Snap tie-dye tank with James Jeans jeans, a Rebecca Minkoff clutch, and Havaianas thin-strap animal-printed flip-flops. Serena has breakfast with Blair wearing an Adam cowl-neck tank with silk chains, Rich & Skinny sleek jeans in busted black, and a Loeffler Randall Bedelia D Ring satchel. She's trapped in the elevator with Dan wearing a Vena Cava Honeycomb high-neck dress with Chanel belt, holding a Botkier Gladiator small shoulder bag. No doubt chosen for him by Catherine, Nate wears a Brooks Brothers suit and shirt and Steve Madden shoes to B's party.

Music: The episode opens with the second Santogold song of the season, "Lights Out." Vanessa and Nate's hangout is interrupted by Catherine's texts to "It's A Lot" by The 88. Blair's party starts with The Fashion's "Like Knives." Dan and Serena's elevator scenes are to "I Can Feel a Hot One" by Manchester Orchestra. Ne-Yo's "Closer" is playing when Nate arrives to Blair's party.

Michelle Hurd as Laurel

Raised in an artistically inclined family — her parents met while acting together in a play — Michelle Hurd is an accomplished theater, film, and television actress. Michelle has worked on numerous series, including *The O.C.*, but is best known for her role as Detective Jefferies in the first two seasons of *Law and Order: SVU.* Her role on *Gossip Girl* as Eleanor's no-nonsense right-hand woman was unusual for her. "It was fun for me," said Michelle, "as I often play cops and lawyers and doctors and this time I had the opportunity to play a mean fashionista . . . and wear cute outfits and heels."

"What Dan Humphrey does with the other serfs in the village is his business, but when he brings his new maiden to court, it's a declaration of war. Sound the trumpets, strumpets."

2.04 the ex-files

Original air date: September 22, 2008

Written by: Robert Hull
Directed by: Jim McKay
Guest cast: Laura-Leigh (Amanda Lasher), Purva Bedi (Clare), Jonathan Freeman (Butler), Kayte Grace (Melissa Murphy), Tyler Johnson (Jenns), Whitney Vance (Kelsey), Remy Zaken (Frightened Girl #2)

The return to school starts Dan and Serena's race to be the first to move on. Vanessa's refusal to be bought leads to the end of the British Invasion of the Upper East Side.

Having failed to break up Marcus and Blair three times now, Chuck tries another angle. Playing puppet master, he circuitously brings about the rise of the House of van der Woodsen. He capitalizes on Serena's breakup with Dan to force her into a power position with the Blairites, succeeding despite S's best intentions to preserve her friendship with Dan and not be jealous or competitive. Kind, considerate, and respectful or selfish, reckless, and superior — the question of S's identity that she struggled with at the end of the first season rears its head again. Dan condemning Serena for her "no fault" mantra pushes her to the dark side. If he doesn't believe in her, why should she bother?

While Blair begins her senior year concerned with ruling her queendom (picking suitable projects, casting aside the victims, protecting S from persons of interest), she is soon distracted by a more pressing problem. She handles the Catherine/Marcus affair brilliantly — banishing them, restoring the Archibalds' fortune, and not letting her hurt feelings get in the way. But after asking her for help, Vanessa loses faith in B and ruins the plan. Vanessa not trusting Blair is a wise move, but not trusting Blair to properly exact revenge on Catherine is misguided. Ironically, confiding in Blair in the first place hurts her friendship with Nate, while her distrust of Blair hurts his family's well-being. Double fail. Leave the scheming to the pros, V.

Vanessa isn't the only one who's miserable by the end of the episode. The return to Constance–St. Jude's has brought out the worst in everyone: Dan is judgmental, Old Serena is back, Jenny is lying, Lily is lonely, Chuck is destructive, Nate is friendless, and Blair is masking her real problems with schoolyard pettiness. The Humphrey kids have taken "total social pariah" to a new level of isolation. Jenny flees Constance for the atelier while Dan is left stunned in the wake of Queen S and her followers.

"It's not so bad when you get used to birds flying into your head and automatic doors never opening."
— Dan gives Jenny lessons on being invisible

JTLYK:

- Lily's back, and while the rest of the Constance girls have returned, Hazel is AWOL.
- Top story on Gossip Girl: "*D & S Two Point . . . No?* Our favorite star-crossed lovers are calling it quits again. And this time it looks like it's for good. Guess opposites don't really attract. Someone pass the Kleenex. Tears. :("
- When Dan and Serena first see each other in the courtyard, he gives her an awkward wave, just like the one at the end of their first date in "The Wild Brunch."
- Gossip Girl's first blast on Dan and Amanda reads: "*Serena Who?* Looks like Dan Humphrey wasted no time finding a new lady friend. We all know lunch leads to dinner, which leads to dessert, which leads to, well, you get the idea . . ."
- The girls in their field hockey uniforms confronting Amanda in the hallway harkens back to "Poison Ivy." But in that instance, Serena was the target, not the one being defended.
- Gossip Girl's blast after D and A's first date: "*Defiant Dan.* Spotted: Lonely Boy no longer down but out . . . at STK, Serena's home court. And by the look of the faces of her fans, we have quite the match brewing. Can't wait to see the look on S's face when she sees the highlight reel tomorrow . . ."
- When Vanessa sees Catherine and Marcus together, it's a nod to the scene from *Atonement* Blair mentioned in "The Dark Night." Both Catherine and Keira Knightley's character look stunning in green dresses when they are caught in illicit embraces in a library.

Secrets & Lies:

- Chuck doesn't tell Eric the real reason he has one of the Constance girls' files with him.
- Vanessa is cruel to be kind, telling Nate she doesn't want to be friends with him.
- Vanessa catches Marcus and Catherine making out.

- Beneath a thin veil of faux friendship, Blair and the girls tell Amanda to stay away from Dan.
- Vanessa confides in Dan and he suggests she turn to Blair Waldorf, Queen of Revenge, for help.
- Blair blackmails Catherine and Marcus into leaving town and paying Captain Archibald's restitution . . . but Vanessa also tells the Duke.
- Chuck has a master plan to make Serena queen of the school: set Dan up with the perfect girl and drive S mad with jealousy.
- Amanda was in Chuck's employ and had no interest in Dan (or in attending Constance).
- Jenny lies to Laurel so she can avoid the Mean Girls' torture.
- Blair explains her absence with a lie to Serena, saying she wasn't feeling well, not telling her about the Catherine/Marcus affair.

Scrap!: Blair drops her field hockey stick on Amanda's foot. Penelope chucks a Nairtini at Amanda.

You'll B a Woman Soon: Blair returns to her duties as Queen of Constance — choosing worthy lowerclassmen for inclusion in her group. She also uses her power at school to protect Serena, even though S doesn't approve of what she starts with Amanda. Blair handles Marcus and Catherine and throws a good deed in on top, getting Nate his old life back. B can control just about everything but that Brooklyn girl.

The Original Gossipverse: In *Only in Your Dreams*, Blair finds out that Marcus's relationship with his cousin is more than familial.

The X-Files (dir. Rob Bowman, 1998): The FOX sci-fi show *The X-Files* spawned the theatrical release *Fight the Future*. In 35,000 BC a creepy prehistoric alien fights a pair of prehistoric alien-hunters. Alien wins. Cut to the present day when a little boy falls into a cave and unwittingly speeds up an interspecies conspiracy. An alien virus will take over Earth and use humans as hosts unless someone can stop it. The heart of the movie is Fox Mulder (David Duchovny) and Dana Scully (Gillian Anderson) who find themselves unsure of their place inside the FBI now that the X-Files have been closed. With a background in science and a medical degree, Scully brings conventional thinking to her partnership, balancing Mulder's "expect the unexpected" conspiracy theories, hunches, and off-the-books methodology. This case nearly tears their partnership apart with Scully ready to quit the FBI, feeling she's done nothing but hold Mulder back. But Scully is the one who makes him whole, says Mulder. Just as the two are about to have a much-anticipated romantic moment, a bee infected with an alien virus stings Scully and it's a race against time (and to Antarctica) to save her . . . and the world.

The chemistry between Dan and Serena and between Chuck and Blair make for compelling television, just like Mulder and Scully's dynamic made *The X-Files* a hit show. In "The Ex-Files," Chuck Bass is the one spreading a pathogen among the *Gossip* kids. Silently putting plots into motion like Cancer Man, Chuck uses Dan, Serena, and his secret weapon Amanda to get to his real target: Blair. An unwitting victim in his scheme, Serena is infected with the Mean Girl virus and turns on Dan before threatening Queen B's status. Dan is reminded that at Constance–St. Jude's, you can trust no one.

Welcome to the Real World:

- Amanda is named after *Gossip Girl* producer and writer Amanda Lasher.
- Construction on the Met steps began in May 2008 and was due to finish in April 2009, meaning Blair and Serena's *entire* senior year will be sans steps.
- Rufus and Lily have a mini Harry Dean Stanton film festival. Of the actor, Roger Ebert said no movie he's in "can be altogether bad"; he starred in *Repo Man* (1984), *Paris, Texas* (1984), and in *Pretty in Pink* (1986) as the dad of a daughter who makes her own clothes and has trouble fitting in with rich kids.
- Dan compares Rilke to Albom at STK. Rainer Maria Rilke's *Letters to a Young Poet* (1929) and Mitch Albom's *Tuesdays with Morrie* (1997) both contain wisdom from a mentor passed to his apprentice, but Rilke's *Letters* has not yet been featured on *Oprah* or turned into a television movie.
- Jenny tells Laurel that she has the day off from school for Women's Suffrage Day, which is not in September but on August 26.

Locations:

- The exterior of Constance–St. Jude's was filmed at Packer Collegiate

home is where the art is

With the houses of Bass and van der Woodsen now united, a lot of *Gossip Girl* action happens in their shared home rather than at the Palace. (The family has moved back into the apartment Lily was renovating in season 1.) "The van der Woodsen apartment is composed of clean, simple lines, shapes and rhythms," said production designer Loren Weeks to *InStyle*. "But in keeping with Upper East Side tradition, it is still very formal in its presentation and layout." Contrasting it with the ornate Waldorf resident and informal Humphrey loft, Weeks used a palette of primary colors to achieve a modern look. Its simplicity keeps the focus on Lily's art collection.

Kiki Smith's "Carrier" (2001) is in the foyer. **Elmgreen & Dragset**'s "Prada Marfa" (2005) points the way into the apartment. By the kitchen is a print of **Jessica Craig-Martin**'s photograph "Watermill Center Benefit Gala 2007 (Showing Pink)," which Aaron recognizes in "The Magnificent Archibalds." Martin's photography is known for capturing high society in its off-kilter and unguarded moments. **Marilyn Minter**'s photographs explore what she calls the "pathology of glamour"; she's responsible for the sparkling eye in S's room, the jeweled high-heeled feet, and the hand grasping a globe. On the wall by the fireplace is **Ryan McGinley**'s haunting "Blonde." **Richard Phillips**' "Spectrum" (1998) hangs on the stairway wall. Phillips makes a cameo in "Chuck in Real Life" and said to the *New York Times* that the show covers issues he has in his art: "lost virginity, teen pregnancy, divorce, rape, manslaughter, suspected homicide, teen suicide, gay sexual identity, eating disorders, criminal blackmail, theft, as well as drug addiction and sex with multiple partners." A group of six black-and-white photographs of celebrities by **Patrick McMullan** hang in the living room. McMullan also makes a cameo in "Remains of the J."

The production team on *Gossip Girl* connects with the artists through the Art Production Fund, a non-profit organization that helps contemporary artists reach a broader audience through these sorts of collaborations.

Institute in Brooklyn (170 Joralemon St) and the Museum of the City of New York (1220 Fifth Ave at 103rd St).

- The *Gossip* kids hang out at STK (26 Little W 12th St) two nights in a row.
- Blair invites Marcus and Catherine to brunch at Centrolire (1167 Madison Ave).
- Marcus says he can't wait to take B to Warkworth, a village in Northumberland that boasts a medieval castle.

Oops: Nair may be an effective hair remover, but it doesn't work at the

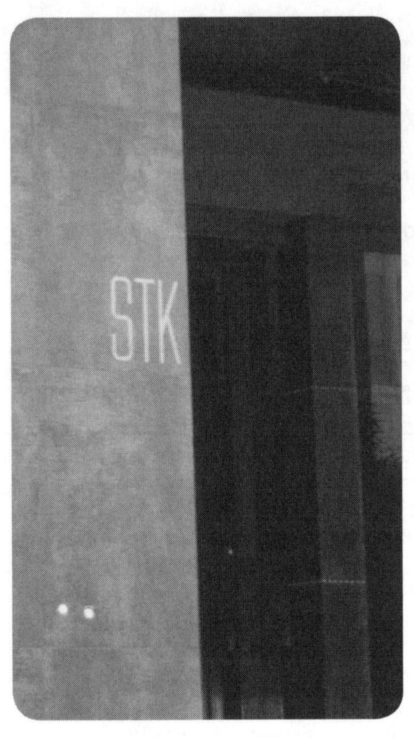

speed of light. Maybe Penelope added an extra burning agent into the Nairtini. Also, *Gossip Girl* loves unexpected pop-bys, but it was overkill in this episode. There were eight unannounced trips between Manhattan and Brooklyn, most of which could have been avoided by a phone call or text. And this show has a mobile telephone company for a sponsor. The check Catherine gives to Vanessa says her name is "Catherine Mason," not Beaton. It could be her maiden name, but why bother writing the check out to cash if it's not from a shared account?

The Look: Eric van der Woodsen, your day has finally arrived: the blond highlights are no more. Hanging out with Chuck definitely has its style benefits. Chuck also knows the easy way to attract Dan to Amanda: put her in a vest. Blair's first-day-of-senior-year headband is a double row crystal scallop by Jennifer Behr and her blouse is from Alexandra Vidal's spring/summer 2008 collection. For S's first day, she's in her French Toast uniform skirt, James Perse relaxed casual tee, Maison Martin Margiela vest, and light grey Nine West shoes. Lily visits Rufus in a floral-patterned Stella McCartney blouse from the spring/summer 2008 collection, a gorgeous turquoise Van Cleef & Arpels necklace, and Hermès Kelly bag. Blair gets the bad news from Vanessa in a Cynthia Steffe dress. Serena goes on a date with Amanda and Dan wearing a silver and black Hervé Léger bandage tank dress. Serena returns to Constance as Queen in her French Toast uniform skirt and tie, Viktor & Rolf T-shirt, Schumacher vest, Veronique shoes, Kateri Daman bracelet, and LAI bag. Blair finds she's been dethroned in a Susan Daniels headband, bone Zara blouse, Coach scarf, navy Cynthia Steffe skirt, Brooks Brothers belt, and Cole Haan shoes with a red Gianfranco Ferré bag. Penelope has a L.A.M.B. multi stirling tote when she and the Mean Girls fawn over Serena. If the last scene at Constance is sign of the *Gossip Girl* future — headscarves over headbands — there will be riots. The scarf works on Serena; she's easygoing and flowy. But Blair and the Mean Girls need the rigidity and preppiness of the hairband.

Music: The episode opens with "Morning Tide" (The Little Ones). Draft Day at Constance is to Nappy Roots' "Good Day." Catherine visits Vanessa at the gallery where "The Observer" by Chris Chavez plays. Vanessa shows Dan the photo of Marcus and Catherine to "Buildings & Mountains" by The Republic Tigers. Miss Eighty 6's "Came to Party" is playing on Dan and Amanda's date. When Dan, Amanda, and Serena are on their ill-advised three-way date, MGMT's "Electric Feel" is on at STK. Jenns the lacrosse dude tells his boring story to "Hold Up" by Young Mennace. Queen S reigns to "Please Remain Calm" by Cloud Cult. Dan is completely ignored in the courtyard and dressed down with Serena's Death Stare to "Shove It" (Santogold ft. Spank Rock), a brilliant choice for the moment: "We think you're a joke, shove your hope where it don't shine."

"What would Fashion Week be without a fashion victim?"

2.05 the serena also rises

Original air date: September 29, 2008
Written by: Jessica Queller
Directed by: Patrick Norris
Guest cast: David Patrick Kelly (Noah Shapiro), Jill Flint (Bex), Jim Ford (Joe), Jo Newman (Attractive Woman in Bar), Maureen Sebastian (Headset Girl), Ray Weiderhold (Holding-Cell Cop), Alexandra Carl (Laurel's Assistant)

Serena hits the runway and Blair hits the roof during Fashion Week. Dan goes down the rabbit hole with Chuck.

A companion episode to season 1's fashion-themed Blair/Serena showdown "Bad News Blair," "The Serena Also Rises" continues the regime change that started in "The Ex-Files." Serena nonchalantly gets the attention and praise that Blair scrambles for every day of her life. Enjoying her new life as a socialite, Serena knows she has to be careful or Blair will be hurt again.

But that "Poppy person" gives Serena sound (if a little cheesy) counsel: she should be her best and most vibrant self. Serena tells Blair that she's always held herself back for fear of bruising Blair's ego. And S's incredible bluntness demonstrates the truth of her words: she's not holding back any longer. If the future of S and B's friendship depends on Blair being supportive and *not* competitive, are our favorite besties dunzo? It doesn't look promising when you compare the end of this episode to the friends-forever impromptu photo shoot that closed "Bad News Blair." Now Serena's in front of the cameras with a new friend, while wounded Blair looks on alone.

More than just for Serena, Poppy's advice not to "hide your light" applies to the rest of the episode's storylines. Rufus asks Jenny to put her career on hold when all Jenny wants to do is shine — as an invaluable, fashion-show-saving intern and as a designer in her own right. Though Bart says he's protecting the family by spying on Lily and destroying the Mapplethorpe, a part of her past, she refuses to hide who she is or was. (Save that one little secret.)

With Bart shutting down Chuck's attempts to reach out, Chuck dulls his own potential and doesn't try to be more than his father thinks of him. His unlikely moment of friendship with Dan turns ugly when Chuck realizes

D was using him, and C is left alone again. If only he and Blair could be together. She feels utterly ignored and useless. Jenny is the only one who is kind to her, acknowledging how hard she works for what she has and admiring her for that.

Seeing his little sister in her flurry of Fashion Week prep, Dan discovers he too has to work hard to achieve greatness in his writing. But after following Noah Shapiro's advice to be ruthless and drawing out Chuck's secret, Dan finds he can't use it. Learning what happened that made Chuck who he is changes the way Dan feels about the guy who, a short year ago, attacked his little sister. While we've long known that Chuck's mother died, finding out that she died in childbirth adds a untold pathos to Chuck, who not only never got to meet his own mother but believes his father holds him responsible for her death.

Dan: "How do you know so many twins?"
Chuck: "Twins find me."

JTLTK:

- Nate's off at his grandparents this week, and Vanessa is likely hiding in Brooklyn after royally screwing up last episode.
- Top story on Gossip Girl: "*Dethroned?* Oh how the mighty have fallen. Sorry, Blair, but it looks like the girls of Constance Billard have a new Queen Bee: Serena van der Woodsen. However, we know how much Queen Bee status means to Blair so we're pretty certain the battle for power isn't over quite yet . . ."
- Blair's "Serena, Serena, Serena!" is very Jan Brady, who complains about sister Marsha getting all the attention.
- Blair borrows her own move from "The Blair Bitch Project" and uses Rufus to take down Jenny Humphrey.
- Holding out two pills, Chuck invites Dan to go down the rabbit hole with him, echoing Morpheus in *The Matrix* (who was referencing Carroll's *Alice's Adventures in Wonderland*).
- Noah Shapiro compares D's Charlie Trout character to a young Mephistopheles, the demon who makes a deal with the scholar Faust — his soul in exchange for expanding the limits of his knowledge and experience. Dan, in a Faustian move, seeks out his own demon in Chuck to advance his writing career.

- The dress Jenny wears to the fashion show is the same one Rufus admired when he arrived home from his summer tour in "Never Been Marcused."
- Thinking Jenny put the dress in the fashion show on purpose, Eleanor compares her to Eve Harrington (see page 117).

Secrets & Lies:

- Jenny lies to Dan about having a substitute teacher for French class.
- Lying to both Eleanor and Headmistress Queller, Jenny skips school to work at the atelier.
- Blair tattles on Jenny to Rufus, and even though he knows B's a schemer, "facts are facts."
- Fashion show sabotage! Blair tells the models the show was overbooked and sends them home. She gives Serena Jenny's dress to wear, hoping to humiliate Serena, Jenny, and her mother with one move.
- Chuck realizes Dan was using him as fodder for his fiction.
- Lily finds out Bart has a "Lily Bass dossier" and isn't amused. She still has one secret kept from her children, and Bart knows what it is.
- Jenny lies to Headset Girl and denies Rufus admittance to the fashion show.

Scrap!: Dan punches the boyfriend of the girl who dresses like a high-class call girl.

You'll B a Woman Soon: Blair's jealousy and competitiveness overcome her. As she gets more and more out of control, scheming and screaming, her actions seem ever more childish in comparison to Serena's composure and Jenny's accomplishments. She doesn't realize that sabotaging them doesn't make *them* look bad, it makes *her* look crazy and immature.

The Original Gossipverse: It's Serena, not Lily, who poses for a famous photographer (the fictional Remi brothers) in the first book; the photograph is a close-up of an unidentified body part that could be mistaken for a belly button. In *Because I'm Worth It*, Serena models in the Les Best show during Fashion Week. Blair is jealous of Serena when she sees her in the society pages with fashion designer Bailey Winter in *Only in Your Dreams*.

That's How It's Done in *The O.C.*: In "The Brothers Grimm," Caleb Nichol tells his wife Julie that he had a P.I. investigate her before they were married and he knows all her secrets. Of course, he has to cover up a porno she made in the '80s, not an artistic nude photograph.

The Sun Also Rises (dir. Henry King, 1957): Adapted from Ernest Hemingway's 1926 novel, the film is set in Paris in 1922 after the Great War and amid the Lost Generation who live as if they "were about to die." American Jake Barnes (Tyrone Power), an ex-pat newspaper man, was wounded in the war and is impotent. The woman he loves, Lady Brett Ashley (Ava Gardner), returns to see him in Paris, drunk and flitting from suitor to suitor but is miserable, "paying now for the hell she put others through." Jake, sick of the life in Paris, goes on a trip to Pamplona for the Fiesta and running of the bulls. There he, his friend Robert Cohn (Mel Ferrer), Lady Ashley and her fiancé Mike (Errol Flynn), and Bill Gorton (Eddie Albert) drink heavily and tension builds between them. A young bullfighter, Pedro Romero (Robert Evans), comes into the picture and Ashley flirts with him, making him one more fool for her love. She's characterized as Circe, tempting men into acting like pigs and then playing the innocent bystander. Increasingly weary of it all, Jake still cleans up Ashley's messes. Like Robert Cohn, scorned and hopelessly in love, Jake wants what he can't have.

Though the "Serena" play on the film's title connects the episode to our blonde heroine, the stronger link is to Chuck and Dan roaming New York City getting drunk and high and disorderly. Their nights of hedonism are characterized by the same listlessness of the Lost Generation. It's Chuck's boredom with his life that leads him to agree to hang out with Dan in the first place. The drinking and brawling are a thin veil for Chuck's feelings of bitterness and emptiness. Like Jake Barnes, what Chuck wants — love from his father, Blair, a mother — he can't have, so he fills his life with pain-dulling distractions.

Welcome to the Real World:

- The 2008 New York Fashion Week ran from September 5 to 12; though this episode aired on September 29, the date of Eleanor's show is the 12th.
- Lily asks Bex to buy a Mapplethorpe she posed for. Photographer Robert Mapplethorpe (1946–1989) was a controversial artist whose subjects were mainly portraits of well-known people, nudes, and flower still-lifes.

- Shapiro advises Dan to find his Charles Bukowski (1920–1994), a poet and novelist known for dirty realism and hard drinking, and to remember that Truman Capote (1924–1984) didn't create the masterpiece *In Cold Blood* by judging the murderers who are its subjects.
- Laurel cruelly says Kiki's stint in rehab barely made headlines. Kirsten Dunst entered rehab in February 2008; in 2007 she had starred in *Spider-Man 3*.
- Among the guests on the seating chart for Eleanor's show: Jessica Morgan and Heather Cocks from GoFugYourself.com, Anna Wintour (scandalously seated in the second row, noted *Vanity Fair*), Viktor Horsting of Viktor & Rolf, French designer Jacques Granges, Tory Burch, *New York* editor Adam Moss, Leanne Marshall from *Project Runway*, New York writers Moe Tkacik and Ian Spiegelman, Lydia Hearst, and It girl Josephine de la Baume.
- American editor-at-large of *Vogue* André Leon Talley loved the finale dress in Eleanor's show.

Locations:

- The photo in *Women's Wear Daily* of S and Poppy was taken at STK where the "Ex-Files" action went down.
- Eleanor's show took place in the ballroom at Capitale (130 Bowery St).

Oops: The invitation to the fashion show says it starts at 6:00 p.m., but when Jenny ignores a call from her dad before the show, her phone says it's 8:45 p.m.

Spotted: After chatting with Little J at the White Party, Tinsley Mortimer is back. At the fashion show, she's with fashion designer Michael Kors and Cristina Greeven Cuomo, editor-in-chief of *Hamptons* and *Gotham* magazines, socialite, and wife of *Good Morning America*'s Chris Cuomo.

The Look: The scarf returns! Chuck has his signature patchwork scarf on when he taunts Blair at school. Both *Gossip* moms wear purple this episode. Lily meets with Bex in a purple Rebecca Taylor ruffle top. Serena's wearing a yellow Catherine Malandrino Butterfly dress in the photograph in *WWD*. Jenny has a blue Katherine Kwei bag and Tarina Tarantino jewelry with her uniform, which she wears over a Zara blouse. Blair's wearing a Milly lily-print silk blouse and ribbon bow cardigan when she decides to go after Little J. Serena's wearing a brown What Comes Around Goes Around deco top when she and Blair argue at the Waldorfs. S wears a LaROK metal fringe halter dress to Eleanor's show and carries a purple Chanel 2.55 Reissue flap bag. The green dress Serena models is made by Eric Daman and he paired it with metallic gold python Jimmy Choo Sweden pumps. The dress Jenny is wearing at the show is also designed by Eric Daman, with a red necklace and bracelet by Tarina Tarantino, as is Blair's dress with a blue headband by Sami Rattner.

Music: Over the Fashion Week montage, "NYC–Gone, Gone" by Conor Oberst plays. Rufus makes waffles to "Made Concrete" by The Republic Tigers. Guests arrive to Eleanor's show to Lady Gaga's "Poker Face." Dan gets into an altercation at the bar to "This Ship Was Built to Last" (Duke Spirit). The socialites walk the runway to "Fille Atomique" par Nous Non Plus. "Raise the Dead" by Phantom Planet plays over the closing montage.

In all its glory and lovingly transcribed, here is D's story that fails to impress Noah Shapiro.

"Untitled" by Daniel Humphrey

The cigarette dangled from her cherry red lips. She took long drags from the cancer stick like an asthmatic would take from an inhaler. "I can make your wildest dreams come true," she whispered into his ear.

He laughed and shook his head. "No, I can make your wildest dreams come true. Do you know who I am? I'm Charlie Trout."

The lady of the night was taken aback. Who exactly was this imperious man standing in front of her? And was man even the right word for this hedonist? At just 17 years young, Charlie Trout really should only be considered a boy. However, he was far more practiced than his high school counterparts at the exclusive St. Charlie's School for Boys. Charlie Trout had seen and experienced things his classmates had only witnessed on screens at multiplexes, or had read in their summer reading books. He had a penchant for women, booze and all things turmoil. Clad in his signature necktie, Scotch in hand and a town car as his carriage, New York City was his playground. No chaperones, no boundaries, no rules . . .

Charlie Trout slumped forward, head in hands.

"My God," he groaned.

"After so much scorched earth, can either side claim victory?"

2.06 new haven can wait

Original air date: October 13, 2008
Written by: Alexandra McNally, Joshua Safran
Directed by: Norman Buckley
Guest cast: Byron Jennings (Dean Berube), Reed Birney (Mr. Prescott), Matt Burns (Leader of the Skull and Bones), Krysta Rodriguez (Jordan Steele), Molly Camp (Ms. Steinberg), Alexandra Carl (Laurel's Assistant), Bill Kux (History Professor), Jenny Sterlin (Shirley), Roarke Walker (Skull), Aaron Dean Eisenberg (Bones), Charlie Hewson (Yale Guy)

Field trip! Blair, Chuck, Nate, and Dan are off to visit Yale. When B tells S she's not Yale material, Serena goes too.

The sequel to "Poison Ivy," "New Haven Can Wait" explores some of the same issues and character pairings. In "Poison Ivy" Dan was envious of Nate's legacy at Dartmouth. A year later Nate's the one wishing he could be Dan, even for one day. When the Yale students know exactly who his father is, Nate adopts Dan's identity to escape. Not taking kindly to the impersonation, Dan has the same blinders on that he did last year and dismisses Nate's difficulties in the face of his own need for a reference letter. Dan is the one with the enviable life. His father is right: if Yale doesn't accept him, it's on Yale, not on him. Nate, on the other hand, is without that kind of encouragement or direction. By sending the Skull and Bones guys after Dan, Chuck inadvertently repairs the dynamic between Nate and Dan. They leave New Haven with an easier friendship, while Chuck has driven Nate away with his cruelty. Nate doesn't think Dan is "less than nothing" and never has.

As we first saw in "Poison Ivy," Dorota is Blair's surrogate mother. She brings B breakfast, expresses pride at B's accomplishments, and is a sounding board for her. Without Serena, Blair's life is pretty empty. Threaten to take away Yale and she flips into crazy mode. Serena knows exactly how Blair will react to her actions, but S takes no joy in tormenting B. The fight scene was delightful, with S going for B's hairband and B targeting S's sparkles-in-the-sunshine hair. The girls' easy reconciliation after such a major battle was less moving than the scene in Central Park last season, but "New Haven Can

Wait" otherwise achieved that same crackerjack mix of humor and heartfelt emotion.

"I'm sick of always looking like Darth Vader next to Sunshine Barbie."
— Blair and Serena work out the terms of their truce

JTLYK:

- Top story on Gossip Girl: "*Serena Takes Manhattan.* Serena Van Der Woodsen isn't just on top at Constance Billard. She's New York's newest 'it' girl and is taking the city by storm. You can't seem to open a newspaper without seeing Serena's long locks and ever longer legs staring at you. You got it, girl. Work it."
- Blair has her first Audrey Hepburn–inspired dream since "The Blair Bitch Project." This time it's *My Fair Lady*: Blair is Eliza Doolittle pre-transformation, Dean Berube is Henry Higgins, and Serena is Eliza dressed for the races. Once again, the position Blair desires has been usurped by her rival.
- Lily went to Brown, so Serena's mysterious father went to Harvard. (In "Poison Ivy," she mentions where her parents went but not who went where.)
- Vanessa mentions she's applying to NYU. Thanks to Nate making her take the SATs in "Desperately Seeking Serena," she can!
- The scene at the Dean's party is a companion to the Ivy Week mixer in "Poison Ivy." Blair and Serena interrupt each other's conversations and Blair puts Serena on the spot in front of a crowd.
- A term added to the *Gossip Girl* lexicon: pseudononymous (pseudonym + anonymous) sex.
- Josh and Stephanie asked Blake Lively and Leighton Meester to model their fight after the one between Shirley MacLaine and Anne Bancroft in Herbert Ross's 1977 film *The Turning Point.*

Secrets & Lies:

- Nate lies to his new Yale love interest, pretending to be Dan Humphrey.
- Chuck tells Serena Blair's answer to the Dean's question.
- Dan busts Nate on his Dan Humphrey impersonation.
- Blair bribes Shirley for an invite to the Dean's party.
- Blair changes Serena's answer to "Pete Fairman."

- Chuck tells the Skull and Bones guys that Dan is Nate. Chuck also gathers incriminating evidence on them so he can control them when they are one day running America. Long-term plotting!

Scrap!: Blair and Serena have their second throwdown of the series. After B throws her purse at S, S shoves her and things get messy. B says, after the fight, that she had S in a chickenwing, a wrestling move where she hooked S's arm with her own and pulled up. Nate starts a fight at the bar with the Skull and Bones guys, but escapes unharmed.

The Original Gossipverse: Instead of a Marc Jacobs handbag, Serena has a perfume named after her in *Because I'm Worth It*. In *You Know You Love Me*, Blair kisses her Yale interviewer. In *Nobody Does it Better*, S and B attend a New York Loves Yale party hosted by an influential alumnus; Serena charms him while Blair acts ridiculous.

That's How It's Done in *The O.C.*: Seth botches his interview for dream school Brown in "The Pot Stirrer" and makes it worse by chasing down faculty members in "The College Try." Blair's insults about Brown students form a pretty accurate description of Summer's transformation when she attends the school in season 4.

Heaven Can Wait (dir. Warren Beatty and Buck Henry, 1978): Joe Pendleton (Warren Beatty), a football player just overcoming his knee injury and ready for the big game, gets in a car accident and an angel pulls him out of his body and into heaven a moment too soon — he wasn't going to die but now he can't have his own body back. Joe ends up back on Earth in the body of billionaire industrialist Farnsworth, a man about to be murdered by his wife and her lover. Joe as Farnsworth turns his world upside down, changing his companies' policies from destructive to people friendly and making a friend in Ms. Logan (Julie Christie) along the way. But all Joe really wants to do is play ball, so he buys the Rams and starts training with his old coach. Destiny doesn't align with Joe's plans and he's pulled from Farnsworth (who ends up down the well). Put into the Rams' quarterback injured in the big game, Joe gets his big football moment. In his new body he loses knowledge of his previous life, but when he meets Ms. Logan she sees a sparkle in his eyes and recognizes Joe's soul.

Like Joe, Nate takes on a different persona in "New Haven Can Wait" and has a difficult time adjusting to the world in another man's shoes. Like Joe yanked from his life too soon, since Nate's father's arrest and his family's fall from fortune, N has been displaced from the life and future he was supposed to have. Coming out of his demoralizing relationship with Catherine, Nate needs an escape and finds it for, oh, about an hour before Dan kicks him out of his shoes.

Welcome to the Real World:

- Dan is right: more presidents than Humphreys graduated from Yale — William Taft, Gerald Ford, George H.W. Bush, Bill Clinton, and George W. Bush.
- C says N's family practically owns Yale. Among his other philanthropic acts, Cornelius Vanderbilt (1843–1899) donated a great deal of money to Yale. Several buildings on campus owe their existence to the Vanderbilts.
- During the American Revolution, the British invaded New Haven Harbor on July 5, 1779.
- The mocked courses, the Role of Sex in Art and Great Hoaxes in Archeology, are indeed offered at Yale.
- Captain Archibald is described by a Yalie as a "modern Milkin." Michael Milkin, nicknamed the Junk Bond King, went to prison after an insider trading investigation got him indicted on close to 100 counts of racketeering and securities fraud. (But he only served two years in jail.)
- Blair's perfect answer to the Dean's question is his favorite author. Prolific writer George Sand (1804–1876) was a famous, controversial, and independent woman. She wore men's clothes and smoked in public and wrote frankly about women's lives. Wrote Sand, "The world will know and understand me someday. But if that day does not arrive, it does not greatly matter. I shall have opened the way for other women."
- Jordan asks Nate his opinion of Nobel Prize–winning author Gabriel García Márquez's 1988 novel *Love in the Time of Cholera.*
- Speaking in French to the professor, Serena says that French filmmaker Claude Lelouche's *Roman de Gare*, released in the U.S. in 2008, was one of her favorite films of the year.
- Serena corrects Blair at the Yale party. She knows her popes from watching *The Tudors*; Henry Cavill plays Charles Brandon.

- Blair tackled New York Senator Chuck Schumer's daughter for wearing a sweatshirt from her father's alma mater, Harvard.

Locations:
- Lily needs a dress for a dinner at the Frick (1 E 70th St).
- Some of the Yale scenes were filmed at Columbia University (Morningside Heights campus main entrance at 116th St and Broadway).

The Look: For her Yale interview, Blair pairs a yellow Catherine Malandrino blouse with a dark green Diane von Furstenberg Martine skirt, striped tie, and cardigan. Serena wears a stunning white Ralph Lauren Collection Breanna double peplum jacket with thin purple stripes and Ralph Lauren crest, a rather plunging white Alice + Olivia shirt, Rich & Skinny jeans, Michael Kors boots, and Celine Watch Me Work bag. To the Dean's party, B wears a dark green belted Catherine Malandrino shirt dress, which gets totaled along with her grey Susan Daniels headband. Serena's coal Black Halo cut-out Jackie O dress fares better in the battle. Blair goes a bit overboard on her second-day Yale outfit with a chevron-patterned Anna Sui blouse, diagonal plaid L.A.M.B. skirt, and one-size-too-big Coach hat. S keeps it simple with a cream Joie Larissa sweater dress.

Music: An instrumental version of "The Rain in Spain" from *My Fair Lady* plays during B's dream. Blair and Dorota talk Yale to The Submarines' "The Wake Up Song." When Nate catches the eye of the pretty Yale girl, "White Diamonds" by Friendly Fires kicks in. Nate's make-out session to "Wooden Heart" (The Duke Spirit) is interrupted by D's arrival. The Section Quartet's cover of Muse's "Time Is Running Out" provides a suitably dramatic soundtrack to the Dean's reception. Nate waits for Chuck to show up at the bar to "Dragstrip Girl" by Jamie Blake.

"You made your bet. Now you have to lie in it."

2.07 chuck in real life

Original air date: October 20, 2008
Written by: Lenn K. Rosenfeld
Directed by: Tony Wharmby
Guest cast: Chuck Cooper (Horace Rogers), Whitney Vance (Kelsey), Zach Poole (*InStyle* Reporter)

Bart's new rules for the van der Woodsen–Bass household get Serena's knickers in a twist (and then she forgets to wear them). To counter Vanessa's good intentions, Blair busts out her best Cruel Intentions imitation.

The center event of "Chuck in Real Life" is the van der Woodsen–Bass housewarming party, and suitably, the characters grapple with issues of family and finding a place to call home. Chuck is surprised to find himself at ease in an outer borough: he takes a shining to the Brooklyn Inn (on his second visit) and to Vanessa, and he earnestly wants to help. Like Dan saw in "The Serena Also Rises," Vanessa sees another side to Chuck, especially when she overhears Bart berate him. Like she told Nate in "The Dark Night," V believes C deserves better than the treatment he receives from his father. But just as he begins to see the potential in himself Vanessa sees, Blair puts a halt to their tentative friendship. She doesn't want C to feel at home with anyone but her. The blossoming bromance between Dan and Nate is nearly over when Dan admits he knows that Nate is squatting in an empty, repossessed house. Ashamed of being without a home or family, Nate pushes Dan away. With a little push back from Rufus, Dan decides to be the person who doesn't give up on Nate and brings him back to the Humphrey homestead.

Angry that Bart is masking his self-interest with family values, Serena goes on a tear, flaunting the new household rules. Her real bitterness, as she realizes, comes from years of her mother's neglect. Learning about how Serena and Eric spent their childhood makes S's wild child days and E's depression even more understandable. The family accord at the end of the episode felt forced and Bart gets off the hook rather easily. Conspicuously absent from that happy family moment is Chuck. Instead he's with the person who understands him best and can torment him the most. Taking

Vanessa's comment that he deserves better to heart, Chuck refuses to put out until Blair tells him that she loves him.

"Tights are not pants!"
— Blair presides over a disciplinary hearing for Kelsey's fashion crime

JTLYK:

- Top story on Gossip Girl: "*A New Lonely Boy?* Karma's a bitch, C. Looks like our favorite schemer is totally friend-less. Even Dan Humphrey seems to have more friends. Now that's just sad. Chuck Bass, party of one."
- Serena compares Lily to a Stepford wife (from the 1972 novel and two film adaptations), who are attractive, agreeable fembots mindlessly following their husbands' wishes.
- Dan has his Lincoln Hawk tee on again.
- Blair shouldn't try so hard. The last time she set up an over-the-top, candles everywhere, sexy-times bedroom (for Nate in the pilot), it was also a failure.
- The backstory on the van der Woodsen family dynamic doesn't quite gel with "Blair Waldorf Must Pie!" Serena and Eric were shocked to learn that Lily had been a hard-partying groupie — wouldn't the Klaus cocaine party have been a tip-off to earlier adventures?

Secrets & Lies:

- Lily has a pattern of adopting her boyfriends' interests, rather than being true to herself.
- Vanessa uses the photo of Marcus and Catherine together to blackmail Blair into helping her.
- Chuck tells Serena what Bart's real motivations are for the new rules.
- Blair devises a plot for Chuck to "seduce and destroy" Vanessa.
- Over breakfast, Blair pretends not to have any interest in Chuck when Serena notices her Bass-inspired smile. She doesn't tell Serena about her plan to humiliate Vanessa and sleep with Chuck.
- On the phone, Dan fibs to Nate and doesn't tell him he's in N's seized house.
- Nate lies to Dan about the way things are at Casa Archibald. He's also lied to his mother, saying he was staying with Chuck.

meta moments

Without breaking the fourth wall, *Gossip Girl* likes to toss out self-references. Here a few of the best from a show that isn't afraid to poke fun at itself.

- "Oh my effing god!" says B on discovering Nate and Catherine *in flagrante delicto* in "Never Been Marcused." Blair's line is a big old wink at the camera imitating the much-discussed promotional images for *Gossip Girl*, which showed steamy stills stamped with OMFG.
- In "The Dark Night," Dan and Serena discover they have a fandom and they have haters. Mini Serena, Mini Blair, and Mini Mean Girl, the "should they, shouldn't they" forums Dan starts trolling — it's like the show's creators are hugging the audience.
- "No one watches TV on TV anymore." So says Eric van der Woodsen in "Chuck in Real Life" and so say the creators of *Gossip Girl*. Its audience doesn't sit down at a prescribed time to watch must-see TV on a TV set. Through online broadcasters and digital downloads, on computers or portable media players, *Gossip Girl* is ready when you are.
- Vanessa explains to Nate what will make her documentary about the school play in "The Age of Dissonance" compelling: "wealth, privilege, atrocious acting." Just what critics said about *Gossip Girl* when it premiered.

- Vanessa apologizes to Chuck for misjudging him. He is about to be honest with her when Blair texts him.
- Serena's angry with Bart for being a hypocrite and doesn't believe he had Eric's best interests in mind when he suggested Jonathan not come to the party.
- Bart assumes Chuck was trying to sneak the Brooklyn Inn deal past him, and feels his son betrayed his trust. (Chuck had no dishonest business intentions.)
- Vanessa eavesdrops on Bart's conversation with Chuck.
- Serena overshares with the *InStyle* reporter while Lily pretends their family is something it's not.
- Blair pretends to be bored with the bet when she's actually jealous, and she tells Vanessa the truth about why Chuck was helping her.

Scrap!: An angry Brooklynite throws an iced beverage at Chuck Bass, not helping with inter-borough relations.

You'll B a Woman Soon: When Blair sets out to destroy, she almost inevitably ends up being the one left the worse for wear. Her plan to humiliate Vanessa backfires as Chuck takes to the sweet, sassy girl from Brooklyn and leaves Blair in the cold. Avoiding emotional transparency at all costs, Blair takes it upon herself to embarrass Vanessa by telling her that they've been toying with her. But hurting V costs her a night with C. Will Blair learn anything from Chuck's appreciation for Vanessa's emotional transparency and say those three words?

The Original Gossipverse: Dan only has one guy friend in the book series, Zeke, and he ignores him.

That's How It's Done in *The O.C.*: When her mother starts putting on airs, being hypocritical, and keeping secrets, Marissa spills a big secret in a public setting in "The Perfect Couple." Like Nate in his seized townhouse, Julie Cooper-Nichol loses her formerly fabulous lifestyle and lives in a trailer park in season 3. Sandy Cohen, like Dan Humphrey, finds himself with no guy friends until "The Metamorphosis" when he forges a friendship. They play golf instead of soccer.

Dan in Real Life (dir. Peter Hedges, 2007): Widower, father, and advice columnist Dan Burns (Steve Carell) takes his three daughters to a family reunion weekend. Dan meets the charming Marie (Juliette Binoche) at the local book and tackle store, completely unaware that he's hitting on the girlfriend of his brother (Dane Cook). Lots of awkward situations crop up over the weekend as Dan and Marie pretend not to have met. Dan falls in love with her and can't seem to do anything right, alienating his daughters and pissing off his brother. Dan hasn't allowed himself to love anyone since his wife passed away and has filled that void with work and parenting. His wise children help him realize that denying himself is only making him (and them) crazy.

Navigating the perils of parenting is a large part of "Chuck in Real Life." Where one of Dan Burns' daughters tells him that he's a good father but sometimes a bad dad, with Lily the opposite is true: she's a good mom, but not the best mother. The delicate balance between being a devoted parent and having a life of your own is off for both Dan Burns and Lily. Lily is also fortunate to have a wise and insightful child; Eric's gentle honesty helps Lily see the valid cause of Serena's anger. Jealousy brings out the worst in all kinds of people, advice columnists and Upper East Side princesses alike. Dan Burns behaves as terribly when he has to watch his brother with Marie as Blair does seeing Chuck with Vanessa. Both are deceitful not only to others but to themselves, denying that they are in love. Blair's master plan falls apart when Chuck turns the tables on her. If only she could accept what Dan Burns does: plans don't work out, so plan to be surprised.

Welcome to the Real World:

- The name of the girl who gave mono to the lacrosse team is Lauren Goldenberg, a.k.a. *Gossip Girl*'s script coordinator.
- At home on a Saturday night, Serena is reading *Answered Prayers* by Truman Capote.
- Lily would jet off to Mustique, a private island in the West Indies, or Ibiza, a Spanish island known for its partying scene.
- Joe Kennedy (1888–1940), father to John F. Kennedy, made good money bootlegging during Prohibition, and according to *Gossip Girl*, he hung out at the Brooklyn Inn.
- Eric's ringtone for Lily was Kelly Clarkson's 2004 hit "Since U Been Gone."

Scandal: the van der Woodsen–Bass apartment isn't on the Upper East Side. With an East 55th Street address, the Milan Condos are actually in Midtown.

- Nicolas Sarkozy, president of France since 2007, would likely have dated Lily between 2005 and 2007 when his second marriage was basically over but he hadn't yet become involved with his third wife-to-be, Carla Bruni. He and Bruni went public with their relationship by going to Disneyland Paris.

Locations:
- Vanessa's campaign is to save The Brooklyn Inn (148 Hoyt St, Brooklyn).
- Serena tells Bart she's going with the girls to 1Oak (where she left her phone in "Woman on the Verge," 453 W 17th St) and Bijoux (57 Gansevoort St).
- Blair texts Chuck that she's on her way to J Sisters (35 W 57th St, 3rd Flr), presumably for their legendary waxing service.

Oops: Eric agreeing with Bart's suggestion that he might not want to come out in a national magazine makes zero sense. Jenny and Asher's party was last May and Gossip Girl posted the "gay bomb" that night. Anyone who googled Eric van der Woodsen would know, and more importantly everyone who Eric cares about already knows. It's not a secret.

Spotted: Assistant managing editor of *InStyle* Honor Brodie and managing editor Ariel Foxman are guests at the housewarming party. Artist Richard Phillips is also at the party for the official unveiling of "Spectrum," which hangs on the stairway wall of the apartment.

The Look: Serena carries a purple Bryna Nicole Loyola bag to school and wears a sequined silver Rebecca Taylor cardigan with her uniform. At breakfast with B, S wears a Cake Primary Ikat V-neck sweater, Rich & Skinny jeans, and Christian Louboutin Ginevra boots. Jenny makes fun of her big brother in a charcoal and purple striped Splendid dip-dye tee. The beaded crimson dress Chuck bought Blair, which just happens to match C's suit, is from Nodresscode and she wears it with a Pas Comme les Moutons headband. A tad outside her price range, Vanessa wears an Eskell Dahlia dress and Gabriela de la Vega necklace to the housewarming but keeps it real with an H&M bag. Lily's red dress is Armani, her jewelry is Van Cleef & Arpels, her Rosazissimo shoes are Christian Louboutin, and her hair is terrible. What happened, Lil? Serena decides to attend the housewarming party, and she wears a McQ by

marquise de waldorf & vicomte de bass

"Chuck in Real Life" borrows *heavily* from the *Liaisons Dangereuses* story. Originally from an 18th-century French novel, the story of rivals who relentlessly toy with others and each other for their own sick enjoyment has been re-imagined many times, most notably in two film adaptations: *Dangerous Liaisons* (1988) and *Cruel Intentions* (1999).

Dangerous Liaisons (itself based on a play adaptation by Christopher Hampton) pairs the Marquise de Merteuil (Glenn Close) and Vicomte de Valmont (John Malkovich) as competitors in a game of seduction and destruction. The Marquise requests Valmont make his next target Cécile de Volanges (Uma Thurman), the virgin who is betrothed to the Marquise's former lover, but he has his eye on Madame de Tourvel (Michelle Pfieffer), a married woman known for her virtue. Her plot is for revenge; his is to make a woman betray all that she believes in. Once Valmont discovers Cécile's mother has been bad-mouthing him, he says why not take on two seductions at once? The deal is sweetened when the Marquise promises Valmont that she'll spend the night with him once both seductions are complete. Using Cécile's innocent blossoming love with the Chevalier Danceny (Keanu Reeves) as an excuse for secret meetings, Valmont beds Cécile. Madame de Tourvel proves a more difficult target and Valmont inadvertently falls in love with her goodness. When he has finally broken her down and she acquiesces, he is overwhelmed with her candor and their extraordinary lovemaking. The Marquise forces Valmont to completely break off his relationship with Tourvel, promising that if he does that, she will finally sleep with him. He does, repeating the phrase "It is beyond my control" (he says it about 100 times), and Tourvel falls desperately ill with heartache. Jealous that Valmont no longer loves her but Tourvel, the Marquise balks on their bargain, angering Valmont. The Marquise declares victory over him and he declares war on her. She has seduced the Chevalier so Valmont takes him away from her by using Cécile. The Marquise fights back by telling the Chevalier about Valmont's affair with Cécile. They duel and Valmont is fatally injured. As his last act, he sends Tourvel letters that show how dastardly the Marquise is. The Marquise is publicly scorned when the Chevalier publishes them. Valmont dies, and upon hearing the news of his death, Tourvel does too.

The plot of *Cruel Intentions* is the same save a few differences. Instead of 18th-century France, it's set in turn-of-the-21st century Upper East Side among spoiled teenagers. Kathryn Merteuil (Sarah Michelle Gellar) appears to be a perfect and morally upstanding girl but really she's a diabolical sex addict who teases her equally twisted stepbrother Sebastian Valmont (Ryan Phillippe). At the end of the movie, Sebastian is killed saving Annette (Reese Witherspoon), the girl he seduced and fell in love with, from oncoming traffic in Central Park. Epic.

The structure of the Blair/Chuck plot has the same basic outline: Blair asks Chuck to seduce Vanessa and sweetens the bargain with the promise of sex, C finds V initially resistant to him, C finds himself strangely enjoying hanging out in Brooklyn with V, B gets jealous and destroys what C is building with V. But unlike the Marquise or Kathryn, Blair's willing to let Chuck "claim his prize." Chuck is the one who refuses her. To quote B, "Are. You. Kidding?"

Alexander McQueen Blue Tonic blazer (with no apparent shirt underneath) and her skirt is Rag & Bone. Blair's red lingerie is from Agent Provocateur.

Music: Breakfast at the Bass–van der Woodsens is to "Snowflakes" by White Apple Tree. Vanessa brings Chuck to meet Horace at The Brooklyn Inn while The Black Keys' "Psychotic Girl" is playing. The housewarming party begins with "Take Back the City" by Snow Patrol. Bart and Chuck talk business in the kitchen to Morrissey guitarist Alain Whyte's "City Nights." Another track from Whyte, "NYC Streets," plays as Serena and Eric talk. Whyte's "Martini Lounge" plays when Blair calls off the bet with Chuck. B tells C to meet in her room for his reward and "One Week of Danger" by The Virgins kicks in. (It also played in "Seventeen Candles" when B had a flashback to her first hookup with Chuck.) Chuck returns to The Brooklyn Inn and Horace is listening to Mildred Anderson's "Hard Times." Chuck dares Blair to say she loves him to Guillemots' "Sea Out."

"Sorry J, but in the real world you can't take a note to the principal when a drunken model eats your homework."

2.08 prêt-a-poor j

Original air date: October 27, 2008
Written by: Amanda Lasher
Directed by: Vondie Curtis Hall
Guest cast: Willa Holland (Agnes Andrews), Wade Allain-Marcus (Max)

As Serena and Dan try to be friends, he gets roped into helping Blair get Chuck. Jenny gets a new rocker look, wild friend, bad attitude, and steamy love interest.

After the previous episode's *Cruel Intentions* knock-off, the show bounces back to form with new characters (Aaron and Agnes), couples (Jenny and Nate!), co-conspirators (Blair and Dan), enemies (Jenny and Eleanor), and no small measure of humiliation and embarrassment. Using Dan's "drive him crazy" suggestion, Blair tries over-the-top seduction tactics with Chuck and her frustration is comic genius. But once she decides to take the big leap — telling Chuck she loves him — the mood of this plot turns. After Dan deliberately shakes her confidence, Blair is overcome by her insecurities and she chickens out, opting to rehash his wrongs rather than tell him the truth. In a moment of bravery for Chuck, he later comes to her and tells her that they can't be a normal, boring couple. From her pitch-perfect bitchy asides to that solitary tear, Leighton Meester's performance in "Prêt-a-Poor J" is outstanding.

For a girl so headstrong, Jenny Humphrey falls under other people's influences rather easily. Last year it was the Mean Girls and now it's Agnes. After a summer and then some slaving away at the atelier, Jenny feels entitled to more respect and gratitude from Eleanor than she's getting — especially when it's her dresses that are catching the eyes of the buyers. Tired of being treated like a child (and called one) by her father and by Eleanor, J gets swept up in Agnes's rock-glam lifestyle and big ideas. Nate walking in on their bra-dance-party was one of the best secondary-embarrassment moments of *Gossip Girl* thus far. But the moment that followed was even better: Jenny kissing Nate and him kissing her back. Definitely the most passionate new couple moment since Chuck and Blair.

"I can skip dinner now that I'm so full on humiliation."
— Blair reports back to Dan on her failed attempt to seduce Chuck

JTLYK:

- No Lily this episode.
- Gossip Girl quotes Donna Summer in her top story: "*Working Girl?* Ever since Jenny dropped out of Constance she has been logging countless hours at Eleanor's atelier. Little J works hard for her money so you better treat her right."
- The scene of Blair walking with Chuck, who rides alongside her in his limo, is an echo of their similar conversation in "Seventeen Candles" when Blair was leaving confession the morning after she lost her virginity.
- Both Blair and Chuck have to take things into their own hands, so to speak, when sex is off the table until one of them says I love you.
- Another candlelit sexy setup fail!
- Agnes's MySpace profile says she's 16 years old and her mood is evil.
- Aaron Rose's installation at Rufus's gallery (and his art in future episodes) was created by artist Nathan Nedorostek, who worked with the producers and writers to create an artistic persona for Aaron that was "honest, but slightly pretentious."

Secrets & Lies:

- Eleanor reneges on her promise to let Jenny into the buyers' meetings.
- Blair can't tell Chuck the truth (she loves him) because if she does, she'll lose their game.
- Just as Chuck is falling for Blair's seduction plot, a text from Serena revealing how cocky B is ruins the moment.
- Serena has an ulterior motive for bringing Blair to the gallery: to see Aaron again.
- Jenny is caught in her lie when Eleanor reveals Laurel saw the photos of her and Agnes partying the night before.
- Vanessa didn't tell Dan about Chuck and Blair using her as "catnip" because she was embarrassed.
- Dan intentionally crushes Blair's confidence so she won't tell Chuck how she truly feels.
- Jenny tells Nate to lie to Rufus if he asks where she went.
- Jenny doesn't tell her dad or brother that she quit Eleanor's.
- Chuck and Blair finally have an honest conversation about their relationship.

You'll B a Woman Soon: So close! After her seduction game fails, Blair is very nearly able to tell Chuck what she's been hiding in plain sight for over a year: she loves him. And though neither can say it, their final conversation is at least honest and provides them both with some peace. What will B do with all her spare time now that they've pressed pause on their game?

The Original Gossipverse: Aaron Rose appears in the second *Gossip* book, complete with a dog named Mookie. A high school senior, Aaron is a dread-locked vegan who starts dating Serena in *All I Want Is Everything*. Jenny is in trouble with the headmistress and Rufus when photos of her partying (with The Raves) appear on the Page Six website in *Nobody Does it Better*. In *Nothing Can Keep Us Together*, Little J decides to ditch Constance after her freshman year, opting for boarding school (and a spin-off book series, *The It Girl*) not homeschooling.

That's How It's Done in *The O.C.*: Seth could have been classmates with Aaron Rose at RISD; he was accepted at the school in the season 3 finale. Willa Holland, who plays Agnes, played bad girl little sister Kaitlin Cooper in seasons 3 and 4.

Prêt-à-Porter (dir. Robert Altman, 1994): A satire of the fashion industry set during Paris's fashion week, this Altman-length film features more cameos and subplots than you can count. Kitty Potter (Kim Basinger), a TV host, helps stitch together the pieces (a murder plot, a fashion line being sold to a boot company, a love affair between two luggage-less journalists) of a wild, fast, and loose world of fashion and freakish characters. Not well received by film critics or the fashion industry, *Prêt-à-Porter* is a mixed bag, full of clever homages to classic film and people stepping in dog poop. Its big finish is an all-nude runway show, which leads Kitty to realize that all this fashion world hysteria is itself a load of dog poop. Oddly entertaining, the film presents the world of fashion as more sensationalism than substance.

Throwing herself in, Jenny navigates the wacky world of the fashion industry. She leaves the staid mentorship of Eleanor Waldorf for the guidance of the entertaining but unreliable Agnes. J loves fashion more than anything, but will she love the fashion world or will she, like Kitty, declare Agnes and her act to be nothing more than a show?

Welcome to the Real World:

- Aaron went to the Rhode Island School of Design (RISD) in Providence; it's one of the highest-ranked fine art schools in the U.S.
- Isabel's godfather, Warren Buffett, was ranked by *Forbes* as the world's second-richest billionaire (with a net worth of $37 billion) in 2009.
- Charlize Theron signed a contract to become the face of Dior back in 2004. Apparently B does not *J'Adore* her.
- The porn DVD Chuck picks up is *Ticket 2 Ride*, which costars a woman calling herself Dru Berrymore.
- Serena's knowledge of welding comes from 1983's *Flashdance*, which follows Alex, a welder by day, dancer by night. Let's hope S knows the "Maniac" dance too.
- The beloved center fielder William Hayward "Mookie" Wilson played for the New York Mets in the '80s, and Nana Rose loved him enough to name Aaron's dog after him.
- Serena met Aaron at Camp Suisse, held at a resort in Torgon, Switzerland (not too far from the banks of Lake Geneva). Campers aged 7 to 17 stay for two weeks and participate in cultural and sports activities, language education, and learn how to make perfectly crafted licorice rings.

Oops: When Blair flops back onto her bed after Dorota's interruption, the headboard wobbles like a prop. When Blair turns to face Chuck in his limo, she does the action twice from two different camera angles.

The Look: Blair sits on the hood of the limo in a navy and black Marc by Marc Jacobs Scribble houndstooth skirt. Her red bag is Celine Orlov. When Serena first meets Aaron, she's in a burgundy Valentino sweater, J Brand jeans, black Jonathan Kelsey boots, and has a metallic python Devi Kroell hobo bag. Attempting to seduce Chuck, Blair has a drink with him wearing a Nanette Lepore Magic Wand silk dress in, of course, purple. Carrying a Kate Spade Spring Island 2 Evan with Rose tote, Blair wears a Temperley London Zola mini dress to tell Chuck she loves him. Jenny attends the Aaron Rose opening wearing a J. Humphrey original (a.k.a. an Eric Daman original) with a David & Young marbled knit beret, Rachel Leigh short necklace, Pinkyotto long necklace, and Rachel Leigh and Nine West bracelets. Serena wears a plum Foley + Corinna dress, a leather Doma bomber jacket, and has a Gianfranco Ferré bag.

Music: Blair's back-of-the-limo fantasy is to Robyn's "Crash and Burn Girl." J is out for drinks with Agnes at a bar playing "Partie Traumatic" by Black Kids. Chuck sees Blair lighting candles in Serena's room to "With Light There Is Hope" by Princess One Point Five. Mad Staring Eyes' "Walking in the Streets" is the soundtrack for the impromptu photo shoot at the bar. Jenny hangs with Agnes and Max to "Robot Talk" by Alain Whyte. The song that

Willa Holland as Agnes Andrews

Best known for her role as Mini Coop, Marissa Cooper's bad-ass little sister Kaitlin, on *The O.C.*, Willa Holland was "discovered" by none other than Steven Spielberg when he told her mother that Willa had to be put in front of a camera. He was echoing Willa's stepfather, filmmaking legend Brian de Palma. An actress and model, Willa was in two independent feature films in 2008, *Middle of Nowhere* with Susan Sarandon and *Genova* with Colin Firth. Of her character on *Gossip Girl*, Willa said, "She has good intentions, but she goes about it the wrong way. . . . She's kind of flaky."

is so awesome that Agnes has to dance around with her top off is t.A.T.u.'s cover of The Smiths' "How Soon Is Now." "Dark on Fire" by Turin Brakes plays as Chuck and Blair realize why they can't say "I love you."

"I spy with my little lie someone getting busted."

2.09 there might be blood

Original air date: November 3, 2008
Written by: Etan Frankel, John Stephens
Directed by: Michael Fields
Guest cast: Willa Holland (Agnes Andrews), Patricia Kalember (Mrs. Boardman), Stella Maeve (Emma Boardman), Michaela Annette (Mini Serena), Stephen Beach (Cop), Gonzalo Escudero (Buckman), Jabari Gray (Man with List), Eva Kaminsky (Housekeeper), Robert Stoeckle (Head of Society)

Jenny launches her clothing line with a guerrilla fashion show. Blair plays babysitter while Serena moons over her new love interest.

Why the charity gala is the *only* chance *ever* for Jenny to launch her fashion line is never explained, but the result is good fun. Sometimes the ends have to justify the means, says Jenny to Nate, and she seems to believe it. She so badly wants to prove herself and be a success that she is back to her old ways: lying to her family, sneaking around, and doing quasi-illegal things. The success of the fashion show just reinforces her convictions. Failing to get a reference letter for his ho-hum stories, Dan decides that his little sis knows what she's doing and comes over to her side. The dark side, if you ask Rufus. The showdown between Rufus and Jenny drives her right out of the loft; she's determined to make it on her own.

Blair also toys with the "any means necessary" philosophy. Discovering Mrs. Boardman having an affair provides Blair with the perfect bargaining chip to get what she desires most in life: a spot at Yale. Like Jenny with Rufus, Blair refuses to listen to Serena's do-gooder advice. It's only when she sees her own lifelong issues reflected in Emma that she decides against blackmail. Like B, Emma suffers from a mother who's overbearing and emotionally distant. Knowing what that feels like (as well as how a parent's infidelity can hurt), Blair gives Emma the same advice Dan gave her in "Bad News Blair":

tell your mother how you feel. Her act of kindness is rewarded with a promising call from Dean Berube.

Romance on the Upper East Side is no less complicated. Nate and Jenny's new relationship barely gets started before it's ground to a halt with Dan and Vanessa freaking out over it. With Nate leaving town for the Hamptons and Jenny wandering the streets, who knows if these two lovebirds will ever reconnect. Serena can't stop thinking about Aaron, but doesn't want to settle for being one of a harem. Will she be able to resist his licorice rings, awkward facial hair, and inability to give a straight answer to a serious question?

"Just so you know, while there are few things I consider sacred, the back of the limo is one of them."
— Chuck Bass, so skeezy and so sweet in the same sentence

JTLYK:

- Top story on Gossip Girl: "*Little J vs. The Queen Mum*. Move over, B. J has a new Waldorf enemy: Eleanor. We just hope Little J knows what she's doing. We don't want to see her go from fashion star to fashion victim."
- Chuck calls Emma's suitor "Humbert Humbert," the protagonist of Nabokov's *Lolita* (1955) who falls for the 12-year-old title character.

- The girl who takes the picture of Nate and Jenny kissing is Little Serena from "The Dark Night."
- The Gossip Girl blast on N and J reads: "Spotted at the Palace! Nate Archibald and Little J. Like the song says, 'How long has this been going on . . . ?'"
- Blair thinks God wants her to blackmail her way into Yale. The last time she mentioned the Man Upstairs was in "Seventeen Candles" when she thanked him for bringing Nate back to her with a diamond necklace in tow.
- What Rufus doesn't know is that this is the second time Jenny's nearly been arrested. The first was in "Dare Devil" when she was caught in Eleanor Waldorf's store.
- It's rather unlikely that both Nate and Dan would have a *very* important letter to mail *that* morning, but the mail montage was such an old-school TV moment where characters have painfully obvious parallel experiences. Was it U.S. Postal Service product placement?

Secrets & Lies:

- Nate pretends not to know that Jenny quit Eleanor's.
- Agnes and Jenny lie to Dan and Nate saying they're going to eat pizza and watch *Project Runway* when it's actually time for Project Guerrilla Runway.
- Emma hides who she really is from her mother, putting on a show of being prissy, well-mannered, and innocent.
- J and Agnes are caught on their way out of the loft.
- Emma threatens to ruin B's chances to get into Yale if Blair rats on her.
- Vanessa suggests that Dan cover for Jenny rather than tell Rufus what she's up to. Rufus overhears the conversation and makes the choice for him.
- Serena and Blair lie to Emma about the charity event being a good place to pick up.
- Jenny says she's Erica van der Woodsen to sneak into the gala.
- Using his tried-and-true talking-to-grownups voice, Nate helps Jenny out with a lie to Lily, saying J's there as his date.
- Emma's mother is having an affair and Blair takes an incriminating photo.
- Dan hides the Gossip Girl photo of Nate and Jenny from Vanessa and

Rufus, but nearly reveals Nate's affair with Catherine to Rufus in the cab.

- Serena warns Blair that she shouldn't blackmail her way into Yale.
- Dan confronts Nate and Nate apologizes for kissing Jenny but tells Dan he has no right to judge him about the Catherine affair.
- Chuck gets Gossip Girl to post a fake story about Muffy to stop Emma from sleeping with Serge.
- Vanessa sees Jenny and Nate kissing.
- Blair keeps Mrs. Boardman's affair a secret.

Scrap!: Confronting him about the Gossip blast, Dan shoves Nate. Agnes stomps on glassware, likely giving *someone* at least a little cut.

You'll B a Woman Soon: Nothing like seeing a little version of yourself trying too hard to remind you what's important in life. In Emma, Blair sees who she used to be not too long ago: a girl competing with her friend and desperate to lose her virginity, even if it's to someone who shouldn't necessarily be trusted — slimeball Serge or slept-with-S Nate. Empathizing with Emma leads Blair to do the Serena-sanctioned right thing — get the girl home safe and don't use another's misfortune to profit. Blair is rewarded for her good deed. And the icing on the cake? She got to trade barbs with Chuck while they chased after the little vixen.

The Original Gossipverse: In *You Know You Love Me*, Nate and Jenny start hanging out and smoking pot together and soon they're kissing. There are photos of Jenny posing in her bra in *You're the One That I Want*, but it's for an official modeling gig.

That's How It's Done in *The O.C.*: Sadly, Blair Waldorf did not invent the word "lacrossetitute." In "The Man of the Year," one of Kaitlin's boarding school friends (played by *Privileged*'s Lucy Hale) says it.

There Will Be Blood (dir. Paul Thomas Anderson, 2007): Daniel Plainview (Daniel Day-Lewis) is a prospector in search of silver but finds oil in California at the turn of 20th century. He takes in an orphaned baby boy, H.W., and as he raises him he builds an oil empire. Finding oil on land in possession of the Sunday family, Plainview makes an offer to buy it; as

John Patrick Amedori as Aaron Rose

Born in 1987 in Baltimore, John Patrick Amedori began working as an actor in the late '90s but landed his first major role as the young Evan in *The Butterfly Effect* and has worked steadily since. He played Max Collins on the short-lived TV series *Vanished.* He and Penn Badgley often ran into each other at auditions, where they were up for the same parts. When John arrived on the *Gossip Girl* set, he was happy to see a friendly face. Said John of his time on the show, "Everyone's really nice, really cool. They don't make me feel like an outsider, which is fortunate for me." Also musically talented, John Patrick wrote and performed "Love Song" for the Jeff Bridges film *Stick It*, as well as playing the role of Poot.

he builds his oil derrick, so Eli Sunday builds his new church. The two men have different ideas about how to run things, religion, and the town's future. While tension builds between them, the vast ocean of oil beneath the ground overwhelms the derrick. It explodes and H.W. loses his hearing. Plainview trusts a con artist and then kills him; H.W. is sent away when he commits arson. Plainview is alone in his life. A plan to build an oil pipeline is complicated by a piece of land not owned or easily acquired by Plainview: he must convert to Eli's church. A non-believer, Plainview agrees and is humiliated in his baptism. Turning even more to his work and to drink, Plainview ends up an angry old man in a mansion who humiliates and alienates his son and destroys Eli.

Plainview's single-minded determination to succeed as an oil man leads him to do terrible things — manipulating, betraying, lying, cheating, and murdering. While Jenny only disrupts a charity event, she has that same ambition, that compulsion to succeed, which she showed last year in her climb up the Constance social ladder. The way she says to Nate, "The ends *have* to justify the means" reveals a crack in her resolve, a moral code she doesn't want to break. Hopefully she won't meet an end analogous to Plainview's: success achieved but at the cost of everything important and dear.

Welcome to the Real World:

- Jenny and Agnes would've been watching reruns of Bravo's fashion design competition show *Project Runway*. Season 5 wrapped up in October.

- Serena went to Karl Lagerfeld's birthday; the German fashion designer who once helmed Chanel and now runs Fendi and his own label celebrated his birthday on September 10 but is cagey about how old he turned. (Rumor has it he changed the year on his birth certificate from '33 to '38.)
- Mrs. Boardman is off to see friends from Bryn Mawr, the women's liberal arts college in Pennsylvania, one of the Seven Sisters colleges.
- Waiting for Emma, Blair's flipping through the October 2008 issue of *InStyle* with Meg Ryan on the cover.
- The side Emma shows her mother is sweet and innocent little Holly Hobbie, who has nothing but alliteration in common with Jenna Jameson, once known as the Queen of Porn, who Blair describes Emma as to Serena.
- At the fictional New York Philanthropic Society's gala, J's looking for potential investors from companies like media conglomerate Hearst and luxury brand holding companies LVMH and PPR.

Locations:

- Jenny buys her fabric at Mood (225 W 37th St, # 3).
- Emma's plan is to go to Socialista (505 West St) and then Beatrice (285 W 12th St).
- Both Emma and her mother end up at 1Oak (453 W 17th St, pictured below).
- Nate's address is 4 East 74th Street.

Spotted: Providing a distraction for Emma to take advantage of, Scott Sartiano says hi to Serena at 1Oak. Sartiano is the mastermind behind *Gossip* favorites Butter and 1Oak and is known on the gossip pages for his past relationships with Anne Hathaway, Ashley Olsen, and Jamie-Lynn Sigler.

The Look: Having tea with Mrs. Boardman, Serena's wearing a rather low-cut grey Iisli sweater dress with Chloe booties and has a Valentino Petale Rose tote. Blair's in a pomegranate-red Catherine Malandrino ruffled sleeve shirt dress. As she chases Emma around town, Blair wears a plum Nanette Lepore Lucky Stars cardigan with black beading over a Milly sequined shift dress. At her guerilla fashion show, Jenny's cream and black dress is H&M with Aldo shoes (so income-bracket appropriate), her necklace is DebraJill Designs, and her fascinator is I Love Factory. J's jacket is Nanette Lepore's

music supervisor alex patsavas

Raised and educated in Illinois, Alex Patsavas described herself in her early music fanatic days as "that kid who had the bad '80s haircut who went to all the clubs and shows." Booking bands to play at her college led to a job at Triad (now William Morris) where she worked her way up from the mailroom before making the leap to BMI's film and television department. It was there that she discovered the job of a music supervisor existed. "I liked it because I've always been interested in all sorts of music, including classical," said Alex. "And I saw music supervision as a way to not only keep really current on music, but to use all of my music tastes." She went to work for the legendary filmmaker Roger Corman at Concorde Films and music supervised more than 50 B-movie classics over the course of three years. In 1999, she formed her own company, Chop Shop Music Supervision, and worked on a couple of movies (the excellent *Happy, Texas* and the terrible *Gun Shy*) before focusing her company primarily on TV series. Starting with *Roswell*, Alex has gone on to music supervise *Carnivale*, *Boston Public*, *Fastlane*, *Private Practice*, *Chuck*, *Without a Trace*, *Rescue Me*, *Mad Men*, *Supernatural*, *Numb3rs*, and, most famously, *Grey's Anatomy* and *The O.C.* In 2007, Alex formed a music label named after her company, Chop Shop Records, and landed a deal with Atlantic Records. Among her more recent film projects is a little movie called *Twilight;* its soundtrack was released on Chop Shop Records and debuted at the top of the Billboard 200.

For *Gossip Girl*, Alex works closely with executive producers Josh Schwartz and Stephanie Savage to establish what an episode's music should sound like and how much of it there should be. Because of the setting, she chooses a lot of New York–based bands, but her selections run the gamut from pop to indie rock to classical, and from established

Cheek to Cheek velveteen leopard coat in coffee bean. Serena's dress for the event is Just Cavalli; her mother's in Vera Wang. Runaway J is wearing the gorgeous cashmere Jamison Rollins stripe wrap hooded sweater in pepper.

Music: The episodes opens with a cover of the Ramones' "Sheena Is a Punk Rocker" by Thurston Moore and Jemina Pearl, which also plays during J's guerilla fashion show. Dan and Vanessa talk in the café to "The Host's a Parasite" (The Henry Clay People). Jenny and Nate talk outside the Palace while "The Preafterlife (The Air Is All Around You, Baby)" by Porterville plays in the background. Kinky's "Papel Volando" is playing at 1Oak when the girls catch up with Emma. Serena and Blair argue over what to do about the Boardmans to "The Only One" by Deathray. The "Summer"

artists to the totally unknown. Each week, Alex and her music coordinating team send comps (compilation CDs) of music that they think might work to Josh, Stephanie, and the picture editors who review them. Explained Alex, "Song spots [in an episode] become obvious as we view the footage as it comes in, and we work closely together to fill those particular spots. Each episode has a budget and sometimes we can't afford every single song that we hope to use, so we have to replace things based on budget. Basically we put in as many songs as an episode requires." Finding and organizing music has become easier for Alex since she started music supervising over 10 years ago. What used to be analog is now digital; any song that Alex loves she files in a digital system so she and her team can find it anytime. And with her success and high-profile projects, Alex receives about 500 submissions of music per week, in addition to the stuff she seeks out herself by going to shows, reading blogs, and checking out MySpace. In the not-so-distant past, having a song on a show like *Gossip Girl* would have been selling out for an independent band, but now it's seen as a great opportunity, especially if it's a show Alex works on. "We use music respectfully and we're fans of the bands we use. [We try to] use a song in a place where their music can ring out and fans can really hear it."

Considering whether the instrumentation and lyrics fit the scene and whether the song can be cleared for use, Alex selects songs that "enhance the drama" of a moment. One special scene in "There Might Be Blood" was Jenny's guerrilla fashion show. Alex wanted to find a song that was "New York, punk rock, rebellious" as well as fun and lively; the Ramones' song "Sheena Is a Punk Rocker" came to mind. After Stephanie Savage found out that Thurston Moore of Sonic Youth had referenced *Gossip Girl* during a recent concert, she and Alex approached him about doing a modern take on the classic song. With Jemina Pearl from Be Your Own Pet, he recorded the cover version just for *Gossip Girl*.

movement of Vivaldi's *Four Seasons* is playing when Nate and Dan have their run-in at the Palace. The closing montage is to "No New Tale to Tell" by Love and Rockets.

"Every Bass will have his day."

2.10 bonfire of the vanity

Original air date: November 10, 2008
Written by: Jessica Queller
Directed by: David Von Ancken
Guest cast: David Patrick Kelly (Noah Shapiro), Brennan Brown (Mr. Smith), Peter Francis James (James Wolf), Daniel Stewart Sherman (Deep Throat), Gonzalo Escudero (Buckman), Justin Keyes (Robert), Joy Nakayama (Danielle)

On the eve of her 18th birthday, Blair meets her mother's new boyfriend. Dan takes on his first assignment: an exposé on Bart Bass.

Lesson of the week? Choose your business partner wisely. Jenny figures out pretty quickly that banking her livelihood on a 16-year-old model who likes to party was maybe a bad idea. As Jenny tries hard to realize her ambition, Agnes escalates from unreliable to full-on crazytown. Jenny's dresses are all she has left — having alienated her family and friends, dropped out of school, and quit her job, but they go up in flames as Agnes's punishment for Jenny's betrayal — fitting if you're a 15th-century Catholic but a punishment far outweighing the "crime" in this case. Besides the dress fire, there are other flames in "Bonfire of the Vanity": Bart is guilty of having a building burned down in Midtown, he reads Dan's story with his roaring fireplace behind him, and Serena and Aaron's musical theme is "Sex on Fire."

Just as Dan tricks Bart into spending time with him under false pretences, so does Blair with Cyrus. Both Dan and Blair have to make a decision: reveal the information they've discovered, causing destruction to get what they want, or stay quiet. Blair chooses destruction, telling her mother about Cyrus's affair in Vietnam and crushing Eleanor's happiness. Of all the cruel things Blair's done in the show so far, this moment is particularly difficult to watch. Luckily for Eleanor and for Blair, Cyrus is resilient and can outmaneuver B, winning over both her and the audience. Though Dan decides to keep Bart's secret, it's not before he does a cruel thing to his parent, telling Bart that Rufus isn't a good enough role model for him. *Ouch*. Dan knows the history between Bart and Rufus; it's a pretty low move. But Dan chooses not to write the story with the weight of his father's advice and Chuck's plea not to. Instead he shares his Charlie Trout story and helps to bring about the only emotionally honest conversation Chuck and Bart Bass have ever had.

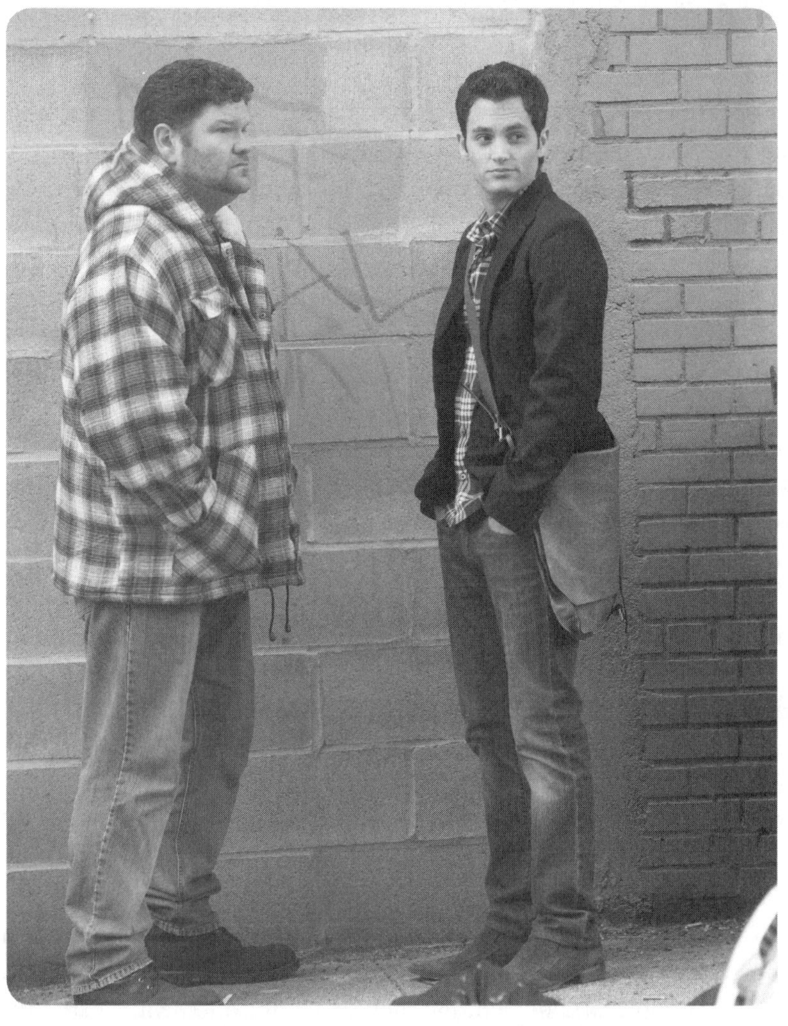

At Fulton Landing in Brooklyn, Penn Badgley films a scene with an actor brave enough to snitch on Bart Bass.

"A guy starts out in his Blue Period and everything's great. But it's only a matter of time before he's all into Cubism and it's some other girl's eye coming out of her forehead."
— B warns S about the dangers of being Aaron's muse

JTLYK:

- Nate, Vanessa, Lily, and Eric are all missing in action this week.
- Top story on Gossip Girl: "*Little J Fashion Star*. After a hugely successful guerilla fashion show it looks like Little J is on her way to designer fame and fortune. Pretty impressive for a fifteen year old from Brooklyn. We just hope Little J's lasts longer than fifteen minutes."
- The *Falò delle vanità*, or bonfire of the vanities, is a religious ceremony where material things that could tempt one into sin are tossed into a fire.
- The Waldorfs' everyday china is Bernardaud, the Constance pattern.
- Says Gossip Girl, "Every Bass will have his day," a play on Hamlet's oft-quoted line: "Let Hercules himself do what he may,/ The cat will mew and dog will have his day."
- Dan says his meeting with the informant was just like *All the President's Men*, the 1976 film about Bob Woodward and Carl Bernstein, the journalists who broke the Watergate story for the *Washington Post*.
- Why wasn't Chuck at Blair's birthday party?
- In "Never Been Marcused," Rufus returned home and admired the fruits of his children's work, Jenny's dresses and Dan's writing. Now those very passions have led them away from what he thinks is the right and moral path.
- Gossip Girl combines an *Annie* reference (Little Orphan Jenny and Daddy Warbucks) with a shout-out to *A Tree Grows in Brooklyn*, a coming-of-age novel by Betty Smith about a young, poor Brooklyn girl.
- As Serena and Aaron traipse off, Gossip Girl closes the episode with a namedrop of *Barefoot in the Park*, Neil Simon's play about a New York couple, one of whom is more of a free spirit than the other.

Secrets & Lies:

- Rufus tries to act like he's OK with Jenny staying with Agnes.
- Dan tells Bart he's interested in the construction business and flatters him so he can spend time with the mogul and get material for his exposé.

- Jenny snoops in Agnes's purse and sets up a meeting without her.
- Chuck spots Dan meeting with the *New York* people.
- Unlike Harold, who cheated on her, Eleanor likes Cyrus because she can trust him.
- Dan finds out a major secret about Bart Bass: he had a building burned down in the '80s to collect insurance money.
- Blair finds out about Cyrus's past and uses it against him, telling Eleanor that he cheated on his ex-wife.
- Dan lies to Bart, saying he overheard the arson story and wants Bart's explanation.
- Chuck tells Bart about the *New York* story and asks Dan to keep his father's secret.
- Cyrus was wise to Blair's plan and managed to outmaneuver her with Cyndi Lauper.
- Dan gives Bart his story, revealing how Chuck actually feels about his father.
- Jenny doesn't tell Rufus that she can't stay at Agnes's anymore and crashes at the gallery.

You'll B a Woman Soon: On the eve of her official entry into adulthood, Blair gives maturity a shot, repeating her mantra ("I am Grace Kelly. Grace Kelly is me.") to overcome the disgust she has for her mother's choice of boyfriend. When she reverts to underhandedness, she is ashamed. As she spits out Cyrus's secret to hurt her mother, her disgust with herself is visible. Cyrus's birthday present to her is not Cyndi Lauper at her party but, as B tells Cyndi, a conscience.

The Original Gossipverse: Considerably less personable, Cyrus Rose is in the picture from the very first *Gossip Girl* book and Blair does not like him. She finds him physically repulsive and déclassé.

That's How It's Done in *The O.C.*: In "The Lonely Hearts Club," Seth acts completely unprofessional in a meeting with Zach, Summer, and a comic book publisher and ruins the deal. Like Blair to Cyrus, Kaitlin is mean to her would-be stepfather, eager for more time and attention from her mother, in "The Shake Up."

The Bonfire of the Vanities (dir. Brian de Palma, 1990): Based on the 1987 novel by Tom Wolfe, the film is narrated by writer Peter Fallow (Bruce Willis) and bookended by scenes of him at the height of his fame, hopelessly drunk. The crux of film's theme comes from Mark 8:36, which Fallow recites in his narration, "For what does it profit a man if he gains the whole world and loses his soul." Living in luxury on the Upper East Side, Sherman McCoy (Tom Hanks) is in a loveless marriage to Judy (Kim Cattrall) and having an affair with Maria (Melanie Griffith). The lovers take a wrong turn on their way to her apartment and end up in a bad neighborhood in the Bronx; Maria hits a black teenager with the car and they drive away. The boy, Henry Lamb, ends up in a coma, and the black community, led by Reverend Bacon, uses this incident as a symbol of the race and class divide. Peter Fallow is roped in as the journalist who will break the story, and piece by piece, Sherman's life falls apart as he takes the fall for the crime. Losing everything, Sherman repents his selfish waste of a life. In his trial, the only way for the truth to be revealed (that Maria was driving) is for Sherman to lie (about how he obtained key evidence). Fallow publishes the story of Sherman McCoy, a man who started with wealth, lost everything, and gained a soul, and when the book is an unparalleled success, Fallow realizes he's the opposite — he started with nothing, gained everything, but lost his soul in the process.

Dan finds himself in the same position as Fallow: a writer with a scoop that will make his career but destroy a man. Rufus's argument against writing the story and the conclusion Dan comes to himself saves Dan from Fallow's fate, a man who compares himself to a whore (but the best in the whorehouse). Distanced from his father, who has always disapproved of him, Sherman McCoy is given one brief moment of closeness with him when his father reaches out before the trial to say he'll always love him and support him. Chuck gets the same kind of moment with Bart, an unusual break in Bart's stone-faced façade. Though the film was not very well received, *The Bonfire of the Vanities* is a complementary portrayal of the Upper East Side to *Gossip Girl*'s and one worth watching, if only to see Kirsten Dunst as a precocious six-year-old.

Welcome to the Real World:

- Blair compares Aaron to Picasso. Spanish-born painter Pablo Picasso's moody Blue Period (roughly 1901–1904) predated his more famous and influential Cubist work, which began with 1907's *Les Demoiselles d'Avignon*, a painting of not just one woman, but five.

- Blair and her mom love Cyndi Lauper, but *Vibes* wouldn't have been their first DVD purchase. The 1988 comedy starring Cyndi and Jeff Goldblum wasn't released on DVD until February 2009.

Locations:

- Aaron puts Serena onscreen in Times Square (Broadway and Seventh Aves).
- Agnes nurses her hangover by a Vitamin Water display at Mangiami (9 Stanton St).
- Chuck spies Dan meeting at *New York* magazine's offices (75 Varick St).
- Cyrus buys out Cyndi's gig at Joe's Pub (425 Lafayette St).
- One of Serena's favorite places in Manhattan is the old puppet theater, the Swedish Marionette Theater in Central Park (West Side at 79th St). Aaron's favorite spot is the Cloisters (Fort Tyron Park).

Oops: It made for a dramatic moment — all that neon crinoline on fire — but Jenny would have just knocked the matches out of Agnes's hand. When your life's work is at stake, I think you'd get a bit more defensive of it. And how old is Aaron Rose? Cyrus's story of Kim Lee (which I'm pretty sure doesn't mean "Golden Lion") implies that he and Aaron's mother Alice broke up near the end of the war, 1975. But if Aaron was just a few years older than Serena at camp, there's no way he's 34 now. Did Cyrus and Alice get back together and have Aaron and then split up again? Finally, does no one get punished for their crimes on the Upper East Side? Bart Bass committed arson and is responsible for someone's death, but not reporting it is presented as the unequivocally right thing to do.

Spotted: Dorota's favorite singer, Cyndi Lauper, makes a special appearance at Blair's birthday party. Lauper hit the big time in 1983 with "Girls Just Want to Have Fun" from her *She's So Unusual* album, and over the intervening two decades, she's released 11 albums and sold over 25 million of them. Her 2007 album, *Bring Ya to the Brink*, was nominated for a Grammy. In addition to her spot on *Gossip Girl*, Lauper also popped by *30 Rock* for its season 3 finale.

The Look: Blair convenes the Party Planning Committee wearing an Alice + Olivia ruffle-front Ombre tee, Marc by Marc Jacobs Bright Plaid Skirt, and her "bW" Alex Woo diamond necklace. Serena goes to Times Square wearing a grey EDUN Althea top under her winter white Gryphon "The Drum Major" jacket (from the fall 2008 collection) and Giuseppe Zanotti crystal stud suede booties, and carries a Miu Miu Patch shoulder bag. At their business meeting, Jenny has a grey lace-print ruffle Ra Ra dress on (from Topshop) and Agnes wears a black Natori Sonia chemise and a leather hooded Joie Amita jacket. To meet Cyrus, Blair puts on a charcoal polka-dot Milly Georgette dress. Blair goes to school in a black Giovanni beret, Cynthia Steffe top and Grace miniskirt, Isabelle V-neck cardigan by Lynne Hiriak, and Manolo Blahnik slingback pumps. Posing for Aaron, S is in Chloe's sequin

"5.19.91" by Daniel Humphrey

His hand held a firm grip around the glass [of] Scotch. It was like the glass was a part of him and if he let it go he'd lose a piece of himself. He took one long gulp and finished off the glass.

"Keep them coming, Joe," he spoke across the bar. The surly bartender poured some more of the brown liquid into his glass. He tilted it towards Joe and took a sip. As it hit his mouth, his lips curled and he swallowed. The glass was still clutched in his hand.

Charlie Trout had spent every Birthday at this bar since he was thirteen years old. And this year was no exception. Charlie sat on the exact same stool, drank the exact same brand of Scotch and ordered from the exact same bartender year after year. One would think Charlie Trout's Birthday party would be full of friends, sexy women and located at an exclusive Manhattan club. But that was not the case. Charlie's Birthday was always just a party of one. Or two, if you count Joe the bartender.

Charlie's Birthday didn't just signify his aging. It also represented the anniversary of his mother's death. She died while giving birth to him all those years ago and Charlie's been living with that grief ever since. Charlie's father, media tycoon Bernie Trout, had never once wanted to celebrate his son's Birthday. There were no elaborate Birthday parties for little Charlie. There weren't even Birthday cakes. Nor any wrapped gifts. A Lego set or a toy fire truck were never waiting at the foot of Charlie's bed when he awoke on his Birthday morning. All he ever got was just a deposit into a savings account.

This caused Charlie to believe his father held him responsible for his mother's death. If it weren't for Charlie, Bernie's beloved wife would still be alive. It was Charlie who killed her, Bernie must have thought. And that was why Bernie could never truly love Charlie.

jersey dress from the fall 2008 collection. Blair bickers with her mother over breakfast in a magenta and black Marc by Marc Jacobs Brilliant Scribble houndstooth printed silk dress. To her birthday party, Blair wears a modified Bill Blass Flamenco backless blouse. Serena wears an Emporio Armani dress to B's party with Gryphon's "The Sequin Armor" coat. Eleanor announces that Cyrus is moving in while Blair is in an Alice + Olivia trellis-print dress.

Music: Dan gets an offer he can't refuse from Noah Shapiro to "Let You Down" by Alain Whyte. Aaron asks Serena to model for him and he and Serena kiss in Times Square to Kings of Leon's "Sex on Fire." Jenny confronts Agnes at the café while Doug Burr's "Graniteville" is playing in the background. During the photo shoot with Aaron, "Closer" by band-of-the-episode Kings of Leon plays. Blair's birthday party starts with "Echo" by Cyndi Lauper. "Be Somebody" by Kings of Leon kicks in as Agnes lights the dresses on fire. Serena talks to Cyrus at the party to "Manhattan" by Alain Whyte. Dan decides to give Bart his story about Charlie Trout to Youth Group's "What Is a Life." At the end of the episode "Satellites" by We Know, Plato! plays.

Wallace Shawn as Cyrus Rose

Educated at Harvard and Oxford, actor and playwright Wallace Shawn was born and raised in New York City on the Upper East Side, the son of the editor of the *New Yorker*. His memorable character roles are almost countless, but highlights include Vizzini in *The Princess Bride*, Mr. Hall in *Clueless*, and himself in *My Dinner with Andre*. Before becoming an actor, he briefly worked as a teacher and encountered students he described as "*Gossip Girl* characters in the making": "The parents on the show really remind me of some of the parents I met then. I literally do think, 'Oh, where have I seen that before?' And I say, 'Oh, it was in reality.'" Before he began filming *Gossip Girl*, he picked up the season 1 DVDs to find out what he'd gotten himself into and was addicted after watching just a few episodes.

"On the Upper East Side, the holiday returns to its roots: lying, manipulation, and betrayal."

2.11 the magnificent archibalds

Original air date: November 17, 2008
Written by: Joshua Safran
Directed by: Jean de Segonzac
Guest cast: Sam Robards (Howie "The Captain" Archibald), John Shea (Harold Waldorf), Francie Swift (Anne Archibald), Dion Graham (FBI Agent), Kelly McAndrew (CPS Counselor)

Thanksgiving brings some families and friends back together, while others are driven apart.

It's hard to be a moral compass on the Upper East Side: temptation lurks everywhere and when you stick to your convictions or impose them on others, everyone resents you. Just ask Dan or Vanessa or Rufus. The one guy who can pull it off with grace is Nate Archibald. Nate's relationship with his father has been strained since we first saw them jogging together in Central Park. The Captain's unexpected return throws Nate's already destroyed world into greater chaos. But as he did in "Much 'I Do,'" the Captain inadvertently brings Nate back together with friends Chuck and Vanessa. In the real world, it's absurd for Nate to ditch his mother on Thanksgiving and leave her alone in a house with no electricity after her husband's been carted off by the FBI, but in the *Gossip* world, Nate and Chuck spending the holiday together getting drunk just feels right.

You don't have to be blood to be family, and seeing Lily step in to help Jenny and Rufus sort out their problems was touching, as was Eleanor's maternal gesture of putting her shawl on the shivering, whimpering Little J. That girl needs a mom. Jenny's return to her family, symbolic raccoon-eye makeup removed, the Humphrey hug, and the reconciliation with Vanessa were just as moving as J's return to the fold last season in "All About My Brother." Too bad V had to spoil the moment by stealing J's love letter.

Serena has her own trust issues to contend with — can Aaron trust her? Moments after becoming Aaron's only lady, S finds herself fibbing about her past and then full-on lying. S is not herself in this relationship: she lacks self-confidence, she worries about impressing Aaron and holding on to him, she's hiding her past, and she's ditching family and friends (Blair on her birthday!) to be with him. Choosing her love interest over her family . . . sound like any van der women we know? Not this Thanksgiving. With Eric in tow, Lily returns to the place that feels most like home to her: the Humphrey loft. Valuing her children over her husband by walking out on Bart will do wonders to heal the resentment Serena and Eric have for her history of doing just the opposite. Is this the end of the Bass–van der Woodsen union? Bart's lack of trust and his violation of their right to privacy seems like a deal breaker.

Lily: "How did you get so wise?"
Eric: "The nanny."

JTLYK:

- Top story on Gossip Girl: "*Nate the Not So Great*. And we thought living in Brooklyn with the Humphrey's was hitting rock bottom. Looks like Nate is now MIA. We hear he's holding up in the Hamptons . . . with his mom. Oh, prince of the UES, when will you return?"
- Like in last year's Thanksgiving episode, Gossip Girl takes a holiday from narrating.
- Blair compares Aaron and his non-exclusivity clause to Bill Paxton's polygamous character on HBO's *Big Love*.
- Drew Barrymore played a 10-year-old trying to divorce her parents who were separated themselves in 1984's *Irreconcilable Differences*, which Eric and Jenny watched in preparation for the meeting with the counselor.
- How long has Bart Bass been spying on the van der Woodsens? He proposed to Lily in "Roman Holiday," and the safe bet is that he already had his P.I. digging up their dirt. That would mean that when he gave Eric the Marlins jersey, he knew that Eric hadn't really been in Florida but at the Ostroff Center. Twisted.
- Telling Jenny that at least her father cares enough to be that angry with her, Blair echoes what Chuck said to Dan in "The Serena Also Rises."
- Nate's letter, in part, reads: "Dear Jenny, I always try to be as honest as I possibly can. That's kind of hard when you come from a family like mine. Honesty isn't really something [I was] taught. [. . .] But I can't hide the way I really feel about you. The emotions are too strong for me to just

pretend that they don't exist. I think about you all the time. Now that your brother knows about us, I have to stay away from you. But I don't want to. I really care about you. I just don't know what to do. Nate."

Secrets & Lies:

- Jenny has been secretly staying at Eric's, and both Jenny and Eric kept it from Lily, Bart, Serena, Rufus, and Dan.
- Captain Archibald misleads his wife and son into thinking he only has their best interests at heart, when he's trying to scam the van der Bilts for money.
- Serena pretends to be "nearly a teetotaler" to Aaron so he will stay interested in her.
- Dorota spills to Blair about Eleanor's engagement.
- Dan overshares information about S's past with Aaron, and Aaron pretends to know what he's talking about.
- Chuck goes along with Serena's ruse but calls her out for lying to Aaron.
- Bart Bass has had his P.I. spying on the van der Woodsens, which Eric finds out while snooping in BB's safe.
- Dan covers for Serena, telling Aaron he was the one who lied. Dan and Serena apologize to each other, and Dan warns S that the "truth always comes out."
- Lily and the van der kids confront Bart about the dossiers of secrets.
- Eric lies about not reading Lily's file and asks her why she kept her stay in an institution from him.
- S admits to Aaron that she lied to him and gives him her file.
- Blair spills the secret of Eleanor and Cyrus's engagement after she finds out her dad's visit was the surprise Eleanor was keeping from her.
- Vanessa steals Nate's letter to Jenny and, saying she's calling her parents, sneaks away from dinner to read it. Federal offense! (And sneakiness fail: she turns her back to the door but then stands in front of a *mirror* so anyone could see what she's up to.)
- Bart asks his P.I. to pry into the reason why Lily was institutionalized.

You'll B a Woman Soon: One thing Blair Waldorf does not like is people messing with her daddy's pie. Eleanor did it last Thanksgiving and Cyrus does it this year. Delicious as it very well may be, the pie itself is not what gets B's goat. So many of her family's traditions were lost with her parents' divorce and now B feels left out of the new family forming in her apartment. Thinking her mother cares no more for her than she does for Cyrus's "Corn: Grain of the Future" nephew, Blair pouts like an ignored child. But seeing distraught Jenny brings out kindness in B, and she tells Jenny how much she envies the fierce love her father has for her and encourages her to go home. Blair finds that she underestimated her parents — they know exactly how meaningful that pie is to her.

The Original Gossipverse: The intercepted letter in the books (*Would I Lie to You*) is written by Serena for Nate. Blair finds it and destroys it. In *You Know You Love Me*, Eleanor announces her engagement to Cyrus, much to Blair's chagrin.

That's How It's Done in *The O.C.*: Like Captain Archibald, Jimmy Cooper returns and makes a show of rebuilding his family, but he's still in serious money trouble in "The Shape of Things to Come."

The Magnificent Ambersons (dir. Orson Welles, 1942): The story of the magnificent Ambersons begins in 1873 in a town developing into a city and headed by the conspicuously wealthy Ambersons. Miss Isabelle Amberson (Dolores Costello) makes the sensible if loveless choice between two suitors and has just one child, George Anderson Amberson Minafer, whom she spoils. George is a brat and a terror and the whole town hopes for the day when classist, self-centered Georgie will get his comeuppance. When George (Tim Holt) is a young man, the other of his mother's suitors, Mr. Morgan (Joseph Cotten), returns to town with his beautiful daughter Lucy (Anne Baxter). George tries to woo her. Morgan is an inventor and is having some success with a horseless carriage (that's old-timey talk for a car), which George irrationally disapproves of. After making some bad investments, George's father dies, Mrs. Minafer begins spending time with Mr. Morgan, and George's plan not to have a career ends his chances of marrying Lucy. Finding out about his mother's relationship with Mr. Morgan from his meddling old maid Aunt Fanny drives George bonkers and he ultimately forces his mother to choose him over her one true love. After traveling abroad with George, Mrs. Minafer returns ill and dies, never having seen Mr. Morgan again. While the Morgans prosper, the Ambersons are now penniless, and George, forced to work a dangerous job, is injured in a car accident. He's finally got his comeuppance. Asking Mr. Morgan's forgiveness, George's destitution has led him to a change of character, and the film ends with the promise of a future for him with Lucy.

As is made clear in the title of the episode, the Archibalds are the family once magnificent, now ruined. Nate finds himself alone at the beginning of this episode like George is near the end of the film. But while George Amberson is unlike any part of N's character, he does resemble the worst in Chuck. C frowns on those he deems riffraff, like Dan Humphrey, and feels entitled to the luxury which surrounds him. Hopefully Chuck won't need total emotional, financial, and physical ruin to come to the same realizations that George does. Like George meddling in his mother's personal life, so Blair tried to drive away Cyrus in "The Bonfire of the Vanity"; where George succeeded, Blair failed, but both realized their wrongdoing and apologized for it.

Welcome to the Real World:

- V's family is spending Thanksgiving at a Washoe reservation. The Washoe people are Native Americans who originally lived around Lake Tahoe and currently have four communities, three in Nevada and one in California.

Just steps away from Central Park on East 74th at Fifth, the Archibald home is finally back in the family's hands.

- Vanessa's Thanksgiving plan is to watch German filmmaker Rainer Werner Fassbinder's *Berlin Alexanderplatz*, a 15-and-a-half-hour film (originally a TV movie series) made in 1980, restored in 2007, and released by Criterion. The film follows Biberkopf, a man who has the conviction, like our dear V, that "although the world may be an evil place, humankind is good natured."
- Poor Aaron Rose. Blair calls him Warren Jeffs, the leader of the Fundamentalist Church of Jesus Christ and Latter Day Saints, now in prison, who was a polygamist and landed on the FBI's Most Wanted List in 2006.

Locations:

- Cyrus takes Eleanor to Jean Georges (1 Central Park W) for dinner.
- Blair's favorite restaurant is Gramercy Tavern (42 E 20th St).
- Lily and Bart return from the private Necker Island, owned by Sir Richard Branson, in the British Virgin Islands.
- The Humphreys buy groceries for Thanksgiving dinner at Union Market (754 Union St, Brooklyn).
- Feeding ducks at the Boat Pond in Central Park (east side at 74th St) soothes Blair.

Oops: Why wouldn't the FBI just follow Nate back to the apartment where he's staying and arrest the Captain? Chuck tells Eric the (rather easy to guess) password for the safe, but Connor Paolo hits 8764, not 8769.

The Look: Lily walks with Rufus while wearing a Brunello Cucinelli coat. The seemingly impossible has been proven possible: Blake Lively does not look good in everything. Serena's awful Thanksgiving outfit is a Porter Grey silk charmeuse shirt with a too short, too high-waisted skirt and dark red suede Nine West Ginga, Boutique 9 pumps. Lily wears a brown Hugo Boss dress, Miu Miu pumps, and jewelry from Stephen Dweck. J wears a red and black plaid D&G shirt dress with black Nine West Cuzza boots. Blair wanders the Upper East Side in a Sretsis fall 2008 coat over her green Alexandra Vidal dress with Jimmy Choo Peony tall leather boots. Serena pops by the Waldorfs to give Aaron her file wearing a tweed Mayle Odette coat and carrying a Chanel black quilted crepe flap shoulder bag. Back at home, Jenny's in a Kova & T Amsterdam tee in burnout black and purple leggings with an

Alexis Bittar pearl-and-chain necklace and Tarina Tarantino cameo ring.

Music: The episode opens with Mates of State's "My Only Offer." Serena has dinner at Aaron's to "Bad Man's World" by Jenny Lewis. At the supermarket where Dan and Rufus run into Aaron, "Danger! (Ice Cream Shout Remix)" by The Sound of Arrows plays. A hilarious choice, Dorota's ringtone for Eleanor is Britney Spears' "I'm a Slave 4 U." The happy Thanksgiving moments montage is set to "Reasons to Sing" by The Crash.

"Snowflake or snow fake, either way it's gonna be a ball."

2.12 it's a wonderful lie

Original air date: December 1, 2008
Written by: Robby Hull
Directed by: Patrick Norris
Guest cast: Natalie Knepp (Lexi), Jennifer Damiano (Blair Knock-off), Jake O'Connor (Chuck 2.0), Kevin Stapleton (Andrew Tyler)

Aaron's ex-girlfriend comes to town in time for a double date to the Snowflake Ball. As things cool down between Lily and Bart, the old Rufly flame reignites.

Last year Little J was playing Cinderella, sneaking into the masked ball with help from Vanessa, who hooked her up with a beautiful ballgown. At the Snowflake Ball, the tables are turned: Vanessa is the one going, but her fairy godmother is an evil stepsister in disguise. The concept of a storyline that makes allies of Jenny and the Mean Girls against Vanessa is inspired, but the execution was terrible. Putting a girl with a perfect body in a barely see-through dress is hardly public humiliation. (That 1980s Cosby sweater she was wearing at the café was more embarrassing.) And while *Gossip Girl* is not known for its gritty realism, the slow-motion laughter of *everyone* at the ball was farfetched enough to dilute the sting in the prank. But Jessica Szohr made the most of it, playing her scenes with a tender honesty and earnestness. Sorry for ever being mean to you, Vanessa.

"The Handmaiden's Tale" was our introduction to Vanessa: a girl who wanted nothing to do with the Upper East Side, didn't understand the Humphreys' fascination with it, and put being a good person over getting what you want by any means necessary. Now she's stolen Nate's letter to Jenny and advised her to forget about him; she finds this kind of manipulation to be repulsive in others, and as it turns out, in herself. Vanessa's remorse for her deceit is earnest; seeing that, Nate forgives her almost instantly. Jenny takes a different route by handing out punishment instead of forgiveness.

The episode's other love triangle involves Lily, Bart, and Rufus. Since marrying Bart, Lily has found that life as Mrs. Bass is much like she feared: his focus is on his work and she's left alone — trying on Serena's dress to feel young again, trying to get Rufus to hang out with her to ease her loneliness, or trying on a Stepford persona to impress Bart. Lily seems ready to give her husband another chance after his impassioned "I'll do whatever I need to do to keep you" speech (well, impassioned for BB), but discovering the invoice from the P.I. is enough to drive her to Rufus. Chuck asks Lily to respect his father and give him the conversation he deserves before moving on with Rufus (and in public). But it looks like that's a conversation she'll never get to have. And she'll never know that Bart had been telling the truth about calling off the P.I.

Just as Lily is moving on too quickly for Chuck's liking, Serena and Dan realize that maybe they're not ready to move on and sleep with someone else. Especially not when it's the ever-condescending Aaron Rose and his awful ex-girlfriend Lexi. (Those two should get back together. They are quite the pair.) At least the uncomfortable double dating forced the conversation at the ball between Dan and Serena about their misgivings. Having already told Blair that the single greatest day of his life was when Serena said "I love you," Dan now says that the single greatest night was the first time they slept together. There is a "mythological tie" between them; the audience feels it as much as D and S do. As awful an interruption as Lily's is, at least it saves Serena and Dan from going home with their dates.

Chuck and Blair also find they just can't move on. The Upper East Side's other One True Pair dreams up another game to play with each other: a bet on who can find the perfect date for the other. It's a considerably kinder bet than their last one when poor Vanessa was toyed with (well, this one's kinder to everyone but Dorota). The punch line of the bet, while rather predictable, points to what so clearly can't be ignored: Chuck and Blair are perfect for each other. How will their relationship change after Bart Bass's accident?

"Facebook! I joined few groups."
— Dorota defends her strategy for finding Chuck's date to the ball

JTLYK:

- Top story on Gossip Girl: "*Serena Gets Serious?* Looks like S has a new boy in her life. Guess she really is over what's his name? We're happy for S. She deserves a good man. And this Aaron guy seems nice, soulful, artsy and wait a minute he sounds a bit familiar . . ."
- Anne Archibald was asked to step down from the Snowflake Ball organizing committee after Howie's legal troubles in "Blair Waldorf Must Pie!"
- Gossip Girl blast on N&V: "Spotted: N swapping spit with a girl from an outer borough. Ew. Ew. Ew."
- Serena references 1989's *When Harry Met Sally* about how a man and a woman's relationship developed over chance meetings in New York City.
- Serena's reply of "Can't she just vote?" to Aaron saying that Lexi sleeps with guys on the first date "as a political statement against the male-dominated sexual hypocrisy" was perhaps the most annoying thing ever uttered on *Gossip Girl*. In a one-two punch, it mocked feminism with

it's britney, bitch

More than any other pop culture figure, Britney Spears gets loads of attention from *Gossip Girl*.

- S tells B to imitate Britney with the umbrella ("The Blair Bitch Project")
- Gossip Girl asks if Little J will "go from Brady to Britney" ("Dare Devil")
- Is compares S's Guitar Hero playing to Brit at the VMAs ("Seventeen Candles")
- Shoeless Chuck "pulls a Britney" ("The Handmaiden's Tale")
- Gossip Girl mentions Madonna and Britney's kiss ("All About My Brother")
- B insults and S defends the good people of Kentwood ("Never Been Marcused")
- Dorota's ringtone is "I'm a Slave 4 U" ("The Magnificent Archibalds")
- A brilliant promo for the show set clips of Chuck Bass to Britney's "Womanizer"

Lexi's over-the-top attitude and belittled the serious inequalities that exist between the genders with S's comment. Argh!

- Bart was paying his private investigator $25,000 quarterly to follow the van der Woodsens, Chuck, Rufus, and Jonathan.
- When Rufus and Alison broke up, the first thing he did was go to Lily's. Lily hasn't even told her husband she's leaving him and she's back in Rufus's arms.
- If Bart's accident proves fatal, then the last real conversation Chuck had with him was when Bart blamed him for his failing marriage. Awful.

Secrets & Lies:

- Vanessa keeps her relationship with Nate a secret from Jenny, telling her she should move on and hiding a call from him.
- Nate and Vanessa are busted by one of Gossip Girl's spies.
- Bart tells Lily he's done with the snooping, spying, and controlling, and will do whatever it takes to save their marriage.
- Penelope, Hazel, Is, and Jenny hatch a plot to humiliate Vanessa at the Snowflake Ball.
- Lily thinks Bart has lied to her and is still working with the P.I.
- Vanessa admits to Nate that she stole his letter to Jenny.
- Rufus reveals to Lily how he feels about her.

It's a Wonderful Life (dir. Frank Capra, 1946): A perennial Christmas movie, *It's a Wonderful Life* is the story of George Bailey (James Stewart), a good man whose big dreams were left behind again and again as he put others before himself. Faced with financial ruin after a great deal of money is accidentally lost, drunk George throws himself off a bridge but is saved by an angel, Clarence (Henry Travers), who will get his wings if he can help George see the worthiness of his life. Clarence takes George into an alternate reality where he never existed, and George comes to realize all the good his "small" life has done. With the desire to live again, George is put back into his life, on Christmas, and the town has rallied to save his business and family. Writes Clarence to George in a copy of *Tom Sawyer*, "No man is a failure who has friends."

Each character in *Gossip Girl* could use their own Clarence to come down and sort them out. In "It's a Wonderful Lie," rather than being full of appreciation for their lives, friends, and families, everyone is not quite where they want to be — in the wrong relationship, unable to be with the person they love, fighting with a friend — and are bitter or sad because of it. But the person who could use a Clarence the most is Bart Bass. . . .

Welcome to the Real World:

- Serena thinks of the Snowflake Ball as Tolstoy's epic Russian love story *Anna Karenina* (1877) imagined by *Vogue* editor-in-chief and fashion icon Anna Wintour.
- Vanessa compares her wardrobe malfunction to Janet Jackson's exposed breast at the end of 2004's Super Bowl halftime show with Justin Timberlake.

Locations:

- Grab a Jacques Torres hot chocolate, as per Gossip Girl's instructions, at 285 Amsterdam between 73rd and 74th Streets.
- Vanessa has a gift certificate to Grimaldi's Pizza (19 Old Fulton St, Brooklyn).
- Norman Mailer's Brooklyn townhouse was on Columbia Heights with a view of the East River.
- The Snowflake Ball was filmed in the same location as the Kiss on the Lips party last season, at The Foundry (42–38 9th St, Queens).
- While there aren't Blair and Chuck lookalikes available there, Canal Street is known for vendors of designer knock-offs.

Spotted: Tied for the most Olympic medals and World Championship titles for a U.S. gymnast, Nastia Liukin is beat out by Blair for Chuck's attention at the Snowflake Ball.

The Look: Reviewing her options for a date to the ball, Blair wears an argyle Brooks Brothers cashmere cape and a navy bow tie. Talking with Dan at school, Serena wears a sparkly Marc by Marc Jacobs Etta sweater with her uniform and carries a gold Mullberry women's mirror metallic Bayswater tote. Making a deal with Chuck, Blair's in Alice + Olivia's Jabot dress with a yellow horseshoe belt, Rachel Leigh bangle, and Marc by Marc Jacobs kitten heel patent pumps. For the walking tour of Brooklyn, S is in a Valentino leather jacket, J Brand jeans, and White + Warren wrap-up cashmere scarf with Celine's Watch Me Work bag. Blair's gown for the ball is from Carolina Herrera's fall/winter 2008 collection, and she wears the Erickson Beamon necklace Chuck gave her in "Seventeen Candles." Not to be out-sparkled, Chuck wears a glittering CoSTUME NATIONAL blazer, Brioni shirt, Fred Perry pants, and H&M shoes. As on her wedding day, Lily wears a white gown by Vera Wang to the ball; this one is from her 2009 bridal collection. Both Vanessa and Jenny's dresses are designed by Eric Daman. J's wrap is Anna Sui. Serena's gown is Bill Blass.

Music: Accompanying Gossip Girl's guide to winter in NYC is "Lady Jesus" by The Asteroids Galaxy Tour. Serena and Aaron talk Lexi at the gallery to The Metros' "Sexual Riot." "Steady" by Alain Whyte is playing when Jenny brings Vanessa the dress. The Snowflake Ball kicks off with The Asteroids Galaxy Tour's "The Sun Ain't Shining No More." Lily and

Amanda Setton as Penelope Shafai and Dreama Walker as Hazel Williams

Amanda Setton, from Great Neck, New York, has been working at her acting career since high school, where she was the president of the drama club. At Ithaca College, she studied acting and landed bit parts in big movies like *Sex and the City* and *What Happens in Vegas*. Playing Penelope on *Gossip Girl* is her breakthrough role and she's thrilled with the "vicious" character and the show itself. "We have such a good time on set [and] it's amazing to be able to work on a show in New York," said Amanda. Though she doesn't get to keep the designer clothes she wears as Penelope, Amanda does get front row seats during Fashion Week.

Like her onscreen bestie, Dreama Walker also had a bit part in the *Sex and the City* movie. Florida-born Dreama describes her character Hazel as "a little Upper East Side brat with not a care in the world!" The second season of *Gossip Girl* was a busy year for the actress, who also appeared in *Gran Torino*, a pilot for a Showtime series co-starring Matthew Perry, and *This Side of Truth* with Jonah Hill and Tina Fey. As for Hazel's future on the show, Dreama wondered if she'd still be as catty after senior year. "I would hope that girls are at their mean peak in high school because you're still immature enough to be that way," she said to the *Observer*. "Then you grow up and you realize there are more important things than being terrible. So hopefully they become more docile in the third season."

Rufus dance to "Breakdown" by Dearheart. Vanessa arrives at the ball to "Saturday Morning" by Afternoons. Chuck and Blair dance to "Hero" by The Asteroids Galaxy Tour.

"On the Upper East Side, sometimes the dead still speak."

2.13 o brother, where bart thou?

Original air date: December 8, 2008
Written by: Stephanie Savage
Directed by: Joe Lazarov
Guest cast: Kevin Stapleton (Andrew Tyler), Dennis Higgins (Priest), Daniel Neiden (Rabbi)

One wedding and a funeral. Bart Bass stirs up even more trouble as he's laid to rest.

Part of what makes "O Brother, Where Bart Thou?" so tragic is seeing Chuck orphaned — by the death of his father and by him cutting all ties to those he's grown close to over the past year. When *Gossip Girl* began, Chuck was a near orphan: his father's presence in his life was only to scold him, his only true friend was Nate. As Chuck fell in love with Blair and as Bart fell in love with Lily, Chuck found he was no longer alone. He had a little brother in Eric, an annoying sister in Serena, a mother figure in Lily, a soul mate in Blair, and he even managed — shockingly — to have brief moments of closeness with the formerly reviled Dan and Vanessa. Most important of all these relationships to Chuck was the one with his father. When Chuck did win Bart's approval — his investment in Victrola, being best man in his wedding — the victories were always fleeting; Bart would soon see failure in Chuck, whether it was real or just his perception. The two retreated back to their same distant positions each time. With the help of Dan's Charlie Trout story, Bart began to understand his son and reached out to him, taking him up on the Rangers game. But even that closeness was temporary: in their last face-to-face conversation, Bart blames Chuck for driving Lily away. For his whole life, Chuck strove to win his father's love and approval. In Bart's death, Chuck has lost the chance to ever be accepted by him. He embraces his new mantle of orphan and pushes away the van der Woodsens and Blair.

Cattano
REALTORS
12-555-0144

Stephanie Savage wrote this episode, the last before the winter break, and there's a discernable difference to it. Tightly crafted, it contains many references to moments from *Gossip Girl* gone by — Chuck's penchant for twins, Rufus singing "Everytime," a key scene in Grand Central Station, Blair finally being able to say those three words. The tone, a perfect mix of pathos and *Gossip Girl*'s signature wit, was set in the first five minutes with breakfast scenes at the van der Woodsens and the Waldorfs — both matriarchs admiring the photo of Bart and noting the necessity of sending a thank-you to the photo editor. In many more small moments like that one, our Upper East Siders try so hard to be there for each other and to follow their hearts: Blair being there for Chuck; Eric reaching out to Chuck; Rufus telling Lily that he'll wait six months or six years; Jenny making amends with Eleanor by creating her wedding outfit; Dan thwarted as he tries, too late, to declare his love to Serena; Blair turning to Cyrus for comfort (and turning Jewish); Dorota a bridesmaid; Mister Chuck sitting on B's bed; Blair waking up alone and with that letter. Ed Westwick's performance of a grieving, raging, broken Chuck is masterful, as is Leighton Meester's when Blair gives up the games they've been playing all season and tells Chuck she loves him.

Why did Serena go to Buenos Aires with Aaron? If she has feelings for Dan but can't be with him, should she have gone away with Aaron, her next-best-available choice? Lily was in a similar situation last season. In love with Rufus but unable to be with him because of Serena and Dan, she chose to marry Bart. Perhaps both women would rather try to make it work with Aaron or Bart than give up on love entirely. But who can tell with these van der Woodsen women. They sure can hold on to a secret. Lily and Rufus had a child — a great cliffhanger. Will a new member of the *Gossip Girl* family soon arrive on the Upper East Side?

"We're Chuck and Blair. Blair and Chuck. The worst thing you've ever done, the darkest thought you've ever had, I will stand by you through anything."
— Blair tells Chuck she loves him

JTKYK:

- Top story on Gossip Girl: "*Bye Bye Bart.* This is so shocking and sad I don't even know what to write. My thoughts are with the Bass/van der Woodsen family and I urge everyone to respect them in their time of mourning. I think this says it best -- :("

- How did Bart Bass die? There was an "accident," presumably in the limo, but the P.I. is alive and well and selling secrets. On a show like this, it's hard not to wonder if he's actually, factually dead.
- Cyrus inverts the line from the Book of Common Prayer, "In the midst of life we are in death," to "In the midst of death we are in life."
- Like with most of Lily's interactions with Serena and Eric, she could have used a second take in her conversation with Chuck. She immediately regrets what she says and her slap, but her later conversation with him is heartfelt.
- Dan carries the garment bag and is just as awkward as Baby with her watermelon in 1987's *Dirty Dancing*.
- Hopefully he doesn't remember, but in "Chuck in Real Life," Chuck quipped to his father that their new family meant "less money for me when you die."
- Rufus and Lily planned to take a trip in "School Lies"; Lily was the one to show up without luggage.

Secrets & Lies:

- Lily secretly meets with Rufus in Central Park and Cece follows.
- Chuck meets with Andrew Tyler, the P.I., to make a bid for Lily's secret.
- Lily listens to the last voicemail Bart left her, in which he tells her he knows her secret.
- Rufus doesn't tell Dan about him and Lily when Dan tells him what Chuck said at the funeral.
- Lily asks Cece to pay to keep the truth quiet. Cece suggests now is the time for a clean slate.
- Blair finally tells Chuck that she loves him.
- Serena and Dan are unable to communicate their feelings for each other so Dan makes up a lame excuse about muffins and takes off.
- Serena overhears her mother and Cece talking about Lily and Rufus.
- Jenny advises Dan to tell Serena how he feels about her.
- Chuck buys the secret from the P.I.
- Serena tells Dan that their parents are back together.
- Cece lies to Lily about paying off the P.I. and Lily finds out that Chuck knows.
- Taking Lily's words to heart, Chuck burns the evidence he just bought.
- Despite Rufus's protestations, Cece tells him Lily's secret. Is it a boy or a girl?

Scrap!: Chuck grabs Dan and gets in his face at the funeral. Lily slaps Chuck.

You'll B a Woman Soon: In the wake of Bart's death, Blair acts with sustained grace and maturity, which she's only shown glimpses of in the past. She worries about Chuck when she can't be with him, she cares for him when he's raging and drunk, and she asks permission to be there for him and lays bare her feelings. When Chuck rejects her, she takes help and comfort from Cyrus, and in that hug accepts him into her family.

The Original Gossipverse: Eleanor and Cyrus get married in *You Know You Love Me* with Blair as the maid of honor and Serena one of the bridesmaids.

That's How It's Done in *The O.C.*: The Bart Bass of Orange County, Caleb Nichol, dies at the end of season 2 just as his marriage to Julie is nearing its end. In "The Dearly Beloved," bereaved Kirsten drinks too much and causes a scene at her father's wake. Like Chuck's with Bart, her last interaction with her father was full of venom. In "The Case of the Franks," Kirsten reveals that she kept a pregnancy secret from Jimmy back when she was a teenager.

O Brother, Where Art Thou? (dir. Joel and Ethan Coen, 2000): Loosely based on Homer's *Odyssey*, *O Brother* follows three escapees from a chain gang in Mississippi in the Great Depression. Smart-talking and slick-haired Ulysses Everett (George Clooney) leads Pete (John Turturro) and Delmar (Tim Blake Nelson) on an adventure to find hidden money from a robbery. On their way they run into a variety of characters and situations (including recording a hit song as the Soggy Bottom Boys) before Everett admits that there isn't any treasure, that he just needed to get home before his wife remarried. After more misadventures, the boys survive the lawmen on their tail and the flooding of the river valley to declare their adventuring days over and the age of reason upon them. In crafting *O Brother, Where Art Thou?*, the Coens drew from a wide range of cultural influences; beyond the *Odyssey*, the film alludes to the Southern Gothic tradition (the work of writers like Faulkner and Flannery O'Connor) and popular movies (*The Wizard of Oz*, *Cool Hand Luke*, *Sullivan's Travels*). The almost monochromatically dusty look and the omnipresent music are critical pieces of the film. The creators of *Gossip Girl* build their episodes in the same way with a collage of rich cultural allusions, evocative music, and a suitably baroque look.

Welcome to the Real World:

- For Eleanor's bridal outfit, she references Bianca Jagger's, who married Mick on May 14, 1971, in a white Yves Saint Laurent jacket but no shirt underneath it.

Oops: When Blair embraces Chuck in her room, her arm position switches depending on the camera angle. As Lily headed off to Grand Central, there was one person completely forgotten: Eric. Forget about not mentioning the secret love child to its father, she forgets about Eric — the boy who just lost his stepfather and his stepbrother, whose sister is off to South America, and who tried to commit suicide a short year ago. Were we to assume Eric was happily spending Christmas with Cece, having gin toddies all the live-long day? One throwaway line to account for Eric would have solved this oversight.

The Look: To Bart's funeral, Blair wears a Kay Unger cropped jacquard jacket in navy over a simple black DvF dress and Basha and Shaindy head-band. Forgetting that impossibly short skirts are maybe *not* for funerals, Jenny puts together an otherwise excellent outfit in varying shades of black: Nanette Lepore jacket, H&M dress, Henri Bendel gloves, Zephyr tights, Be&D peep-toe slingbacks, and a Bodhi safety clutch. Serena is in a Burberry coat, Sigerson Morrison shoes, and has a Chanel bag. Blair wears a beige 3.1 Phillip Lim silk fan evening gown to her mother's wedding, and Serena wears Alice + Olivia Ruched Grecian dress with beaded trim. And for the first time ever, Dorota is out of her uniform and in a lovely bridesmaid dress. Love!

Music: The episode opens with "Signs" by Bloc Party. Breakfast at the Waldorfs is to Mozart's "Piano Concerto No. 21 in C Major." Chuck meets with the P.I. to "The Mourning Son" by Xu Xu Fang. Chuck confronts Dan at the funeral to Bloc Party's "Biko." Rufus is singing Lincoln Hawk's "Everytime" when Dan comes home. Nate and Blair arrive with Chuck at the funeral reception to Chopin's "Waltz in B Minor." Cece encourages Lily to go and speak with Chuck to Beethoven's "Kreutzer Sonata for Violin &

Piano No. 9 in A Major." Blair tells Cyrus about her heartache to the finale from Dvorak's "American Quartet." Another song from Xu Xu Fang, "These Days," when Chuck has his second meeting with the P.I. Aaron tells Serena he may be falling in love with her and Blair lies with Chuck to The National's "Slow Show."

"Pop quiz: what do you get when you cross Chuck Bass, a billion dollars, and Bart cold in the ground? Free fall."

2.14 in the realm of the basses

Original air date: January 5, 2009
Written by: John Stephens
Directed by: Tony Wharmby
Guest cast: Linda Emond (Headmistress Queller), Sue Jean Kim (Beth), Henny Russell (Helen), Christa Scott-Reed (Second Colony Woman)

The winter school term begins with Jenny back at school, but Chuck missing — until his uncle Jack drags him home.

The two girls who cared the most about high school politics last year are now so completely over it. On J's return to Constance, she plans to save Nelly Yuki from the torture she once endured, only to discover Nelly was making a power play herself. In her encounter with the argyle-uniformed Colony Club ladies, Blair realizes high-school cattiness isn't confined to teenage years, but lasts a lifetime. Jenny and Blair are done with social climbing.

Blair turns her attention back to Chuck at just the right time: his downward spiral has worsened since Bart's funeral. While his devil-may-care attitude can be rather entertaining (like telling the headmistress that hash is a softer high), Chuck's self-destruction moves from hookers and hookahs to a near-death walk along the edge of a roof. He screams his signature phrase — "I'm Chuck Bass!" — not as a point of pride or as a pickup line but as a declaration of his emptiness and worthlessness.

As Chuck is lost without his father, Rufus can't think of anything but finding his son. Both are spiteful to the women who love them the most and dismissive of those they normally care deeply for — Rufus with Dan and Chuck with Eric. Chuck's turning point is hearing Blair tell him how much she needs him. Knowing how awful it is to lose someone so close to you, he comes down from the (literal and figurative) edge. Rufus softens when Lily shows him her vulnerability and her fears about how her children will react to the news of their sibling. He finally sees the situation for what it was: giving the baby up for adoption was a difficult decision to make, but the right choice for her.

With each chapter in their story, Dan and Serena are more and more like star-crossed lovers. Dan can't tell Serena the huge, life-altering secret he knows. Just as they reconnect, their parents' past threatens to tear them apart.

"The only way Nelly is leaving is in a body bag."
— Penelope turns up the crazy

JTLYK:

- Nate and Vanessa are MIA.
- Top story on Gossip Girl: "*All Chucked Up*. Little Orphan Chuck. His dad dies and he skips town. :(We've heard absolutely 0 about him in the past few weeks and have no idea where he's hiding out. Sadness. When will Chuck finally show his face on the UES again? Your guess is as good as mine. Pls come home soon, C."
- How times have changed. In "The Wild Brunch," Rufus said to Lily, "You don't think I'm really going to tell my kid who he can and can't date." Now Rufus doesn't want Dan with Serena.
- Now that Serena is back with Dan, she has all the time in the world for helping her friends, which she didn't when she was with Aaron.
- On the rooftop, Chuck sings "Spanish Ladies," a sea shanty that dates back to the 18th century. The lyrics go on to say, "For we will be jolly and drown melancholy."
- In "Hi, Society," Rufus found out that Cece gave Lily a Rufus-or-the-inheritance ultimatum back in the day, and Lily chose the inheritance, leaving Rufus to move on to Alison. Was putting the baby up for adoption part of that deal?

Secrets & Lies:

- Rufus lies to his kids, saying he went on a trip to look for an artist.
- Jenny is left out of the Humphrey loop, not knowing that D and S are

back together or why there's a cold front between Dan and Rufus.

- Penelope lies to her father and the headmistress, saying that Jenny is bullying her.
- Serena and Dan rifle through Rufus's things looking for the real reason R and L went on a trip.
- Nelly spills to Eric and Jenny about Penelope's secret affair.
- Rufus won't tell Dan what the secret is, and asks for time so the situation can be handled properly.
- Chuck tells Dan about his half-sibling.
- Blair is at first dishonest with the Colony Club ladies, saying she disapproves of Serena, before she gets her priorities in order and tells them the truth.
- Using Nelly's secrets as leverage, Jenny wins the battle against the Mean Girls.
- At his father's and Lily's insistence, Dan keeps the secret from Serena.
- Blair and Jack have a major secret of their own: what happened on New Year's. Has Blair been playing double Bass?

You'll B a Woman Soon: B laid her soul bare for Chuck and then he left her. Now she doesn't want to appear weak but has a hard time maintaining her façade. Rushing from Victrola where Chuck cruelly mocked her to her meeting with the Colony Club ladies, Blair allows herself only one moment to break down — a gutting portrait of an overwhelmed girl who tries so hard to control the world around her and fails. Once again Blair is brave for Chuck, asking him to come down from the ledge because she needs him. With her honesty she saves his life.

The Original Gossipverse: Aaron's the one to break up with Serena in *Because I'm Worth It.* She cries one solitary tear just as she's shooting a print ad for her perfume, which comes to be known as Serena's Tears.

That's How It's Done in *The O.C.*: Kaitlin Cooper takes on her school's Queen, who's too bossy to her underlings in "The Summer Bummer." After Kaitlin throws a superior rager, the Queen concedes defeat and says she'll serve Kaitlin's command. But Kaitlin just wants the girl to be nicer to her friends.

In the Realm of the Senses (*Ai no corrida*, dir. Nagisa Oshima, 1976): This controversial film is based on a real incident where a woman accidentally killed her lover during sex and cut off his member. Set in Toyko in the 1930s, prostitute Sada Abe (Eiko Matsuda) and hotel owner Kichizo (Tatsuya Fuji) begin a passionate and all-consuming affair at a time when the army is increasing its presence and control over the lives of the Japanese. Isolating themselves from the world, the two lovers "attempt to be free of all inhibition and repression." Their experimentation, which explores morbidity and death, leads to accidental strangulation, and Sada cuts off Kichizo's penis and writes on his chest in his blood. Though heralded as a masterpiece, *In the Realm of the Senses* was also banned and censored for its explicit sexual content.

While Chuck and Blair's relationship has not reached a point where anyone will cut anything off the other (and it's safe to assume it never will), they have always been overcome with passion for each other like Sada and Kichizo. Their games are not always sexual, but psychological. Exploring power dynamics and the lengths they can push each other has proven dangerous. Blair said in "O Brother" that she must be a masochist to love Chuck; in "Prêt-a-Poor J" she acknowledged the "exquisite pleasure" in being denied satisfaction in their relationship. Sada and Kichizo's downfall came in large part from hiding from the suffocating nature of the outside world. Chuck will have to emerge from hiding in his self-destructive behavior and reenter the land of the living.

Welcome to the Real World:

- Formed in 1903, the Colony Club is the oldest social club for women in New York City.

Locations:

- The Battle at Pinkberry was filmed at their Midtown location at 1039 Second Avenue.

The Look: Blair, in a Diane von Furstenberg Nueva short-sleeve jacket and red Christian Dior Lady Dior handbag, catches up at school with Serena in a Joie Eileen sweater vest. To snoop at the Humphreys, Serena wears a black Mackage leather jacket. Chuck smokes up at school and B's in a Nanette Lepore ruffle-necked cardigan and Walter skirt with a red Milly coat and red

Marc by Marc Jacobs pumps. Lily agrees to tell Rufus whatever she can in a long black Organic by John Patrick sweater, Tory Burch Thalie top, black J Brand skinny ankle jeans, and Christian Louboutin Miss Tack shoes. Blair meets with the Colony Club women in a black wool Milly cap-sleeve rhinestone sequin dress.

Music: The opening montage is to "No One Does It Like You" by Department of Eagles. Nelly plays servant to the Mean Girls at Pinkberry to "Who's Crying Over Who" by The Temporary Thing. The Little Ones' "Like

Desmond Harrington as Jack Bass

Playing uncle to Chuck is Desmond Harrington, who was born in Georgia but raised in the Bronx. After high school he worked in construction and as a bartender to pay for acting classes. His dedication paid off when he booked the first film he auditioned for, Luc Besson's *The Messenger: The Story of Joan of Arc.* Desmond has built a loyal fan base with his roles on Spielberg's miniseries *Taken*; TV series *Dexter*, *Dragnet*, *Sons & Daughters*, and *Rescue Me*; as well as in films like *Ghost Ship*, *Wrong Turn*, *We Were Soldiers* (which Taylor Momsen also acted in), and 2009's *TiMER,* costarring John Patrick "Aaron Rose" Amedori.

a Spoke on a Wheel" provides the soundtrack to the tense breakfast at the Humphreys. Jenny makes her power play at Pinkberry to "Will Scarlet" by Magic Bullets. When Blair tracks down Chuck at Victrola, "I'm Not Cool" by Sohodolls is playing. The Victrola party starts with "Mayday" by UNKLE featuring Duke Spirit. Shiny Toy Guns' "Ricochet!" is on when Eric talks to Chuck at Victrola. Serena catches up to Dan at Victrola to "Circles" by The Sugar Migration. Jack drives off with Chuck in the limo to "E.S.T." by White Lies, which plays over the closing montage.

"Careful Bass, now that you're a big fish there are a lot more sharks in this pond."

2.15 gone with the will

Original air date: January 12, 2009
Written by: Amanda Lasher
Directed by: Tricia Block
Guest cast: Joseph Adams (Miles), Michaela Annette (Mini Serena), Stevie Ray Dallimore (Chris Rosson), John Hillner (Albert), Lydia Grace Jordan (Mini Mean Girl), Ellie Pettit (Mini Blair), Thomas Schall (Pete Holmberg), Anne Torsiglieri (Renee Rosson)

Lily and Rufus search for their son as Dan keeps the secret from Serena. Chuck inherits the majority share of Bass Industries.

If you are ever invited to a brunch at the Palace Hotel hosted by or celebrating a man named Bass, do not go. A life-altering secret will be revealed, causing you to storm out of the brunch, and the reserved éclairs will go uneaten. Double tragedy. This brunch was definitely a bigger disaster than last year's "The Wild Brunch." Jack Bass is officially the worst uncle: tricking his grieving nephew into losing control of a billion-dollar company so he can take it himself. Desmond Harrington plays the villain so well, making Jack delight in his victory over Chuck.

Sarkozy may be a bad kisser, but Dan Humphrey is a bad liar. He does the same things Serena did when Georgina came to town: acting cagey, avoiding hangouts and phone calls, and giving vague answers. With Blair on Chuck watch, Penelope, Hazel, Is, and Nelly break rules that B wouldn't in their quest to find out Dan's secret. As mean as Queen Blair can be, she has boundaries to her evilness. You don't out Eric without his permission, and you definitely don't reveal to the world that Lily and Rufus have a secret love child that Dan knows about but Serena doesn't. The school needs its Queen back.

After Blair's best efforts to be a loyal friend to Chuck, he insults her devotion by getting high with hookers and pushing her away again. Though his apology, complete with bouquet of peonies, is sincere, it's too much to ask her to endure after such a difficult few months. Dan and Serena feel they can endure the new obstacle in their path, deciding that while the existence of a shared sibling changes things, it doesn't change the depth of feeling they have for each other. For Lily and Rufus there could be nothing better to come home to after learning their son has died than the new Brady Bunch eating PB&J together at the Humphrey loft.

"Tuna fish? Why does he make it so hard for himself?"
— Blair gets the Gossip Girl blast on Dan's brown-bag lunch

JTLYK:

- Top story on Gossip Girl: "*Boy Billionaire?* With the recent passing of his father, Chuck Bass has been left with sorrow, grief and a big fat inheritance. If you thought C was rolling in $$ before just wait. You ain't seen nothin' yet. And remember, money changes everything."
- Jack makes another pass at Blair, but what happened between them remains a mystery.
- Attention Nate: a two-month anniversary is not a good enough reason to miss a brunch in honor of your best friend whose father just passed away.
- "Talk about failing upwards." The Mini Mean Girls return! The trio was last seen together in "The Dark Night."
- Gossip Girl's blast about the love child compares Dan and Serena to Romeo and Juliet, but then specifies that R and J didn't share DNA. Um, neither do D and S.
- On his father's desk where Chuck's partying with his lingerie-clad coquettes are pills, booze, lines of cocaine, and cigars.
- Remember back in "School Lies" when Serena told Lily she'd rather be Chuck's sister than Dan's? Now the poor girl is pseudo-sister to both.

- Nate knows how important it is to have friends show kindness when painful personal details are made public, and he reaches out to Dan.
- While Dan points to Toni Morrison, Flannery O'Connor, and Russian aristocrats for precedents of love between pseudo-siblings, Serena cites *Clueless*. Cher (Alicia Silverstone) falls in love with her stepbrother Josh (Paul Rudd). *Clueless* is based loosely on Jane Austen's *Emma,* wherein the title character and her brother-in-law fall in love.

Secrets & Lies:

- Unable to tell Serena the secret, Dan avoids her and lies to her.
- Serena says Lily is too honest about her relationships with men, but S doesn't know about the major secret her mother is harboring.
- Penelope, Is, and Nelly overhear Dan say he's lying to S and get Gossip Girl to put out an APB on D's secret.
- Jack puts on a show of sincerity and care for his nephew while plotting to humiliate him and steal Bass Industries from under his nose. Even though B knows not to trust him, she gets embroiled in his scheming.
- Blair pretends not to have a "flare-up of Chuck fever" when S asks her about it.
- Dan tells Vanessa his secret.
- Serena goes to Vanessa on a "boyfriend snooping" mission, and Vanessa lies to her.
- With Dan's phone, the Mean Girls intercept V's text and learn the secret.
- Chris Rosson, the adoptive father, tells Rufus and Lily a whopper of a lie: that their son died in a boating accident when it was actually his other son who died. The Rufly child is still alive.

That's How It's Done in *The O.C.*: Suffering from the same "never good enough" relationship with her father, Kirsten is surprised to receive a personal letter from him at the reading of his will in "The End of Innocence."

Gone with the Wind (dir. Victor Fleming, 1939): Adapted from the 1936 novel, this epic romance centers on Scarlett O'Hara (Vivien Leigh), a Southern belle with a strong will and sharp tongue, and the two loves of her life, Ashley Wilkes (Leslie Howard) and Rhett Butler (Clark Gable). As the world around her changes over the course of the Civil War, Scarlett fights to survive and preserve what's left of her family and estate, but in that fight she develops a meanness of spirit that nearly destroys her and what she holds dear. But Scarlett is a fighter 'til the end.

Jack Bass in his roguish determined ways is not unlike Rhett Butler at his worst, and his any-means-necessary grab for Bass Industries is like Scarlett at hers. Losing her daughter and her husband in quick succession, Scarlett proves to have a great amount of endurance in the face of loss, the quality that Rufus and Lily demonstrate when they learn of their son's death. Just as they nearly destroy Scarlett and Rhett's marriage, petty gossips threaten Dan and Serena's union. But in both cases, the stories spread are true and must be faced. Let's hope Dan and Serena fare better than Rhett and Scarlett.

Welcome to the Real World:

- Jonathan and Jenny are planning an Edith Head/Alfred Hitchcock film festival. The legendary costume designer worked with the legendary director on 11 films, including *Notorious*, *Rear Window*, *Vertigo*, and *The Birds*.
- Dan makes Vanessa swear secrecy on her Simple Machines 7 inches, the now out-of-print compilation records produced by the indie-rock label run by Jenny Toomey and Kristin Thomson in the '90s. The label produced bands like Tsunami, Monorchid, Retsin, Ida, and tunes by future Foo Fighter Dave Grohl.
- Jack and Chuck talk gonorrhea medications: Suprax and Rocephin are antibiotics that kill the gonorrhea bacteria.
- Rufus reminds Lily of the time the drummer from alternative rock band Buffalo Tom, Tom Maginnis, groped her.
- Would Jenny really want to watch 1995's cult classic *Showgirls* with her brother? Winner of 13 Razzies, the movie stars Elizabeth Berkley as Nomi Malone, a stripper-turned–Vegas showgirl who can't correctly pronounce Versace.

Locations:

- Vanessa and Dan buy candy at Dylan's Candy Bar (1011 Third Ave).

Oops: Chuck mentioned his sexual awakening with Gina, his Italian au pair, in "The Magnificent Archibalds," and here he even more explicitly says he lost his virginity to her. But in "Woman on the Verge," he says he lost it to Georgina in the sixth grade. Perhaps C is muddled in his grief.

The Look: Jenny's excited about movie night with Jonathan and Eric in a grey embroidered Nanette Lepore Day & Night sweater coat with a silver Valentino bag. Blair goes to the reading of the will in a DvF Bette Glitter plaid suit, Urban Outfitters tights, Robert Clergerie Luna shoes, and a Flavio Castellani black cape with a Lady Dior Cannage bag. Serena turns to Vanessa for help in a navy Vena Cava Kashmir top. In a black Dolce & Gabbana dress, Blair is stood up by Chuck. To the brunch in Chuck's honor, Jenny wears a black Barneys CO-OP turtleneck under a cream and black Temperley London jumper. Serena is in Armani with necklaces by Finn and Helen Ficalora and charcoal Loeffler Randall Yvette cutout booties. Blair wears a butterfly-patterned ribbon-tie Milly top and See by Chloé tweed skirt.

Music: "Mirror Error" by The Faint bookends this episode playing when Blair, Chuck, Nate, and Jack meet at the Palace for the reading of the will and again from Chuck taking off Bart's tie to Rufus and Lily returning to the loft. Nelly impresses the Mean Girls with her thievery, and Franz Ferdinand's "No You Girls Never Know" plays in the background. The Gossip Girl blast on Dan and Serena's half-sibling goes out to "Watchman, What Is Left of the Night?" by Greycoats. At the restaurant where Rufus and Lily meet with their son's adoptive father, "At Least" by Dan Cray Trio is playing.

Yin Chang as Nelly Yuki

Before *Gossip Girl*, New Yorker Yin Chang's acting credits were a ton of commercials, the short film *Paper Girl*, and a stint on both *Law and Order: Criminal Intent* and *Special Victims Unit*. Yin was featured in *Nylon*'s 2009 Young Hollywood issue alongside Dreama Walker, Amanda Setton, and Nicole Fiscella. "Nelly is a nerd. But she's not only book smart. She really struggles to fit in and conform to the group. But she's a fashionable nerd," Yin told the magazine. Her interests aren't limited to just acting: she writes, she's classically trained in piano and ballet, and she makes jewelry under the brand name LeliMelo. (Vanessa wears a LeliMelo necklace in "The Grandfather" and in "Remains of the J.")

"New beginnings require something else to end."

2.16 you've got yale!

Original air date: January 19, 2009
Written by: Joshua Safran
Directed by: Janice Cooke
Guest cast: William Abadie (Roman), Jan Maxwell (Headmistress Queller), John Shea (Harold Waldorf), John Bolton (Bruce Caplan), Tom Dooley (Usher), Thomas Schall (Pete Holmberg), Jessalyn Wanlim (Pauletta Cho)

It's Yale Day and Opera Night on the Upper East Side.

It's sometimes easy to forgot that *Gossip Girl* is a show about teenagers who are (mostly) in their senior year of high school with ordinary concerns like college and keeping up good grades — in addition to attending will readings and society functions, dealing with dilemmas regarding shared half-siblings, pseudo murders, and who will take the helm of a billion-dollar corporation. But Rachel Carr, the new teacher at Constance, doesn't realize where she's landed and doesn't play by the — well, by Blair's rules. Giving Rufus an Opera 101 lesson, Eric recites a line from *The Magic Flute*, "The vengeance of hell boils in my heart"; like the Queen of the Night, Blair is on a rage-filled warpath by the end of "You've Got Yale!"

If you took all of the worst parts of Chuck Bass and let them fester in Australia for years and years, you'd end up with Jack. The attack in the powder room was frightening, perhaps made worse with Kelly Rutherford visibly pregnant. This is the third sexual attack on *Gossip Girl* — Serena, Jenny, and Lily, each one more violent than the previous — and none have been reported. Criminal actions deserve consequences, don't they? Proper punishment aside, Jack's attack on Lily created an opportunity for Chuck to realize who he no longer is, and who Lily and her family have helped him become. Instead of being the attacker, he was the one who recognized something was wrong and took swift action to help Lily. As cruel as Chuck was to her after he heard her on the phone with Rufus, he was right to suggest she exercise a little more tact, and think of others — her children and Chuck — before, um, parading her mistress around. Chuck's been paying attention: he knows that Lily has put the men in her life ahead of her children in the past.

With Lily now Chuck's legal guardian and him moving back in with them, it feels as though he's taken an important step away from the self-destructive behavior of his first stage of mourning. As Rufus leaves, Chuck shakes his hand, showing that he no longer holds him, or Lily, responsible for his father's death. A huge moment for him.

As Chuck comes to terms with Lily's relationship with Rufus, Dan and Serena realize how difficult it is to go on double dates with their parents. The four years of college they would have spent together, away from everyone and building a new life, will not happen now that Serena's chosen Brown over Yale. Dan ignoring S's call is a sign that Rufus and Lily's relationship may be too much for him to get over.

"Witch hunts are my valium, Serena."
— Blair returns to terrorizing the halls of Constance

JTLYK:

- Top story on Gossip Girl: "*Yale or Bust!* For Blair it's either go Yale or go home. She's been dreaming about the school since like forever. We're eager to see what B's fate will be. Although you can be sure our favorite fighting bulldog won't go down easy."
- On the CW's first GG show, *Gilmore Girls'* Rory went to Yale in season 4.
- Wagner's Ring Cycle (*Der Ring des Nibelungen*) is composed of four operas; that's about 15 hours Dan sat through. No wonder he felt like Alex in *A Clockwork Orange* with his eyes pinned open.
- The opera that the characters attend is *Tristan und Isolde* (1859), also by Wagner, and tells a story of doomed lovers. Rufus prepared to see Mozart's *The Magic Flute* (1791).
- Pauletta Cho, now head of publicity for Bass Industries, was the woman Chuck thought Bart was sleeping with in "Victor, Victrola."
- Giving us an otherwise Chair-free episode, the one shot of Blair running across the lobby while Chuck sips champagne at the bar was comedy gold.
- The newspaper story "'Bass' Exit to Brooklyn" is a pun on *Last Exit to Brooklyn*, the controversial 1964 novel by Hubert Selby, Jr.
- The picture at Serena's bedside was taken at the debutante ball ("Hi, Society").

"It's funny because they came into this as these fashion-naïve kids from L.A. . . . They are like New Yorkers now — real, fashionable New Yorkers." — Eric Daman

"It's fun to push men's fashion and let straight guys know they can dress fashionably too."

"We couldn't make
the show without the generosity of designers behind us."

"She is someone who has been working on her look for years." — Eric D on B

smart with an edge

old hollywood glamour

a little more coco chanel

XOXO

- After being told the son she gave up for adoption has died, Lily adopts a new son, Charles.
- Dan is reading John Updike's *Rabbit Redux* when Rachel arrives at the café.
- Your eyes do not deceive you: Headmistress Queller is played by a different actress in this episode and the rest of the season.

Secrets & Lies:

- Chuck's plots against his uncle keep failing; their scheming minds work too similarly.
- Serena lies to Blair and Dan about Yale, but tells Ms. Carr she got in.
- Blair is determined to smoke out the Constance student who got into Yale.
- Blair and the Mean Girls plot revenge against Ms. Carr. Blair misleads Serena into thinking the Carr plot is dead when she gets S's spot at Yale.
- Nate doesn't tell Vanessa he was going to bring her to the opera until Dan mentions it.
- Eric says that people in high society say one thing and mean another, but in Lily's case, he was wrong.
- Blair's trick on Ms. Carr is to falsely invite her out to dinner and the opera, a halfhearted scheme if ever there was one. Once she finds out Ms. Carr tried to fix her grade, Blair tries to right her wrong.
- By legally adopting Chuck, Lily thwarts Jack's master plan to run Bass Industries.

Scrap!: Jack sexually assaults Lily, and, coming to her rescue, Chuck punches Jack.

You'll B a Woman Soon: Blair's internal moral debate is made humorously external with Penelope playing devil and Is reluctantly playing angel. Blair knows exactly what the right thing to do is, but it's not what she *wants* to do. Blair's battle is bigger than going black ops on Ms. Carr; she is evolving from a girl who always goes after what she wants and does what she pleases to a woman who shows restraint and compassion. But she apologized to Ms. Carr and her Yale acceptance is *still* in jeopardy — it looks like Blair will slip back into her old ways.

The Original Gossipverse: In *You're the One That I Want*, Blair is wait-listed for Yale and Serena gets in everywhere she applied. Nate gets into Yale too, but keeps it from Blair. Every school Chuck applied to rejects him. Dan gets into four schools, including Brown and NYU.

That's How It's Done in *The O.C.*: Wanting to go to different colleges brings tension to Summer and Seth's relationship in "The Game Plan," as it does to Dan and Serena's. In "The Day After Tomorrow," Seth lies about his college acceptance, but unlike Serena, he pretends he got into Brown when he didn't.

You've Got Mail (dir. Nora Ephron, 1998): Set in New York in the days of dial-up internet connections, Kathleen Kelly (Meg Ryan) runs the beloved children's bookshop her mother left her. Though she has a boyfriend, she's more interested in an email friend she's never met. But that friend, Joe Fox (Tom Hanks), happens to run the big-box chain bookstore that's moving in around the corner from her store and threatens to destroy it. The two are soul mates online and enemies in person. Joe finds out that she is his email pal. Deciding that he does love her, he builds a friendship with her, and once he thinks she is ready to forgive him for destroying her business, he arranges a meeting. Kathleen is relieved that her real-life and online love interest are one and the same.

Blair goes to the mattresses on Ms. Carr, setting up her "come to the opera! oh no, wait alone" ruse. She thinks of Ms. Carr as Kathleen Kelly does Joe, an enemy who must be taken down. Kathleen thinks Joe is out to destroy the thing she values most, her store, but finds that there's a charming man behind the corporate face. Similarly, Blair sees Rachel as out to destroy her dream of Yale, the thing she values most, but realizes that it's a person she's hurting, not an abstraction.

Welcome to the Real World:

- A non-profit organization, Teach for America places teachers in low-income neighborhoods, but currently none of those placements are in Alabama where Ms. Carr says she was working.
- Jack calls Lily his Mata Hari (1876–1917), foreshadowing his later violent sexual assault of her. Mata Hari was an infamous courtesan executed by the French on charges of espionage during World War I.

"Refresh, refresh, refresh!" Blair and her minions await her Yale acceptance on the steps of the Museum of the City of New York, a.k.a. Constance–St. Jude's.

- Like pregnant women, says B, Chinese gymnasts get special treatment. At the 2008 Beijing Olympics, a scandal emerged that some members of the Chinese gymnastic team were too young to be eligible competitors.
- Chuck gets Jack on Megan's List, which makes information about registered sex offenders available to the public.

Locations:

- The opera scenes were filmed at St. George Theatre (35 Hyatt St) in Staten Island.
- Rachel waits for Blair at the Boathouse in Central Park (E 72nd St and Park Dr N).
- Rufus and Lily suggest stopping at Newport Creamery for milkshakes

on visits to the kids at college. There's a location in Providence (673 Smith St) and 10 others in Rhode Island.

- Angelica Kitchen (300 E 12th St) serves "organic plant-based cuisine." They make their own seitan (concentrated wheat protein) on the premises.

the shakespeare club

In January 2009, there was a post on CW's official *Gossip Girl* blog about the new club Serena was starting at Constance with the help of Ms. Carr: the Shakespeare Club. Maybe S had picked up on how very Shakespearian the Upper East Side is.

If Chuck and Blair are Benedick and Beatrice (see page 176), then Dan and Serena are Romeo and Juliet. Gossip Girl loves calling Dan and Serena her star-crossed lovers after that famous pair, whose love for each other was tragically doomed by the expectations, rules, and demands of the society surrounding them.

Blair also has a connection to Juliet. Like the Nurse is to Juliet, so Dorota is to Blair. The Nurse in *Romeo and Juliet* is a substitute mother to Juliet; she cares for her and helps in Juliet's plan to marry Romeo, just as Dorota takes care of Miss Blair and assists her in all schemes related to Mister Chuck. Both the Nurse and Dorota serve as comedic foils to their precocious teenage charges.

From one tragedy to the next, *Gossip Girl* casts our poor Chuck Bass in the role of Hamlet, the Danish prince whose father dies suddenly and leaves his son wallowing in grief, attacking those who try to reach out to him — his mother Gertrude, his love interest Ophelia, his friends — and swearing vengeance for his father's murder. As the King's death leaves a throne empty, so Bart Bass's death leaves Bass Industries in need of a new ruler. Hamlet had to contend with his murderous uncle, Claudius, who stole the kingdom for himself. With the arrival of Jack Bass, Chuck finds he also has a ruthless uncle, one determined to take the company, power, and wealth that is rightly due to Chuck. In Lily, Chuck has a Gertrude stand-in: a mother figure who has moved on to a new man too quickly for his liking. And though, like Hamlet for his mother, Chuck cares very deeply for Lily, in his rage and grief he abuses her, calling her a whore and blaming his father's death on her and her lover.

As for dear sweet Ophelia? Blair plays the part of the girl who loves so deeply and is treated so cruelly. From echoes of scenes (a near fight in a graveyard) to tiny references (like the King, Bart Bass is always referred to as dying "like, a month ago" despite the actual timeline), the first episodes of *Gossip Girl*'s winter return could've been set in Denmark just as easily as the Upper East Side.

Oops: Shirley from the Dean's Office has a different accent than she did in "New Haven Can Wait."

The Look: On Yale Day, B's wearing a cream and black Milly coat, navy Yves Saint Laurent Preppy pumps, a Brooks Brothers blazer, Oscar de la Renta blouse, H&M skirt, and she carries a red Valentino Jardin Rose Framed Duffel. Nelly's coat is Missoni and her sweater and bag are Tory Burch. Penelope has a cream Walter coat, David & Young scarf, leopard-print Rebecca Taylor silk and cashmere cardigan, and hot pink tights. Hazel's in a Coach coat with a Tarina Tarantino bag and bright blue tights. Under her grey Lauren Moffatt coat, Serena wears a blue plaid Smythe equestrian jacket with her uniform and brown Te Casan by Fay Baldock Fenny boots. Lily wears a BCBG Max Azria beaded satin gown to the opera. Blair's coral dress is from the Christian Dior resort 2009 collection. The red plaid blouse B wears to her final meeting with Queller is D&G Dolce & Gabbana, which she wears under her red plaid Dolce & Gabbana fall/winter 2008 coat. There could not have been more plaid in this episode.

Laura Breckenridge as Rachel Carr

Born in 1983, Laura Breckenridge is just as educationally inclined as her onscreen persona in *Gossip Girl.* Attending Princeton University while keeping her acting career thriving has been Laura's double life since 2002, when she enrolled in what Blair called a "trade school" but the rest of the world recognizes as a top-notch university. Laura studies classics as well as theater and takes time off when she lands a role. She trained as a dancer but decided to give it up to focus on acting. Not long after making that decision, she appeared on Broadway in *The Crucible.* The role may have been small, but Arthur Miller himself was present for the play's rehearsals and Laura described the experience as "a master class." Before *Gossip Girl,* her best-known role was as Rose Sorelli on the WB's *Related.* Shortly after Laura's first episode of *Gossip Girl* aired, said Laura, "I was walking down the street, and suddenly a guy pointed and yelled, 'Gossip Girl! You're awesome!' It took me a moment to realize he was talking to me, and then I couldn't help but laugh. Only in New York."

Music: Cold War Kids' "Against Privacy" opens the episode. Eric gives Rufus an opera lesson while listening to Mozart's "Der Hölle Rache kocht in meinem herzen" from *The Magic Flute*. "The Double" by We Fell to Earth begins as Vanessa and Nate sit in the box and builds as Jack confronts and then attacks Lily. Blair's meeting with Queller goes sour to "Mexican Dogs" by Cold War Kids.

"Once something is set in motion it can't help but build momentum."

2.17 carrnal knowledge

Original air date: February 2, 2009
Written by: Alexandra McNally, Lenn K. Rosenfeld
Directed by: Liz Allen
Guest cast: Jan Maxwell (Headmistress Queller), John Shea (Harold Waldorf), Kate French (Elle), Kate Levy (Attorney Parent), Kathy Searle (Realtor), Alexis Suarez (Courier)

New rules at Constance–St. Jude's lead to an eerily prophetic rumor about the new teacher.

OMFG! Dan Humphrey is the new Pacey Witter. As apparent as it was that Dan and Rachel wanted to hook up from the moment they swapped anti-UES barbs, the moment of Dan actually going through with it felt unexpected. His relationship with Serena has been over for less than a day and he's at Rachel's doorstep. Besides the teacher/student obstacle, Rachel is the perfect match for Dan — she's an outsider who doesn't agree with the way things are done on the Upper East Side and loves literature and praising Dan's stories. She's like a real-life Sarah (a.k.a. Georgina's alter ego) crossed with Amanda (a.k.a. Chuck's plant in "The Ex-Files"). As Dan feels connected to and understood by Rachel, he pulls further away from his father. Rufus's relationship with Lily had already placed a strain on the close father/son dynamic, and it's worsened when Dan feels betrayed by Rufus's vote to fire Rachel. Dan feels betrayed by Serena as well, who first believes the rumor might be true and then gives Blair the misleading photo.

Serena is caught in the middle of a tricky situation. Like Dan, she feels understood by Rachel, a teacher who finally encourages her and takes the time to develop her work. At the same time, Serena's best friend's future is on the line, a future that Serena has already shown a willingness to protect by giving B her spot at Yale. But Serena isn't blind. Seeing the connection between Dan and Rachel and the distance between Dan and her, she easily believes the rumor to be true. Serena regrets handing over the photo (and apologizes to Rachel and Dan), but she doesn't regret breaking up with Dan. Showing an altogether alarming lack of regret, Blair feels that since she got back into school that "everything is perfect again." But Harold has seen Blair's duplicitous side and been embroiled in one of her schemes, and he doesn't like it. The person whose opinion Blair values most in the world disapproves of her.

Can we pretend the whole Chuck Bass *Eyes Wide Shut* plot doesn't exist? Just one thing for the record: mysterious nanny/call-girl Elle isn't the most beautiful woman Chuck's ever seen. Blair is.

"Dorota, give Handsome to a homeless man. Make sure he has kind eyes."
— Blair gives up on a future that includes Yale

JTLYK:

- Top story on Gossip Girl: "*Carr-Wreck?* No one crosses Blair Waldorf and gets away with it. You can be sure B is on a warpath to bring Ms. Carr down while trying to reclaim her spot at Yale. Watch out, Ms. Carr. You're not in Iowa anymore."
- Serena's essay on *King Lear* reminds Rachel of a Cordelia reference in Dan's story. Rachel's storyline casts her in a similar plight as Cordelia, the daughter of Lear who refuses to pander and is banished for it.
- The secret society sex party took place on January 29.
- The Penelope/Blair exchange — "This is madness." "This. Is. Constance." — is a hilarious nod to *300*, where King Leonidas replies to his adversary by yelling, "Madness? This is Sparta!" before kicking him into a pit.
- Blair's effort at a rousing speech borrows from *Gladiator*: Maximus rallies his men by saying, "What we do in life echoes in eternity," while B opts for "What we do here today echoes through eternity."
- Chuck Bass's version of Narnia is *Eyes Wide Shut*. Nate and Vanessa play the film's theme on the grand piano while Chuck explores the house. In Kubrick's 1999 film, Dr. Harford (Tom Cruise) attends a masked orgy where a mysterious woman warns him he's in danger, and after the party

he tries to find her and discovers her dead.

- The building where the party was held is selling for $38,650,000.
- For telling on Blair, Vanessa calls Dan "Templeton," the rat in *Charlotte's Web*.

Secrets & Lies:

- Blair puts on a martyr act in front of her father, but is actually having Dorota do her detention dirty work.
- Dorota sneaks contraband phones to Blair and company.
- "When the truth fails you, you have no choice but to abandon it," says B. So she starts a rumor about Dan and Rachel Carr.
- Serena confronts Dan about the Gossip Girl rumor and he tells her there's no truth to it.
- Serena breaches the teacher/student information divide telling Ms. Carr about the rumor and about Gossip Girl.
- The realtor purposely leaves her file unattended so Chuck can get her client's contact information.
- Nelly Yuki confirms Dan's accusation that it was Blair who started the rumor about Ms. Carr.
- Blair lies to her father's face, saying the Gossip Girl post is true.
- Harold overhears Blair gloating to Dan and realizes she lied to him.
- Serena and Dan have been lying to themselves about their ability to overcome the challenges facing their relationship.
- Bart Bass was in a secret society that even his snoopy son didn't know about.

You'll B a Woman Soon: Blair has damaged reputations before, but never threatened someone's livelihood. With a teacher as a target (even a really short, really young teacher), Blair draws attention from the authority figures in her life — her headmistress and her father — both of whom she's always aimed to please. Her father saw her scheming side in "Roman Holiday," but when he sees the lengths to which she'll go, he gives Blair a worse punishment than no Yale — his disapproval.

That's How It's Done in *The O.C.*: Taylor Townsend and Dean Hess are having an affair; when the Dean threatens Ryan's academic future, Summer uses cell phone evidence to get him fired in "The Perfect Storm." In "The

Safe Harbor," the gang petitions a school board meeting to have Marissa re-admitted.

Carnal Knowledge (dir. Mike Nichols, 1971): Way less sexy than the title suggests, *Carnal Knowledge* opens with a voiceover of two young men talking about women, sex, and love — and that's the focus for the rest of the film. Jonathan (Jack Nicholson) and Sandy (Art Garfunkel) are college boys eager to lose their virginity, and they both end up with Susan (Candice Bergen), only Sandy doesn't know his best friend's sleeping with his girlfriend. Susan chooses Sandy, who trusts her, over Jonathan. In the next part of the film, years later, Jonathan is a man who cares only about sex and money, but has been experiencing some technical difficulties. Lucky for him he meets Bobbi (Ann Margret), whose cleavage is ample enough for Jonathan. Sandy married Susan but their sex life is dull so he takes a lover. Both men gripe continuously about women. Bobbi and Jonathan's affair goes from playful to poisonous and she takes too many painkillers after a particularly bad fight. The coda is Jonathan's slideshow of ballbusting women he's known. Sandy watches it with a young woman who looks to be his daughter but is (of course) his lover. Jonathan visits a prostitute who talks him into an erection by praising his strength, power, independence, and manliness, all the while insulting awful ballbusting women. A heartwarming tale.

Blair and the Mean Girls feel wronged by Ms. Carr in the same misplaced and misguided way that Jonathan and Sandy feel hard done by the women in their lives. Blair's actions destroy a woman's career and reputation (or very nearly do), and like the pathological Jonathan, she has little to no remorse for her actions. In one of the only interesting conversations in the film (zing!), Susan talks about the fluidity of identity, how people play different roles, acting differently, for example, with their friends than with their father. Blair has always played fast and loose with her various personas and shows the wrong side to her dad.

Welcome to the Real World:

- Ms. Carr mentions Henry David Thoreau (1817–1862); some of his ideas are no doubt anathema to Blair. To wit: "Most of the luxuries and many of the so-called comforts of life are not only not indispensable, but positive hindrances to the elevation of mankind." Hairbands included.

- Blair compares Ms. Carr to Mary Kay Letorneau, who began a sexual relationship with one of her 12-year-old students and later was convicted of and served jail time for statutory rape. Letorneau bore two children by the student, and they married in 2005.
- Blair quips that she could still apply to Ohio liberal arts college Oberlin.
- Blair loves *Damages*, the award-winning FX series starring Glenn Close as ruthless lawyer Patty Hewes.

Locations:
- The secret club's party is held at 678 East 63rd Street.
- Rachel meets with Dan at Le Petit Oeuf, which is in Brooklyn and not at the address, 547 East 78th Street, written in her daybook. It doesn't make much sense that she (and Serena) would go from Central Park to Brooklyn and back to the Upper East Side in such a short time.

The Look: Another color explosion at Constance: Nelly Yuki's yellow jacket is French Connection's Knickie. Penelope is wearing an Alice + Olivia purple bubble coat. Under the red H&M coat, B has a cream Nanette Lepore Songstress cardigan on with a bow tie (which she's been wearing to show her heart still belongs to a certain bow-tie wearer?) and a BGN skirt; her black bag is Robert Clergerie (Titan) and so are her shoes (Fillesat). S gives Rachel her essay wearing a black Rag & Bone "Great Coat," a Nuti New Yorker ostrich hobo purse in purple, and DvF boots. Ms. Carr's purse is Hogan. B arrives with the exculpatory evidence wearing a red Catherine Malandrino floral sleeve top and jade Nanette Lepore Kiss Me coat. Harold takes Handsome away and B's wearing a Milly beaded cardigan and knit tank.

Music: "It's a New Day" by will.i.am starts the episode as Dorota does B's detention clean-up for her. Light FM's "Black Magic Marker" plays in the background when Serena finds Dan and Rachel having coffee. The girls learn about the new cell phone rule at Constance and "Mission Control" by The Dandy Warhols kicks in. Rachel and Dan's misleading meeting is to "Kiss Me Again" by Jessica Lea Mayfield. Dan and Rufus talk the morning after Rachel is fired to Brighton, MA's "Bet You Never Thought." Rachel puts the moves on Dan to "With a Heavy Heart" by Does It Offend You, Yeah?

Kate French as Elle

Born into a New Jersey family of photographers and models, Kate was a model herself before moving into acting. Best known as Niki Stevens on *The L Word*, she also appeared as a recurring character on *Wicked Wicked Games* and *South of Nowhere* (and had a bit part in the film *Accepted*, which starred Blake Lively). A newbie when she started on *The L Word*, Kate said she was "extremely intimidated because [the cast] has all done such amazing work." But her experience on that show prepared her for her steamy role on *Gossip Girl* as Elle.

"Before Gossip Girl there was
Edith Wharton, and how little has changed."

2.18 the age of dissonance

Original air date: March 16, 2009
Written by: Jessica Queller
Directed by: Norman Buckley
Guest cast: Jan Maxwell (Headmistress Queller), Kate French (Elle), Beau Gravitte (Mr. Campbell), Harmon Walsh (Julian Rawlins), Bess Rous (Fiona), Whitney Vance (Kelsey), Carrie Yaeger (Teacher)

No one but the stage manager seems to care about the senior class play. Chuck gets duped by Elle.

The creators of *Gossip Girl* have always acknowledged Edith Wharton's novels of high society in 19th-century New York as an inspiration for the show. Here Jessica Queller weaves the narrative of *The Age of Innocence* explicitly and deftly into the episode's plot. With the play as the main event, Blair tries to find the person destroying her, Dan pursues Rachel and battles Rufus, Serena hatches a Cyrano plot to win Julian, inadvertently causing Nate and Vanessa to argue, and off-campus Chuck plays the hero to a woman who doesn't need saving, just cash.

Though the Elle plotline proved to be the most useless of the season, it did alter the Gossipverse in two important ways. After losing his father and being betrayed by his uncle, Chuck chooses to help someone he thinks is in danger instead of continuing his self-destructive behavior. (And though he definitely has the hots for Elle, his motivation is more than simple lust. Finding attractive women to sleep with has never been a problem for Chuck.) Elle also brought Carter Baizen back, the guy who gets under Chuck's skin like no one else. And judging by his hand on Blair's leg at the end of the episode, he's after someone much more precious to Chuck than Elle.

For a guy who's popular, handsome, and (sometimes) wealthy, Nate gets kicked around a lot and by those closest to him — his parents, girlfriends, and best friends. Seeing Nate give a piece of his mind to Julian was a wonderful moment of him standing up for himself, and publicly. From Nate's little dance in the dressing room in the opening montage through his tomato-analogy fight with Vanessa, Chace Crawford was finally allowed to be funny.

Taking a step not unlike Newland Archer, Dan defies his father and the rules that govern society and pursues Rachel. A guy with a strict sense of right and wrong (which has caused him to be more than a little judgmental in the past), Dan has been pushing his moral boundaries this year: dating up a storm, partying with Chuck Bass, deliberately sabotaging Blair ("Prêt-a-Poor J"), not reaching out to Jenny when she ran away, experimenting with exploitation for personal gain (his Chuck and Bart stories), and now sleeping with a teacher. As he discovers how to be the person he wants to be as an adult, his world is no longer black and white. Admitting his mistake with Rachel, Dan asks his father for room to falter. Ah kids. They grow up so fast.

She's acted crazy before (in "The Serena Also Rises" and "New Haven Can Wait" this season), but "The Age of Dissonance" is a portrait of Blair Waldorf unhinged. Already hiding the hurt her father's disapproval caused her, Blair loses Yale and can no longer pretend that everything's perfect. No one will indulge her witch-hunt and Nelly Yuki shuts her down: "People aren't jealous of you. They hate you." Even true blue Serena loses faith in Blair, telling her, "Bottom line is, betrayal is in your nature." Ouch. Like Dan, Blair has struggled to become the person she imagined she'd be at 18, to put aside the scheming and embody Grace Kelly. Serena, Vanessa, and the Mean Girls finally get through to her: they've had enough of the Old Blair. She realizes there's no one to direct her rage at but herself. Her punishment for Ms. Carr, to simply live with her wrongdoing, signals how awful B feels about who she is. It's about time Blair felt remorseful for her actions. But hooking up with Carter Baizen? A surefire path to feeling more remorse.

"I hate these clothes, I hate this play, and I hate pretentious asshats who try to steal other people's girlfriends."
— Nate shares his feelings with the "lame dilettante director"

JTLYK:

- Lily is mysteriously absent and unable to help Rufus deal with the aftermath of Teachergate.
- Top story on Gossip Girl: "*Constance Teacher Back for More?* Looks like Ms. Carr didn't move back to the farm. She's returned to Constance, teaching the works of Shakespeare, Joyce and other dead white guys. We assume since Ms. Carr's a teacher again she and Dan Humphrey are over. But we all know what they say about those who assume? Makes an a$$ out of you and me . . ."
- The episode opens with "Hong Kong Garden" in homage to *Marie Antoinette*, a major inspiration for the look and feel of *Gossip Girl.*
- Gossip Girl takes the play as an opportunity to quote Shakespeare: "All the world's a stage" from *As You Like It* and a name check for *All's Well that Ends Well.*
- Will any of Vanessa's countless Constance–St. Jude's documentaries ever be shown?
- Last seen in "Hi, Society" escorting Serena to the debutante ball and getting punched by Nate, Carter Baizen is back.
- Rufus intercepts Rachel's reply to Dan's note. Attention *Gossip* folks: don't send handwritten letters! Rufus intercepted the note from Alison's lover in "Roman Holiday" and Vanessa stole Nate's to Jenny in "The Magnificent Archibalds."
- Maybe Serena didn't see all of *Cyrano de Bergerac*? Serena casts herself in the role of Christian, the lover who needs help wooing the object of his affection, and puts Vanessa in Cyrano's spot, who tells Christian what to say and do to win her affection but falls in love himself and must keep it a secret. Depending on the version, Cyrano either dies of heartbreak or ends up with the girl.
- Blair inverts Nina's speech from Chekhov's *The Seagull.* In act 4, Nina says, "I'm a seagull — no, no — I'm an actress."

- Chuck finds Elle at the Eastview Hotel, where Serena "killed" Pete Fairman.
- When the camera pans over the audience, at least six people are so bored they're playing on their cell phones.
- Blair says to Dan, "Don't you gaslight me," an expression derived from the 1944 thriller *Gaslight* where Paula (Ingrid Bergman) is relentlessly manipulated and driven crazy with suspicion by her husband, who's out to get her.

Secrets & Lies:

- Chuck gets a doctor's note for acute stage fright to get out of the mandatory participation in the school play.
- The other teachers gossip about Ms. Carr.

constance billard and st. jude's present *the age of innocence*

In the school production of *The Age of Innocence*, Dan Humphrey plays Newland Archer, the man who questions the rules and customs of the New York's high society. Dan's romantic interests parallel Newland's — Serena (playing Newland's fiancé May) is a part of the very society that he questions, and Rachel, as a stand-in for Countess Ellen Olenska, shares his ideas. Like Newland helping Ellen reintegrate into society, Dan helps Rachel adjust to life at their tony private school. As Rachel returns to Constance after her brief firing and the student-affair rumors, so too does Ellen return to New York disgraced by the failure of her "bad marriage" and by rumors of an affair. The gossips whisper about Ellen and Rachel; Newland and Dan feel compelled to protect her.

Serena is a friend to Rachel as her character May Welland is cousin and friend to Ellen. Serena is welcoming, helpful, and appreciative of Rachel, but also suspicious of her relationship with Dan, just like her *Age of Innocence* counterpart. At the beginning of the episode, Blair doesn't see how she suits the Countess Olenska role, having pictured herself as "Winona." The persona that Blair presented to the world, at school and with her father, was very May Welland — perfectly groomed, compliant, well mannered, and eager to carry on the traditions of high society, which includes "ignoring the unpleasant." But as Blair's "perfect life" crumbles, she finds she's right for the role of the Countess.

As Nate says in his onstage meltdown, he understands Julius Beaufort perfectly. Like Captain Archibald, Beaufort is a man who has a "regrettable family history" but has married into one of New York's top families, the Mingotts, so he's accepted, especially because he throws lavish balls

- Elle is calling herself Hayley.
- Jenny passes secret notes between Dan and Rachel.
- Vanessa plays Cyrano in Serena's attempt to woo Julian, inadvertently leading Nate to believe she's the one flirting with Julian.
- Carter is a member of the secret society.
- Elle dupes Chuck into thinking she's into him, when really she just wants his money.
- Blair accuses Nelly, Vanessa, and Dan of being the ones out to destroy her. Serena accuses Blair of putting out the blast about her.
- Nate explodes onstage, telling everyone how he really feels.
- Dan realizes it was Rachel behind the Gossip Girl stories and tells Blair about their romp in the costume closet.
- Rachel tries to punish Blair by revealing the secrets she has on her: calling

and has business interests with all of New York. Just like the Captain, Beaufort falls into financial ruin, his family is disgraced, and he loses scads of money for others. When his wife reaches out to Granny Mingott (Nelly Yuki in a fat suit), she turns her away, like Anne Archibald was by the van der Bilts. And if Chuck Bass hadn't been excused from the play, he would have been cast as Larry Lefferts, a fashionable man who has no shortage of extramarital affairs.

Outside of the similarities between *Gossip Girl* characters and their *Age of Innocence* alter egos, "The Age of Dissonance" also alludes to Wharton's story by echoing plot points. Agreeing to finally consummate their relationship, Newland sends Ellen a letter containing a key; she changes her mind when May steps in; the letter is returned to him unopened. Rufus intercepts Rachel's key-enclosed note and returns it to her with a warning. At the theater, Newland watches a scene between two lovers; the man approaches his love from behind, picks up a ribbon from the back of her dress, and kisses it. This "farewell" scene is reenacted by Newland and Ellen in their own manner at later points in the story. In the costume closet with Rachel, Dan reenacts a scene between Newland and Ellen, kissing her wrist. That scene is later acted out by Dan and Blair onstage. (In the costume closet, Dan changes Newland's words to avoid mentioning the inevitable failure of their relationship.) Says Ellen to Newland in their passionate embrace in the carriage, "Is there anywhere we can be happy behind the backs of people who trust us?" Like Ellen, Rachel abruptly leaves town, and for good. In Rachel's farewell note to Dan, she quotes Ellen in a farewell scene with Newland, shortly before he marries May. Though Rachel doesn't quote the end of Ellen's speech in her letter, it is appropriate for the end of this affair: "I can't love you unless I give you up."

Dean Berube, sending Gossip Girl information about Marcus's affair with Catherine, and spilling the reason S was accepted by Yale.

- Serena sees Julian is a total fake but doesn't acknowledge that she was being fake herself.
- Dan tells Serena that it was Rachel, not Blair, who put out the story about her.
- Blair doesn't blame Serena for not believing her, since it was the type of thing she would do and lie about.

The Original Gossipverse: Starring in a remake of *Breakfast at Tiffany's*, Serena falls for her co-star, whom she finds out is gay, in *Only in Your Dreams*.

That's How It's Done in *The O.C.*: Seth and Summer are forced into helping out with the school play in "The Shape of Things to Come."

The Age of Innocence (dir. Martin Scorsese, 1993): Adapted from Edith Wharton's Pulitzer Prize–winning 1920 novel, the film begins at the opera in New York City in the 1870s among the society whose descendents would walk the streets of the Upper East Side and the halls of Constance Billard. Newland Archer (Daniel Day-Lewis) hastens the announcement of his engagement to May Welland (Winona Ryder) after the return of her cousin, the Countess Ellen Olenska (Michelle Pfieffer), sets the gossips' tongues wagging. Newland becomes a friend to Ellen, helping her navigate the "hieroglyphic world" of high society where the real thing is never said or done or even thought. Unlike the traditional and perfectly rule-abiding May, Ellen is worldly, unusual, and independent, having had a strange upbringing and a bad marriage to a Polish count. Newland and Ellen fall desperately in love, but he marries May nonetheless and finds it less trouble to conform to tradition than break out on his own. After the matriarch Mrs. Mingott falls ill and Ellen returns, Newland feels the suffocating falseness of his life and tries to consummate their love. But May meets with Ellen, having more insight than Newland gives her credit for, and tells her she's pregnant. Ellen leaves the city. The rest of May and Newland's life is spent in domestic peace as they raise their children and the world changes around them. In his old age, Newland is given a chance to see Ellen again but finds he is too "old fashioned" and does not.

In the film, Scorsese puts visual emphasis on the rituals of the society, which are heavily laden with meaning: the details of the clothing, elaborate dinners and balls, manners and customs of the characters. Opera, flowers, and a character's style of dress are symbols chosen with the same deliberateness that marks both the *Gossip Girl* characters' choices and those of the show's creators.

Welcome to the Real World:

- Julian's impressive résumé includes working with Eric Bogosian, the playwright and actor perhaps still best known for *Talk Radio*.
- Vanessa and Julian drop lots of classic film references. Among dozens of others, director William Wyler is responsible for *The Little Foxes* (1941), *The Heiress* (1949), as well B's favorite *Roman Holiday* (1953). British film director Jack Clayton made *The Great Gatsby* in 1974 from a script by Francis Ford Coppola.
- Caught off-guard, Serena recites lyrics to the song "Bette Davis Eyes," best known from Kim Carnes' version, but there's also a cover by Leighton Meester on YouTube.
- Julian paraphrases Uta Hagen (1919–2004), actress and acting teacher whose books, such as *Respect for Acting*, are required reading for drama students.

Locations:

- Chuck runs into Carter and Elle at Park Avenue Winter (100 E 63rd St).
- Carter tells Chuck he met Elle at Apothéke (9 Doyers St).

Oops: In the repeated shots of Dan reaching to kiss Rachel in the storage closet, the arm he reaches with switches back and forth. In the stage wings at various points during the play, Serena, Vanessa, Nate, and Jenny talk loudly with no concern of interrupting the performance. For a play with such a lavish budget, the actors would be miked for their performance, so Blair and Dan's angry whispering onstage would be heard. Rufus's ice cream handling switches from shot to shot.

Spotted: *New York Times* critic Charles Isherwood attends the Constance–St. Jude's production of *Age of Innocence*. On accepting the invitation to do the cameo, Isherwood wrote, "As someone who makes a living assessing the achievements of people who have the courage to risk making fools of themselves every day — to be a good actor is to be fearless about emotional self-exposure — I knew it would be cowardly to say no."

The Look: Serena's gown as May Welland and Blair's as Countess Olenska are both from the Marchesa fall 2008 collection. Vanessa attends the play in a Lauren Moffatt dress with a bright yellow Rebecca Minkoff Rendezvous clutch. Blair's post-play outfit is stunning: a Nanette Lepore "black tie" top, Diane von Furstenberg velvet skirt, and Susan Daniels headband.

Music: The episode begins with Siouxsie and The Banshees' "Hong Kong Garden." At Park Avenue Winter, where Chuck sees Carter with Elle, "North London Trash" by Razorlight is playing. The New Monarchs' "Kiss Me at the Gate" is the Rachel and Dan theme for the episode, as they pass notes through Jenny and when they sneak into the costume closet. The overture from Mozart's *Don Giovanni* (an opera which includes a pivotal scene of a man who refuses to repent his sins being dragged to hell) begins as Blair takes the stage as Countess Olenska. Blair and Dan bicker onstage to Mozart's "Piano Concerto No. 21 in C Major." Blair drinks alone to Bizet's "La fleur que tu m'avais jetée" from *Carmen*. (This is the second time a distraught Blair has been accompanied by *Carmen*; the first was in "Bad News Blair.")

"The problem with calling someone's bluff is that even if you win, you risk them walking away from the table for good."

2.19 the grandfather

Original air date: March 23, 2009
Written by: Robert Hull, Etan Frankel
Directed by: J. Miller Tobin
Guest cast: James Naughton (William van der Bilt), Aaron Tveit (Tripp van der Bilt), Jill Flint (Bex), Holley Fain (Maureen), Marlene O'Haire (Upper Crust #1), Karen Culp (Upper Crust #2), Emily Fletcher (Society Matron), Robert Emmet Lunney (Dean Wheeler)

Vanessa helps Nate reconnect with the van der Bilts and Dan tags along. The New Blair Waldorf emerges while Serena and Chuck try to resurrect the Old B.

If timing is everything, then Chuck and Blair are nothing. As Chuck reaches out to B he finds she's just beyond his grasp. Blair first spirals out of control as she casts off her old self, doing whatever Old Blair wouldn't: sleeping with Carter, shoplifting, getting drunk, and spilling secrets among the elite of the elite. She says hurtful things to Chuck, including mocking his near suicide, which ranks high on the cruelty meter alongside some of the things he's said to her in the past. Her destructive behavior can't be controlled by Chuck; only the reassurance Nate gives can calm her. Nate represents the best of who she aspired to be growing up, and he knows exactly how it feels to have the life you planned pulled out from beneath you. But he's still standing proud. His speech about bringing out the best in yourself and living up to your potential strikes a chord with Blair, who had lost hope and faith in herself. Though Nate tells Vanessa that his grandfather believes in him, it is his belief in himself that's enabled him to endure the trials he has. He's been without family in his life for a long time. Choosing the van der Bilts over Vanessa is understandable, but heartbreaking for V, who has always tried to be there for Nate when no one else was.

More Carter Baizen please! Sebastian Stan clearly gets along with cast members Connor Paolo and Matthew Settle (not to mention Leighton Meester).

As Blair struggles to redefine her identity and Nate finally accepts that his family legacy is part of his, Rufus and Lily create drama for themselves with the hairbrained list-making. Oh, the wacky things people do in relationships. Like Serena's bad-girl past, Lily's has always been an issue — with Rufus, Bart, her mother, and her children. Rufus finally says that her past doesn't matter, it's their present relationship that does, and accepts her without lingering doubts.

"Do you think the Humphreys have a crest? Something Jenny can stitch onto one of my cardigans?"
— Dan proves once again that he's funniest when he's feeling awkward

JTLYK:

- Top story on Gossip Girl: "*Blair In Despair?* Why so blue, B? Things must be really bad if you're resorting to drinking your pain away. Maybe you need something, or rather someone, to help you out of your rut?"
- Rufus met Bex in "Bad News Blair" and dated her in "The Thin Line."
- Carter first mentioned being in Santorini with Serena in "Hi, Society," saying he woke up and she was gone. This episode takes Blair and Serena's Guys They've Both Slept With count to two.
- When Chuck offers to bribe Dorota, she says, "How much? [In Polish] Have you lost your mind, you little shit? I work for Miss Blair and not for you. What did you think you were going to do — buy me!?"
- Suffering from his touch-football injury, Dan tells Jenny that the van der Bilt reunion was less like F. Scott Fitzgerald's *The Great Gatsby* (1925) and more like Chuck Palahniuk's *Fight Club* (1996).
- Blair quotes George Sand, the writer she was going to use as her answer to the Dean's question in "New Haven Can Wait," from her novel *Mauprat* (1837). Edmée, trapped in a horrible life, finds it is pointless to mourn what she has lost and the hardships she's endured. She has nothing left to lose when she says, "We cannot tear out a single page from our life, but we can throw the whole book into the fire."
- Chuck says to Blair, "This isn't you," just like she said to him at Victrola in "O Brother, Where Bart Thou?"
- Names of note from Lily's List include the obvious (Rufus, Bart), the rock stars (Slash, Trent Reznor), the Klauses, and a whole slew of names borrowed mostly from *Gossip Girl* crew members. (Crew members were

used as seat fillers for the Eleanor fashion show chart as well). But the one name missing? Van der Woodsen.

Secrets & Lies:

- Chuck steals Serena's phone to see if Blair's changed her number.
- In order to save face, Lily pretends she knew Bex and Rufus dated.
- In the interest of full disclosure, Rufus and Lily decide to share lists of everyone they've ever slept with.
- Carter tells Chuck that seducing Blair began as a move in his game with Chuck.
- Serena has a secret on Carter bad enough to make him leave town when she tells him to. What happened in Santorini?
- Lily hides half her list from Rufus.
- Chuck tries to bribe Dorota for information on B's whereabouts.
- Vanessa follows Dan and Jenny's advice and shares her concerns about the van der Bilts with Nate.
- Blair didn't tell Serena or Chuck that she was still trying to get into college.
- Blair spills as many secrets as she can think of at the van der Bilt party, including telling Serena about D's extracurricular activity in the costume closet.
- Tripp tells Vanessa about N's internship before he has a chance to himself.
- Rufus finds the other half of L's list and pouts for a while before telling her he knows she lied.
- Dorota tells Mister Chuck that Miss Blair is sleeping, when she's awake and Nate's with her.

Scrap!: Playing with the roughhousing van der Bilts, Dan sustains a touch-football injury. Serena slaps Dan for sleeping with Rachel.

You'll B a Woman Soon: Cut adrift from the future she vividly imagined for herself, Blair proves she can be nearly as self-destructive and just as cruel as Chuck at his darkest hour. She feels punished for the wrongs she's done other people, and her remorse manifests in self-loathing. Nate helps her see that despite the bad there is in being Blair Waldorf, there's also a lot worth embracing.

The Godfather (dir. Francis Ford Coppola, 1972): Spanning 1945 to 1955, *The Godfather* is the story of an Italian mob family headed by Vito Corleone (Marlon Brando), a.k.a. the Godfather. While one daughter gets married, another of his children returns home from the service wanting to break out from his family and prove he's different. Michael (Al Pacino) has a girlfriend, Kay (Diane Keaton), who's not too interested in a life as part of a notorious crime family. The Godfather helps a cousin land a part in a Hollywood movie that leads to the famous horse-head-in-the-bed trick. When the Godfather refuses to get into the drug trade, his eldest son goes rogue with another mob family, the Tattaglias. The conflict escalates and one mobster after the other ends up sleeping with the fishes. Visiting his father in the hospital, Michael gets roped into mob business and proves a ruthless leader, suggesting an assassination or two, which he describes as not personal but business. The Godfather returns to power, negotiates a ceasefire with the warring mob families, and Michael is sent to Sicily. Upon his return, he takes over the family, at first hoping to make it legit, but after his father's death, he's in for good and does some house cleaning. He kills a whole bunch of people to assert the Corleones' power and get the assassins off his back. Michael becomes the new Don Corleone.

When Vanessa first mentions her concern about Nate and the influence of his family, Dan quips that their name is van der Bilt, not Corleone. Like Kay, the girl from a different world, Vanessa sees Nate's potential and wants him to make his own choices. Both inside and out of his family, Grandfather "The Godfather" van der Bilt is a powerful force. Like Michael, Nate is drawn back into the family fold. Celebrating his family's history, acknowledging how much his legacy is part of who he is, Nate finds his grandfather's made him an offer he can't refuse.

Welcome to the Real World:

- Lily and Bex look at a painting by British artist Cecily Brown. Stephanie Savage was awestruck that Brown granted them permission to use the painting: "She's one of the greatest contemporary artists of our time and she's a fan of *Gossip Girl*."
- William van der Bilt gives us some family history, which is not the actual Vanderbilts' story. The real-life family patriarch came to America in 1650 and his descendent Cornelius built a shipping and railroad empire.
- When the young girl answers the townhouse door, Chuck says Polanski

must be in town. Film director Roman Polanski pleaded guilty to unlawful intercourse with a minor after an incident with a 14-year-old girl in 1977.

- Blair's last resort is Sarah Lawrence College, a liberal arts school north of New York City known for its academic excellence and low student-to-faculty ratio.
- Blair and Chuck have their heated encounter next to a replica of Van Gogh's "Road with Cypress and Star" (1890), the last painting he produced while in an asylum. (The original is in Kröller-Müller Museum in The Netherlands.)

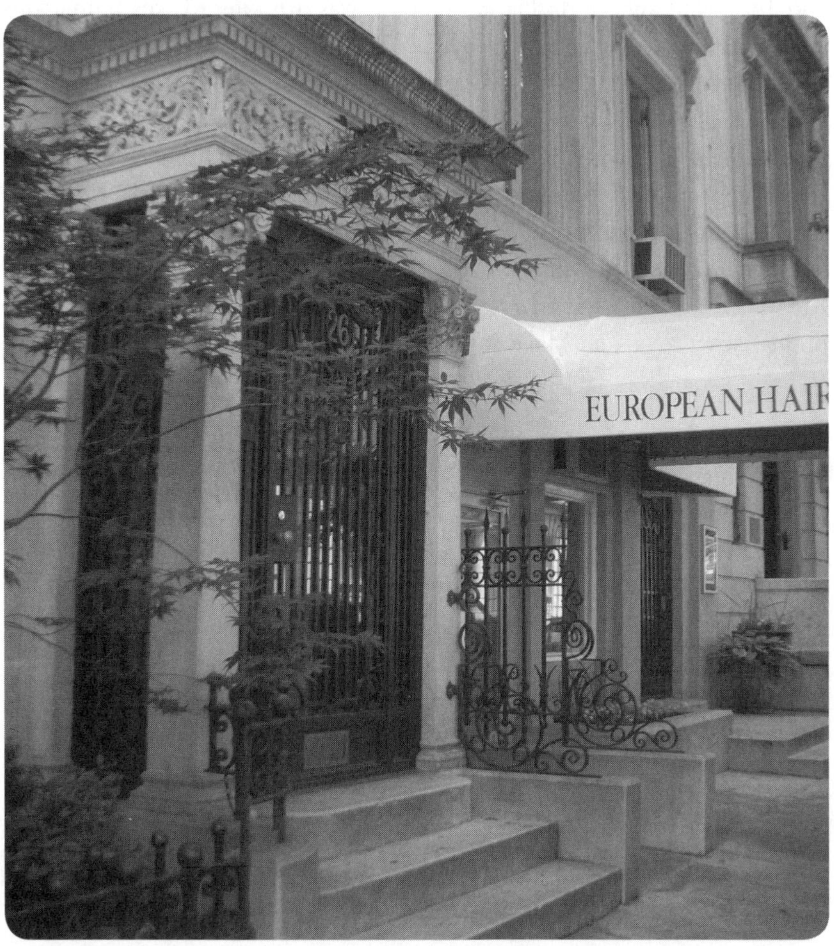

Blair pleads with the Dean of Sarah Lawrence at his home on East 73rd at Madison.

Locations:

- The van der Bilt estate is Old Westbury Gardens (71 Old Westbury Rd, Old Westbury, New York), built for the Phipps Family in 1906. Scenes in *Age of Innocence* and *Cruel Intentions* were also filmed there.

The Look: At Nate's, Vanessa's cardigan is Marc by Marc Jacobs. Blair goes shopping with S in a Diane von Furstenberg jacket over a red Milly dress and bright red bad-girl lips. Serena wears a 3.1 Phillip Lim racerback sequin tank when she and Bass boot Carter out of the country. To the van der Bilts, Blair is wearing a navy and white Hervé Léger bandage dress with a Joie cardigan and Tomassini anchor necklace. (When S was drinking too many martinis and competing with Dan in "The Ex-Files," she was also wearing a Hervé Léger bandage dress, though a different style and color.)

Music: Vienne's "Be Alright" plays as Lily asks Rufus what the deal is with Bex. Blair uses her five-finger discount to "Slip Away" by The Shore. The van der Bilts play football to MGMT's "Kids." Nate assures Vanessa that nothing will change between them at the gallery café to One Silver Astronaut's "Band-Aid for a Fracture." Blair asks Nate to stay and Chuck sees the Archibald crest on the jacket to "I Can Make You Feel It" by Home Video.

James Naughton as William van der Bilt

Two-time Tony winner James Naughton brings 30 years of acting experience with him to the role of William van der Bilt. Connecticut-born Naughton studied at Brown and Yale Drama School and has appeared in plays, in film, and on television in roles that vary from Angela's ex-husband on *Who's the Boss?* to Billy Flynn in *Chicago* on Broadway. Naughton directed *Our Town* in 2002–2003, which starred his dear friend Paul Newman. Not only an actor, Naughton also performs as a singer, mounting critically acclaimed cabaret shows and releasing an album, *It's About Time.*

"Nobody gets what they want without losing something they love. Like their integrity."

2.20 remains of the j

Original air date: March 30, 2009
Written by: Sarah Frank-Meltzer
Directed by: Allison Liddi-Brown
Guest cast: Cecilia Foss (Shana), Aaron Schwartz (Vanya)

Serena throws a party for Jenny's Sweet Sixteen. Chuck and Vanessa make unlikely bedfellows.

Jenny has a major storyline! After being such a central character in season 1, Jenny has been relegated to the backburner (delivering notes, online shopping) since her return to Constance. Serena and Jenny's first fight is fun to watch. They've been friendly since the pilot episode, with J helping S out with an invitation and S returning the favor with fashion advice. Jenny's right about Serena's misplaced motivation, but the way she handles it is childish. But her speech about wanting to stay a Humphrey and not pretend to be someone she's not shows just how much she's changed from 15 to 16. Jenny has a strong sense of self, much like Serena used to; in contrast, S now finds herself bored with her life and ready for its next phase. But is Poppy Lifton and her condescending socialite ways the answer?

Blair is desperate to rush back into dating Nate, but he tempers her haste with consideration, suggesting that friendship was what their relationship lacked in the past. So wise. But while he treats Blair with tenderness and care, he's rather callous with Vanessa, telling her that there's no one else when there kinda sorta is, even though technically he and Blair aren't physically involved yet. Chuck sees opportunity in Vanessa's hurt and anger, but even he seems surprised when she kisses him. Awesome. He makes the good girls go bad.

"I liked my social grave. I dug it myself and was happy to lie in it."
— Jenny turns 16

JTLYK:

- Top story on Gossip Girl: "*Back to Brooklyn?* Is it finally over between our prince and his pauper? Okay, so maybe V isn't totally destitute but she definitely doesn't like the sweet life like N. Have fun back in the BK. Tell Dan and the rest of the Humphrey's hi from us. It was nice knowing ya."

- Nate breaks up with Vanessa at a Greek diner; the first time they ever went out together, they met at a Greek diner ("Desperately Seeking Serena").
- Blair compares her spark-less relationship with Nate to Maurice Chevalier and Gigi (played by Leslie Caron) in 1958's musical *Gigi* about a young girl groomed to be a courtesan.
- In the elevator of the dee-luxe apartment, Dan can't help but sing the theme song to *The Jeffersons*, "Movin' On Up."
- Vanya the Doorman, who is seen for the first time, was mentioned back in "Chuck in Real Life" as the one who signed permission slips for the van der kids when Lily was away. He also appears in the webseries *Chasing Dorota* (see page 307).
- Serena had a Patrick McMullan photography book in her room in "Prêt-a-Poor J" and now he's a guest at their party. His photography also hangs in the living room.

Secrets & Lies:

- Blair tells Serena she's at home in her PJs when she's on her way to Nate's. Then she hides behind some shrubbery.
- Also hiding behind a planter, Vanessa sees Blair leaving Nate's. Chuck brought her there by sending her an email from Nate's account.
- Rufus lies to Dan about not having the Yale package with him.
- Vanessa asks Nate if there's someone else who's come between them and thinks he's lying when he says there isn't, which drives her to Chuck.
- Dan tells Jenny about the call from the realtor.
- Serena says she threw the party with only Jenny's interests in mind, but later admits she was also trying to spice up her own life and prove to herself (and Poppy) that she's interesting.
- Seeing Blair and Nate at the party, Vanessa kisses Chuck to make Nate jealous.
- Overheard talking to Lily, Rufus has to tell Dan about the financial aid problem with Yale.
- Chuck and Vanessa plan to keep their "purely physical" relationship on the down-low.

- Scott's parents intercept the call from Dan, lie to him, and delete the record of it from their son's phone.

You'll B a Woman Soon: Poor B. The adjustment from playing games with Chuck where there's an instant physical connection to slow-and-steady "friendship first" with Nate was a doozy. With a bruised ego, she complains to Dorota and comes on strong to Nate, but she identifies what's most important to her: her friendship with Nate, not winning in a competition against Chuck and Vanessa.

The Original Gossipverse: The day after Jenny's party, Dan's in a Strand T-shirt. In *Only in Your Dreams*, Dan works at the Strand for the summer. In *Would I Lie to You*, for a *very* brief moment, Vanessa finds Chuck attractive based solely on his looks; his personality's a stinker.

That's How It's Done in *The O.C.*: In season 2's "The Rager," a birthday celebration for Trey turns into an insane party. On Kaitlin's 15th birthday in "The Pot Stirrer," her hopes for a family night watching *The Sound of Music* fall through and she sabotages the birthday party Julie and Marissa throw for her.

Remains of the Day (dir. James Ivory, 1993): Stevens (Anthony Hopkins) is a butler at Darlington Hall and his life is his work — ensuring every last detail is correct, maintaining order and control over his environment, and repressing his emotions and personal opinions. Set primarily in the lead-up to World War II, the world outside Darlington Hall is changing and its flux invades the tightly wound world of Mr. Stevens. Housekeeper Miss Kenton (Emma Thompson) is equally as strong a presence in the household. Their relationship is complicated, and Stevens' lack of emotionalism leads her to marry another when her heart belongs to the butler. Lord Darlington (James Fox) is a Nazi sympathizer, and Stevens is pushed to the limits of his unquestioning servitude when asked to fire Jewish girls on his housekeeping staff. After the war, Lord Darlington, ashamed of his political role in it, dies a broken man, and Mr. Stevens denies his knowledge of what went on in the house, still unable to show Miss Kenton, now Mrs. Benn, his feelings for her.

Feeling trapped in a controlled and rigid life analogous to the household of Darlington Hall, Serena does what neither Mr. Stevens nor Miss Kenton can: she asserts herself. Mr. Stevens hides behind the rituals and order of Darlington Hall and loses himself in it. Having already had one round playing at Park Avenue princess, Jenny sees falseness in that lifestyle and doesn't want to mask who she really is and what she really feels. Unwilling to lose her identity as a Brooklyn Humphrey, Jenny mirrors Miss Kenton's strength of character as she holds onto her personal integrity.

Welcome to the Real World:

- Gossip Girl says the Nikkei, the index for the Tokyo Stock Exchange, is on the rise.
- Vanya is reading Ann Coulter's 2009 book *Guilty: Liberal "Victims" and Their Assault on America*. I must disagree with Dorota: some enemies are best to just ignore.
- Penelope is happy to be hit on by members of the Bronfman family, whose empire was built on the Seagram company and currently has interests in Warner Music Group.

chasing dorota

As part of Verizon's V-Cast sponsorship, Dorota starred in her very own six-part webseries. With the exception of the always wonderful Zuzanna Szadkowski, it was not very good (sadly), but here's what you missed.

Episode 1: "Upper East Server," a.k.a. Gossip Girl for the hired help, tells us that when no one else is home the maids get together for martinis. Dorota reveals she loves *Tyra* and wishes she had a boyfriend. Why not Vanya the doorman at the VDW, asks one of her maid pals. It can never be, says Dorota, who keeps getting mysterious texts.

Episode 2: Getting facials at the Waldorfs, the three maids are giddy when Vanya shows up to return B's hairband and asks Dorota out. They make jokes about Verizon's great service. After Vanya leaves, a mystery man arrives — a "ghost of Polish past"?

Episode 3: With Dorota's favorite flowers (hydrangeas) in hand, Stanislaw reveals he found Dorota through Facebook and was surprised to learn her fave movie is *Sabrina*. With a new handsome look and English learned from *O.C.* DVDs, Stanislaw asks Dorota to come back to Poland with him. Who is he? Her husband!

Episode 4: Dorota reveals to her girlfriends that her parents made her marry Stanislaw. She dreamed of living in America so she ran away. Stanislaw declares his love for her, but she thinks he's only after one thing — her title. Dorota is a Polish countess.

Episode 5: Stanislaw reminds Dorota of the good times they shared — formal balls and lavish brunches. But Vanya makes his plea too. He's loved Dorota since she first dropped Miss Blair off at Miss Serena's. The men start to fight and Dorota is forced to choose.

Episode 6: Dorota, with bags in hand, appears to have chosen Poland. But no! It's the dry cleaning. She signs her divorce papers and kisses Vanya. She opens a package from her parents. A note from them says all they care about is what kind of person she becomes. Inside is her tiara. The maids and Vanya toast to no more secrets.

Locations:

- Both Blair and Serena hit Via Quadronno (25 E 73rd St, pictured on facing page) for morning coffee and pastries.
- Serena takes Jenny shopping at Missoni (1009 Madison Ave).
- Rufus and Lily see *Billy Elliot: The Musical* at the Imperial Theatre (249 W 45th St).

Spotted: New York celebrity photographer and columnist Patrick McMullan snaps a photo of Serena and Jenny.

The Look: Bringing Nate coffee and hiding from S, B's in a BCBG Max Azria forest plaid tweed coat, purple Kate Spade hat, and Pour La Victoire pumps with a red Isabella Adams bag. New-Haircut Poppy wears a Gryphon fur vest. Shopping with Jenny, Serena wears a yellow Elie Tahari Aimee blouse. Choosing her dress for J's party (she settles on DvF), Blair wears a black and silver patterned Milly dress with a Rachel Leigh cuff. Jenny gathers up the board games wearing a heather gray Line Marlene ruffle wrap. The birthday girl wears a Missoni dress, black leather Doma jacket, Alexis Bittar earrings, David Aubrey and Landver bracelets, hot pink heels, and carries a gold Forever21 clutch. Vanessa's draped in a Catherine Malandrino dress; how could Chuck not stare at her boobs when she's wearing purple? That color is his Kryptonite.

Music: Serena calls to check up on Blair to "Baby Boombox" by The Handcuffs. Rufus makes chili and lies to Dan to Sorta's "Gone Away." J tries on dresses at Missoni to "Money Honey" (Lady Gaga). The restaurant where Nate meets with Vanessa is playing Two Hours Traffic's "Sure Can Start." "Dance Till Dawn" by Hearts Revolution welcomes Dan and Jenny to the party; it repeats on Chuck and Vanessa's arrival. The party turns into a rager with Mongrel's "Hit From the Morning Sun." Blair leaves and Vanessa approaches Nate to "We Got It Boy" by 5 Alarm Music. Alana D's "Break it Down" is playing at the bar when Poppy suggests Serena come to Spain. The final montage is to "Lights Off" by The Dears.

"On Passover we ask why is it that this night
is different than any other night?"

2.21 seder anything

Original air date: April 20, 2009

Written by: Amanda Lasher

Directed by: John Stephens

Guest cast: James Naughton (William van der Bilt), Aaron Tveit (Tripp van der Bilt), Holley Fain (Maureen), Will Rogers (Wes), Marilyn Bernard (Ida), Francesca DiMauro (Seamstress), Sofia Sokolov (Anna), Tom Titone (Allan Levy), Sarah Wilson (Corinne), Kaley Cuoco (Rebecca Dubrovich)

Blair skips Passover Seder to be with the van der Bilts, but everyone else shows up for Eleanor's first and disastrous attempt to host one. Everyone but Elijah.

A Seder dinner commemorates the Jewish people's freedom from slavery, both their physical and spiritual redemption, and though the Gentiles on the Upper East Side blunder and step on pretty much every sacred tradition that the ever-patient Cyrus tries to uphold, the theme resonates with the characters. Jenny and Chuck have been quietly co-existing since his attack on her at the Kiss on the Lips party and her minor measure of vengeance against him in "The Handmaiden's Tale." Seeing him with his lady friend is difficult for Jenny, especially when Chuck tells her not to worry if she hears screams. She makes it clear to him that she hasn't forgotten what happened and knows exactly how pathetic his life would be without the van der Woodsens. And Chuck knows it too. He's now seen a woman he cares for assaulted and knows how Dan felt that night. The cocky villain who attacked J in the pilot episode is not the same man who regrets his actions today. His simply worded apology was an important moment for him, for Jenny, and for the show itself.

Finding it hard to resist her old ways of using manipulation and leverage to get what she wants, Blair slips before catching herself. She apologizes to Nate and to Cyrus for mixing up what's important to her. Heeding the selfless advice from Chuck, Nate accepts Blair's apology and shows her that he still believes in her. Like Dan with Rufus, Serena and Lily try to work out their relationship. Serena is no longer a wild child but nearly an adult and needs more freedom. Just as Dan did in "The Age of Dissonance," Serena asks for room to make mistakes. Considering that Gabriel's up to some kind of no good with Poppy, it looks like S is going to need it.

"Yes, you're the wife of the landed gentry and I'm a cater waiter at a Seder."
— Dan can't help but be bitter

JTLYK:

- Dorota gets the weekend off, as do Eric and Vanessa. And Aaron Rose apparently doesn't celebrate holidays with his father.
- Top story on Gossip Girl: "*Blate on a Date!* Am I having a middle school flashback or is our beloved couple from the past actually back together? It's quite fitting that N&B would find themselves in each other's arms once again. I mean, they really are the highest members of the UES high school royal court. Long live the king & queen."

- Blair has her second *My Fair Lady* dream (the first was in "New Haven Can Wait"), but it's the first time she's not competing with Serena or Jenny, but herself. She's both Eliza as poppy-selling pauper and Eliza as lady going to the races. Nate's grandfather is the waiter who boots her out of the restaurant.
- Blair quips that firstborns are supposed to be spared. On Passover, first-born sons fast in commemoration of being spared from the plague of the firstborn in Egypt.
- The catering company is Le Petit Oeuf, the same name of the café where Dan met with Rachel Carr.
- A girl following in her mother's multi-matrimony footsteps, this is Serena's second fake marriage. Her first was at the age of eight with Aaron at Camp Suisse.
- Very fitting for a clothing designer, Jenny's Monopoly piece choice was the thimble.
- Lily brought Rufus to an event at Eleanor's once before ("The Handmaiden's Tale"). Though she had an ulterior motive then, Lily told Rufus it was so he could meet important people good for his business, which is her only reason this time. At the Seder, Serena is the van der Woodsen using a Humphrey as a fake date, not Lily.
- Nate feels betrayed by his grandfather when he finds out that Gramps was the one who instigated the SEC's investigation into the Captain. Nate's quick forgiveness may spring from the fact that Nate himself turned his father in. In "Victor, Victrola," after his father refused to seek help for his drug problem, Nate had the NYPD arrest him.

Secrets & Lies:

- Chuck catches Serena in her lie about her trip to Spain, having run into Poppy the week prior.
- Blair and William van der Bilt agree on a mutually beneficial arrangement: Blair gets Nate to attend Yale and Blair gets on the Whitney Junior Committee and a spot as a bridesmaid.
- Serena doesn't tell Blair that she is going to meet Cyrus.
- Dan gets a job catering but keeps it from his father.
- Dan overhears Serena talking to Cyrus about her secret maybe-marriage.
- Nate won't tell Blair what Tripp told him at lunch.

- Lily had ulterior motives for inviting herself and Rufus to the Seder.
- Serena covers for Dan when Rufus arrives, saying she invited him.
- Nate spills the secret in his speech: William van der Bilt was the one who tipped off the SEC about the Captain's wrongdoings.
- Serena lies to Gabriel, saying Dan is her boyfriend, and Dan goes along with it, but the way they describe their love for each other rings true.
- Jenny reminds Chuck that she's keeping a very big secret from her father and Lily.
- After explaining why he turned Captain Archibald in, Nate's grandfather vows to only tell the truth to his grandson.
- Dan admits that he's a cater waiter.
- Gabriel and Poppy are seeing each other behind Serena's back and plotting something bad.

You'll B a Woman Soon: With a halfhearted Plan B of life as a socialite, Blair finds it difficult to be at the bottom again — being too new to matter in those circles. William van der Bilt tempts her with a shortcut and B agrees to take it. As witnessed in her drive to keep Lord Marcus when she found out about his title, Blair aspires to high social standing but now realizes it's not important enough to her. Being trustworthy and kind to her boyfriend and family matters more to B. The change in her character over this season is nowhere more apparent than in her immediate willingness to apologize to and appeal for help from Nate and Cyrus.

That's How It's Done in *The O.C.*: In season 1's "The Nana," the Cohens host a wacky Seder with Sandy's mother in town. Kiki Cohen always had a glass of wine in her hand, until her alcoholism got out of control. Our Lily van der Woodsen always has wine too — a cover for Kelly Rutherford's real-life pregnancy or trouble for Lily down the road?

Say Anything... (dir. Cameron Crowe, 1989): High school graduation leaves Lloyd Dobbler (John Cusack) with only one last chance to ask Diane Court (Ione Skye) out. Overachiever Diane is detached from people her age, spending all her time studying, working at her father's retirement home, and with her father (John Mahoney), who's her best friend and to whom she can say anything. Outsider Lloyd has a nervous talking thing, just like Dan Humphrey. Lloyd takes Diane to an after-grad party and the two start hanging out and falling in love. Under pressure from her father, Diane breaks up with Lloyd just after he tells her he loves her. To win her back, Lloyd's best friend Corey (Lili Taylor) advises, "Don't be a guy; be a man. The world is full of guys." Caught for defrauding the elderly who live in his retirement home, Mr. Court has lied to his daughter and done wrong in her name. Diane turns to Lloyd and he brings her to visit Mr. Court in prison before they both leave for England where Diane has a fellowship. Diane still loves her father despite his wrongdoing.

The most important things in the world of *Say Anything…* are honesty, fighting for love, and standing by those you do love. In "Seder Anything," Blair struggles to be trustworthy and honest, and Nate decides to stand by and believe in her despite her wobbles. If only Dan Humphrey were just a little bit more Lloyd Dobbler, he and Serena could still be together; he has Lloyd's quirky charm but lacks his perseverance. Get a boombox and blast "In Your Eyes," Dan. It will work.

Welcome to the Real World:

- B shows Cyrus a photo of her and Nate at the Young Fellows Ball, which starts charity ball season. It was held at the Frick on February 26, 2009.
- While experimenting with lesbianism is not, Toni Morrison's Pulitzer Prize–winning novel *Beloved* is definitely on some NYU course syllabi.
- Chuck's date is the lead ballerina of the Bolshoi Ballet, the Russian company with over two hundred seasons of history.
- Eleanor, pay attention: Hadassah Lieberman is married to Joe, the United States Senator from Connecticut; the Haggadah is the text followed during a Passover Seder.

Locations:

- Chuck says he ran into Poppy at Rose Bar in the Gramercy Park Hotel (2 Lexington Ave).
- Blair wants to get on the Junior Committee for the Whitney Museum of American Art (945 Madison Ave).
- Tripp and Maureen's wedding (and rehearsal) is at St. James Church (865 Madison Ave, pictured opposite).

Oops: Cyrus would know that Serena's wedding in Spain is not legally binding. Even Serena should know — the Heidi and Spencer wedding in Cabo was more official than Gabriel waking up a priest at midnight and *it* didn't count.

The Look: Blair meets Nate at the church in a green coat by Milly. Serena goes to the Waldorfs wearing a Burberry sequin cardigan, Joie leaf-print tank, and J Brand Woodstock jeans; her aqua trench coat is Robert Rodriguez. Want to achieve the cater waiter look? Dan pulls it off with a J. Crew vest, white Theory shirt, H&M tie, and Marc by Marc Jacobs jeans (a.k.a. what he wears every day). At her rehearsal dinner party (which Nate totally ruins), bride-to-be Maureen is in the Lorick Heart Beat dress. Blair's in a D&G printed silk organza halter dress, Jennifer Behr rosette headband, and Kara by Kara Ross gold-plated cuff.

Music: Blair's dream soundtrack is "Anitra's Dance" from Grieg's *Peer Gynt*. "Graffiti Eyes" by Stellastarr* plays at the Humphreys when Jenny suggests Dan work for the catering company. A remix of Dinah Washington's "Is You Is Or Is You Ain't My Baby" plays at the rehearsal dinner when Blair tries to talk to Nate. "Hatikvah," the Israeli national anthem, is playing when Rufus

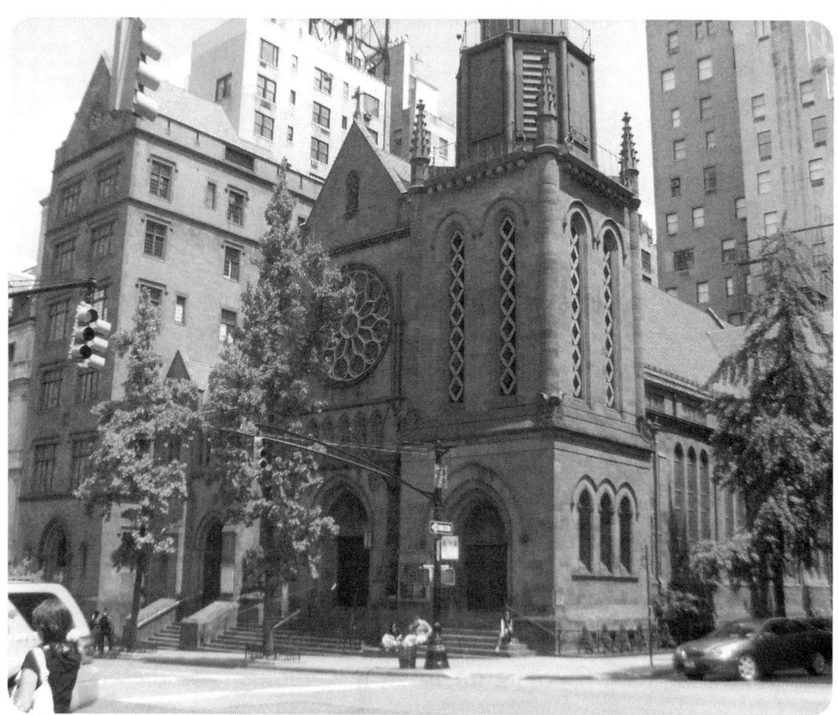

and Lily arrive at the Seder. Blair asks Tripp what he told Nate to a Gotan Project remix of Sarah Vaughan's "Whatever Lola Wants." Eleanor invites Gabriel to stay and Flo Rida's "Right Round" kicks in as the plots thicken. Miss Eighty 6's "Inside Outside" is on when Blair decides to do the right thing and not manipulate Nate. Chuck apologizes to Jenny to "Runaway" by the Yeah Yeah Yeahs.

Armie Hammer as Gabriel Edwards

Great-grandson of oil tycoon Armand Hammer, Armie Hammer was raised in Los Angeles and has appeared on *Veronica Mars*, *Arrested Development*, *Desperate Housewives*, and had a recurring role on *Reaper* as Morgan. He was signed on to play Batman in the much-delayed *Justice League: Mortal* film. Gabriel's backstory — his family acquired their wealth through the tobacco industry — isn't too far of a stretch for the actor whose great-grandfather is a controversial figure for his company's environmental and labor practices. But Armie's never considered changing his name. "I'm proud of my family name," said Armie. "The only time it hurt was in junior high school when the nicknames started. I also get a lot of questions about baking soda."

"Sometimes a queen has to make a choice: a castle with a white knight or a quest with a dark prince."

2.22 southern gentlemen prefer blondes

Original air date: April 27, 2009
Written by: Leila Gerstein
Directed by: Patrick Norris
Guest cast: Redman Maxfield (Co-op President), Cathy Trien (Camp Counselor)

Blair butts into Serena and Gabriel's relationship, enlisting Chuck's help and alienating Nate.

Unable to resist an adventure for even one episode, Blair decides to find out where Gabriel is "poofing to" to great comical effect. The New Blair

Waldorf may have sworn off hurting people, but she can still use her greatest skill set for good, can't she? Though her tactics are somewhat questionable, Blair proves to be a good friend to Serena. She's protective and persistent, sensing something sketchy in Gabriel even if she has her own Chuck-related motivation for investigating him. Once again, Blair proves to be eerily prophetic: Gabriel and Poppy are up to no good and Serena's misplaced trust brought her mother, the co-op board, and Rufus into their scheme. Oopsy!

Though Nate just resolved to trust Blair at the end of the previous episode, he still has a hard time trusting Chuck — and with good reason. Chuck still toys with B. The boys get into a pissing contest, with N asking Blair to move in with him when he knows Chuck is listening and C orchestrating a night in the back of a limo. The good, old-fashioned love triangle from the days of debutante balls and fistfights outside school is back.

And so is Georgina. But she's reformed, or pretending to be. Georgina Sparks has decided she's sick of the person she was, so she's found Jesus and happiness. She's not the only one who has changed.

In his "I Never" drinking game, Dan Humphrey actually utters to Vanessa, "You get no judgment from me. Everyone makes a mistake at least once." And he means it. Dan reserving judgment — who knew the day would come? Both Humphrey kids put their father's happiness above their misgivings and support him in his hope to marry Lily. Jenny's advice to her dad, to risk falling flat on his face, may just happen as he unwittingly throws his money into the Gabriel/Poppy scheme. Poor Serena's attempt at a mature relationship, free from scheming and spying, turns out to be a con. Gabriel makes a show of choosing her over money when he's really up to the exact opposite. But hell hath no fury like Blair Waldorf on a mission, and with the show's season finale approaching, Gabriel and Poppy better watch out.

"Say hi for me. I have so much love in my heart for that girl."
— Born-again Georgina sends greetings to the girl she roofied

JTLYK:

- Gossip Girl throws out a *Streetcar Named Desire* reference in her top post: "*Southern Comfort.* Hey y'all, looks like S nabbed a real southern gentleman. Good for her! She so deserves a peach after that long string of prunes she's dated. Let's hope this stranger's kindness is one S can depend on."

- The *Gossip Girl* writers' MLB team of choice? The Mets. Aaron's grandma, Nate, and Dorota are all fans.
- The Nelly Yuki Sabotage Party was in "Desperately Seeking Serena."
- In "Chuck in Real Life," Chuck told Blair that they could never be a regular couple who do regular couple things like holding hands. But they finally do — while sleeping — in the back of the limo.
- Rather than partying with guys with ironic moustaches, Georgina reveals that she and a passed-out Serena spent the night before the SATs watching MTV's *The Hills*.
- Gossip Girl quotes Elvis's 1963 hit "Devil in Disguise" as Georgina gets in the cab with Chuck. Uh oh.

Secrets & Lies:

- Blair wants to spy on Gabriel, and Serena wants to trust him.
- Blair goes ahead and spies on Gabriel and catches him embracing Poppy after leaving the VDW.
- After Gabriel tells S his story about Poppy, Serena says she hates lying but agrees to keep their relationship from Poppy for one more week.
- Blair declares trust the most important thing in a relationship.
- Unable to get through to Serena, Blair turns to Chuck for help in exposing Gabriel, but their plan fails when Gabriel chooses Serena over money.
- Vanessa tells Dan about sleeping with Chuck and about Rufus's financial problems.
- Rufus doesn't tell Jenny why he's upset, but she succeeds in giving him good advice nonetheless.
- Gabriel says he met Serena at Butter, but both Chuck and Blair know that's a lie.
- Serena refuses to get sucked into the Blair and Chuck hysteria and asks Blair to show her and her relationship the same respect she's shown Blair's.
- After going on the mission with Chuck, Blair realizes he was just trying to get her away from Nate and didn't need her help.
- Georgina claims to have found God and rejected her old scheming ways — has she?
- Gabriel and Poppy are running a scheme and have duped the co-op members and Rufus.

- S catches Gabriel in a lie, and returns to his hotel room to find he's gone.

That's How It's Done in *The O.C.*: In season 3, friendly outsider Charlotte earns Kirsten's trust in an attempt to con her and the Newpsies with a scam charity.

Gentlemen Prefer Blondes (dir. Howard Hawks, 1953): Dorothy (Jane Russell) and Lorelei (Marilyn Monroe) are friends and showgirls. Their taste in men is completely opposite: Dorothy goes for the looks, Lorelei goes for the money. Engaged to Mr. Esmond, a wealthy man whose family doesn't approve of her, Lorelei boards a ship to Europe with Dorothy as her chaperone. Unbeknownst to them, there's a P.I. spying on Dorothy. After he gets some incriminating evidence, the girls and a wealthy man named Piggy drug him and destroy it. Lorelei convinces Piggy to give her his wife's beautiful diamond tiara. After having a wonderful time in Paris, the girls find out they're in trouble due to a misunderstanding with the tiara. Dorothy ends up posing as Lorelei in court, wearing a blonde wig. The tiara is tracked down and eventually returned to its rightful owner. Everything's cleared up, declarations of love (Dorothy's for the P.I.) and materialism (Lorelei's for money) are made, and the musical comedy ends with two weddings.

"Southern Gentlemen Prefer Blondes" inverts the film's "diamonds are a girl's best friend" characterization of Lorelei, framing Gabriel, not blonde bombshell Serena, as the one willing to use his charms for monetary gain. The heart of the film carries over to this episode: the friendship between the two girls. Like Dorothy for Lorelei, Blair will do anything to protect her blonde friend.

Welcome to the Real World:

- Serena proudly tells Gabriel that the co-op board repeatedly turned away Bernie Madoff, who defrauded thousands of investors an estimated $65 billion with a Ponzi scheme, the largest pulled off by a single individual in history. He served on the co-op board of his Upper East Side apartment building for years.
- Blair compares her morning hair to Speaker of the House of Representatives Nancy Pelosi's.

Locations:

- Blair resists public transportion outside the Bleecker Street Station (Lafayette and Bleecker).
- Nate and Chuck play basketball at Sara D. Roosevelt Park at E. Houston and Chrystie Streets; they played there as part of the lost weekend in "Bad News Blair."

The Look: On her jaunt to the Village, Blair's black-and-cream coat is Betsy Johnson and her green bag is Nancy Gonzalez. The gold-yellow ruffle shirt she wears at the beginning of the episode is Milly. Blair tells Nate about catching Gabriel with Poppy in Nanette Lepore's gorgeous red and black Very Cherry dress. When Gabriel tells Serena about his situation with Poppy, she's in a Vena Cava shirt. Blair wears a green and gold jacquard Phillip Lim shift dress and gold Rachel Leigh cuff to the cocktail party and Serena's in the cream and rust Papyrus bodice Vena Cava dress she tried on while shopping with Blair. (The blue dress she tried on was Stella McCartney.)

Music: "Some How" by Downsyde plays as Nate shows Blair the Village and repeats again when Nate and Chuck play basketball. Serena and Blair talk about Gabriel to Anya Marina's "Waters of March." Vanessa chugs beer and tells D about sleeping with C to "Is This Sound OK?" by Coconut Records. Lying on the floor at the Humphreys, D and V talk and "Your Way" (Xu Xu Fang) plays. Serena finds out that Gabriel has been lying to her to "Clam Man" by Hot Seconds. Chuck and Georgina get into the cab back to NYC and The Kills' "U.R.A. Fever" kicks in. (The Kills' songs were also used in "All About My Brother" and "Woman on the Verge" for moments of Georgie evil.)

Tamara Feldman as Poppy Lifton

Kansas-born Tamara Feldman is no stranger to the CW. In addition to playing Poppy Lifton, she's had roles on *Supernatural* and *Smallville*. Tamara took the leap into her career with the encouragement of an acting teacher who suggested she move to Los Angeles. The move paid off. She was cast in *Rez Bomb*, *A Woman Called Job*, the campy horror film *Hatchet*, and her most notable TV role to date is as Natalie Kimpton on *Dirty Sexy Money*.

"The more you twist the tighter the trap."

2.23 the wrath of con

Original air date: May 4, 2009
Written by: Sara Goodman
Directed by: Janice Cooke Leonard
Guest cast: John Bolton (Lily's Business Manager), Jeff Joslin (Russian Tea Room Maitre'd), John Roney (Cop)

Chuck returns to the city with Georgina Sparks. The gang tries to take down Poppy, but Lily has plans of her own.

Serena and Lily's relationship has always been a rollercoaster: when it's good, it's great, and when it's bad, it's downright awful. It goes from one extreme to the other in this episode. Lily gives Serena her great-grandmother's bracelet to recognize the wonderful woman she's become but then uses it to control her, incarcerating her so Lily can make sure this "adult scandal" is handled the right way — *her* way. And her way is more than a little morally suspect: no punishment for the criminals, restitution made from her own fortune, and no concern for potential future victims. Lily's prime concern is "protecting" her family, but her methods are just as unsavory as Bart Bass's were in having the van der Woodsens followed. Gabriel betrayed Serena's trust and used her for monetary gain, but Lily betrays Rufus's trust by trying to secretly give him money. As difficult as it must be for Lily to have oodles of cash and watch Rufus suffer, she should know better. Lily has always oscillated between caring about appearances and putting her kids' feelings first. She kept Eric's stay at the Ostroff Center a secret, forced Serena to go to cotillion and changed her statement, and put on a show at the housewarming party, then realized the error of her ways. Will she this time? Will Serena forgive her?

At odds with her mother, Serena is fortunate to have others in her life that she can rely on. Beginning last season with the Georgina plot, Serena has become increasingly reliant on Chuck. Their transition from enemies to siblings was unlikely, but her cries to Blair to call Chuck as she's being arrested show just how much she's come to rely on him.

Nate and Chuck's battle for Blair comes to an end when both Nate and

Blair ask Chuck to make an honest move or give up the game. Leighton Meester gives us one more solitary tear as Blair is gutted to hear that it is just a game to Chuck. Even more heartbreaking for the audience is his confession to Serena that he is sacrificing his happiness for hers. Even as he pushes B away, Chuck shows his closeness to his "sis" by telling her the truth behind his lie.

"Poppy's so evil she makes the Old Georgina look like the New Georgina."
— Blair encourages Serena to go ahead with the plan

JTLYK:

- Top story on Gossip Girl: "*OMJC!!* Oh Lord. Could it be? Has Georgina Sparks really ditched scheming and plotting for Jesus? The reformation of Georgina can only be a true miracle from God. Hallelujah."
- Gossip Girl quotes the Beatles' "A Little Help From My Friends" in her opening narration.
- Points for consistency: Serena's liked bone-dry cappuccinos since "The Wild Brunch."
- While Rufus does the proposal setup, Jenny distracts Lily with the details of the epic love of *Twilight*'s Bella and Edward.
- Blair's favorite Biblical passage is Ezekial 25:17, which Samuel Jackson's character in *Pulp Fiction* famously quoted.
- Georgina as Sherilyn calls herself a "Charlotte" and Poppy a "Carrie." *Sex and the City*'s Charlotte was a prissy do-gooder, while Carrie was worldly and wise.
- Though this episode aired a week earlier, the date of Serena's arrest is May 11.

Secrets & Lies:

- Serena doesn't tell her mother about the Gabriel con when Lily gives her the bracelet.
- Serena is trying to figure out what about Gabriel was real and what was a con.
- The "clichéd but effective" pregnancy ruse brings Gabriel to the Palace where Serena and Chuck get the full story on his Ponzi scheme.
- Dan tells Lily what's going on in the hopes that she can fix it. She assures him that Serena will forgive him for breaking her confidence.

- Despite having nothing but Gabriel's word, the word of a man who *just* conned her, Serena believes him and lets him leave.
- To save the family from any public scandal, Lily's solution is to keep everything a secret and just pay back the investors herself.
- Lily takes the opportunity to put Rufus on an allowance without his knowledge. She lies about it to Dan when he questions why R got a call about dividends.
- Blair convinces Georgina to participate in the trap for Poppy, despite it being against G's new moral code.
- Nate thinks Chuck is lying to himself about how he feels for Blair.
- Rufus discovers Lily's plan to pay him.
- Poppy and Georgina both pretend to be someone they're not.
- Chuck lies to Blair, saying their relationship is just a game to him.
- Lily falsely charges Serena with theft and has her arrested.
- Blair thinks Georgina deliberately sabotaged the Poppy plot. Whether she was earnest about her conversion or not, by the end of the episode the New G is gone and the Old G is back.

You'll B a Woman Soon: Blair deftly manages Serena's crisis and her own: counseling her bestie, transforming Georgina, forcing Chuck to give her an answer, accepting it even though it's not what she wanted to hear, and being honest with Nate about not wanting to move in with him.

Star Trek II: The Wrath of Khan (dir. Nicholas Meyer, 1982): The second *Star Trek* movie — and still the one most fans consider the best — is a vengeance story. Exiled by Captain Kirk (William Shatner), Khan (Ricardo Montalbán) seeks revenge on him by infecting an exploratory team with a creepy in-your-ear eel parasite that renders them under his control. Khan wants to get his hands on the Genesis Device, which can reorganize molecular matter and render a planet hospitable. Not under Captain Kirk's watch! Good battles evil and in the epic final battle, Spock (Leonard Nimoy) makes the ultimate sacrifice, repairing the *Enterprise*'s warp drive to save the crew, knowing he will die. Through the aging Captain Kirk and Spock, *The Wrath of Khan* deals with mortality and the nature of friendship between those who've known each other forever. In Spock's death, Kirk is forced to deal with a no-win scenario, something he has avoided and even cheated his way out of facing.

"The Wrath of Con" is also a story of vengeance, a battle between good and evil on the Upper East Side. Despite the *Gossip* gang's best efforts, they find themselves in a lose-lose scenario with Poppy escaping and Serena arrested. Like Spock sacrificing himself for the good of others, Chuck gives Blair the answer she needs in order to move on with Nate, so they can . . . live long and prosper. Chuck sacrifices his own happiness to ensure hers.

Welcome to the Real World:

- "Jesus, Take the Wheel" is Carrie Underwood's 2005 Grammy-winning song, not a life choice, as Blair tells Georgina.
- What is more frightening? Children in developing countries using their free wireless access to post to Gossip Girl or to download Kirk Cameron's *Left Behind* movies?
- Serena's taken to the 55th Precinct in the New York City Police Department, which doesn't exist in real life but is often used on TV shows. (It was the fictional precinct on NBC's *Third Watch*.)

Locations:

- Lily is coming out of Petrossian (182 W 58th St, pictured opposite), where the family had brunch, when she runs into Dan.
- Jenny goes to see an exhibit at the Fashion Institute (Seventh Ave at 27th St).
- Poppy is lured to the Russian Tea Room (150 W 57th St, pictured at the bottom of facing page).

The Look: Serena is wearing a beautiful dawn grey Helmut Lang zip-away lambskin leather jacket when Lily gives her the diamond bracelet. When Dan meets her on the street, Lily is carrying a Hermès Birkin bag and wearing J Brand skinny jeans and black Christian Louboutin round-toe pumps. Blair schemes in a Diane von Furstenberg blouse with a pink Tibi Ainsley bow-weave skirt. Outside the Palace, Serena's coat is Marc by Marc Jacobs and her magenta scarf is Magaschoni. The outfit Blair picks out for Sherilyn Philips (a.k.a. Georgina) is a Milly sheath dress with gold-tone chain waist detailing, purple leather Tasha headband, Christian Louboutin leopard peep-toe pumps, a Nanette Lepore tweed coat, and a pink Nancy Gonzalez Crocodile tote. Blair arrives at the Russian Tea Room in a black Lyell silk Georgette lace fan dress, Rachel Leigh Audrey bangle, Wolford stage tights, and Sigerson

Morrison pumps; her blue overcoat is Nanette Lepore's Emperor's New Coat. Serena gets arrested in Haute Hippie's gold and black sequin tank dress, a quintessential S look. Her black wool coat is Tivon and her shoes are Sergio Rossi platform sandals.

Music: Say Hi's "Oh Oh Oh Oh Oh Oh Oh Oh" plays when Serena calls Chuck to tell him about Gabriel. Georgina's ringtone is "Praise to the Lord." Georgina follows Poppy and the episode wraps up with "Heart's a Mess" by Gotye.

"Shoulder pads may come and go, but a BFF is forever."

2.24 valley girls

Original air date: May 11, 2009

Written by: Josh Schwartz, Stephanie Savage

Directed by: Mark Piznarski

Guest cast: Brittany Snow (Lily Rhodes), Krysten Ritter (Carol Rhodes), Andrew McCarthy (Rick Rhodes), Cynthia Watros (Young Celia Rhodes), Shiloh Fernandez (Owen Campos), Ryan Hansen (Shep), No Doubt (Snowed Out), Matt Barr (Keith van der Woodsen), Abby Pivaronas (Veronica), Bess Rous (Fiona), Miles Fisher (Klemmer), Joe Hickey (Lily's Limo Driver), Jerrika Hinton (Waitress), John Roney (Desk Sergeant), James Schram (Doorman), Danicah Waldo (Prom Guest)

As Serena stews in jail, Lily flashes back to 1983 and the events leading up to her own night in the slammer. Dan busts S out of the pokey in time for prom.

There was a lot of anticipation for this backdoor pilot of a *Gossip Girl* spin-off series centered on Lily's life in the Valley in the '80s. Too much hype and too heavy-handed an attempt to connect 2009 to 1983 made it not entirely successful. The only episode this season written by both Josh and Stephanie, "Valley Girls" suffered from an overkill of parallelisms in the mother/daughter and sister/friends stories. Lily's present-day struggles to parent her willful teenage daughter lead her to understand and forgive Cece for her less-than-wise past choices. In the flashback, we see that Lily's always blamed her mother, favoring her absentee father, and like Serena, she also struggled for her own identity and found herself in trouble now and again. Just as Serena finds support in her friends when her mother fails her, in the flashback Lily finds that in Carol.

Prom night is a great opportunity for writers to fill girls' heads with dreams of grand romantic gestures from their high school sweethearts and *Gossip Girl* delivers two. Hearing that Serena is still in jail, Dan decides to bust her out. Going to Cece for help, getting Jenny to procure S a dress (which she presumably picked up from the VDW rather than sewed herself), and making sure the cabbie didn't scope S while she changed, Dan proves that even though they're not boyfriend and girlfriend, they still have that special "mythological" tie between them. Orchestrating the perfect prom for Blair based on her adorable childhood scrapbook, Chuck proves that he actually *can* make Blair happy despite his fears otherwise. Romance aside, the sweetest moment in the episode is Blair and Serena sitting on the steps in their gorgeous gowns, happy to just be together.

"I would rather give my kids up for adoption than end up like you. Oh wait, you did that."
— Serena hits Lily where it hurts

JTLYK:

- Like the pilot episode of *Gossip Girl*, this backdoor pilot for the spin-off was written by Josh and Stephanie and directed by Mark Piznarski.
- The non-judging Breakfast Club rides again! Chuck, Blair, and Nate rallied to get Serena out of trouble in the penultimate episode of season 1, as they do again here.
- Lily was arrested on April 17, 1983.
- Just like Serena's, Lily's father wasn't around for her when she was a teenager.
- Dan may be 18 years old, but Cedric the Cabbage Patch Kid still sits on his bookshelf.
- The prom queen ballot counter is Fiona, first seen when she was stage-managing *The Age of Innocence*.
- Is Keith van der Woodsen the father of Serena and Eric? If so, that means Lily and Carol totally slept with the same dude.
- Lily's hopeful stare out the bus window at the end of the episode was a nod back to Serena's in the pilot episode.

Secrets & Lies:

- Serena doesn't know that her mother was arrested back in '83.
- In the flashback, Lily tells Cece she'll follow her home but heads for L.A. instead of Santa Barbara.
- Lily insults Carol's decision to be an actress in front of her father, but tells Carol she thinks she's talented.
- Eric reveals to Cece that Lily and Rufus's son died, something even Cece didn't know.
- Blair pretends not to have her prom scrapbook sitting out on her bed.
- Nate asks Chuck if he's sabotaging prom and Chuck says he isn't. And technically he's not lying. He's not *sabotaging* their plans; he's *improving* them.
- Penelope, Nelly, Hazel, Is, and Chuck all commit prom election fraud. But (of course) Chuck's candidate wins.
- Dan apologizes for telling Lily about the Gabriel scheme and Serena forgives him.
- Carol keeps her family's wealth and position a secret from her L.A. friends.
- Keith van der Woodsen cheated on his girlfriend with Carol and is

holding the music video hostage so Carol will talk to him.

Scrap!: Shep punches Keith and an all-out brawl breaks out with Lily jumping on Keith's back and bashing him on the head with her handbag.

You'll B a Woman Soon: As B says to Nate, she's always strived to make real life resemble the movie in her head, and with her perfect prom night, she realizes that "fairy tales end when they do for a reason." Despite her affection for and friendship with Nate, their love feels like a relic of her teenage years. B's ready to move on.

That's How It's Done in *The O.C.*: Kirsten has brief flashbacks to the '80s in season 4's "The Case of the Franks." Seth and Zach are both into Summer, but only one can take her to the Junior Prom where she wins Prom Queen in "The O.Sea."

Blair and Serena have an epic friendship moment on the steps of the stately Tweed Courthouse, a designated NYC landmark.

the rufly timeline

With the flashback in "Valley Girls" comes some important tidbits of information helpful in piecing together just when Rufus and Lily hooked up.

- Lily's birth date on her driver's license is March 9, 1966, making her 17 in the flashback to April 1983.
- Rufus once mentioned his marriage lasted 18 years. He and Alison were married in 1990.
- Both Dan and Serena were born in 1990. (Jenny and Eric were born in 1993.)
- Rufus said to Lily that she's had 19 years to deal with the existence of her child, meaning that Scott was born in 1989. At the earliest, Lily became pregnant with Scott in April 1988 when she was 22.
- Precisely when Lily met Rufus and took those iconic photos of him in Lincoln Hawk is still unclear, but their relationship was definitely over by the time his band hit the big time in the '90s. (He was with Alison and already a father to Dan by 1990.) One thing we do know is that Lily had a busy few years between 17 and 22, falling in love with both Owen Campos and Rufus Humphrey. (And at some point she managed to attend Brown University.)

Valley Girl (dir. Martha Coolidge, 1983): Pretty and popular Julie (Deborah Foreman) is tired of her boyfriend Tommy and spots a guy with a hot bod at the beach. Turns out he's Randy (Nicolas Cage) and he and his friend crash the party in the Valley where Julie and her friends are. Randy and Julie hit it off but jealous ex-BF Tommy beats him up. Randy sneaks back into the party and takes Julie and her friend out to a rocker club (his home away from home) where he promises the friend she won't catch any diseases. There's a Randy and Julie dating montage to "Melt With You," but just when everything seems *totally* perfect, Julie's friends start pressuring her to get back together with Tommy so they can be "the most bitchin' couple at school." She chooses Tommy, and Randy tries his best to win her back by showing up everywhere she goes. With the help of his friend, Randy sneaks into prom and beats up Tommy, then takes the stage with Julie as she wins prom queen. Julie and Randy go off in the limo (which Tommy rented) to the hotel room (also Tommy's). Like, as *if*, right?

"Valley Girls" draws its basic elements from *Valley Girl*: a girl disillusioned with her life meets a rocker guy, he takes her to a grimy club where everyone knows him, there's a party where the rockers don't fit in, a brawl, and (in present day) a prom. But Josh and Stephanie add more to those basics — family drama, sister-friends together, Chuck as prom fairy godmother — to make the episode a more heartfelt 42 minutes than the film's 99 tepid ones.

Welcome to the Real World:

- Lily's kicked out of the Thacher School, a boarding high school in Ojai, California.
- Blair's right: Lindsay Lohan served 84 minutes of jail time after a DUI arrest in 2007, and Nicole Ritchie served 82 minutes for her arrest in 2006, so Serena's got them beat.
- Keith van der Woodsen's uncle is film mogul John Landis, who directed Michael Jackson's "Thriller" video, *Animal House*, *The Blues Brothers*, and *An American Werewolf in London* around the time of the flashback.

Locations:

- Lily stops to use the payphone beside Neptune's Net, a beachside restaurant in Malibu (42505 Pacific Coast Highway).
- Lily meets her father (and mother) at Geoffrey's (27400 Pacific Coast Highway) in Malibu.
- The Constance–St. Jude's senior prom was filmed at the Tweed Courthouse (52 Chambers St).

Spotted: The second group to perform on *Gossip Girl*, No Doubt appears as Snowed Out. Hailing from Anaheim, California, No Doubt broke into the mainstream in the '90s. Returning from a four-year hiatus, No Doubt's appearance was in advance of their summer 2009 tour.

The Look: Lily of 1983 liked her Ralph Lauren: her first outfit is his tweed riding jacket argyle sweater, button-down shirt, and Jodhpur patch pants, with a Gucci flat messenger bag and walnut brown Stuart Weitzman boots. At prom, both Penelope and Isabelle's headbands are SBNY. Penelope, Hazel, and Is are all wearing Phoebe Couture dresses (H in the origami dress in rose, I in the ruffle zipper dress in hot pink). Serena's prom dress is Dior and worth over $19,000. Blair wears Marchesa, spring 2008 collection, with a necklace by Robert Rose, Noir ring, no corsage (good call, Chuck), and — the crowning touch — a Prom Queen tiara.

Music: Totally '80s hit parade! The episode opens with '82's "Destination Unknown" by Missing Persons as young Lily heads to L.A. Lily meets her father for lunch to Huey Lewis & The News's '84 hit "I Want a New Drug." The diner where Carol works is playing 1980's "Mirror in the Bathroom" by The English Beat. As Lily and Owen shake hands, "I Melt With You" by Modern English plays; that song, from '82, was the theme in *Valley Girl* for Randy and Julie. Dan decides to bust Serena out of jail and young Lily tries on Carol's clothes to Billy Idol's 1981 song "Dancing with Myself." No Doubt make a guest performance as Snowed Out, covering the 1981 Adam & the Ants song "Stand and Deliver." The tape Carol plays in her Impala is the B-52s' "52 Girls" from 1978. New Order's "Blue Monday" is on at the party Carol, Lily, and company crash. Shep, Lily, and Owen dance (and they want to) to Men Without Hats' 1982 hit "The Safety Dance." The brawl breaks out at the party to 1977's "I Hate the Rich" by California punk band The Dils. Back in 2009, Blair and Nate slow-dance to Fountains of Wayne's "Prom Theme" (from 1999). The episode ends with Freur's "Doot Doot" from 1983.

Brittany Snow as Lily Rhodes

From Tampa, Florida, Brittany Snow was born in 1986, not too long after the time of the Lily flashback. She began modeling at age three, and by 12 she had a recurring role on *Guiding Light* as Susan Lemay. She played Meg Pryor on *American Dreams* and Ariel Alderman on *Nip/Tuck*. The lead in *John Tucker Must Die*, she acted opposite Penn Badgley. In *Hairspray*, Brittany played Amber von Tussle and had a solo song, "New Girl in Town." For the part of Lily Rhodes, Brittany didn't have to audition; the producers approached her. A fan of *Gossip Girl*, she was honored to be asked but wasn't sure if she was the right actress. "I don't think I really look like Kelly Rutherford," she said, "but we're taking some chances on that." Instead of trying to copy Kelly Rutherford's speech patterns and mannerisms, Brittany decided to play Lily differently from how she is on *Gossip Girl*. "A lot of things happen to her that make her more closed off and uptight," said Brittany. "I thought I'd start her off very sweet and naïve to this world, and because of what happens . . . she becomes a little bit harder."

"You wanted to meet Gossip Girl?
You just did. I'm nothing without you."

2.25 the goodbye gossip girl

Original air date: May 18, 2009
Written by: Joshua Safran
Directed by: Norman Buckley
Guest cast: Jan Maxwell (Headmistress Queller), James Naughton (William van der Bilt), Chris Riggi (Scott), Stella Maeve (Emma Boardman), Reed Birney (Mr. Prescott), Barbara Andres (Bursar), Carrie Yaeger (Teacher)

Graduation! The seniors move on and Jenny moves up.

"The Goodbye Gossip Girl" captured that nervously excited, bittersweet feeling of leaving high school, but that last mystery of high school will never be solved. The "Who is Gossip Girl" plot was frustrating because there can never be a definitive and satisfying answer. Not only are there too many inconsistencies to overcome with identifying someone as Gossip Girl, but without the anonymous blogger, the show falls apart. That said, the fake-out with Jonathan was appreciated, as it gave him and the under-used Eric more screen time.

Gossip Girl's labels had the most effect on "weak" Blair and "irrelevant" Serena. Exposing their most insecure spots drove each girl's actions for the rest of the episode — Serena tried to get everyone together under her direction to smoke out Gossip Girl while Blair gathered her courage and resolved to try again with Chuck. Her real strength was not just in her earnest appeal to Chuck, but in the way she soldiers on after he rejects her again. Though it's a short week later that Chuck *finally* says those three words, Blair was ready to spend the summer in contemplation.

Jenny's plot to overthrow the dictatorship at Constance nearly sucks her back into being the person she was last season: using secrets for leverage. But her last battle with the Mean Girls brings J her once most unlikely ally: Blair. The one person she so desperately wanted approval from finally gives it to her. Blair passing her crown to Jenny instead of to Blairite Emma was a great gesture to show how much both girls have changed.

Less dramatic but no less significant an overhaul from last year is Lonely

Boy's. Dan graduates high school as the "ultimate insider" even though he still feels in many ways an outsider. ("Congratulations, Don" didn't help.) But Blair's list of his achievements helps him realize how much a huge part of his life the Constance–St. Jude's kids have become. It's not surprising that a week after finishing high school he misses it, even Chuck's close-talking and B's "ego demolitions."

With the senior class's graduation, a *Gossip Girl* era has ended and the future lies ahead — so full of promise but also full of potential disaster. Teen shows have a notoriously hard time making the leap to college. Like a high school graduate setting out into the strange unknown world of college, so *Gossip Girl* sets out for its third season: characters going in different directions, new ones popping up, a wedding on the horizon, and old enemies as new allies.

"I love you too."
— Chuck

JTLYK:

- No Hazel at graduation or in the entire finale. Actress Dreama Walker was attending her sister's wedding.
- Top story on Gossip Girl: "*Golden Couple Ends Their Rule.* I suppose with HS coming to a close it was only a matter of time before our king and queen parted ways. Kinda sad. We were actually rooting for B&N this time around. Oh well. Looks like the chapter in the fairy tale that is the romance of Blair Waldorf and Nate Archibald has finally ended. :("
- Why doesn't Alison come to Dan's graduation?
- Calling Dan the "ultimate insider" is a nod back to "The Wild Brunch" when Gossip Girl called Serena the "ultimate insider" turned "total outsider."
- The second Gossip Girl suspect the gang considers is Fiona, stage manager and ballot counter.
- The previous times Blair and Eleanor have spoken in B's room as she gets ready have been just the opposite of this episode's tender moment: Eleanor criticized her ("Pilot"), manipulated her ("Victor, Victrola"), and Blair broke Eleanor's heart ("Bonfire of the Vanity").
- If Nelly Yuki has been secretly in love with Dan this whole time, maybe that's why she was so pleased with herself for stealing D's phone in "Gone

With the Will." She had ulterior motives to break up Dan and Serena. Tricky, Nelly Yuki, tricky.

- Blair's striptease was her second for Chuck. The first was in "Victor, Victrola."
- Finally, the Jack and Blair secret is revealed! Promos for "Gone With the Will" showed Jack telling Chuck about his night with Blair, but at the last minute the producers cut the scene, opting to save it for the finale.
- As with season 1's finale, this episode jumped one week later for its final scenes.
- Blair uses Cyrus's catchphrase — "Not enough!" — when she makes Emma shoo over for Queen J to sit down.
- Dan says to Scott, "It's good to be that guy," which he also said of Nate in "Prêt-a-Poor J."
- In "Much 'I Do,'" Blair was the one packing for Europe and Serena was dealing with a broken heart. This year they've swapped roles.
- Scott tells his parents he's in Portland, the same place Georgina pretended Sarah was from. (Are they working for the Dharma Initiative?)
- For the final scene of the episode, a "foiler" was also shot in the hopes of keeping that glorious moment from being spoiled. Paparazzi photos of Leighton filming kissing scenes with both Chace and Ed hit the internet.
- What was in the third present Chuck had for Blair? This is the second gift C's given B that the audience doesn't get to see. The first was in "The Grandfather" when he brought her a present and found Carter with her.

Secrets & Lies:

- Serena has told Blair what Chuck said to her about loving B.
- Defying their Queen, the Mean Girls want the juiciest piece of untold gossip to determine who reigns next year.
- Serena wants to know the biggest secret of all: who is Gossip Girl?
- Nate does some damage control and tells his grandfather about his affair with Catherine.
- Jenny finds a big secret among Gossip Girl's untold hordes and nearly spills it to win Queen.
- Gossip Girl reveals all the secrets she's been keeping.
- Chuck denies having told Serena that he loves Blair.
- Resolved not to be weak, Blair tells Chuck exactly how she feels about him.

- Scott doesn't tell Dan who he is. He's also told his parents he's in Portland, not New York.
- Blair and Jenny team up to take down the Mean Girls by revealing their secrets.
- Georgina tells the registrar at NYU that she and Blair are besties.
- Carter's had a P.I. looking for Serena's father and has found him.

You'll B a Woman Soon: Finally finishing the conversation Chuck and Blair started in "Summer, Kind of Wonderful," Blair heads into her first year

gossip bombs

Thanks to Jonathan's hacking skills, we get a peek into Gossip Girl's inbox.

- Neil Gabrielson's family lost all their money [to] Madoff.
- Chuck Bass thinks he killed his mother.
- Liz Edwards had to repeat the 2nd grade.
- Sarah Monteith steals her little brother's Ritalin and sells it.
- Nate Archibald has a small…
- Blair Waldorf hooked up with Jack Bass on New Year's Eve!
- Chuck and that weird Brooklyn Girl had sex. More than once.
- Serena van der Woodsen got fake married in Spain.
- Guess who saw Jenny Humphrey with no shirt on? Nate Archibald! And then he kissed her. Um, perv much?
- Eric van der Woodsen dyes his hair.
- Serena van der Woodsen hasn't spoken to her dad in years. No wonder the girl has lots of daddy issues.
- Why is Annie Leitenberg so skinny? She takes Alli before every single meal.
- Dan Humphrey wrote a tell all article about Chuck Bass' dad, Bart. It never got published but still. How rude!
- Blair Waldorf stole a pair of sunglasses. Can you say klepto?
- Omg this is so sad! Nate Archibald was a squatter earlier this school year. He lived in his apartment with no…
- I hear Serena van der Woodsen has an unhealthy obsession with all things Harry Potter. She totally crushes Ron Weasley. What an effing dork!
- Blair had Chuck pretend to fall for Vanessa. Too bad, Chuck actually, gulp, sort of fell for her ??
- Dan Hess has a porn problem. He's addicted and it's getting out of control.
- Um, Serena and Aaron Rose never had sex. What the hell is up with that??

of college bolstered not only by requited love, but a strong friendship with Serena, healthy relationships with her mother and stepfather, and a fully functioning conscience.

The Original Gossipverse: The gang graduates high school in *Nothing Can Keep Us Together*. Vanessa got into NYU in *Because I'm Worth It*.

That's How It's Done in *The O.C.*: Seth, Ryan, Marissa, and Summer graduate high school in season 3's finale, "The Graduate." *The O.C.* had an episode called "The Goodbye Girl" in season 1.

The Goodbye Girl (dir. Herbert Ross, 1977): Written by Neil Simon, *The Goodbye Girl* is a charming comedic story of Paula (Marsha Mason), an aging dancer and mother to Lucy (Quinn Cummings), a whip-smart, charming 10-year-old. When Paula's boyfriend leaves them in the lurch and sublets their New York apartment, Paula has no choice but to live with Eliot (Richard Dreyfuss), the subletter, an actor who plays guitar in the nude in the middle of the night and meditates at the crack of dawn. Paula and Eliot do *not* get along, but they do share affection for Lucy. As life keeps throwing them hardships — Paula's broke, unemployed, and then robbed; Eliot's off-Broadway performance playing a gay Richard III is panned — they fall in love. Paula is scared that Eliot, like every other man she's ever been with, will abandon her, the Goodbye Girl. After winning her trust, Eliot is offered a great job opportunity that will take him away for four weeks and Paula sees the same pattern emerging. Realizing that she'll survive her heartbreak if he doesn't come back because she's grown up in the past few months, Paula gives him her blessing to go. After asking her to come with him, Eliot goes but leaves his guitar, his most sacred possession, at the apartment with Paula and Lucy. He can be trusted.

In her relationship with Chuck, Blair is the Goodbye Girl. She puts herself on the line for him time and again and is rejected time and again. The two bicker and banter like Paula and Eliot, driving each other mad but understanding each other better than anyone else. Like Paula, Blair finally has the strength to survive on her own. In both cases, the Goodbye Girl gets her perfect love scene: the object of her affection proving he's trustworthy standing in a phone booth in the pouring rain for Paula, and outside the Plaza with peonies for Blair.

Welcome to the Real World:

- Eric found a mention of Serena's arrest in Russian newspaper *Pravda*.
- Once upon a time, Rufus performed a cover of Whitney Houston's 1985 song "How Will I Know." Flashback to *that*, please.
- Dan says he used Loopt, the geo-social network, to find Serena.
- Georgina's enrolled in Gallatin at NYU, a school for interdisciplinary and individualized study.
- Chuck brings Blair macarons from Pierre Hermé Paris, the *pâtissier* known as "The Picasso of Pastry."

Locations:

- Serena and Blair have a pre-graduation breakfast, and Blair and Jenny thwart the Mean Girls at Rouge Tomate (10 E 60th St).
- Serena tries to lure Gossip Girl to The Oak Room (The Plaza Hotel, 10 Central Park South).
- Chuck is waiting for Blair outside The Plaza Hotel, pictured below.

by any other name . . .

The nickname love continued in season 2. The *GG*ers were also known as:

Dan: Playboy (Gossip Girl), Downer Dan (Blair), Invisible Boy (Jenny), Humdrum Humphrey (Chuck), Mr. Soccer (Jenny), Lonely Boy (Gossip Girl), Brooklyn Pig (Mini Mean Girl), Ghost of Boyfriends Past (Blair), Financial Aid-iot (Blair), Templeton (Vanessa), Newland Archer (Serena), Don (St. Jude's)

Serena: Sis (Chuck), Blondie the Bombshell (Lexi), Prodigal Daughter (Chuck)

Blair: Miss Blair (Dorota), Waldorf (Chuck), Blair Bear (Harold), Our Girl (Chuck), New Blair (Gossip Girl)

Nate: Archibald, Nathaniel (Chuck), Lost Lamb (Gossip Girl), van der Bilt Promiseland (Blair)

Chuck: Bass, Motherchucker (Blair), Rich Boy (Random Brooklynite), Mister Chuck (Dorota), Bassian Desert (Blair)

Jenny: Little J, Little Orphan Jenny (Gossip Girl)

Vanessa: Weird Documentary Girl, Brooklyn Betty (Penelope)

Eric: Junior (Chuck), Sherlock Holmes (Nate), Kid (Chuck)

Lily: Whore (Chuck), Mata Hari (Jack)

Marcus: Call Boy, Princeton, Untalented Mr. Ripley, Not–James Schuller, Bertie Wooster, Lord Fauntleroy (Chuck)

Catherine: Mrs. Robinson (Vanessa)

Amanda: Little Miss Hannah Montana (Jenny)

Manhattan: Serenaville (Blair)

Aaron: Pablo, Warren Jeffs (Blair)

Lexi: The Enforcer (Serena), The Lexicoaster (Blair)

Cyrus: Danny DeVito, The Gnome (Blair)

Emma: Lohan, Little Red Riding Hood (Blair)

Serge: Humbert Humbert (Chuck), Big Bad Wolf (Blair)

Rachel: Miss Iowa, Cornflower Mary, Commie Cornhusker (Blair), Midwestern Mother Theresa (Hazel), Mrs. Robinson (Gossip Girl)

Gabriel: The Foreigner, North Caroliar (Blair)

Georgina: New Georgina (Blair)

B's date: Prince Uncharming, Beta Bass (Blair)

C's date: Canal St. Knock-off, New Blair (Chuck)

Nelly: The New Old Jenny Humphrey (Eric), Drunky (Nate)

Penelope: Sad Blair Wannabe (Vanessa)

The Constance Girls: Mean Girls, Merry Band of Psychos (Jenny), Little Mini Blairites (Jenny), Trio of Ugly Stepsisters (Gossip Girl)

Oops: If the top story on Gossip Girl is about Nate and Blair's breakup, then why doesn't Chuck know? Also, the headline on the *Daily News* is missing an apostrophe: "Diamonds Are a Girls Worst Friend." And one of GG's gossip bombs is about Jenny's photo shoot, but in "Prêt-a-Poor J" her narration included Jenny being "caught in her knickers by Nate."

The Look: To graduation, Blair wears DvF's Sophia Loren dress with a Leifsdottir faux pearl pointelle cardigan, DKNY tights, a pearl necklace by David Aubrey, Paige Gamble headband, and carries a black Chanel flap bag. S wears a Susan Hanover stone cuff with her blue Jay Godfrey Maxi jersey dress. Serena decides not to do up her gown at graduation and opts to pin the tassel into her hair rather than wear a cap like every other graduate in the history of graduations. Oh, S. Vanessa wears a Rory Beca Watercolor dress and blue Monrow Motorcycle jacket to graduation. Blair's post-grad seduce-Chuck outfit is perfect: a modified Philosophy di Alberta Ferretti dress, Simon Tu necklace, Jennifer Behr headband, and Wolford stockings. Jenny's strapless black dress is Acne Jeans' Baroque tiered bustier dress. Nelly Yuki's orange bow dress is Marc by Marc Jacobs. To her coronation, Jenny wears a Nanette Lepore jacket, Joie top, Theory skirt, and fishnets. Penelope's in a Rebecca Taylor double-breasted blazer, and Emma's in a Nanette Lepore tea party cardigan. In the coda, Vanessa's wearing an aqua cheetah-print Nanette Lepore top. Georgina's brief appearance is in a black Rag & Bone piped jacket and a gray Gary Graham draped tank with a black and white Botkier Margot satchel. Serena's travel outfit is a blue Mike & Chris Eliseo leather hoodie over a Bally glass sequin beaded cami. When Chuck finally tells her he loves her, Blair is in Nanette Lepore's green ferry boat coat over a yellow embellished Milly cardigan, gold bow David Szeto blouse, Marc by Marc Jacobs skirt, gold knotted Jennifer Behr headband, Pour La Victoire shoes, and Stuart Weitzman bag.

Music: The Hotpipes' "The Future Is Where We Belong" opens the finale. Nate and Vanessa catch up pre-graduation to "The Stars Just Blink for Us" by Say Hi. As graduation starts, so does "Season of Love" by Shiny Toy Guns; it plays again at the end for Chuck and Blair's much-awaited moment. Nate's party kicks off with The Handcuffs' "I Just Wanna' Be Free, Man." Gossip Girl interrupts Blair and Chuck and starts dropping bombs to "Zero" by the Yeah Yeah Yeahs. "Bet You Never Thought" by Brighton, MA is on at the

Humphrey loft where Rufus and Lily reminisce. At The Oak Room, Say Hi's "November Was White, December Was Grey" plays. Nate meets up with Dan and Vanessa to "The Summer" by Coconut Records. Jenny's coronation is to "Are You Just a Dream?" by Daniel May.

Questions for Season 3:

- Will Serena return from her summer trip with Mr. van der Woodsen? Will she and Carter become romantically involved?
- Dan, Vanessa, Blair, Georgina, and Scott are all attending NYU. Nate is in the city at Columbia. Will Serena actually attend Brown or find a reason to move back to the city?
- Will Chuck run Bass Industries? The company was his when he turned 18. (His birthday is May 19.)
- Will Jenny be changed by being the new Queen and having access to the Bass fortune? Is Emma her new enemy?
- Will Nate and Vanessa return from their pierogi tour a couple? Or is this more end-of-season misdirection?
- Can Chuck and Blair work as a couple or is their self-destruction inevitable?
- When will Scott reveal that he's Lily and Rufus's child? Will they be able to survive that and/or the return of Eric and Serena's father?
- Will there be a musical episode? Leighton Meester, Taylor Momsen, Ed Westwick, Matthew Settle, and even Penn Badgley are all musical talents. It worked for *Buffy*. . . .

sources

"Behind the Seams at *Gossip Girl*," *People*. September 28, 2008.
"Behind the Scenes . . . with *Gossip Girl*," *People*. April 7, 2008.
BlairandChuck.com
CWSource.com
CWTV.com
ElleGirlblog.com
"Eric Daman," Revolve Fall 08 Style Guide. RevolveClothing.com.
FabSugar.com
FilmReference.com
Gay, Jason. "Dirty Pretty Things," *Rolling Stone*. April 2, 2009.
"Gossip Girl Chic Preview," *InStyle*. September 2008.
GossipGirlInsider.com
GossipGirlFan.org
GossipGirl.net
GossipGirlOnline.net
Harris, Mark. "OMFG! It's the Gossip Boys," *Details*. November 2008.
"Heating Up," *People*. May 12, 2008.
InStyle.com
Internet Movie Database. imdb.com
Johnson, Steven. *Everything Bad Is Good for You*. New York: Penguin, 2006.
Keith, Bill. "School Ties," *Out*. Online. Accessed December 1, 2008.
LaFerla, Ruth. "Forget Gossip, Girl; the Buzz Is About the Clothes," *The New York Times*. Online. July 8, 2008.
Levine, Madeline. *The Price of Privilege*. New York: Harper Paperbacks, 2008.
MacSweeney, Eve. "The Girls Can't Help It," *Vogue*. March 2008.
MediaLookBook.com
NYMag.com
NYTimes.com
People.com
People Style Watch. stylenews.peoplestylewatch.com
Pressler, Jessica and Chris Rovzar. Daily Intel blog, *New York*. Online.
Pressler, Jessica and Chris Rovzar. "The Genius of *Gossip Girl*," *New York*. Online. April 21, 2008.
Schwartzman, Zibby. "Secret Admissions," UpperEast.com. Accessed November 15, 2008.
ShopDiary.com
Stack, Tim. "'Gossip Girl': Four Rumors — and the Reality," *Entertainment Weekly*. Online. September 12, 2008.
Style.com
Usborne, Simon. "Teenage kicks: How Gossip Girl changed TV," *The Independent*. Online. May 6, 2008.
von Ziegesar, Cecily. *All I Want Is Everything*. New York: Little Brown, 2003.
——. *Because I'm Worth It*. New York: Little Brown, 2003.
——. *Don't You Forget About Me*. New York: Little Brown, 2007.
——. *Gossip Girl*. New York: Little Brown, 2002.
——. *I Like it Like That*. New York: Little Brown, 2004.
——. *Nobody Does it Better*. New York: Little Brown, 2005.
——. *Nothing Can Keep Us Together*. New York: Little Brown, 2005.
——. *Only in Your Dreams*. New York: Little Brown, 2006.
——. *Would I Lie to You*. New York: Little Brown, 2006.
——. *You Know You Love Me*. New York: Little Brown, 2002.

——. *You're the One That I Want.* New York: Little Brown, 2004.
Warner, Tyrone. "Producer Says We Are All Gossip Girl," CTV.ca. February 13, 2008.
Wikipedia.org
Wolcott, James and Smith, Krista. "Who's Up? Hollywood's Next Wave," *Vanity Fair.* August 2008.
YouKnowYouLoveMe.org

An Auspicious Beginning

Bellafante, Ginia. "Poor Little Rich Girls, Throbbing to Shop," *The New York Times.* Online. August 17, 2003.
"Cecily von Ziegesar: Between the Buns," BookBurger.typepad.com. September 18, 2007.
"Cecily von Ziegesar Interviews," BookWrapCentral.com. Accessed October 12, 2008.
Dawson Parks, Mackenzie. "Gossip Girl," *Colby Magazine.* Online. Fall 2006.
Deahl, Rachel. "Alloy Makes a Go of It in Hollywood," *Publishers Weekly.* Online. November 19, 2007.
Hill, Amelia. "Sex and drugs tales to tempt teen readers," *The Observer.* August 25, 2002.
Lodge, Sally. "Gossip Girl Dishes On," *Publishers Weekly.* April 3, 2006.
Maughan, Shannon. "Gossip Girl's Got Legs," *Publishers Weekly.* May 14, 2007.
Mechling, Lauren. "A nice girl's guide to misbehaving," *The Daily Telegraph.* Online. October 17, 2002.
Morrison, James. "Protests at sex and drugs in teen publishing sensation," *The Independent* (U.K.). August 25, 2002.
Newman, Andrew Adam. "'Gossip Girl' DVD Extra Tries to Steer Buyers to the Books," *The New York Times.* Online. August 17, 2008.
Nussbaum, Emily. "Psst, Serena is a slut. Pass it on." *New York* magazine. Online. May 21, 2005.
"PopGurls Interview: Josh Schwartz," PopGurls.com. July 18, 2007.
Staino, Rocco. "Make Way for Luxe Lit," *School Library Journal.* Online. September 24, 2008.
Webb Quest, Sara. "The Gossip Girl Speaks," Time Warner Bookmark. Online. October 17, 2004.
Wolf, Naomi. "Young Adult Fiction: Wild Things," *The New York Times.* Online. March 12, 2006.
Wyss, Trudy. "Lifestyles of the Rich and Adolescent," Borders.com. Accessed October 12, 2008.

You're Nobody Until You're Talked About

Adalian, Josef. "Dawn Ostroff," *Variety V Plus.* September 12, 2007.
Andreeva, Nellie. "Schwartz to 'Gossip' on CW Pilot," *Hollywood Reporter.* August 21, 2006.
Andreeva, Nellie and Nordyke, Kimberly. "TV 'Gossip': Busy Week for Schwartz," *Hollywood Reporter.* January 4, 2007.
Atkinson, Claire. "Josh Schwartz, 27; 'The O.C.,'" *Advertising Age.* August 1, 2005.
Cohen, Sandy. "Talking to: Josh Schwartz," The Associated Press, *The Record* (Bergen Country, NJ). April 3, 2006.
D'Alessandro, Anthony. "Stephanie Savage," *Variety V Plus.* July 31, 2008.
Freeman, Hadley. "The Making of a Golden Boy," *The Guardian Weekend.* Online. January 22, 2005.
Goodman, Lee-Anne. "Canadian Gossip Girl Creator Stuck to Dreams," *Winnipeg Free Press.* June 12, 2008.
High, Kamau. "Gossip Girl," *Billboard.* September 27, 2008.
Hughes, Robert J. "'Cho' and Tell," *Wall Street Journal.* August 15, 2008.
Itzkoff, Dave. "Tax Credits Bring More TV Shows to New York City," *The New York Times.* Online. September 25, 2008.
"Josh Schwartz," *The Independent on Sunday* (U.K.). March 23, 2008.
Konigsberg, Eric. "Awaiting a Glimpse of Their 'Gossip Girl' Kin," *The New York Times.* Online. December 1, 2007.
Levine, Stuart. "Dawn Ostroff," *Variety V Plus.* October 3, 2008.
Mahmud, Shahnaz. "Stephanie Savage," *Adweek.* April 21, 2008.

Portuguez, Enid. "'Gossip Girl's' Professor of Teen Angst," *Los Angeles Times*. Online. July 27, 2008.
Posner, Ari. "'The O.C.' Rewrites the Rules of TV Writing," *The New York Times*. Online. March 21, 2004.
Ryzik, Melena. "Omigosh! 'OC' With Warmer Duds?," *The New York Times*. Online. September 12, 2007.
Shaw, Jessica. "Psst . . . did you hear?," *Entertainment Weekly*. November 23, 2007.
Soloman, Deborah. "Gossip Guy," *The New York Times Magazine*. Online. October 14, 2007.
Strachan, Alex. "TV Backbone Consists of Creative Writers," Canwest News Service, *Calgary Herald*. September 6, 2008.
Whitmore, Margo. "'Hopefully, the musicians feel like we're honoring their music,'" *Billboard*. April 23, 2005.
Wood, Mikael. "One-Stop (Chop) Shopping," *Billboard*. September 13, 2008.
Wyatt, Edward. "'The OC': A Fast Start, A Faster Finish," *The New York Times*. January 6, 2007.

Great Adaptations

Donaldson James, Susan. "'*Gossip Girl* Triumphs Over *O.C.*,' Say New York Preppies," ABC News. Online. September 20, 2007.
Malcolm, Janet. "Advanced Placement," *The New Yorker*. March 10, 2008.
McAdam, Carrie. "Chatter in Classes," *Sunday Herald Salon Fresh Online*. March 15, 2008.
Soll, Lindsay. "'Gossip Girl': Going Off the Books," *Entertainment Weekly*. Online. October 24, 2007.
Stanley, Alessandra. "Reading, Writing and Raunch: Mean Girls Rule Prep School," *The New York Times*. Online. September 17, 2007.
Vena, Jocelyn. "'Gossip Girl' Author Is a 'Faithful Watcher' of the TV Series — Although One Thing Was 'Ruined,'" MTV News. Online. October 16, 2008.

Blake Lively

"Accepted: Adam Herschman, Blake Lively, and Director Steve Pink," TheMovieGuy.com. Online. August 9, 2006.
"Blake Lively and Penn Badgley," *E! News* via BlakeLivelyWeb.com. February 21, 2008.
"Blake Lively — Gossip Girl Interview," BlakeLively.org. August 30, 2007.
"Blake Lively: Summary," TV.com. Accessed January 15, 2009.
Elvis and Annabelle. Online. www.elvisandanabelle.com
Fahner, Molly. "Everyone's Talking About Blake Lively," *Cosmopolitan*. September 2008.
Franklin, Garth. "Elvis & Anabelle Open SXSW," Dark Horizons. Online. January 28, 2007.
Freydkin, Donna. "'Gossip Girl' Lively tries to ignore the rumors," *USA Today*. August 5, 2008.
"*Gossip Girl* Actress Blake Lively," GoodPrattle.com. September 13, 2007.
Lee, Michael J. "Blake Lively," *Radio Free Entertainment*. Online. July 29, 2006.
McDonald, Kathy A. "Blake Lively," *Variety V Plus*. October 3, 2008.
Rosenberg, Carissa. "Blake Lively," *Seventeen*. August 2008.
Stanley, Alessandra. "East Side Story," *Vogue*. Online. February 2009.
Shaw, Jessica. "Forever in Blue Jeans," *Entertainment Weekly*. Online. June 6, 2005.
Widdicombe, Ben. "Blake Lively match isn't just 'Gossip,'" *New York Daily News*. Online. December 24, 2007.

Leighton Meester

Fahner, Molly. "The *Gossip Girl* You Love to Hate," *Cosmo*. June 2009.
"Fashion Résumé," *Marie Claire*. December 2008.
Gay, Jason. "The Gossip Girl Next Door," *Rolling Stone*. December 11, 2008.
Goldman, Eric. "Gossip Girl's Leighton Meester on Being Bad," IGNTV.com. August 29, 2008.
"*Gossip Girl* Actress Leighton Meester," GoodPrattle.com. September 19, 2007.
"'Gossip Girl' star Leighton Meester talks new album," CTV.ca. February 22, 2008.

"In Blossom," *InStyle*. March 2009.
"Leighton Meester's March 2009 Photo Shoot," InStyle.com. February 18, 2009.
O'Leary, Kevin. "Leighton Meester: Her Untold Story," *Us*. October 6, 2008.
Rogers, Thomas. "Everyone's favorite mean girl," Salon.com. August 29, 2008.
Rosen, Christopher. "Blair Waldorf Is Only as Awesome as Leighton Meester," *The New York Observer*. Online. October 21, 2008.
Syme, Rachel. "The Talk of the Town," *New York Post Page Six Magazine*. September 3, 2007.
Waterman, Lauren. "New York Doll," *Teen Vogue*. February 2009.

Penn Badgley
Barker, Lynn. "Penn Badgley Joins Cast of 'Gossip Girl,'" TeenHollywood.com. September 12, 2007.
"Behind the Scenes: Penn and Blake," *The Tyra Banks Show*.
Dos Santos, Kristin. "Gossip Guy Penn Badgley Takes On Seth Cohen and His Character's Sexuality," EOnline.com. October 16, 2007.
"Fall TV Preview," *Entertainment Weekly*. Online. September 13, 2002.
Gallagher, Brian. "Set Visit: Take a Stroll Through the World of *The Stepfather*," MovieWeb.com. March 21, 2008.
"Gossip Girl — Interview with Penn Badgley," CW Television. www.youtube.com/user/CWtelevision. September 29, 2007.
"Gossip Girl's Penn Badgley Interview," *E!'s Watch With Kristen* via DuckyDoesTV.com. October 17, 2007.
"Interview with Penn Badgley," The CW Source. www.youtube.com/user/TheCWSource. November 14, 2007.
Jaffer, Murtz. "Exclusive Gossip: Murtz Jaffer Interviews Gossip Girl's Penn Badgley," PrimetimePulse.com. September 25, 2007.
James, Caryn. "New TV Season in Review; Do Over," *The New York Times*. Online. September 19, 2002.
Levesque, John. "A moment with . . . Penn Badgley, actor," *Seattle Post-Intelligencer*. Online. July 27, 2002.
McFarland, Melanie. "On TV: Seattleite is the talk of 'Gossip Girl,'" *Seattle Post-Intelligencer*. Online. November 5, 2007.
"Penn Badgley Talks Sexy," InStyle.com. May 28, 2008.
Pressler, Jessica and Chris Rovzar. "The Wit and Wisdom of Penn Badgley," Daily Intel blog, *New York*. Online. April 21, 2008.
Warner, Tyrone. "'Gossip Girl' star Penn Badgley just 'fell into' acting," CTV.ca. December 10, 2007.

Chace Crawford
"17 Questions with Chace Crawford," *Seventeen*. Online. Accessed January 12, 2009.
Bawden, Jim. "Chace Crawford next teen sensation," *Toronto Star*. Online. September 18, 2007.
Calvert, Gemma. "I'm Looking for Lust Not Love," *Fabulous*. January 25, 2009.
"Chace Crawford," *You* (U.K.). October 12, 2008.
Garcia, Jennifer. "Chace Crawford Pairs Up with Leona Lewis," *People*. Online. December 20, 2008.
"Uptown Boy," *The Independent on Sunday*. August 3, 2008.

Taylor Momsen
Chang, Rachel. "Taylor at the Plaza," *Cosmo Girl Prom*. Winter/Spring 2009.
"Interview with Taylor Momsen," The CW Source. www.youtube.com/user/TheCWSource.
"Paranoid Park," NylonMagazineTV. Online. April 25, 2008
TaylorMomsen.org
"Taylor Momsen is 'Naturally Thin,'" JustJared.com. October 12, 2008.

"Taylor Momsen on Paranoid Park," *ElleGirl*. Online. Accessed January 12, 2009.
"The Cast of *Gossip Girl* Talk About Each Other," *People*. May 12, 2008.
Vilkomerson, Sara. "The It Girl of *Gossip Girl*," *The New York Observer*. Online. August 12, 2008.

Ed Westwick

Chang, Rachel. "Ed Westwick . . . Rock Star," *Cosmo Girl*. November 2008.
"Ed Westwick," *Nylon*. April 2008.
Ed-Westwick.org
"Ed Westwick," *TV Guide*. May 2008.
Joseph, Claudia. "Move over Brad — here comes Ed from Stevenage," *The Daily Mail* (U.K.). Online. April 27, 2008.
Michals, Susan. "'Gossip Girl' Swirls Around Ed Westwick," *Venice Magazine*. November 2008.
Shaw, Jessica. "'Gossip Girl' Hotties," *Entertainment Weekly*. December 26, 2008–January 2, 2009.
Shelasky, Alyssa. "Ed Westwick Q&A," *People*. September 2008.
Syme, Rachel. "Gossip Girl's Ed Westwick: Man About Town," *Page Six Magazine*. Online. Accessed December 1, 2008.
Waterman, Lauren. "Bass Appeal," *Teen Vogue*. March 2009.

Jessica Szohr

"Exclusive Interview: Jessica Szohr of 'Gossip Girl,'" BuddyTV.com. April 28, 2008.
Fitzpatrick, Catherine. "Face value," *Journal Sentinel*. Online. August 21, 2001.
"Interview with Jessica Szohr," *The Morning Blend*. Online. December 28, 2007.
McNary, Dave. "Brittany Snow 'Walks' to indie drama," *Variety*. Online. March 20, 2009.
Mitovich, Matt. "Jessica Szohr of the CW's 'Gossip Girl,'" *TV Guide*. Online video. November 12, 2008.
"PopGurls Interview: Gossip Girl's Jessica Szohr," PopGurls.com. September 23, 2008.
Stone, Andrew C. "The Girl Most Likely," *Ocean Drive*. March 2009.
"We Gossip with Gossip Girl Star Jessica Szohr," TheTVAddict.com. April 28, 2008.

Kelly Rutherford

"Beauty part," *People*. July 7, 1997.
Dhalwala, Shruti. "Pregnant Kelly Rutherford Puts Parenting First," People.com. April 8, 2009.
"Interview with Kelly Rutherford of *Gossip Girl*," *CW11 Morning News*. December 3, 2007.
"Kelly Rutherford biography," *The New York Times*. Online. Accessed April 11, 2009.
"Kelly Rutherford talks 'Gossip Girl,'" *KTLA News*. November 15, 2007.
"Kelly Rutherford with Jason C.," The CW Source. www.youtube.com/user/TheCWSource. October 28, 2008.
Lewittes. "L.A. Confidential," *Cosmopolitan*. December 1998.

Matthew Settle

Chi, Paul. "Gossip Girl's Matthew Settle Pop Culture," *People*. September 22, 2008.
"Exclusive Interview: *Gossip Girl* Star Matthew Settle," TheTVAddict.com. May 5, 2008.
Hamm, Liza. "Gossip Dad," *People*. April 13, 2009.
"Interview with Matthew Settle at *Entertainment Weekly* party," The CW Source. www.youtube.com/user/TheCWSource. June 5, 2008.
"Matt Settle talks Rufus," *CW11 Morning News*. September 15, 2008.
"Matthew Settle," *Rachael Ray*. January 15, 2009.
"Matthew Settle Interview at Vitamin Water S2 launch party," The CW Source. www.youtube.com/user/TheCWSource. August 18, 2008.

Episode Guide

"Actor Robert John Burke," GoodPrattle.com. August 30, 2008.

The Age of Innocence. DVD. Sony Pictures, 2001.
All About Eve. DVD. 20th Century Fox, 2003.
All About My Mother (Todo sobre mi madre). DVD. Sony Pictures, 2000.
Aurthur, Kate. "Answering for Antics of 'Gossip Girl,'" *Los Angeles Times*. Online. July 23, 2007.
Bad News Bears. DVD. Paramount, 2005.
Becky Sharp. DVD. Alpha Video, 2004.
The Blair Witch Project. DVD. Lion's Gate, 1999.
The Bonfire of the Vanities. DVD. Warner Home Video, 2004.
Breakfast at Tiffany's. DVD. Paramount, 2001.
Callahan, Maureen. "'Girl' Gone Wild," *New York Post*. Online. November 9, 2008.
Carnal Knowledge. DVD. MGM Video & DVD, 1999.
CelebrityFashionTips.com
The Covenant. DVD. Sony Pictures, 2007.
Cruel Intentions. DVD. Sony Pictures, 1999.
Dan in Real Life. DVD. Buena Vista Home Entertainment/Touchstone, 2008.
Dangerous Liaisons. DVD. Warner Home Video, 1997.
Daredevil. DVD. 20th Century Fox, 2003.
The Dark Knight. DVD. Warner Home Video, 2008.
"Designer Abigail Lorick on Dressing the Gossip Girls," StyleList.com. Accessed March 17, 2009.
Desperately Seeking Susan. DVD. MGM Video & DVD, 2000.
Downie, Stephen. "Mysterious Big Sister Is Watching," *The Daily Telegraph* (Sydney). November 28, 2007.
EliteGossipGirlStyle.com
"Fast Future Generation '09," *Nylon*. May 2009.
"Five Questions: *Gossip Girl*'s Nicole Fiscella Will Tell Her Co-Stars What to Eat," *The New York Observer*. Online. June 19, 2008.
Flynn, Elinor. "Spotted: 'Gossip Girl' Laura Breckenridge '10 drinking coffee in Chancellor Green," *The Daily Princetonian*. Online. March 5, 2009.
Gentlemen Prefer Blondes. DVD. 20th Century Fox, 2001.
The Godfather. DVD. Paramount, 2008.
The Goodbye Girl. DVD. Warner Home Video, 2000.
Gone With the Wind. DVD. Warner Home Video, 2004.
GossipGirlCloset.com
"'Gossip Girl' EP Finally Explains the Great Dumbo/Williamsburg Contradiction!," Daily Intel blog, *New York*. Online. December 3, 2007.
GossipGirlFashion.onsugar.com
"Gossip Girl Interactive Map," *The New York Post*. Online. Accessed December 21, 2008.
Gossip Girl — The Complete First Season. DVD. Warner Home Video, 2008.
Gossip Girl. TV Series. Exec. Prod. Bob Levy, Leslie Morgenstein, Stephanie Savage, Josh Schwartz. The CW. 2007–.
Halterman, Jim. "Interview: Stephanie Savage Touts the Return of 'Gossip Girl,'" TheFutonCritic.com. March 13, 2009.
The Handmaid's Tale. DVD. MGM Video & DVD, 2001.
Heaven Can Wait. DVD. Paramount, 1999.
HeardonTV.com
Hernandez, Greg. "My interview with Armie Hammer," Out In Hollywood. www.insidesocal.com/outinhollywood. October 6, 2008.
High Society. DVD. Warner Home Video, 2003.
In the Realm of the Senses. DVD. Criterion Collection, 2009.
Isherwood, Charles. "Gossip Boy, but Just for a Day," *The New York Times*. Online. March 4, 2009.
It's a Wonderful Life. DVD. Paramount, 2006.
John Tucker Must Die. DVD. 20th Century Fox, 2006.

Kludt, Amanda. "The 'Gossip Girl' Guide to New York," GridSkipper.com. January 15, 2008.
La Ferla, Ruth. "My So-Called Gossipy Life," *The New York Times*. Online. September 16, 2007.
The Magnificent Ambersons. DVD. TCM Turner Classics.
Marie Antoinette. DVD. Sony Pictures, 2007.
Morgan, Spencer. "Lydia Unleashed," *The New York Observer*. Online. November 6, 2007.
Much Ado About Nothing. DVD. MGM Video & DVD, 2003.
MusicFromGossipGirl.blogspot.com
Never Been Kissed. DVD. 20th Century Fox, 2003.
Norris, Michele. "Teens, Sex and TV: A Risky Mix?," *All Things Considered*, NPR. December 2, 2008.
O Brother, Where Art Thou? DVD. Touchstone, 2001.
The O.C. — The Complete Series Collection. DVD. Fox Network, 2007.
Ophir, Edon. "Ithaca's own 'Gossip Girl'," *The Ithacan Online*. August 28, 2008.
Ouzounian, Richard. "Sir Lancelot Stirs the Gossip," *Toronto Star*. September 6, 2008.
Powers, Bill. "Richard Phillips Unveiled on 'Gossip Girl,'" The Moment Blog. themoment.blogs.nytimes.com. September 30, 2008.
Prêt-a-Porter (Ready to Wear). DVD. Miramax, 1999.
Pretty in Pink. iTunes rental. Paramount, 2006.
Poison Ivy. DVD. New Line Home Video, 1999.
Remains of the Day. DVD. Sony Pictures, 2001.
Roman Holiday. DVD. Paramount, 2002.
Say Anything. DVD. 20th Century Fox, 2002.
School Ties. DVD. Paramount, 1999.
Sixteen Candles. DVD. Universal Studios, 2003.
Some Kind of Wonderful. DVD. Paramount, 2006.
Stanley, Alessandra. "What Are Friends For? Power and Pain," *The New York Times*. Online. May 18, 2008.
Star Trek II — The Wrath of Khan. DVD. Paramount, 2000.
Strausbaugh, John. "In the Mansion Land of the 'Fifth Avenoodles,'" *The New York Times*. Online. December 14, 2007.
The Sun Also Rises. DVD. 20th Century Fox, 2007.
There Will Be Blood. DVD. Paramount, 2008.
TheCharmedLife.wordpress.com. May 28, 2008.
A Thin Line Between Love and Hate. DVD. New Line Home Video, 1999.
TVShowMusic.com
Valley Girl. DVD. MGM Video & DVD, 2003.
Victor / Victoria. DVD. Turner Home Entertainment, 2002.
Vena, Jocelyn. "'Gossip Girl' Co-Star Dishes On Dorota's Future," MTV.com. February 17, 2009.
Wharton, Edith. *The Age of Innocence*. New York: Penguin Classics, 1996.
WhatSheWoreFashion.blogspot.com
The Wild Bunch. DVD. Warner Home Video, 2006.
Women on the Verge of a Nervous Breakdown (Mujeres al borde de un ataque de nervi). DVD. MGM Video & DVD, 2001.
The X-Files: Fight the Future. DVD. 20th Century Fox, 2001.
You've Got Mail. DVD. Warner Home Video, 1999.

acknowledgments

Thank you to Jack David and David Caron, co-publishers at ECW Press, for trusting I could write this book and for being the best bosses ever. To all the ECWers, thank you for approaching your work with expertise and passion and for being dear friends. A special thanks goes to Sarah Dunn for being both my expert reader and publicist, and to Rachel Ironstone for doing the production for *Spotted* as well as its glorious photo sections. Thank you to the talented people who put the book together: cover designer Dave Gee and page designer/typesetter Melissa Kaita (who, BTW, pulled off the bows-on-hairbands look long before Blair). Thank you to Tim Forbes at Forbes Creative, Erin Nicole Smith, and Sarah Dunn for generously helping me with the NYC photos. A world of thanks to Lee Weston (leewestonphoto .com) for my author photo; you're the best! *Dziękuję* Jeannette for the enthusiastic translation of Dorota's rant. Fan sites and blogs were an invaluable research tool for me while writing; a huge thank-you to the similarly obsessed out there. A great deal of gratitude to Nikki Stafford for letting me borrow the structure and format of her books; she's perfected the art of the television episode guide, writing about shows like *Buffy* and *Lost.* Thank you!

Thanks to my mum for letting me camp out at her casa (and eat her food) while I was writing; thanks to my da for trying to watch the show so he could talk S and B with me. Love and gratitude to Sarain, Tony, Russ, Erin, and the awesomesauce Ace Gang. Thank you Claire for keeping me company (*Practical Magic* style) even when we are an ocean apart. And thank you Adam for being a tolerant roommate, especially when I reached the "make your own smoke monster" level of delirium.

Thanks also to my friends who join me on the internets, and sometimes even in real life, to discuss the scandalous lives of Manhattan's elite.

Finally, this book owes its existence to my editor Jennifer Hale. She believed I could write it and if there's one thing we've learned from *Gossip Girl*, ~~it's that tights are not pants~~ it's what a huge difference it makes to have someone believe in you and see your potential. Thank you, Jen, for the amazing edit, for your suggestions, improvements, encouragement, and friendship.

about the author

Crissy Calhoun is an editor and writer who blogs at calhountribune.blogspot.com. She lives on the Lower East Side of Toronto, the New York City of Canada. This is her first book.